# French Women's Writing 1848–1994

**BRESCIA COLLEGE
LONDON ONTARIO**

# Women in Context

## Women's Writing 1850–1990s

*Series Editor: Janet Garton (University of East Anglia)*

This new series provides a survey, country by country, of women's writing from the beginnings of the major struggle for emancipation until the present day. While the main emphasis is on literature, the social, political and cultural development of each country provides a context for understanding the position and preoccupations of women writers. Modern critical currents are also taken into account in relating feminist criticism to recent critical theory.

Already published
*Norwegian Women's Writing 1850–1990*
Janet Garton
0 485 91001 2   hb
0 485 92001 8   pb

*Italian Women's Writing 1860–1994*
Sharon Wood
0 485 91002 0   hb
0 485 92002 6   pb

Forthcoming
*Swedish Women's Writing 1850–1995*
Helena Forsås-Scott
0 485 91003 9   hb
0 485 92003 4   pb

In preparation
*German Women's Writing*

**Women in Context**

# FRENCH WOMEN'S WRITING 1848–1994

## Diana Holmes

ATHLONE
LONDON & ATLANTIC HIGHLANDS, NJ

First published 1996 by
THE ATHLONE PRESS
1 Park Drive, London NW11 7SG
and 165 First Avenue,
Atlantic Highlands, NJ 07716

British Library Cataloguing in Publication Data
*A catalogue record for this book is available
from the British Library*

ISBN 0 485 91004 7 hb
0 485 92004 2 pb

Library of Congress Cataloging-in-Publication Data
Holmes, Diana.
French women's writing, 1848–1994 / Diana Holmes.
    p.    cm. -- (Women in context ; 3)
Includes bibliographical references.
ISBN 0-485-91004-7 (hb). -- ISBN 0-485-92004-2 (pb)
    1. French literature--Women authors--History and criticism.
2. French literature--20th century--History and criticism.
3. French literature--19th century--History and criticism.
4. Women and literature--France--History.    I. Title.
II. Series: Women in context (London, England) ; 3.
PQ149.H65    1996
840.9′9287--dc20                                           95-50716
                                                                CIP

Typeset by
Bibloset

Printed and bound in Great Britain by
Bookcraft (Bath) Ltd

# Contents

# *Acknowledgements*

Thanks to all the friends and colleagues who have generously given their time to read and discuss work in progress, and especially to Penny Welch and Elizabeth Fallaize. I am grateful too to all the students both at Wolverhampton University (then Polytechnic) and at Keele University who have studied women's writing with me, and contributed their enthusiasm, ideas and questions.

This book is dedicated, with love, to Nick Cheesewright, to our children Thomas and Martha, to my mother Marie Holmes and to my sister, Anne Marie Holmes.

# Series Foreword

The aim of the *Women in Context* series is to present a country-by-country survey of women's writing from the beginnings of the struggle for emancipation until the present day. It will include not just feminist writers but women's writing in a more general sense, incorporating a study of those working independently of or even in direct opposition to the feminist aim of greater autonomy for women.

While the principal emphasis is on literature and literary figures, they are placed in the context of the social, political and cultural development without which their position cannot be properly understood, and which helps to explain the differing rates of progress in different areas. The volumes therefore combine survey chapters, dealing with women's place in the public and private life of a given period, with more in-depth studies of key figures, in which attention will be focused on the texts. There is no attempt at encyclopaedic completeness, rather a highlighting of issues perceived as specifically relevant by women, and of writers who have influenced the course of events or made a significant contribution to the literature of their day. Wherever possible, parallels with other countries are drawn so that the works can be placed in an international perspective. Modern critical currents are also taken into account in relating feminist criticism to recent critical theory.

Until quite recently women's writing has been virtually excluded from the literary canon in many countries; as a result there is often a dearth of information available in English, and an absence of good translations. *Women in Context* represents a move to remedy this situation by providing information in a way which does not assume previous knowledge of the language or the politics of the country concerned; all quotations are in English, and summaries of central texts are provided. The general reader or student of literature or women's studies will find the volumes a useful introduction to the field. For those interested in further research, there is a substantial bibliography of studies of women's writing in the country concerned and of individual authors, and of English translations available in modern editions.

*Janet Garton*

# Introduction

In February 1848 an insurrection in Paris toppled the monarchy of Louis Philippe and replaced it with a Republic. Like the Revolution of 1789 and the uprising of 1830, it was a moment of great political excitement, accompanied by a collective sense of liberation and empowerment. Wrongs would be righted, all citizens would have their right to a say in the government of the country. This sense of a new beginning belonged to women as well as to men: on 22 March the Committee for Women's Rights sent a hopeful petition to the City Hall: 'You have proclaimed the right of all to vote without exception. We come to ask whether women are included in this general right.'[1] Many of the political clubs which flourished in the revolutionary climate accepted female members, and some of them were for women only. The women who produced the first feminist daily newspaper, *La Voix des Femmes* (Women's Voice), attempted to persuade a reluctant George Sand to stand for the National Assembly. In Seneca Falls, in the same year, American feminists expressed the claims which also underlay the demands of their French sisters: 'We hold these truths to be self-evident, that all men and women are created equal.'[2] 1848 looked initially like a good year for women.

On 6 June the most vociferous and radical of the women's clubs, Eugénie Niboyet's 'Société de la Voix des Femmes', was closed down by order of the Prefect of Police. After the violent events of June, when demonstrations against the government's abandonment of radical policies met with savage repression, the political clubs were dissolved and a new regulation banned 'women or minors' from attendance at political meetings. In September 'universal' suffrage, excluding the female half of the population, was voted through Parliament. The misogynist Proudhon argued in the columns of the left-wing *Le Peuple* that socialism should have nothing to do with feminism. It was almost one hundred years later, in 1944, that French women finally won the right to vote, and were thus acknowledged to be adult citizens of France.

Excluded from the public domain of politics, women were identified with the private sphere of home and family. The Napoleonic Civil Code, the basis of the French legal system since 1804, defined women as the property of their father or husband. Industrialization confirmed and accentuated the division between a masculine world, located outside the home, in workshop, factory, farm, school, Parliament, law courts – the sites of material and intellectual production – and a feminine world, centred in the home, devoted to reproduction and the maintenance of the workforce. The consistently high rates of female employment in France scarcely disturbed this symbolic patterning of gender roles, for many women worked for their husbands, on the land or in small businesses, and for those who did not, low pay marked the fact that their labour was deemed inessential and inappropriate. In the twentieth century, anxiety about the low national birth rate led to a series of policies designed to persuade or coerce women into having more children, policies which further reinforced the identification of women with home and family. While France shares the basic structures of patriarchy with most other Western nations, French gender politics are also in some ways culturally specific. In the period under study here, French culture has shown a particular tendency to emphasize women's specificity as a sex, and to profess a reverence for Woman that conceals the real political and cultural powerlessness of women. Identified, by the feminine gender of 'la France' and 'la République', with the nation itself, and – for the majority of the period – with the Republican state, women have been offered adoration, dutiful service, protection – but rarely the full rights and subjecthood of a human being and a citizen.

This emphasis on gendered difference, and the consignment of many desirable human qualities such as compassion, tenderness, selflessness, to the 'feminine' sphere, have posed acute dilemmas for French women keen to assert their rights and their voices. To insist on women's equality with men, to demand integration into existing economic and political structures, runs the risk of abandoning all that is valuable in the 'feminine' sphere and subscribing to the hegemony of 'masculine' values. But to claim rights on the basis of a specifically feminine contribution to society is equally dangerous, for it leaves women confined to the roles and identities conferred by, and ultimately dependent on, men. The struggle against patriarchy in France constantly returns to this debate between a politics of integration and a politics of difference.

A quarter of a century after French women's belated achievement of the right to vote, despite the state's acknowledgement of the legal and social equality of the sexes, French public life continues to be dominated by men, in politics, in the workplace and in the sphere of culture. In 1949 Simone de Beauvoir's famous, angry definition of women as the 'Second Sex' pointed to the fundamental sexual inequality of Western culture. Both title and book also expressed a spirit of feminist resistance which has been present – sometimes overt and confident, sometimes covert and cautious – throughout the history of modern France. Beauvoir's formulation, and the feminist challenge it implies, both retain their relevance in the France of the 1990s.

Literature is one of the cultural forms through which a society shapes its sense of reality – or, in Raymond Williams's words, 'through which the meanings that are valued by the community are shared and made active'.[3] In the nineteenth century, in the increasingly industrialized and literate societies of Europe, the written word became a primary medium of ideology, defined in Stuart Hall's sense as 'not . . . content and surface forms of ideas, but . . . the unconscious categories through which conditions are represented and lived.'[4] If writing contributes in crucial ways to the establishment of shared meanings, then it is surely a matter of some importance to know who writes. Yet if we are to believe those histories and works of criticism which select from a multitude of texts and determine for posterity what constituted 'French Literature', then we must believe that at least until the 1970s women were as scarce in literature as they were (and still are) on the benches of the French National Assembly.

Most histories of French literature between 1848 and 1968 retain only the names of George Sand, Colette and (considerably less in France than abroad) Simone de Beauvoir, in an otherwise wholly male landscape. Even in the last two decades, with huge increases in both the number and the visibility of women-authored texts,

female and particularly feminist writers tend to be ghettoized as
a separate, minority category, or what one quite recent history of
French literature termed a 'Sectional Interest'.[5]

Has writing been a largely male domain? Were women prevented by lack of education, lack of time, lack of a 'room of
their own' from committing words to paper? Were they entirely
caught up in the ideological web that constructed them as man's
Other? Or is it, rather, that the process of selection and evaluation
has written women out of the canon, judging them against criteria
which identified serious concerns with male concerns?

The answer to both these sets of questions is a qualified 'yes'.
As Virginia Woolf demonstrated in *A Room of One's Own*, women
(like other classes excluded from power) have been prevented from
writing by lack of education, lack of economic independence,
and other more subtle inhibiting pressures.[6] Social, cultural and
educational disadvantage certainly account to some extent for the
paucity of women's texts in the literary canon, but it is also true
that far more women wrote and were widely read than is now
remembered. Many women writers have been discarded by the
canon as trivial or insignificant, when in fact a rereading of their
(often out-of-print) works reveals otherwise. Since the early 1970s
feminist criticism and feminist publishing houses (though rather less
in France than in the USA or Britain) have made it their business
to rediscover women's voices lost to posterity. Feminists have also
engaged in the rereading of the few 'canonized' women writers,
on the grounds that earlier criticism had often employed aesthetic
criteria that mistook the masculine for the universal.

Mainstream histories of French literature rarely foreground the
peculiar fact that they are, on the whole, histories of men's writing.
Women readers, women students, have long been invited to see
the silence of their sex as a fact of life. However, over the last
two decades, and particularly in the late 1980s and the 1990s, a
number of studies have begun to return lost French women writers
to history, to reread literary history as a process shaped by (among
other forces) sexual politics, and to bring to readers' attention work
by contemporary women authors.[7] This book can thus be seen as
a contribution to a feminist project which is, happily, collective.
Its first and most simple task is practical and political: our reading
of a national culture is partial and incomplete if it depends on the

writings of only the dominant group. At one level, the aim of this study must be to demonstrate the presence of female voices in what is usually presented as an unproblematically male literary scene.

It is not enough, however, to add women writers to the existing canon. The implication of a book which seeks out missing female voices is clearly that women's writing will differ in important ways from that of men. This question of difference is a crucial one within feminist scholarship, and has been the subject of considerable debate.

Feminists have broadly agreed on the fact that although women are divided from each other by (among other things) race, class, age and sexual orientation, their gender identity has linked them as a group and placed them as subordinate within patriarchy. Nineteenth-century ideologies of gender, predicated on what Auguste Comte termed women's 'natural inferiority which nothing can destroy',[8] applied – albeit differentially – to women of all social categories. Until 1945, all French women, regardless of class, wealth or ethnicity, were excluded from 'universal' suffrage. The common experiences of sexual harassment, discrimination, unequal domestic responsibilities, domestic violence, cut across the class and racial divisions between women now. Since so many levels of experience are significantly determined by gender, women and men stand in a different relationship to cultural forms, and to their authorship.

The nature of difference and its impact on writing has, however, been theorized very differently. Within Anglo-American feminist criticism the emphasis has been generally on women's social, political and cultural exclusion, on their status as men's 'Other', constantly represented in art and in language in terms of men's needs and desires, and on the problems this raises when women come to take up the pen. Elaine Showalter's trailblazing *A Literature of Their Own* (1978), for example, or in a rather different way Gilbert and Gubar's *The Madwoman in the Attic* (1979), explore the narrative and linguistic strategies employed by women writers to deal with the difficulty of reconciling the female self as other and the female self as author. These range from the straightforward transvestism of adopting a male pen name, to the weaving of a subversive subtext beneath an overtly conformist narrative – the strategy of the palimpsest. One aim of this book will be to identify and explore literary strategies which arise from and implicitly contest the exclusion of women from the dominant culture.

French theory has laid less emphasis on women's social experience and more on the psycho-emotional construction of the gendered subject in early infancy, and the effect of this on language. Recent French theorists of gender, of whom the best-known are Hélène Cixous, Luce Irigaray and Julia Kristeva, have shown little interest in the historical development of gender relations, but have argued (in different ways) that language itself encodes patriarchal power, representing the world in man's image, equating the masculine with the positive, the feminine with absence, silence and negativity. On this model, any attempt to represent the feminine in language must involve experimentation with form, and radical rejection of the dominant linguistic and literary codes. Cixous, in particular, defines feminine writing as an attack on the very structure of language, and a courageous quest for what lies beyond conventional meaning:

> Such is the strength of women that, sweeping away syntax, breaking that famous thread (just a tiny little thread, they say) which acts for men as a surrogate umbilical cord . . . women will go right up to the impossible.[9]

There is a liberating energy in this questioning of 'phallic' language, this assertion of women's potentially positive otherness beyond patriarchy. The idea that a truly subversive feminine writing contests the phallocentric order at the level of syntax and structure will be evoked in the analysis of texts throughout this book, and discussed in more depth in Part III. However, particularly given the historical dimension of this study, it would distort the picture to identify only features such as disjuncture, dislocation of syntax or neologisms as 'authentic' feminine writing. A great variety of literary forms have been appropriated, modified, popularized and merged by the writers under study here, just as feminism itself has shared and refashioned the radical discourses of each age from liberal individualism to postmodernism. Rather than form a league table running from the truly feminine to the merely imitative, the aim will be to explore the complex and evolving relationships between gender and genre, established literary discourses and feminist meanings, appropriation and experimentation.

Thus this book starts not only from a belief in the political importance of redrawing the literary map, to include forgotten women writers and reassess the few canonical figures, but also from a belief that male and female writers differ significantly in their relationship to literary forms and possible discourses – a difference which is not fixed and constant but historically specific and evolving. The intention is to offer a selective but none the less broadly informative account of women's writing in the 1848–1994 period in France, addressing the work of the few 'canonized' female figures from an original and feminist perspective, but also setting them in relation to some of their lesser-known sisters whose work illuminates both the contemporary situation of women and the question of women authors' specific techniques and strategies.

The period 1848–1994 could be subdivided in a number of different ways. The tripartite division here is not intended to correspond to any radical breaks in women's history or their literature, and there will be an inevitable weaving of threads across the dividing lines, particularly in the case of writers whose careers stretch across lengthy periods. The three sections are uneven in terms of years covered, but chosen because they can usefully be seen as having some historical and ideological coherence. The divisions make it possible to situate writers within certain material and political contexts and within what Raymond Williams termed 'structures of feeling',[10] in order to place a critical reading of their work in relation to social and literary practices of their day. Where possible, I have focused discussion on texts which are available in English translation. The problem of the selection of authors and texts has varied considerably from one period to another, for although the 'feminization' of the novel has been greatly exaggerated – one estimate suggests that women already made up 20 per cent of published writers in France in 1909,[11] and the current figure is only 25 per cent[12] – contemporary texts are easily available, and often also translated, whereas the period 1848–1958 demanded a degree of literary detective work.

Part I covers the period 1848 to 1914, a long period and one marked by several changes of political regime, but none the less given some underlying continuity by the gradual, ongoing process of urbanization and industrialization in France, and by the presence of a clearly articulated and powerful ideology of separate spheres for men and women. Against this dominant pattern of thought, an undercurrent of feminism can be traced – varying in degrees of radicalism and forms of expression, but constantly present and contesting the relegation of women to inferiority and silence – thus linking across national boundaries with movements in neighbouring European countries.

George Sand (1804–76) challenged the constrictions on women's sexual, intellectual and legal freedom through a life which combined motherhood with a prolific literary career, political activism and a series of lovers, yet she refused to commit herself to the cause of feminism. Her later work displays a similar ambivalence, subtly contesting contemporary ideologies of gender, yet frequently through the medium of uncontentious literary forms such as the pastoral and the (quintessentially feminine) romance. The narrative of romance is equally central to the popular novels of Gabrielle Reval (1870–1938), Marcelle Tinayre (1871–1948) and Colette Yver (1874–1953), interweaving and at times conflicting with narratives of individual achievement and female solidarity. Rachilde (1860–1953) echoes Sand in that while her life challenged accepted standards of feminine behaviour, she declared herself hostile to feminism. In Rachilde's case, as in Sand's, the tension between revolt against patriarchy and endorsement of its laws is textual as well as biographical, though Rachilde's adoption of the misogynist discourse of Decadence poses the contradiction more sharply.

If narrative fiction dominates this Part of the book, it is because women found it easier to write and publish in this flexible and catholic literary form which required neither a high degree of social mobility nor a classical education. A small number of women did none the less achieve contemporary celebrity as poets. The lesbian love poetry of Renée Vivien (1877–1909) is profoundly marked by her society's construction of the lesbian as erotic spectacle, or as deviant and damned, but it also expresses a defiant resistance and sketches a utopian celebration of imagined happiness beyond the patriarchal order.

Part II encompasses the years 1914 to 1958, and thus two world wars. The theory that the 1914–18 war radically altered the employment patterns and status of women has been thoroughly refuted by historical research.[13] It seems more accurate to see both wars as ushering in periods of social conservatism, as societies attempted to refind the security of prewar patterns of behaviour. The 1920s were marked by an emphatic backlash against the 'New Woman', including draconian legislation to outlaw contraception. Although French women finally gained the right to vote in 1944, the 1950s were also the years of a concerted effort to increase the birth rate and turn women into committed homemakers and consumers. Yet at the same time the experience of war, the disturbance of normal expectations of gendered behaviour, also generate what the French call 'contestation'. In the 1920s and 1930s, as in the 1950s, feminist groups in France continued to argue the case for women's legal and social equality, while women-authored texts frequently engaged in a more radical questioning of the relationship between gender, identity and power.

The journalism of Colette (1873–1954) provides a commentary on French society which subversively mingles the high register of (masculine) Culture with the low register of the (feminine) domestic and the everyday, while her fictions and cross-generic texts propose models of time, identity and ethics which emerge from female experience and articulate a distinctively feminine world-view. With *The Second Sex* (1949), Simone de Beauvoir (1908–86) shocked or inspired her contemporaries, both within and beyond France, with a radical denunciation of existing sexual politics, providing a rigorously researched and argued theoretical base that has remained a central reference point for feminism. In a series of critically acclaimed but largely forgotten novels extending from before World War II to the 1970s, Elsa Triolet (1896–1970) represents women's situation in mid-twentieth-century France in terms of dispossession and homelessness, a figurative exile which is suspended, in the war fiction, by the experience of the Resistance.

Part III covers the period 1958 to 1994, and thus coincides with the history to date of the Fifth French Republic. The contemporary wave of the Women's Movement in France is generally seen as originating in the students' and workers' revolt of May 1968, but its genesis can be traced through the preceding years as campaigns around the legalization of contraception and abortion brought women together. In the decade that followed 1968, feminist activity was a significant part of the social and

cultural scenario of French life, and some of the key debates of
the international Women's Movement originated in France. In the
1980s, the arrival in power of the first Socialist government since
the postwar years brought with it a new Ministry for Women's
Rights, and some important reforms. The disappearance of the
Ministry leaves French sexual politics divided between those who
believe that France has reached an era of post-feminism, in which
equality has been achieved, and those who argue, as Susan Faludi
has for the USA, that the late 1980s and 1990s are, rather, a period
of anti-feminist backlash. Debates and dissension within French
feminism will form one of the prisms through which women's
writing in this most recent period will be viewed.

The sheer number of interesting women-authored texts published and available made selection particularly difficult for this
section. My solution has been to try to provide in the Context
chapter an overview of the range of recent writing, and then, rather
than simply select three or four individual writers, to adopt an
approach which foregrounds critical questions raised and explored
by recent French feminism. Thus the arguments for and against
the existence of a distinctively *feminine* style of writing [*écriture
féminine*] are examined, and the adequacy of such a concept as a
lens for reading is tested through its application to texts by Chantal
Chawaf and Marguerite Duras. The analysis of texts by Christiane
Rochefort and Annie Ernaux demonstrates that realist techniques
– apparently excluded from the category of the truly feminine by
theorists of *écriture féminine* - may also be effectively deployed to
critique and reinvent the meanings of gender.

The final chapter, 'An Open Conclusion: Women's Writing
Now', draws together some of the threads that weave through
the book as a whole, but also attempts to open on to the present
and the future by introducing some significant contemporary texts
by French women writers. If there is one feature that unites the
most inspiring and – I use the word with all the ambiguities and
reservations that surround it – feminine texts studied here, it is their
preference for an open rather than a closed ending.

# PART I
## 1848–1914

# 1
# Women in French Society 1848–1914

In 1880, at the midpoint of the period 1848 to 1914, Emile Zola published his bestselling 'poem of male desires',[1] the novel *Nana*. *Nana* opens in a Parisian theatre, as the audience gather for the début performance of a new star. Word of Nana's beauty has spread, and not only the theatre itself but, it would seem, the whole city reaches a feverish pitch of anticipation before the play – a light, frothy piece of vaudeville – actually begins: 'A shiver of expectation went round the house: at last they were going to see this famous Nana, whom Paris had been talking about for a whole week' (p. 29). The reader is drawn into this build-up of sexual tension, kept waiting, page after page, for the appearance of the woman whose name echoes obsessively through the text. At last she makes her entrance, in the role of Venus, and the audience are briefly shocked to discover that Nana can neither sing nor act. Yet they soon realize that her lack of talent is essential to her performance: Nana's power of fascination lies not in her art but in her body, and any display of trained artistry would disturb the spectators' sense of her as wonderfully natural, passive flesh. A tense, greedy desire holds the audience captive until she leaves the stage.

Nana's ability to provoke intense and irresistible desire is at the heart of Zola's plot. In the course of the novel she will bring about the downfall of some of the most powerful men in society, cause the death of others, and be linked at least figuratively with the destruction of the Second Empire. While Nana is portrayed as acquisitive, mendacious and manipulative, the havoc she wreaks depends not on any destructive intention but on her involuntary sexual magnetism. The dynamics of the plot demand that she be viewed, as in this first scene, externally, through the lens of masculine desire. Anticipating Freud, Zola presents this desire as composed equally of longing and terror: for Nana's spectators, the

body displayed on the stage represents both intoxicating pleasure
– '[she] gave off an odour of life, a potent female charm, which
intoxicated the audience' (p. 38) – and a horrifying symbol of
castration:

> All of a sudden, in the good-natured child the woman stood
> revealed, a disturbing woman with all the impulsive madness
> of her sex, opening the gates of the unknown world of desire.
> Nana was still smiling, but with the deadly smile of a man-eater.
> (pp. 44–5)

*Nana* is about woman as man's Other, as the embodiment of his
deepest drives and terrors. To present Nana as consciousness, to
give her the voice she lacks, would be to destroy the myth on
which the novel depends. The director of the theatre has clearly
understood what his audience wants, and (like Zola) is about to
make a nice profit from Nana's success: 'Does a woman need to
be able to sing and act? . . . Nana has something else, dammit,
and something that takes the place of everything else' (p. 22).

This fictional scene is in some ways emblematic of gender
relations in late-nineteenth-century France. In the spectacle as
in the social world, woman's role was to function in relation to
man, as source of his pleasure or incarnation of his fears. Nana's
lack of a voice raises the problem of the woman writer, of how
she makes her voice heard when what is asked of a woman is not
art, or opinion, but only that 'something else' which signifies the
fulfilment of male needs. Exposed on the stage of man's desires and
fears, successful only provided she neither disappoints nor exceeds
his fantasies, Nana's position may be read as an extreme image of
that of all women in an androcentric society – and of the difficulty
of laying claim to a feminine voice that commands attention.

Reading Zola's text as a woman in itself suggests the problems
posed by writing as a woman. The narration very effectively
positions the reader among the audience which, despite some
references to female spectators, is overwhelmingly characterized
as male. Can the woman reader/writer simply adopt this offered
positioning as a male, and refuse any identification with the body
on the stage? Can the perspective be reversed, and masculine desire
be re-viewed from the point of view of the woman who is so
powerfully constructed as its object? Can the woman writer shout

from the balconies, breaking the sexual tension that makes the scene so compelling? Can she herself view Nana's body with desire, and if so, in what ways is the articulation of this desire different?

The fact that, even as Zola wrote, women were joining together in feminist movements to campaign for economic and legal equality provides one proof of the survival of a female voice in a culture predicated on their silence. Only a few years after Zola had Nana sing her tuneless but appealing songs, the era of feminist congresses in France was beginning; a decade after Zola's fictional heroine narrowly escaped a brutal police raid on streetwalkers, Josephine Butler was visiting Paris to campaign with French feminists for the abolition of police registration of prostitutes. And throughout the years that led from the uprisings of 1848 to the First World War, French women continued to write and be published, in voices that ranged from mimicry of masculine authority to militant assertion of a different, feminine perspective, but mostly negotiated a more complex, and often uncertain, path between these two. Despite their relegation to the status of men's Other, women marked their presence as subjects in history, even if they were 'compelled to act . . . from a place other than that occupied by men'.[2] To understand the nature of that 'other place', we need to examine some of the key economic, political and cultural determinants of women's lives in France between 1848 and 1914.

## WOMEN, LAW AND THE ECONOMY

When, in 1789, the Revolution abolished the old hierarchies and declared the right of men to freedom, equality and fraternity, women too hoped for a new world. There were even some hopeful signs: the age of legal majority was to be twenty-one for both sexes; legislation for divorce by mutual consent was passed in 1792; women met in political clubs in Paris and petitioned the Assembly for equal rights; Olympe de Gouges responded to the Declaration of the Rights of Man with a Declaration of the Rights of Woman: 'This Revolution will only have its effect when all women are aware of their appalling lot and of the rights they have lost in society.'[3] But the demand for political and legal equality between the sexes was declared 'sacrilegious' by the defenders of the Rights of Man, and de Gouges was guillotined in 1793.

The brief liberation of the revolutionary years was followed by a wave of anti-feminist repression and by the inscription of male supremacy in the law of the land.

Napoleon Bonaparte's *Code Civil* (1804) asserted unequivocally the values and priorities of the bourgeoisie, the class which emerged triumphant from the Revolution. Respect for property, the sanctity of the family, the authority of the father and of government: these principles were clearly articulated in the new legal system. A French woman had no automatic right even to her own nationality: this was determined by her husband, and marriage to a foreigner meant loss of French citizenship. Article 213 stated that the wife owed obedience to her husband. This extended to needing his permission for almost all social transactions, to his right to dispose of her earnings and her correspondence, and to the attribution of parental rights only to the father. According to Article 1124 she enjoyed the same legal status as minors and the insane. Moreover, the new emphasis on legitimacy codified unequal standards of sexual behaviour for men and women: a wife's adultery was punishable by a term of imprisonment of three months to two years, whereas her adulterous husband was at most liable to a fine. A woman's infidelity was now grounds for divorce – this was the case for a husband only if he compounded the offence by bringing his concubine to live in the family home. Divorce was abolished completely in 1816.

The *Code Civil* legitimated major differences in rights and power between the sexes, and set the legal framework for the whole of the nineteenth century and beyond. The *Code*'s inscription of gender difference and gender inequality proved an appropriate underpinning to the country's economic development over the next hundred years. For despite six changes of political regime, in terms of economic development the nineteenth century in France can be seen as a period of continuity. As in other Western European countries, the century was one of transition from a predominantly agricultural economy to a society organized around industrialized production and wage-labour, and this meant a new level of gendered separation between a masculine sphere of employment and production and a feminine sphere of domestic work and reproduction.

Although this process of transition took place more slowly in

France than in Britain or Germany, the years 1848 to 1914 were marked by the steady development of industry and communications, and the passage towards a fully industrialized, urbanized society. Changes in government were to a great extent the product of conflicts between classes struggling for survival or advancement in a changing economic climate, so that the revolt of 1848 was fuelled in part by the discontent of an artisanal class threatened by new industrialized modes of production. The hegemonic ideology of this period of industrial expansion was that of positivism: the belief, in the words of Auguste Comte, that:

> the study of nature is destined to provide a truly rational basis for man's ability to intervene in nature, since only the knowledge of and hence the ability to predict natural phenomena can enable us to modify them.[4]

This world-view, confident in the existence of a natural order to all things and in man's ability to observe, understand and hence control, is what Raymond Williams identified in his conclusion to *Culture and Society* as 'the dominative mode . . . one of the mainsprings of industry: the theory and practice of man's mastering and controlling his natural environment.[5] It was a mode of thought which extended easily to a 'rational' justification of the right of the ruling class to understand and control the rest of the population, in the name of productivity and the common good.

For women of all classes, positivism and the 'dominative mode' had a very clear corollary in the concept of separate spheres. Political changes of regime concealed not only the steady growth of industrial capitalism but also the stable and consistent power structure of patriarchy, a system of 'power relations in which women's interests are subordinated to those of men'.[6] Although the forms of women's experience changed as modes of production, technologies and social institutions altered, and although there were vast differences between the lives of women of different classes, a fundamental inequality of power determined a consistent and radical difference between men and women. The Revolution of 1789 proclaimed the Rights of *Man* and, despite some potential slippage of meaning, interpreted 'Man' in the gendered and not the generic sense. The *Code Civil* of 1804 inscribed the dominance of the male sex in a legal system which was to remain in operation for more than a century. The concept of a natural division of humanity into two unequal, different yet complementary halves underpinned industrialization and the social organization of France in the nineteenth and early twentieth centuries.

Although quite a high percentage of French women were classified as employed throughout the years 1848 to 1914 (women forming 33 per cent of the active population in 1866,[7] 37.2 per cent in 1906[8]), this was largely because many of them were engaged in piecework at home, or worked on the family farm. Employment opportunities were severely limited. As the nature of work diversified for men, women's role in the economic process became firmly identified with reproduction and consumption.[9] Middle-class women retreated to the home both to become the principal symbol of their husband's or father's wealth and respectability, and to fulfil the increasingly important economic role of consumer. Working-class women rarely enjoyed the luxury of choice, but had to earn as best they could, even when they were also responsible for dependent children. Women worked outside the home in industry (particularly textiles and the fashion industry), inside the home on piecework and in domestic service (22.5 per cent of the working female population was in domestic service in 1866[10]). Gradually, and increasingly from the middle of the century on, they worked in the retail trade.

The identification of women with their reproductive role, and the very real hardship experienced by pregnant women and mothers of young children in a production system that ignored their needs, meant that despite the high rate of their real participation in production, women could be defined as merely a provisional, reserve workforce, to be called on when the family budget or the economy demanded. This perception of their role was materialized in lower pay: in 1848 a woman's average wage was considerably less than half that of a man, and this changed little across the rest of century. This in turn convinced the male workforce that female competition was a dangerous thing, and contributed to the conservatism of the labour movement on issues of gender. It was the French section of the First International which, in 1866, put forward a motion condemning women's work and declaring their place to be in the home.[11] French trade unions tended more towards a paternalist policy of excluding women from the labour market on the grounds that they were exploited there than towards support for their resistance. The French Trade Union Congress of 1898 also opposed women's work, and 'the iconography of French trade-union propaganda juxtaposed the brawny male breadwinner with his staunch wife and children at home'.[12]

The definition of women's natural role as that of homemakers confined bourgeois women to the private sphere and excluded them from politics, education and large areas of culture. It meant that working-class women functioned as a cheap reserve source of labour and were made personally responsible for the often impossible task of feeding a family on starvation wages.

Women's low pay also served to create a ready supply of prostitutes whose services were a necessary part of the sexual organization of society. The definition of women as by nature concerned with home and children rested on a comfortably androcentric view of the world. This view was mirrored in contemporary thinking on gender and sexuality which neatly enmeshed class economic interests and the gratification of what were presented as 'natural' male sexual desires. The truly feminine woman, worthy of a degree of formal respect, was the chaste wife and mother confined within the home under male protection. 'Because she is by nature an invalid,' wrote Michelet in 1858, 'she is sensitive and abstains from physical pleasure, she is purer than we are.'[13] Yet since the real man was defined as actively sexual and heterosexual, there was clearly a problem of mismatch between his sexual expectations and those of the women he knew, not only before but even within marriage. The answer lay with those women who, often as a rational response to their own and their family's poverty, turned to prostitution.

Paris in the nineteenth century, and particularly under the Second Empire (1851–70), had a Europe-wide reputation as a sexy city, or, in the words of the Goncourt brothers, the world's brothel. Zola's *Nana* is grounded in reality: the city offered frothy, titillating stage shows and a *demi-monde* of *courtesanes* or high-class prostitutes, often themselves actresses or dancers, which attracted not only wealthy French men but also willing clients from abroad. But prostitution spread well beyond this relatively affluent sector. Paris had a higher number of prostitutes than other capitals (in the 1850s London counted about 24,000 prostitutes whereas Paris, with a population half the size, had 34,000[14]), and acknowledged their presence by a system of regulation. Women who registered and submitted themselves to regular medical examination were allowed to practise their trade: 'clandestines' or non-registered prostitutes were liable to imprisonment. Thus the law attempted to make illicit sex safe for the male customers, and punished those women who resisted official categorization as prostitutes.

While the sexual division of labour and the maintenance of male power in the family offered women the idealized role of Angel in the House,[15] the assertion of men's sexual power demanded that the Angel have a demonic sister, the object of desire, the representation of the feared and forbidden power of female sexuality. This role was often assumed by precisely that class of women for whom the gendered division of labour, and women's low wages, made economic survival impossible. The close connection between the economic and the sexual implications of separate spheres can be seen in the high percentages of both registered and clandestine prostitutes who came from the lowest-paid sectors of female employment. Between 1878 and 1887, for example, 30 per cent of the unregistered prostitutes sent to the police Dispensary for medical checks were garment workers – among the lowest-paid women workers – and 39 per cent were domestic servants. In 1890 more than half of the unmarried mothers who gave birth in the public hospitals of Paris had been working as maids or cooks.[16] Thus rigid differentiation of roles and restrictions on economic independence underpinned and legitimated the sexual exploitation of women.

WOMEN AND POLITICS

The nineteenth century was a period of political instability and variety in France, with six changes of political regime between 1800 and 1871. The years 1848 to 1914 saw three major political upheavals: in 1848 the banishment of Louis Philippe led to the establishment of a Second Republic, but only four years later a *coup d'état* installed Louis Napoleon as the Emperor Napoleon III. His reign ended with France's defeat in the Franco–Prussian War of 1870, and the Third Republic was declared on 4 September 1870.

Thus throughout the period political groups in France were numerous and in a constant process of change: the terms monarchist, Bonapartist, republican, radical, socialist each stood for a variety of positions and strategies. However, three broad political groupings can be identified without distorting the picture. On the Right, the Catholic Church was identified with conservatism, and can be seen as the centre of an anti-republican, frequently monarchist grouping opposed to democracy and to the secular state. Occupying the middle ground, the Republicans denounced the pernicious influence of a Church whose teaching encouraged superstition and blind obedience, claimed to represent the Revolutionary principles of 1789, but defended the rights of property and class against the proletariat. Socialists attacked these rights in the name of the working class and sought, by reformist or revolutionary means, to end the domination of capital and create a classless society. What interests us here is the way in which each group incorporated into its vision of reality the naturalness and necessity of women's subordination to men, and the way in which the same central division of male-positive/female-negative reappeared in modified form in each philosophy.

The Catholic Church was a powerful force in the lives of French women in the nineteenth century. The daughters of the aristocracy and the upper middle class were traditionally educated by nuns, often spending their adolescence in convent boarding schools where they were both safe from temptation and able to acquire the accomplishments expected of a marriageable young lady. Before the introduction of state education the Church also provided most of the primary schools and teachers for both sexes. In 1850 the *Loi Falloux* decreed that primary schools for girls should be provided in towns with a population of over 800. However, since the law did not provide the necessary funding, and since it waived the requirement for teachers to possess the 'brevet' or teaching qualification in the case of religious orders, this ensured that the Church would continue to dominate the female primary sector. Women remained under the influence of, and firmly associated in the popular imagination with, the Church. The figure of the pious woman under the thumb of her parish priest is a hostile stereotype to be found in many of the discourses of late-nineteenth-century France.

The appeal of the Church for women is not hard to understand. Christianity did at least take women's souls seriously, and assume their equal chances of ultimate salvation. The Church provided a social forum for discussion, a socially acceptable outlet for female energies in philanthropic and charitable works. It glorified the situation of the mother and offered a form of activity even within the confined space of the home. 'Prayer', writes Bonnie Smith, 'accorded with [women's] position of physical impotence.'[17]

Yet it was hardly likely that the Church would be progressive on questions of gender. Not only did the fundamental mythology of Christianity propose a bleak choice for women between Eve the temptress and the eternally sexless Virgin Mary, but marriage was seen as essentially a means to reproduction, and the alliance of the French Church with the most authoritarian, least democratic political groups signified its acceptance of natural hierarchies and refusal of the doctrine of social equality. Leo XIII's 1891 encyclical *Rerum Novarum* nicely summed up the vision of female identity taught in the Catholic schools and propounded to the (mostly female) faithful:

> for a woman is by nature fitted for homework, and it is that which is best adapted at once to preserve her modesty and to promote the good bringing-up of children and the well-being of the family.[18]

The Church was willing to promote the importance of women's education and of their charitable and moral activities outside the home, but all this remained firmly within the ideology of separate spheres and a definition of female identity as selfless and by nature domestic.

What, then, of Republicanism? French Republicans fought for and defended the gains of the 1789 Revolution against the reactionary forces of Church, Monarchy and Empire, winning the day briefly in 1848 and much more durably in 1870. Republicans saw and presented themselves as progressive, rational and democratic, and prided themselves on their enlightened views on social matters, including the question of women. It was the Third Republic that introduced free, compulsory state primary education for children of both sexes up to the age of twelve (1880); and in 1879 the Minister of Education, Camille Sée, put before Parliament a bill which introduced the first state secondary education for girls. His speech was self-congratulatory and revealing:

Her vocation is to live in a happy communion of feelings and ideas with her husband and to bring up her children, and thus she has the right to an education worthy of her, worthy of him with whom she shares her life, worthy of the children whose first steps in learning she will guide, worthy finally of the Republic which emerged from the Revolution of 1789 and which was the first emancipator of women.[19]

The record of the Republicans on women's emancipation scarcely justified Sée's rhetoric. His own words make it very clear on what grounds women were to be granted an education. The early years of the Third Republic were beset by fears of the monarchist opposition and their Catholic allies. In order to ensure the survival of the Republic, its leaders needed to forge a new sense of national identity, centred on the secular mythology of a Republican France, resistant to religion and to the romantic attractions of monarchy. In order to do this, they had to win over the hearts and minds of the mothers of the nation, who had no direct political power but did have influence over their children's education. This was the chief motivation behind the improvements in women's education; as Bonnie Smith puts it: 'the retrograde conditions of women's minds suddenly appeared a luxury France could no longer afford'.[20]

The advantages of greater educational opportunities for women were real quite regardless of the motivations of the government, but the concept of female identity which informed state policy inevitably limited its scope. Several contemporary historians – notably James McMillan, Siân Reynolds and Theodore Zeldin – have demonstrated the resemblances between Catholic and Republican thinking and discourses on gender: women were by nature less rational and intellectually competent than men, but could, by a judiciously planned education, be trained to be sensible mothers and companions for their husbands. Men and women belonged by nature to wholly different spheres, both spatially and in terms of activity:

What is man's vocation? It is to be a good citizen. And woman's? To be a good wife and a good mother. One is in some way called to the outside world: the other is retained for the interior.[21]

Primary education provided sewing and cookery lessons for the girls where the boys had sports and military training; secondary education, which in any case catered only for a small proportion of middle-class girls, differed from that of boys in that it offered no Latin, no science or applied maths, and led not to the *baccalauréat* but to a special girls' leaving certificate. These differences maintained the sexual division of labour, avoided the danger of rendering girls eligible for any prestigious employment, and to some extent answered the fears of those many authors and writers of letters to the press who feared the loss of womanly qualities under the impact of too much abstract thinking. The spectre of the bluestocking looms large in French culture in the later nineteenth century, subject of impassioned letters and editorials, of cautionary tales (for example, the novels of Colette Yver) and satirical attacks (for example, *Les Bas-Bleus* (The Bluestockings) by Barbey d'Aurevilly, published in 1878).

The political struggle between Republican state and a Catholic Church aligned with the opposition thus led to a limited improvement in educational provision for women. It also constituted one of the chief Republican justifications for excluding half the population from 'universal' suffrage, on the grounds that the women's vote would mean a Catholic and anti-republican vote, and led to the construction of an image of French national identity which cast familiar iconographies of gender in slightly new forms. The doctrine of male supremacy in France had rarely taken the form of overt misogyny. It tended, rather, to be articulated as the adoration of authentic womanhood and a corresponding scorn for women who failed to live up to this ideal, by what Michèle Sarde terms 'that simultaneously protective and scornful attitude which reflects the admiration mingled with disdain that French men in general feel for women'.[22]

Republican discourse played on this disempowering idealization of women in its characterization of both the native land, France, and the Republic itself as female figures to be cherished, adored and defended, and of the citizen as always and inevitably male. The gendered nature of French nouns served to naturalize this process, since both 'France' and 'Republic' are feminine words, but the school textbooks of the Third Republic consistently taught the lessons of patriotism and gender difference in conjunction, using them to reinforce each other. The selfless, devoted mother and her male child, the nurturing, beloved country and her male children, formed the central axes not only of textbooks on national history and geography but also of grammar books where ideology was concealed beneath apparently neutral, self-evident truths.[23]

If women were identified with nation and Republic (symbolized by the female *Marianne*), then they could hardly be citizens of the nation or defenders of the Republic. Their role was as objects of male veneration, patriotism and political idealism, never as subjects, and this fitted nicely with the refusal to give women the vote. Male Republicans were able simultaneously to refuse women civil rights, equal pay and the smallest degree of self-determination while congratulating themselves on their superiority over other nationalities in their enlightened attitude to the opposite sex. There was no need for feminism in France, wrote Jean Alesson in his 1889 *Le Monde est aux femmes* (The World Belongs to Women), because:

> in no other country is woman more cherished, listened to, considered, admired and respected than in France – so that the Orientals, the Asiatics and the Germans are still quite stupefied by the French adoration of woman.[24]

And if France was the authentic woman, then any woman perceived to be working against national interests by defending those of her class or sex was reviled as the anti-France. This became apparent in the harshness of both speeches and sentences at the trials of women who fought for the Paris Commune of 1871, in an attempt to defend working-class aims against the victory of the bourgeois Republic. The prosecutor's speech clearly articulated the dual vision of woman as mother or whore, incarnation of man's ideal or of his deepest fears. Declaring his love and respect for woman 'so long as she remains wholly within the family', he continued:

> but if, deserting her mission, and under the sway of other influences, she serves only the demon of Evil, she becomes a moral monstrosity. Then woman is more dangerous than the most dangerous of men.[25]

Republicanism, with its declared ideals of liberty, equality and fraternity and its theoretical emphasis on the rights of the individual, offered a logical basis for women's rights even as it denied them – just as the Third Republic colonized foreign peoples in the name of freedom. Socialism would appear to offer a still firmer basis for sexual equality, since it is founded on a refusal of class-based privilege and a belief in social equality. As we shall see below, there were French socialists who acted as the champions of women's rights, but French socialism also carried a powerful strain of downright misogyny, and failed to adopt a clear stance on the question of women. Left-wing misogyny in France has its roots in the work of Joseph Proudhon (1809–65), whose belief in human equality and authorship of such radical slogans as 'Property is theft' and 'Progress is a permanent insurrection' contrast interestingly with his views on women. Proudhon argues strongly for male authority and for the enclosure of women within a purely domestic role, for: 'The woman who departs from the role proper to her sex falls back into the state of mere female', which he defines as 'a gossip, immodest, lazy, dirty, underhand, the agent of debauchery, a menace to her family and society'.[26] In Proudhon's terms, socialism is a highly masculine affair, and the trade-union delegates to the Congress of 1898, who refused to defend women's right to work on the grounds that paid employment 'demoralized' them, or Paul Lafargue, son-in-law of Karl Marx, who wrote that 'motherhood and love would allow woman to reconquer the superior position she had in primitive societies',[27] would have agreed with him. The feminist Madeleine Pelletier's view provides a fitting conclusion to this consideration of the views on women held by the three main political groupings of late-nineteenth- and early-twentieth-century France:

> A woman, like any individual, may choose to be socialist, republican or monarchist according to her convictions, but before anything else she must be feminist, because under a monarchy, the republic or socialism she will count for nothing unless the political equality of the sexes is recognized.[28]

WOMEN AND LITERATURE

Literature, in the broadest sense of the word, played its part in determining how sexual identity was viewed and lived. All over Europe the nineteenth century was the century of the printed word, when the publication of newspapers, reviews and books became both an industry and a central element in the construction of ideology. The role of writer gradually shifted from dependence on patronage to dependence on earnings from sales, though in practice French governments continued to patronize those writers they favoured by providing them with undemanding but well-paid posts in public libraries or the civil service.[29]

It is not surprising that the huge majority of published writers were men, since women lacked the prerequisites of education, social freedom and even the right to dispose of their own income. The doctrine of separate spheres relegated women to the private and domestic world, reserving the public space almost exclusively for male voices. As one literary movement succeeded another, the public persona of the poet/writer continued to be defined in masculine terms. From the heroic rebel of the Romantics, inspired by his female Muse, to the alienated and misogynist dandy of the Decadents; from the Realist scribe of society, as Balzac described himself, to the Naturalist scourge of social evils – both of them dependent on a social mobility denied to women – the identity of the writer assumed a confident place in society which legitimated a critical stance. The encouragement which George Sand offered to the male proletarian writers of the 1840s surely came in part from her identification with their plight: their sense of exclusion on grounds of class matched her own experience as a female outsider.

A small but significant number of women writers none the less achieved literary celebrity. The beginning of the period 1848 to 1914 coincided with the last years of two prolific women authors, whose work is currently starting to be reclaimed by feminist scholars.[30] Marceline Desbordes-Valmore (1786–1859) was an actress turned poet and children's author, whose poems explore the themes of human and divine love, maternity, and nature from an explicitly feminine perspective. Delphine Gay de Girardin (1804–55) was one of France's few successful women playwrights. De Girardin was herself the daughter of a novelist, Sophie Gay, and her plays were frequently 'feminocentric', staging the dramas of female figures from myth and history such as Judith and Cleopatra. They were enormously successful, staged first in Paris, then translated for the theatres of England, Germany, Italy and Spain, and even for the United States. From 1836 to 1848, de Girardin also assumed the pen name of the 'Vicomte de Launay' to write regular chronicles for *La Presse*, the paper edited by her husband. These 'Parisian Letters', with their humorously eclectic interest in all aspects of Parisian life and their explicitly autobiographical voice, look forward to the newspaper columns written by Colette almost a century later.

Another male pen name appearing in *La Presse* was that of Daniel Stern, pseudonym of Marie d'Agoult (1805–76). D'Agoult, for many years a close friend of George Sand, won a 'succès de scandale' with her 1846 novel *Nelida*, a fictionalized autobiography which centred on her ten-year liaison with the composer Franz Liszt. Her most important work, though, was perhaps as a historian, for she wrote a 'History of the 1848 Revolution' (published 1850–53) which drew on research from primary sources and on interviews with participants in the events.

From the last decade of the century, there was a marked increase in the numbers of women writers published and acknowledged in the contemporary press. This confirms the connection between education, civil rights and writing, for this was the generation of women born in the 1870s who had benefited from the Third Republic's reform of female education and from some minor advances in social freedom. The critical reception accorded to their works maintained the identification of great art with masculinity, for if they were not condemned, as Sand was, for trying to be like men, they were consistently relegated (as were Tinayre, Reval, Yver – and Colette) to a minor feminine sphere, and read in terms of the available feminine stereotypes.

The poet and novelist Anna de Noailles (1876–1933), for example, was one of the literary stars of her day, pronounced even by the London *Times* in 1913 to be 'the greatest poet that the twentieth century has produced in France – perhaps in Europe'.[31] Yet reviews of her passionate, lyrical verse couched their praise in terms which placed poems and poet firmly on their own, inferior side of the gender frontier. In a review of her first volume of poetry, *Le Cœur innombrable* (The Boundless Heart, 1901), *Le Figaro*'s critic opined that the poet was:

> completely woman in her sinuous grace and absolute elegance of mental attitude (woman concentrates life within her and does

not externalize, she is passive, perpetually awaiting the orders of nature, she is receptive rather than creative).[32]

Several of these *fin-de-siècle* authors are studied below, but Reval, Tinayre, Yver, Rachilde and Vivien were the contemporaries of many other widely read and celebrated women writers, and particularly women novelists. As a genre, the novel was both more able than poetry to provide a woman author with an independent income, and offered more scope for the discussion of social issues. Playwriting demanded access to the public, masculine domain of theatre management and finance, and the only women to achieve celebrity in the French theatre in this period were actresses, of whom the most famous was Sarah Bernhardt (1844–1923).

Lucie Delarue-Mardrus (1874–1945), for example, wrote at least forty novels as well as nine volumes of poetry and some plays and essays. Although her own highly unconventional lifestyle never led Delarue-Mardrus to espouse the cause of feminism, and although she expressed some singularly reactionary views on gender, some of her novels are explicit and angry indictments of sexual inequality. In *Marie Fille-mère* (Marie the Unmarried Mother, 1908), the story of Marie dramatizes the real dilemma of thousands of young women: seduced at home in the country, she is forced into the city, where she finds work as a domestic servant but must conceal her pregnancy, with all the physical and emotional suffering this entails. Once the child is born, she is unable to support the two of them without a man, and the jealous violence of her new lover ends the lives of mother and child. Although few women writers in this first period were self-declared feminists, their work frequently addressed the same issues as did the feminist movement – and took these issues to a wider audience.

As education for girls expanded and the leisure time of the middle classes increased, the last half of the nineteenth century saw a massive increase in the female reading population, so that one of the first lending libraries in Paris had 10 per cent female membership when it opened in 1862, but 70 per cent by 1898.[33] Resa Dudovitz, in her study of bestsellers in France, speculates that despite their almost total disappearance from literary history, it is probable that many of the novels in circulation were in fact written by female authors, in many cases concealed behind pseudonyms, and that the novel was one important means of communication of meanings and images among nineteenth-century French women. Surviving evidence for this appealing thesis is slim in the earlier part of the period, but around the turn of the century the number of women-authored texts which deal more or less explicitly with the question of female identity and experience suggests a significant circulation and negotiation of women's issues through literature.

FEMINIST OPPOSITION

As a movement, French feminism of the late nineteenth and early twentieth centuries was mild and ineffectual, failing to win the vote or to have the impact of similar movements in Britain or Germany. The relative failure of the early feminists can be explained by the national context: fears for the survival of the Third Republic in the face of monarchist opposition made liberal middle-class feminists unwilling to rock the boat; the fact that universal male suffrage had been introduced in France in 1848 meant that (unlike in Britain or the USA) alliances could not be forged with disenfranchised males. The relative moderation and minority status of French feminism should not, however, conceal its elements of original radicalism, nor its real achievements. The existence of a small but articulate feminist opposition in France is a relevant factor in the discussion of women's writing, even where writers did not specifically align themselves with feminist positions.

Every uprising in France, from 1789 to 1871, had its contingent of angry women who fought both with their men against oppressive governments, and for the specific cause of women. In 1848, the year in which American feminists declared the 'self-evident truth' that 'all men and women are created equal', French women created the first feminist daily, *Women's Voice*, met in women's political clubs, and presented petitions to the new Assembly for equal rights, including the right to vote. Many of these women (Claire Démar, Pauline Roland and Jeanne Deroin, for example) were from modest or impoverished backgrounds, but had found a refuge from marriage and domesticity in the Saint-Simonian communes, where the radical theories of sexual equality proposed by the social theorist Saint-Simon (1760–1825) were put into practice. Feminists attempted to nominate the celebrated female author George Sand to the new National Assembly, but her refusal to stand probably merely pre-empted the veto of her male colleagues. The new Republic defined 'universal' suffrage as male suffrage, and closed the women's clubs and paper.

In 1871 the Paris Commune rose against the conservative government of the new Third Republic, and women set up local women's committees to organize food distribution, childcare and nursing, as well as later fighting on the barricades. The Commune itself refused women any seats on the 90-strong governing Council, and paid little attention to women's rights in their political debates. After the defeat of the insurrection, those women who survived the massacre were doubly reviled at their trials for having transgressed the laws of feminine behaviour: 'We will say nothing of their females. Out of respect for women whom they resemble once they are dead.'[34]

The radicalism of Saint-Simon and of Charles Fourier (1772–1837), for whom 'the extension of women's rights [was] the principle of all social progress',[35] had left a potentially inspiring heritage of ideas, but little practical change. The insurrection of 1848 ended with women like Jeanne Deroin and Pauline Roland imprisoned, and George Sand in disconsolate retreat at her country home. The subsequent overthrow of the Republic led to twenty years of Empire, when the working conditions of proletarian women were at their harshest and the doctrine of separate spheres kept most middle-class women firmly out of the public arena. These are the years which form the background to the second half of George Sand's writing career. It was the coming of the Third Republic, and the visible discrepancy between its proclaimed ideals of liberal humanism and the real constraints on women, which produced a resurgence of feminism.

Feminist activity runs throughout the years from the beginning of the Third Republic to the outbreak of the First World War, taking a variety of forms. There were numerous campaigning groups, some of them short-lived, beginning with Léon Richer's *Association des droits des femmes* (Association for Women's Rights), founded in 1870 and rising by 1901 to fifteen feminist organizations in Paris alone, supported by between 20,000 and 25,000 members, of whom about 2,000 could be counted as active militants.[36] When these figures are set against the 500,000 women who took part in the suffrage demonstration in Hyde Park in 1908, the limits of the French movement become clear, but this does not diminish the significance of a consistent feminist presence throughout these years. The generation of French women writers born in the early years of the Third Republic display different attitudes to feminism, but they all write in awareness of the challenge it poses to entrenched beliefs about gender.

There were other ways of campaigning, too. The years 1878 to 1903 were the great era of the feminist congress in France, with at least eleven of these large public meetings being held over the twenty-five-year period. Forums for the discussion of women's demands, they were usually attended by representatives from government or Parliament, invited international guests, and representatives from working-class organizations.[37]

The feminist press also gave women a public voice. Thirty-five feminist publications appeared – albeit briefly in most cases – between 1871 and 1914, and one of these, Marguerite Durand's *La Fronde*, was published daily from 1897 till 1905, reaching, at the height of its success, a print run of 200,000, equivalent to sales of the most popular 'Home & Beauty' magazine for women, *Petit écho de la mode*. *La Fronde* was written and staffed entirely by women, and carried articles by many of the best-known women authors of the day, including Séverine, Marcelle Tinayre and Lucie Delarue-Mardrus. Renée Vivien had poems published there. The paper carried the national and international news of the day, and campaigned on women's behalf – sometimes successfully, as in the case of the campaign for women to be eligible for the Legion of Honour.

Certain themes and demands recur throughout the different forms of campaign. The right to vote was the sole aim of some feminist organizations, and a demand common to all. The abrogation of the *Code Civil*, with its legal infantilization of women, was another central aim: in 1904 feminists held a counter-demonstration as the state celebrated the *Code*'s centenary, and Nelly Roussel denounced 'this execrable and accursed Law', condemning its supporters as 'evil or stupid worshippers of this monument of infamy'.[38] Feminists were united in their demand for equality of education, for the right to work and to equal pay, and for the recognition of maternity and domestic labour as social functions worthy of respect and – many of them argued

– economic recognition. 'We women, we mothers, are the lowest paid of all workers', argued Nelly Roussel on her well-attended nationwide lecture tours,[39] and congresses in 1900 and 1908 argued for wages and pensions for women whose work was motherhood.

Mainstream feminism did not attack the principle of marriage, though more radical theorists such as Madeleine Pelletier argued that the institution of marriage was incompatible with women's emancipation. Arguments for women's right to control their own bodies were much more generally accepted: the journalist Séverine, who came to feminism in mid–career after acknowledging the inadequacy of her former individualist stance, condemned rape within marriage as not the 'fury of a lover' but the 'violence of the injured property owner taking his revenge'.[40] Roussel's popular lectures emphasized above all women's rights to chosen maternity, hence to contraception and, where necessary, abortion. Roussel even proposed that women should withdraw their labour through a 'womb strike' until their reproductive rights were recognized. In a France already conscious of a declining population and committed to the glorification of maternity, this was heresy, and in 1906 Roussel was brought to trial for publishing 'immoral and antisocial theories' which would lead to the 'weakening and decadence of the nation'.[41] The same accusations of immorality and decadence were levelled at the lesbian or Sapphist group, centred around the American expatriate Natalie Barney in *fin-de-siècle* Paris, whose writings raised the spectre of a female sexuality exclusive of both men and maternity.

As in other European countries, it was perhaps the issues around prostitution which most obliged feminists to confront the difficult question of sexuality. As I explained above, prostitution was tolerated and regulated in France. The starting point in the campaign to abolish regulation was often a conventionally moralizing one which fitted well with the 'separate sphere' allotted to women: women brought up to assume that chastity and marital fidelity were the highest virtues were shocked by the state's protection of male promiscuity. But many feminists moved on from moral indignation to a more political questioning of the concept of male sexuality which made prostitution a necessary counterpart of marriage, and yet punished the prostitute for her role. With the founding of the French Association for the Abolition of Regulated Prostitution in 1878 the issue of sexual morality entered the mainstream of feminist debate in France, and also brought French feminists into closer contact with their British counterparts through links with Josephine Butler's crusade against the Contagious Diseases Act. For middle-class feminists to assume common political cause with prostitutes, recognizing the structural interdependence of their roles rather than seeing them as fallen sisters, was a major advance, even though their campaigns had distinctly less practical success than those of Josephine Butler. Registration of prostitution in Paris did not officially end until 1961.[42]

Recognition of the significance of prostitution also meant consideration of the lot of working-class women. Relations between socialist and bourgeois feminists in France were another cause of the relative failure of the movement, for while on the one hand middle-class women 'had both ideological and material stakes in the continued existence of the republic',[43] and perceived socialism as a threat from below, for socialist women 'class oppression seemed more fundamental than sex oppression'.[44] Bourgeois feminists' attempts to speak on behalf of working-class women were often perceived as 'maternalism'. Socialist women themselves struggled against the Proudhonian heritage of misogyny within the movement, but also against the well-established notion that movements like feminism were a mere digression from the real struggle for socialism, which would put an end to all inequalities. In this they were in a situation very comparable to that of their middle-class sisters who were constantly being told that their demands were inopportune because the crucial thing was to save the Republic – which would, in its own good time, also end injustice. The fact that women's problems transcended class boundaries was none the less frequently recognized in action. With the notion of political solidarity, the concept of a gendered identity ceases to be rooted in biology, as the dominant ideology would have it, and is redefined in terms of shared oppression.

There were achievements during these years. Feminist campaigning contributed to improvements in women's conditions at work, and won women the right to vote for and be voted on to minor bodies such as departmental councils for primary education (1886) and works councils (1900). Divorce was legalized in 1884, women had legal control of their own income from 1907, and in the same year gained the right to be the legal guardians of their own illegitimate children. There were regular, if limited, improvements in educational opportunity. As the war approached it seemed certain that the numerous, often imaginative campaigns for female suffrage were about to be rewarded, as a postal referendum conducted by the newspaper *Le Journal* demonstrated widespread national support, and the socialist leader Jean Jaurès argued women's case in Parliament. As war approached, nationalist fervour led to the assassination of Jaurès by a self-declared patriot, and internal dissent came to be identified with betrayal of the nation. The moment was lost.

As Zola's novel *Nana* ends, Franco–German war is also about to break out, though it is the war of 1870, not of 1914. Nana lies dead, her power destroyed as the masculinity of the nation is reasserted in the virile young recruits marching off to war. Zola's attitude to his story is at least ambivalent, since he wrote with the retrospective knowledge that this war led both to the defeat of France and to the birth of the Republic he believed in: Nana represents the regime whose death he celebrates, yet she also represents the cause of its downfall.

There is an odd and enigmatic moment in the closing scene when Nana's fellow prostitutes, hitherto represented as self-seeking and incapable of solidarity, keep vigil over the body, and Nana's chief rival, Rose, remains last of all to tidy the room and light a candle, hovering anxiously: 'You know it's been a great blow to me. . . . We were never nice to each other in the old days. And yet this has driven me out of my senses . . . ' (p. 469). This fleeting moment of solidarity among women as their world is consumed by war offers a prescient image of 1914 and a rare representation of a female perspective in Zola's novel. Despite the final massed chorus of 'To Berlin!', *Nana* ends with the sound of a female voice which is not performing for a male audience, but trying to articulate an awkward sense of a collective and gendered plight. The voice of feminists in 1914 was considerably more assured, but their situation as women in a society ordered by and for men had not fundamentally changed.

## 2
# George Sand (1804–76)
# and the Problem of Authority

In July 1831, Aurore Dudevant (*née* Dupin) left her husband and children at the family estate in central France and went up to Paris, where she rented – in Virginia Woolf's famous phrase – a room of her own. After nine years of marital incompatibility, Casimir Dudevant had agreed to make his wife an allowance from the Nohant estate so that she could spend half the year in Paris. His agreement was essential, despite the fact that Aurore had inherited the estate from her paternal grandmother, since under the *Code Napoléon* a wife's property was legally controlled by her husband. The allowance was small, but it represented the means to a longed-for independence.

The exhilaration of finding herself alone in her own apartment overlooking the Seine is recalled in Sand's 1854 autobiography *Histoire de ma vie* (*The Story of My Life*), for Aurore Dudevant was shortly to become the writer George Sand. Sand rejoices retrospectively in the sense of possessing her own space: 'I had sky, water, air, swallows and greenery on the rooftops.'[1] Limited income, together with a recognition of women's semi-exclusion from public places, soon led her to adopt the clothing of a male student. Since gender difference was markedly inscribed in costume in the nineteenth century, women's long voluminous skirts and fragile footwear restricting their movement and acting as constant reminders of social constraint, to dress as a man meant a delightful freedom of movement:

> I can hardly tell what delight my *boots* gave me: I could have slept with them on. With those little metal heels I was steady on the pavement. I flew from one end of Paris to the other. I felt as if I could have gone round the world.[2]

A female signature could be compared to female dress in that it too set up powerful expectations of propriety, limitation to acceptably feminine areas, abdication of any pretension to authority. Dudevant's transvestism was thus followed by her adoption of the male pen name George Sand, which similarly afforded her greater freedom of scope and style. To gain freedom through masquerading as a man none the less means to acknowledge the reality of male power, and from the outset Sand's writing career was based on a problematic masking of her own identity as a woman.

Sand was unusually fitted to write as a man, for the circumstances of her birth and education had not been those of a conventional upper- or middle-class woman. First, there was her split class identity, for she was born – in her own words – 'astride two classes', child of a marriage between an aristocratic young officer in Napoleon's army and his working-class Parisian mistress. This meant both conflicting views from mother and paternal grand-mother on what constituted appropriate female behaviour, and the beginnings of that identification with the underprivileged that was to fuel Sand's political commitment. Her father's early death meant that Aurore took his place in the affections of her wealthy, cultured grandmother, and meant too that as she grew up she identified herself with a lost, romantic father figure – particularly, perhaps, because the strained relationship between mother and grandmother left her often emotionally isolated. Finally, her formal education was initially delivered by her father's old tutor and thus followed a 'masculine' syllabus including science and the classics, even though her grandmother subsequently recognized that if Aurore were to have any viable female future, she must unlearn her unaffected demeanour and acquire the appropriate 'cultural capital'³ provided by a convent education.

Marriage, at the age of eighteen, was Aurore's solution to the difficult situation in which she found herself after her grand-mother's death. Living in Paris with her volatile and increasingly tyrannical mother was harder than the isolated life at Nohant, and marriage the only way for a young woman to achieve even a semblance of adult autonomy. Sand writes warmly of the experience of motherhood, but the marriage itself failed to provide the intellectual and emotional companionship she had hoped for. By 1825 Aurore was engaged in the first of a series of passionate friendships with men who shared her interests and enthusiasms, and when she did leave Nohant alone for Paris, this unconventional step was made easier by the presence there of a small network of male friends from her native Berry. Educated to the same degree, dressing like them, Aurore/George was an honorary member of the group of young men. In the terminology of the French sociologist Pierre Bourdieu, Sand was a 'miraculée', one of those exceptional members of disadvantaged groups whose accession to a position of high status functions to make an inegalitarian system appear meritocratic.[4]

Like her male friends, Aurore/George needed to supplement her meagre allowance with an income. The 1830s were a period of massive expansion in publishing due to new technologies and increased public literacy, and soon Aurore had found employment at the newspaper *Le Figaro* and was collaborating with her current lover, Jules Sandeau, on a story and two novels which they published in 1831 under the name of J. Sand. The following year she wrote and published the novel *Indiana* as G. Sand, then *Valentine* using the signature George Sand.

Sand's early novels extend the Romantic themes of individual liberation, passionate love and metaphysical anxiety to women as subjects, rather than as muses and objects of desire for the male hero. Her heroines revolt against loveless marriages and the tyranny of husbands, seek fulfilment in absolute love (Indiana) or accept its impossibility by withdrawing into an austere exile (Lélia). In the play *Gabriel*, written and serialized in 1839 though never performed on stage, the connection between social oppression and the construction of gender is made explicit through a plot which centres on a heroine brought up to believe she is male, who must then discover the servitude of the female role through a painful apprenticeship. The 1830s saw Sand rapidly established as a writer who enjoyed both critical acclaim and popular success, the latter aided by the whiff of scandal produced by the knowledge that the author was really a woman and, moreover, a woman who enjoyed a series of liaisons with famous men.

The early novels have been the focus of much of the critical work devoted to Sand,[5] and they certainly launched her on a long and highly prolific career. Her work can be loosely divided into four overlapping periods: the Romantic period of the 1830s; the politically committed, socialist literature of the 1840s; the pastoral novels written in the period around 1848, and finally the novels and plays produced over the last twenty-three years of her life, which are more difficult to characterize collectively and have received the least critical attention. Between 1832 and her death in 1876 Sand published almost sixty novels (frequently three per year), twenty-five plays, a four-volume autobiography and hundreds of essays, articles and reviews. Since she spent most of her adult life financially supporting the Nohant estate, two children, a succession of impecunious lovers and friends and a number of political causes, she was rarely at liberty to suffer from lack of inspiration.

Popular and critical esteem for her writing went well beyond the commercial success fuelled by scandal. Balzac, Flaubert and Hugo all considered her a writer of major stature. Dostoevsky wrote of her as 'one of the most brilliant, the most indomitable and the most perfect champions [of liberal ideas]'.[6] Patricia Thomson has convincingly demonstrated Sand's success in Britain and the extent of her influence on English-language writers. Although the *Foreign Quarterly Review* in 1834 dubbed her the 'anti-matrimonial novelist', and Thomas Carlyle used the term 'George Sandism' to designate 'tolerance of immorality, romantic effusiveness, lack of common sense',[7] Sand was very widely read and respected in Britain as throughout Europe. George Lewes, John Stuart Mill and Henry James all admired her work, and she was an acknowledged influence on the work of Elizabeth Barrett Browning, the Brontës and George Eliot. Mrs Humphry Ward called her 'that great romantic artist in whom restless imagination went hand-in-hand with a fine and chosen realism',[8] and George Eliot, still Marian Evans when she read Sand in the 1840s, praised in her 'such truthfulness, such nicety of discrimination, such tragic power and withal such loving gentle humour'.[9]

Yet even before she died, Sand's prestige had begun to fade. Under the Third Republic her critical reputation dwindled to that of the author of 'pastoral' novels, which were read as mild eulogies to an idealized rural past consonant with the new nationalism. Despite a recent resurgence of feminist interest, she has disappeared from the canon, is rarely studied on university courses on the nineteenth-century novel, and is accorded little space in histories of French literature. In one typical – if particularly venomous

– modern evaluation of her writing, a critic describes her as a 'congenitally feeble' thinker, and her novels as 'compounded of a jumble of absurd utopian and spiritualist theories . . . , ludicrous idealisations of the peasantry . . . , grotesquely melodramatic stylisations of adultery at its most clichéd'.[10]

Sand's monumental success in the nineteenth century and her subsequent devalorization can usefully be examined in terms of her problematic identity as a woman author. Sand came to writing within a society whose economy and world-view were increasingly constructed on the basis of radical sexual difference. When the author and politician Kératry advised her that 'a woman should not write . . . . Believe me, do not make books, make babies',[11] he spoke as the representative of hegemonic values. Women writers were viewed with hostility because they threatened the frontiers which divided masculine intellect and creativity from feminine instinct and receptivity. Isabelle de Courtivron cites a telling line from Balzac's novel *Béatrix*, in which the androgynous heroine speaks the author's mind: 'only men possess the rod which props one up along these precipices, a strength which turns us into monsters when we possess it'.[12] Even Elizabeth Barrett Browning's sonnets in praise of Sand emphasize the contradiction between her identities as woman and as writer: 'True genius, but true woman! dost deny / The woman's nature with a manly scorn' ('To George Sand. A Recognition').

The difficulty of her position as a woman writer, or the 'anxiety of authorship',[13] led Sand to adopt textual strategies which legitimated her voice – strategies which began, at the most public level, with the adoption of a male pen name. Many features of her later writing seem to me to arise from this anxiety to establish and maintain a textual authority which is in doubt because of the gender of the author. But I also want to argue that Sand's popularity with her contemporary readers, including some whom we might expect to be particularly discerning, was due in part to a concern with the issue of gender difference which addressed contemporary anxieties.

SAND AND 1848

The year 1848 is the starting point for this study because it marks a transition from one regime to another and – for Republicans, socialists and feminists – a transition from optimism to pessimism. Sand was deeply involved in the events of 1848 both practically and emotionally: as one of the best-known and most prolific socialist writers of the day, she was called upon to act as a sort of 'minister for information' for the provisional government (February–April), and produced bulletins, open letters to the population and a play, *Le Roi Attend* (The King Awaits), performed free for the people who are revealed, at the end, to be the true monarch of the nation. When, in June, the newly elected Republican government massacred members of the working class in the streets of Paris, when Sand saw her radical friends and allies deported and Louis Napoléon begin his rise to power, she returned to Nohant, disconsolate, afraid for her own safety and bereft of that political optimism that had sustained her when the Republic was a hope for the future.

The events of 1848 confirmed Sand's political sympathies but severely undermined her political optimism, so that in the changed political climate that followed her work is more cautious, her meanings are less confident and less transparent. The same events revealed Sand's ambivalence with regard to the cause of women. The political clubs that blossomed in the freedom of early 1848 included a number of feminist associations, and it seemed briefly possible that women might make some political gains from the new regime. A group of feminists decided to nominate Sand for election to the National Assembly, thus raising the issue of female eligibility. In a letter often cited to demonstrate Sand's anti-feminism, she declined their nomination, arguing that while in principle women should have the right to participate in politics, in practice the more urgent task was to gain for all women civil and legal equality in the personal domain of marriage and family. The argument is a tenable one, and would be echoed by later feminists: to admit some women into the male political establishment on male terms does not solve the problem of women's fundamental lack of rights as a sex. Moreover, Sand declares optimistically that women's civil rights are 'one of the first questions with which a socialist republic should be concerned',[14] for she sees an analogy between monarchy and patriarchy, republican democracy and egalitarian marriage:

when it is asked how a conjugal association could subsist where
the husband is not the head, the absolute and final arbiter, it is
a little like asking how the free man could get along without a
master, or a republic without a king.[15]

However, despite the validity of the central argument, the letter
also betrays some anxiety to distance herself from her addressees.
Sand maintains a sharp division between herself and the feminists
by referring to them as 'these ladies' and using the second-person
plural rather than the first: 'So, civil equality, equality in marriage,
equality in the family, this is what *you* can and what *you* must
seek and demand . . .'[16] (emphasis added). For a woman who
had exchanged an unhappy marriage for a series of interesting
lovers, she also adopts a strangely pious tone in relation to adultery,
rhetorically demanding whether these 'ladies' were advocating
'promiscuity', and declaring that if so, she would wish to 'dissociate
[her]self personally from them', and 'leave it to public morality to
deal with this regrettable fantasy'.[17] The identification of feminist
political demands with a challenge to the rules of sexual behaviour
is astute, but in the ideological climate of 1848 it is also calculated to
damage women's cause. The letter reveals both an understanding
of what is at stake for women and a profound anxiety to maintain
her own honorary position among a male artistic and political elite
rather than identify with a female underclass. This ambivalence
operates with equal force in Sand's literary texts.

THE PASTORALS

Sand had already written two short novels in the 'pastoral' vein, *La
Mare au diable* (*The Haunted Pool*) in 1846 and *François le Champi*
in 1847. Both these stories purport to be the retelling of tales of
times gone by, told by the village storyteller whose dialect, and
hence whose perspective on experience, they attempt to reproduce
while 'translating' sufficiently to render them intelligible to the
reader of standard French. Although they were later to be read
as apolitical, charming little stories of simple countryfolk, in her
prefaces Sand places her project within a political context of class
conflict. A degree of idealization of the peasantry and the adoption
of their linguistic perspective serve, she argues, to foster the reader's
sympathy towards the apparently alien world of the lower classes.

If there is a radical element in these stories, though, it lies not only in their sympathetic rendering of a peasant class who were in any case, as the elections of 1848 were to demonstrate, politically conservative, but also in what we might term their inscription of Oedipal utopias. One of the most central narratives of the nineteenth-century novel is that of the hero's departure from the maternal home and his discovery of and insertion into the social world, where power is clearly masculine. In terms of the construction of gender roles, this story could also be told in psychoanalytic terms as the son's necessary repression of desire for and identification with the mother, in order to gain access to the privileges of adult malehood. In a strictly segregated economy of gender the girl's development, on the other hand, demands a continuing identification with the mother, but the transfer of desire away from both parents to a new partner and to children.

What happens in Sand's pre-1848 pastorals is that hero and heroine achieve adult status and the gratification of sexual love without any concomitant process of repression. In *La Mare au diable* Germain is an adult man, the widowed father of a family, who is presented at first in a quasi-paternal relationship with the young heroine, Marie. The work of the plot is to eliminate all possible rivals and thus legitimate their final happy marriage, a marriage which also returns Marie to her mother. Figuratively speaking, Marie attains adulthood without having to renounce her desire for the father or her wish to remain with the mother. *François le Champi* is more explicitly Oedipal, for Madeleine Blanchet fosters the orphaned François and raises him as her child. Once grown, he leaves and proves himself as an adult in another village but returns, if not to kill the surrogate father, at least to see him die and to marry Madeleine. The endings of these stories are happy in the fairytale manner: they are optimistic tales in which desire can triumph over repression.

Although they employ the same framework of village storyteller, rural setting and marriage as dénouement, the post 1848 pastorals *La Petite Fadette* (*The Country Waif*, 1848) and *Les Maîtres Sonneurs* (*The Bagpipers*, 1853) are visibly non-utopian. *La Petite Fadette* reveals its difference first in the preface. Written and first published only months after the events of June 1848, the preface to the first edition ironically frames the novel within a political context by disavowing any political intention. Presented as a dialogue between the author and a persuasive friend who wants to hear the story, the preface speaks of the pain and betrayal of recent events, but opts for the telling of pastoral tales as an escape from suffering:

> And we shall dedicate these stories to our friends who are prisoners; since we are forbidden to speak to them of politics, we can only tell them stories to entertain them and help them to sleep. (*Fadette*, p. 12)[18]

The tension between literature as escapism and literature as political activity has apparently disappeared by the later *Bagpipers*, the preface of which simply dedicates the book to a friend who loves the region in which the story is set. None the less, since 1853 is only two years after the *coup d'état* which ended the Republic, this should perhaps be read in the light of the 1851 second preface to *Fadette*, in which Sand explains:

> Since those June days of which current events [i.e. Louis-Napoleon's *coup d'état*] are the inevitable consequence, the author of this tale has set himself [*sic*] the task of being *aimable*, even if he should thereby die of sadness. (*Fadette*, p. 19)

In terms of class politics, the post-1848 Sand thus consciously – and bitterly – renounces her previous optimism about the power of art to act on ideology, and hence on material reality. I would argue that although Sand's position on gender is far less consciously articulated, there too the negative impact of 1848 and its demonstration of the difficulty of achieving radical social change had an effect on her writing. The strategy of 'amiability' was already a part of Sand's repertoire in relation to gender, but 1848 reinforced the need to seek legitimacy, and produced texts whose radical elements are driven underground.

There are several senses in which both *La Petite Fadette* and *The Bagpipers* succeed in being 'amiable', which I take to mean endorsing rather than disturbing the dominant ideology. Although Sand's real identity as a woman was public knowledge from early in her career, she consistently maintained the fiction and the *authority* of the male signature by interposing male narrators between author and reader. In these texts her female identity is doubly concealed by two layers of male narrative voice: that of the male 'George

Sand' in the preface, and that of the old storyteller whose tale he is apparently translating and adapting for the reader. The challenge to male dominance posed by a public female voice is veiled, and the narratives can be taken to signify that belief in an ahistorical, natural wisdom of rural France which would be used to justify many a conservative regime from Napoleon III to Vichy.

Both narratives centre on the formation of a couple, or couples, and thus on the foundation of a productive family unit. *La Petite Fadette* is on one level a love story: Landry Barbeau meets the wild, wilful Fadette, whose family background (a grandmother believed to have the powers of a witch, a mother who abandoned her children to follow the soldiers) and unkempt appearance make her an unlikely bride, but whose transformation through love leads to a happy conclusion. *The Bagpipers* interweaves the story of the narrator's youthful adoration of Brulette and gradual transference of love to the more austere and passionate Thérence, with Brulette's own romance with Huriel. Both novels contain significant secondary narrative lines to which we will return, but in each closure is achieved through marriage, birth and the foundation of new families.

This repeated narrative pattern is conservative in two senses. Closure means the neat tying-off of narrative threads, the res-olution of personal and social issues raised – and thus signifies the reimposition of order. The pleasure of such narratives is a reassuring one, for they promise that conflicts can be resolved and challenges accommodated within the world represented in the text. But here it is not merely the form which is conservative, for the process which leads to closure depends upon reaffirmation of the very concept of sexual difference which underpinned patriarchy in mid-nineteenth-century France. In *Fadette*, in order to win the hero's love the heroine must renounce her unselfconscious pleasure in dance and fun (the young Fadette 'lived like a boy, without any concern for her appearance, and liked only games and laughter' [*Fadette*, p. 121]) and become modest, neat and compliant. She must renounce allegiance to her sexually transgressive mother, whom she defends fiercely in the early part of the book, and herself become the good mother who, like Snow White, cooks and cleans the cottage ('so that you could see yourself in the poor furniture' [*Fadette*, pp. 239–40]) and cares for the male inhabitant, her brother. Fadette undergoes a process of education which transforms her from a clever, irreverent and independent girl to a good wife and mother respectful of convention, and of patriarchal authority in the person of Père Barbeau, her father-in-law.

In a rather similar way, the pleasure-loving and independent Brulette ('the longer I live the more my freedom and my lightheartedness satisfy me' [*Bagpipers*, pp. 83–4][19]) must undergo the trial of caring for a disagreeable infant who, moreover, is wrongly assumed to be her own illegitimate child by the local community, before she becomes 'more gentle in manner, sensible and interesting in her behaviour' (*Bagpipers*, p. 235), and thus deserves her happy marriage. The energetic and unsubmissive younger heroines clearly bear a resemblance to the young Aurore, for Sand devotes several passages in *Story of My Life* to the remembered anguish of being obliged to repress her spontaneous energy and high spirits in order to conform to the feminine ideal: 'when [my grandmother] ordered me not to be restless or noisy it seemed to me that she was ordering me to be dead'.[20] The inexorability of the heroines' transformation within the fiction suggests the author's need to compromise at a symbolic level with an ideological reality which her own success as a writer challenged.

However, although the male narrative voice and the plot's rewarding of female subservience explain how these texts could be co-opted for conservative ends, they cannot be reduced to these meanings alone. Despite their final conformity to nineteenth-century models of selfless, domesticated womanhood, these heroines display qualities of intelligence, initiative and integrity which refuse to fit into a subservient role. They are to a large extent the active agents in the plot. Fadette saves the lives of Landry and his brother through her knowledge of natural lore and her astute readings of their characters, enabling Landry to find his lost brother on one occasion and rescuing him from drowning on another. It is she who insists on her reward for these acts, forcing Landry to dance with her at the fair, and thus initiating their romance. Fadette makes a lucid appeal to Père Barbeau's male pride and his avarice by asking for his advice on how to manage her inheritance, thus ensuring his permission to marry his son; and it is Fadette who understands the illness of Landry's brother Sylvain and, in a scene in which her magical powers come close to those of the psychoanalyst,[21] cures his inertia by having him articulate his unconscious desires and fears.

Brulette's intelligence is emphasized as central to her attraction, and the moral education of the narrator of *The Bagpipers* depends upon his transition from seeing Brulette as object of desire to seeing her as friend, companion and equal. In the contrast between the playful, flirtatious Brulette and the more austere Thérence, Sand also touches on the significance of self-consciousness for women – of playing to, or remaining unconscious of, the male gaze. Thérence is a strong female character largely because she is unaware of herself as object of desire or approval:

> Thérence showed you frankly that she did not want you and even seemed surprised and annoyed if you paid her any attention. . . . She seemed only to wish for the same sort of regard as that that she gave you. (*Bagpipers*, p. 349)

This is the very reverse of the emphasis on appearance as central to women's identity, and echoes Sand's own recollections, in *Story of My Life*, of the frustration of being educated to forgo activity and the open air in order to conform to the visual image of ideal femininity.

The heroines' strength and active roles in the plots are not simply erased for the reader by the closure in marriage. Although, as we have seen, the conclusion of each story in marriage endorses a conservative ideology of gender, marriage does not signify here the confinement of women to domestic space and the definition of the world beyond as male territory. The door of each cottage is, as it were, left open. Fadette – in memory of her own unhappy childhood, and in a diminished version of Sand's socialist ideals – does not retreat into the nuclear family, but 'welcomed into her home all the poor children of the village for four hours each day' (*Fadette*, p. 268), teaching and caring for them alongside her own children. In *The Bagpipers* one of the central and structuring oppositions is that between the people of the flat, agricultural Berry region who are calm, placid and home-loving (Brulette and Tiennet), and the more passionate, restless inhabitants of the hilly Bourbon region (Thérence and Huriel). Here, then, the preference for home territory or for a travelling life is determined much more by a character's regional origins than by gender. The two modes of living are both maintained and fused at the end through the founding of an extended, rather than a nuclear, family. Thus the couple remains part of a wider whole, and the opposition between the static and the itinerant is never aligned with gender.

Also, while Sand's political pessimism at this point means that conforming turns out to be the best strategy, it is important to note that in these texts gender roles are displayed as something learnt rather than innate. Fadette's inclinations go towards an active, independent life and an assertive manner, and in the absence of a suitable role model she has simply not acquired any domestic skills, talent for self-adornment or delicacy of speech, so that Landry reproaches her with an excessive and unfeminine wit. Her decision to 'become a woman' is a conscious one and involves a deliberate learning process. Brulette is a more coquettish character, conscious from the outset of male attention, but she makes a deliberate effort to develop maternal qualities out of love for her own surrogate mother. Still more striking, however, is the sense in which the novels reveal masculinity as a set of attributes acquired through a system of repression and reward.

In both novels the central romantic plot is doubled by another, stranger narrative thread. The working title for *La Petite Fadette* was 'Les Bessons', 'the twins' in the dialect of Sand's region, for the drama begins and concludes not with the Landry/Fadette relationship but with that of Landry and his twin Sylvain. The twins are initially inseparable, refusing individual identity in favour of a complete sharing of tastes, activities and possessions, despite their elders' efforts to force them towards an individuation which collective wisdom holds to be essential:

> They tried giving something they both wanted to only one of them; but straight away, if it was something to eat they would share it, and if it was a game or a little tool they would keep it in common, or pass it from one to the other with no distinction between mine and yours. (*Fadette*, pp. 32–3)

When they are at last separated by force, with the sending of Landry to another farm to work, the difference that emerges between them corresponds to the masculine/feminine divide. Landry is larger, stronger, and succeeds in repressing his attachment to Sylvain and to his mother to become a successful male adult. Sylvain, on the other hand, remains at home, gentle, loving, but dependent and unable to detach himself emotionally from brother or mother. There is no place for Sylvain in the adult world, for as a man his task is to separate from his earliest and closest attachments and found a family himself.

It is Fadette who finally understands him and prevents him from sinking into death. What Fadette recommends is the mirror-image of the choice she has made herself: just as the 'masculine' Fadette opts advisedly for a feminine role, so Sylvain must renounce his 'feminine' passivity and fragility and at least simulate independence if he is to survive. In Sylvain's case, however, the conclusion is not a neatly happy one, for Fadette succeeds only in *transferring* his dependence (in the psychoanalytic sense) to herself.[22] Sylvain's love for Fadette leads to his self-imposed exile, and he ends the novel far from all those he loves as an officer in Napoleon's army – a singularly unfitting fate for this gentle character, and one which resembles suicide.[23]

The romantic plot of *The Bagpipers* is similarly shadowed by a male protagonist who fails to separate from his earliest love-objects, and thus to become a successful adult male. Joseph, like Sylvain, is physically delicate and introspective, contrasting strongly with the conventionally masculine Tiennet who, like Landry, is sturdy and combative. Joseph's initial mystery is explained by his passion for music, and his story is in one sense that of his quest to become the region's finest player and composer of music for the bagpipes, but he is also obsessively attached to Brulette, who in many senses represents a mother figure. Joseph's mother brings up the motherless Brulette alongside her son, to some extent displacing him, since 'a girl wants a mother longer than a boy' (*Bagpipers*, p. 11); he responds by developing an intense dependence on Brulette herself. This passion resurfaces at several points in the narrative, and Joseph remains a curious, solitary character who belongs nowhere, even when his genius as a musician is recognized. Unlike all the other characters, he ends the novel far away from the warm space of the community, dying alone in an icy ditch at the hands of fellow pipers.

Joseph and Sylvain are the elements of narrative which cannot be neatly tied. The casualties of a culture which demands emotional autonomy and authority of its men, dependence and subservience of its women — and in this, perhaps, resembles Sand's own society more closely than the earlier, peasant society in which the narrative is set — Sylvain and Joseph look forward to the equivocally gendered young men of Colette's fiction and signify, within Sand's most apparently orthodox tales, the violent repression demanded by nineteenth-century patriarchal law. Despite those devices which maintain the author's uncontentious air of 'amiability', the pastoral novels expose the cost of conformity to rigidly separate gender roles.

THE LATER NOVELS
Over the next two decades Sand continued to write from Nohant rather than Paris, producing a regular series of novels and seeing twenty of her plays premiered in the capital between 1848 and 1872.[24] Despite her dislike of the autocracy and materialism of the Second Empire, her work of this period is rarely overtly political but deflects opposition on to targets which may be read as within the personal sphere: class prejudice as an obstacle to romantic love; orthodox Catholicism as a doctrine which undermines individual conscience. 'Amiability' continues to prevail: while around her the literary mode of Realism triumphed, and the vulnerability of romantic illusion in a harshly material world became a major theme of fiction, Sand's narratives continued to meander through picturesque settings, more often than not towards an ending of requited and mutual love. The last period of her writing is her least admired, and it is not hard to see why.

However, these works were widely read and appreciated during Sand's lifetime, and their critical interest emerges if we set them in the context of their production and original reception. The specific tone and structure of Sand's later work clearly demonstrate the need to establish legitimacy as a woman author in the face of women's lack of 'natural' authority, but offer an interesting amalgam of these strategies of self-legitimation with more radical features deriving from the earlier work. Sand appealed to a large female readership, and some of her appeal was undoubtedly due to the fact that within a conventional discourse of romantic storytelling she articulated a subtle critique of contemporary beliefs and practices about women.

Pierre Bourdieu writes of 'the "natural" self-confidence, ease and authority of someone who feels authorized';[25] Toril Moi, in an article on Bourdieu's work, of the fact that 'the right to speak, *legitimacy*, is invested in those agents recognised by the field as powerful possessors of cultural capital'.[26] In this final period of her writing career Sand possessed a curious and limited kind of cultural capital, based on a long and successful career as the male narrator 'George Sand' and her more recently acquired respectability as the 'good lady of Nohant', a sort of national mother figure whose rural retreat and edifying tones blurred memories of a much more scandalous past. Sand's writing plays on these dual sources of legitimacy, revealing an absence of that 'natural' self-confidence Bourdieu identifies as the prerogative of the truly authorized – an absence which is unsurprising at a period when her political enemies were ruling France and the legal, economic and political status of women defined them as subordinate and incapable of independent judgement.

The use of a male narrator continues to provide an intratextual reminder of Sand's borrowed male persona as author: extradiegetic narrators are invariably identified as male by masculine adjectives and pronouns, intradiegetic narrators are male characters. The device of the double male narrator recurs, as in *Laura: Voyage dans le cristal* (Laura: Journey into the Crystal), where an artist recounts his meeting with the mineralogist Alexis Hartz, then relays to the reader Hartz's first-person narration of his own story. In wholly or partially epistolary novels, a form favoured by Sand, male and female voices may alternate, but it is frequently the male voice that begins and frames the story (*Adriani* [1854], *Elle et lui* [*She and He*] [1859], *Mademoiselle la Quintinie* [1863]).

At the same time, narratorial interventions often serve to establish a moral framework consonant with female respectability – that is, to legitimize Sand not as an author *per se*, but as a *woman* author within that ideological framework which identifies woman as the moral guardian of the nation. Sand's autobiographical writing censors and selectively represses her own experience: in *Story of My Life* sexual relationships are virtually omitted, and *Elle et lui*, a novel based on her relationship with the poet Musset, repeatedly defines Thérèse, the Sand figure, as *maternal* in her feelings for the young artist Laurent. The scene in which Thérèse agrees to pass from friendship with Laurent to a sexual relationship exemplifies the way in which the writing represents female desire as selfless solicitude:

'. . . you are becoming embittered and it seems to me that if I resist you would hate me and return to your debauchery, blaspheming even our poor friendship. So I offer to God, for you, the sacrifice of my life.'[27]

Thérèse/Sand is repeatedly characterized as selfless, motherly, experiencing desire only as an expression of spiritual and emotional love. This retrospective purifying of the once scandalous Sand persona brings it into line with the moral tone of the later work.

The structure of the narratives also endorses the writer's identity as moral guardian, for it is basically that of the happy romance. The meeting of hero and heroine and the revelation of their mutual love lead, with few exceptions, to a dénouement in marriage, reached after a series of narrative detours caused by obstacles to their union. There is little emphasis on character development since hero and heroine are idealized from the beginning: the work of the narrative is, rather, to display the virtues of the protagonists both to each other and to the reader through setting them to overcome obstacles. Thus in *Mademoiselle la Quintinie*, Lucie and Emile reach marriage once they have uncovered and rejected the machinations of a sinister priest; in *Le Marquis de Villemer*, Caroline proves her lack of self-interest and her resourcefulness, and the Marquis his unqualified love, as they struggle through illness, class prejudice and the tricks of a scheming rival to happiness. The plots represent a world in which heterosexual romantic love is the measure of happiness, and the identification of the narrative voice with this view is reinforced by narratorial interventions: 'and, to put it more simply, in our view the finest natures are those which begin by loving and then bring their wisdom and their poetry into harmony with their emotion.'[28]

None the less, despite the multiple signifiers of respectable amiability, Sand's later work contains elements which make it considerably less bland than the above outline might suggest, and help to explain its popularity, particularly with women, at the time of publication. Despite the male narrative voice, women are always structurally central to these narratives, and what is at stake is the possibility of their finding a happy and fulfilling relationship while maintaining their integrity. Caroline (*Le Marquis de Villemer*) suffers the very real dilemma of an impoverished bourgeois woman whose self-respect depends on her ability to prove that love, not financial need, motivates her marriage to a wealthy man. *Mademoiselle la Quintinie* is the story of a struggle between Catholic fundamentalism and liberal humanism, but the site of that struggle is Lucie's mind and heart, and through the story of Lucie's mother the issue is broadened to become one that concerns all women, since the power of the Church is shown to depend on women's learnt respect for male authority. The consistently happy endings belong to the genre of pleasurable fantasy, but the recognition that female destinies hinge on marriage, the insistence that happiness must be won with minimal loss of personal integrity – these elements address the reality of female readers' lives.

Sand's appeal for legitimacy on conventionally feminine terms does not prevent her from creating the vigorous, independent heroines we met in the pastorals. The later heroines may be angelic in the sense that they have none of the everyday flaws of a more realist discourse (nor do the heroes), but they are never passive, docile or fragile. Sand's self-portrayal in *Story of My Life* is that of a dynamic, determined woman who made her own life against considerable odds; Caroline of *Le Marquis de Villemer* is resourceful, mobile, unconcerned with appearances and frequently the active agent in the plot, while Lucie la Quintinie is assertive, clear-thinking and loved by Emile precisely for these strengths. Sand often draws attention to the issue of the male gaze and characterizes her positive heroines by their unselfconsciousness, their indifference to the gaze as sign of objectification – as in *Adriani*, where Laure de Monteluz looks at the narrator: 'She looked me straight in the eyes with surprise and an absence of shyness which was the supreme expression of a total lack of coquetry.'[29]

If women are central to the plots and characterized in ways which question gender stereotypes, male behaviour is a major theme of many of the narratives. As in all romantic fiction, one of the functions of the story here is to imagine or fantasize a male partner with whom an equal and happy relationship might be possible. This involves both the representation and rejection of negative male figures, and the construction of a satisfactory hero for the purposes of the dénouement. *Mademoiselle la Quintinie* debates and satirizes the principle of paternal authority both in the character of Lucie's absurdly pompous father, whose wholehearted acceptance of each successive regime in France makes him a comical defender of the principle of arbitrary authority, and in the more dangerous figure of Moreali, who links paternal authority with political authoritarianism: '"It is in vain that the revolutionary spirit has restricted and annulled paternal authority; it survives in its entirety in the conscience of the true Christian"',[30] and thus discredits both, when he is proved to be evil and dishonest. If Emile is a suitable husband for Lucie, it is partly because he feels no need to demonstrate male superiority: 'I felt none of that puerile need to dominate her and prove to her that an ordinary man almost always knows better than the most educated woman.'[31]

The theme is still more marked in *Laura: Voyage dans le cristal* (1864), a love story which combines the modes of realism and fantasy. Alexis, a mineralogist, is reintroduced to Laura, a cousin he has not seen since childhood, and immediately falls in love with her. He rewrites the past accordingly, ignoring Laura's reminders of their mutual indifference as children and inventing, instead, nostalgia for 'the time when we were so happy together' (p. 58). Alexis's passion for the adult Laura depends not so much on any real acquaintance with her as on her beauty, by which he declares himself 'dazzled'. The story's fantasy element represents the moral and spiritual education of Alexis, leading to the conventionally happy ending of a marriage only because he has learnt to see beyond the distorting lenses of myth and desire which structure patriarchal perceptions of women, and has thus become a man whom Laura can love.

Alexis and Laura enter a magical world inside the precious stones which Alexis studies, the 'crystal' world of the novel's title. At first this other world is a place of truth in which their love starts to develop, but the appearance of the sinister Nasias, Laura's father, lures Alexis away to undertake a voyage of 'discovery and conquest of the subterranean world' (p. 101). On this dreamlike journey, hovering between realism and science fiction, the discovery of strange and beautiful places gradually becomes less significant than their conquest, for Nasias is a ruthless colonizer. In order to reach the happy dénouement Alexis must reject the heroic masculine myth of the explorer/conqueror, and with it the mythification of Laura, whose only role on the journey has been that of magical guiding light.

With the death of Nasias and the return to the real world, Alexis accepts Laura's insistence: '"Through your magic prism I am too much; through your tired, disillusioned eyes I am too little."' (p. 153). The possibility of a happy marriage, the novel implies, depends on the replacement of the idealization of women – with its corollary of contempt – by the recognition of their imperfect, complex humanity. The fact that Alexis's enlightenment depends on his rejection of powerful myths of masculine heroism suggests an equal and inseparable need to challenge orthodox views of what it meant to be a man.

In a series of articles and a full-length critical study, the feminist critic Naomi Schor connects Sand's idealism (in the sense of positive, hyperbolizing idealization) with her position as a woman, both because her work has been devalued in a critical climate which denigrates idealism by characterizing it as *feminine* ('Idealise only toward the lovely and the beautiful: that is woman's work', advised Balzac[32]) and because idealism served as a literary strategy which avoided reproducing, and thus legitimating,

> a social order inimical to the disenfranchized, among them women. Idealism for Sand is finally the only alternative representational mode available to those who do not enjoy the privileges of subjecthood in the real.[33]

My argument here has emphasized the literary strategies which arise from Sand's female lack of the 'privileges of subjecthood', from her anxiety to establish a threatened legitimacy as an author. In order to be accepted as a voice of authority, to be taken seriously as artist and thinker, Aurore Dupin/Dudevant becomes George Sand, and the male narrators and focalization from a male perspective extend the masculine pen name into the text. As the political climate becomes grimmer and the hope of change recedes, Sand also seeks legitimacy within the framework of the dominant ideology of womanhood, and takes on the voice of woman as Angel, woman writer as guardian of women's morals. The romance-centred, morally ordered world acts as a signifier of female respectability, establishing Sand's credentials as a good woman in a period of deep conservatism when, if not her life, at least her liberty was at stake.

Schor's argument also implies, though, that idealism in the circumstances was an enabling mode for the 'disenfranchized' woman writer. We have seen that Sand's texts are not reducible to the tame and decorative tales they have become in literary history, but engage, albeit often obliquely, with the issues of gender identity and its attendant repression, the mythologization of women (or, in Beauvoir's phrase, woman as man's 'Other'), women's legal subjugation. The mode of romance also allows Sand to conclude her novels with the imagined perfection of joint and equal partnerships between a man and a woman. Sand was a brave and prolific writer whose very ambivalence towards her own sex represents within the text the difficulty of achieving, in life and in fiction, an identity which was strong and creative while securely marked as feminine.

# 3
# Feminism, Romance and the Popular Novel: Colette Yver (1874–1953), Gabrielle Reval (1870–1938) and Marcelle Tinayre (1871–1948)

George Sand saw only the difficult birth and the first four years of the Third Republic. When she died, the new regime's survival was uncertain and its political complexion unclear. This time, though, the Republic was to survive for almost seven decades – socially conservative, respectful of established wealth and property, but none the less a democracy formally committed to human rights and the equality of its citizens.

I have argued above that the Republican definition of gender had a great deal in common with that of the preceding regime and that of the Catholic opposition, but that recognition of the political danger of maintaining an undereducated, Catholic-influenced female population led to the extension of educational opportunities for women. Feminist movements were able to exploit the contradiction between the Republican creed of equality and the reality of women's exclusion from political and legal rights. The arrival of the Third Republic marked the beginning of a new period of feminist campaigning and a widespread anxiety about who women were and what their role should be.

Between 1870 and World War I numerous feminist associations existed in France. They were, on the whole, low in membership and moderate in tone, but they formulated, and thus placed on the public agenda, a set of important demands for civil and legal rights. The eleven international women's congresses held in Paris between 1878 and 1913 were widely – if unsympathetically – reported in the mainstream press, and showed a gradual increase in participation by socialist and trade-union feminists. Thirty-five feminist newspapers appeared and disappeared between 1871 and

1914, the most successful of them, *La Fronde*, published daily between 1897 and 1905. Campaigns for the vote ranged from decorous petitions to Parliament to Hubertine Auclert's refusal to pay taxes on the grounds that as a woman she did not have the rights of a citizen.

The vote was still many years away, but some important reforms were introduced. The legal incapacity of the married woman was slightly attenuated by laws of 1881 and 1897 which gave her the right to keep money in a savings account and to withdraw it without her husband's consent. In 1907 married women gained the right to dispose of their own earnings, and in the same year unmarried mothers were legally recognized as the guardians of their children.

But it was in the sphere of education that the most significant advances took place. Camille Sée's 1880 law established state secondary education for girls and enabled the setting up of female *Ecoles normales* (teacher training colleges) to staff the new *lycées*. The first college was founded at Fontenay-aux-Roses in 1880, the second at Sèvres in 1881. Although initially the state was careful to differentiate the secondary syllabus on gender lines (no Latin, limited amounts of science and applied maths for girls) and to award a special female diploma rather than the prestigious *baccalauréat*, parents and daughters of the less wealthy classes soon saw the employment potential of a secondary education. If there were only a few hundred girls in *lycées* in the 1880s, by 1914 there were 38,000 for about 100,000 boys. This inevitably led to increased access to higher education, with 56 female students in Parisian universities in the year 1889/90 becoming 1,738 by 1918/19 (to 7,358 men).

Even though the majority of French feminists based their claims to civil and political rights on women's responsibilities as wives and mothers, even though the need to extend female education was argued through on these same grounds, the presence of groups of articulate women speaking with a collective voice, and highly educated young women entering the professions, produced considerable anxiety and excitement. Fiction provided a medium in which the meanings and implications of change could be thought through, reassurance about the validity of old values could be sought and given, or the excitement of new roles and opportunities explored. The serious novel, the novel with status, was still a largely masculine domain – Zola, Maupassant, Anatole France, Jules Romains all published during this period, and Gide and Proust made their débuts – but as a privileged site for the discussion of relationships the novel was also legitimate feminine territory.

Jean Larnac, in his hopelessly sexist but immensely useful *Histoire de la littérature féminine en France* (1929), identifies an increase in published writing by women around the turn of the century, explaining this by the general move away from the scrupulously factual and rational modes of realism and naturalism to an emphasis on emotion and intuition. Although the terms of his explanation are questionable, ignoring as they do the relevance of educational reform for a generation of women born in the 1870s, there is certainly evidence of a large number of widely read women authors in the years around the turn of the century. Larnac quotes an earlier writer who found 738 women writers in French library catalogues in 1908;[1] Resa Dudovitz cites much higher figures,[2] and demonstrates the extent to which women writers came into the 'bestseller' category. The obituary of one of these writers, published in 1938 in *Nouvelles Littéraires*, evokes 'that glittering team who, at the dawn of the twentieth century, won for feminine literature a place it had never had before in literary production and in public esteem'.[3]

Gyp (1845–1932), pen name of the Comtesse de Martel de Janville, published at least a hundred novels between 1885 and her death in 1932, selling twenty to twenty-five thousand copies at the peak of her career and thus clearly entering the bestseller lists. Gérard d'Houville (1875–1963, pen name of Marie-Louise de Hérédia), Lucie Delarue-Mardrus (1874–1945) and Anna de Noailles (1876–1933) all wrote widely read novels which largely adhered to the reassuring form of the romance while exploring the social and emotional implications of gendered identity. Three writers in particular succeeded in combining effective storytelling with an exploratory or polemical account of the conflicts over female identity during these years. Colette Yver (1874–1953) was famous for her defence of traditional feminine roles against the threat of the new, while Gabrielle Reval (1870–1938) wrote novels which celebrate the new world of women's secondary and higher education. Marcelle Tinayre (1871–1948) was a bestselling and extremely well-known author, often cited in the same breath as Colette during their early careers, and since then almost totally forgotten. Writing from very different perspectives, defending quite opposed sets of values, all three authors centre their work around the same questions. If women are highly educated, can they and should they continue to identify feminine virtue with a secondary and supportive role, with self-abnegation and caring for others, or is it their duty to achieve as individuals? Is gender identity eternal, ahistorical, and do virtue and happiness consist in fulfilling that ready-made destiny, or can destiny be reshaped as the rationalist, materialist philosophy of their culture would logically imply? If things can change to the extent of women taking on 'masculine' qualities and activities, what impact does and should this have on sexual morality?

COLETTE YVER

Colette Yver was the pen name of Antoinette de Bergevin. Her writing, throughout a long career extending from 1891 into the 1930s, constituted a vehement reassertion of the doctrine of separate and complementary gender roles, in the face of the threats posed by women's increased access to education and employment. Her novels are uncompromisingly committed *romans à thèse* in which the thesis is that women's emancipation challenges the natural order and threatens human happiness. Yver's best fictions are tightly constructed dramas in which all the elements converge to produce this conclusion, but the attraction of the feminist position she opposes is by no means underestimated. *Princesses de science*, winner of the Prix Femina in 1907 and translated into English in 1909 as *The Doctor Wife*, is a good example of such a novel, for despite its firmly conservative thesis it can be seen to address the complex dilemma of the highly educated woman in a society which identified femininity with service and self-denial.

The novel opens with the introduction of Fernand Guéméné, an attractively energetic, philanthropic young doctor. Fernand loves Thérèse Herlinge, daughter of a celebrated surgeon and herself embarked on a promising medical career, and she at first accepts his proposal of marriage. However marriage on Fernand's terms means Thérèse giving up medicine, and this she refuses to do.

Desperate because he has lost her, Fernand at last agrees to marriage on her terms: "'I cannot live without you!' he added in beseeching tones. "I must have the little you will deign to give me of your love'" (p. 75[4]). As both pursue busy professional lives, their home becomes neglected and the couple rarely spend time together. Thérèse's pregnancy is greeted with joy by Fernand, but Thérèse is more dismayed than delighted. Their son dies in infancy, largely because of Thérèse's refusal to breastfeed on the grounds that this would delay her return to work, and the relationship between them becomes progressively more cold and embittered. Fernand gradually falls in love with the selfless, motherly widow of one of his patients, and it is only through her noble renunciation of her love for him that he is returned to a repentant Thérèse, who is now ready to sacrifice career and studies to home and family.

Four subplots are woven through the central narrative, each of them reinforcing the novel's argument. Positive examples of marriage are provided by Fernand's uncle, in lifelong mourning for his beloved and totally devoted wife, and Dina Skaroff, another female medical student, who makes the opposite choice to Thérèse and gives up medicine to embark on a happy life as wife and mother. With perfect symmetry, Yver also provides two negative illustrations of professional women. Jeanne Adeline, an older woman doctor constantly rushing between surgery, visits and home, at first appears to juggle motherhood and career successfully, but she too is finally punished by her husband's decline into alcoholism and her youngest child's near-fatal accident, suffered during his mother's absence. The elegant and successful woman doctor Lancelevée is shown to have won success by cold calculation and the deliberate renunciation of emotion.

The novel defends the concept of natural, polarized and complementary gender identities, a concept which underlay much nineteenth-century thinking, writing and, indeed, the material reality of women's lives. However, in setting this concept to work within a precise – albeit fictional – context, Yver's novel both displays the contradictions of the essentialist view and helps to explain why the perceived threat to its validity provoked such generalized anxiety.

The women doctors of the novel were scarcely representative, since women's entry to medicine had hardly begun at the close of the century.[5] Medicine none the less offered a particularly appropriate field for the demonstration of Yver's thesis. The concept of complementary genders made a clear distinction between the public, masculine world of industry, politics and science, concerned with the great goals of human progress rather than with individual, affective needs, and the feminine domain in which these needs were squarely placed. Women in the role of doctors crossed the gender boundary, and thus represented the potential loss of the personal sphere. Thus several of the scenes which condemn Thérèse accentuate her functionally medical attitude to the human body, and this is implicitly compared with that more 'feminine' attitude which would read the body as signifier of emotion and personality. Guéméné's first proposal takes place in Thérèse's laboratory, where 'a fragment of human brain floated in a bowl' (p. 12), and he is shocked to hear her declare her enthusiasm for dissection and investigation of 'the secrets of the flesh' (p. 25), mentally comparing this to the 'angels of mercy in white cap and apron' (p. 26) who, he feels, represent a more appropriate relationship between women and medicine.

Yver's style is particularly critical where Thérèse deals with parts of the body which carry heavy metaphorical significance. Soon after her rejection of Guéméné's proposal, Yver has the reader observe Thérèse in the act of examining an old woman patient, and the writing emphasizes her impersonal, coldly scientific relationship to the female body:

> unfastening the bedgown [she] laid bare the bosom, where the deformed breasts hung like two folds of flabby flesh. She pushed the left breast to the right and applied to the white chest the black disc of her apparatus. (p. 53)

The black disc reduces the breast and heart, metaphors central to the constructed meaning of femininity, to mere symptoms on the road to scientific discovery. The novel expresses anxiety at the prospect that women's 'masculine' education might reduce human relationships to merely functional transactions.[6]

Yver's evaluation of contemporary changes in women's role was unequivocal, but she wrote in the knowledge that the challenge of feminism was a serious one, and that many of her readers felt its appeal. The novel represents the traditional doctrine of complementary genders within a context of social change, and inadvertently acknowledges the contradictions of the very thesis it defends. The women in the text, consigned to domestic seclusion within the novel's overt scheme of values, are revealed to be the stronger and more independent sex. Fernand, like all the other adult male characters, can achieve professional success and personal happiness only if supported by a woman who takes full responsibility for all his domestic arrangements (food, comfort of the house, domestic finances, children, psychological and emotional support) and becomes depressed, shabby and physically unwell if he is neglected by women. Thérèse, on the other hand, like Jeanne Adeline, Dina Skaroff before her marriage, and Doctor Lancelevée, thrives on a demanding schedule of work and attends to her own domestic needs.

Female self-sacrifice appears to be the prerequisite for a man's success in his career and for his emotional well-being. Fernand explains repeatedly to Thérèse that he can continue to bear 'all the drudgery of [my] profession' only provided that he '"find my fireside sweet, restful and compensating in the society of the wife who rules my home and happiness. I am perhaps selfish, but I am a man and a normal one. I wish you all for myself alone"' (p. 14), and this despite his recognition of her exceptional talents as a doctor and insistence that he sees her as his intellectual equal. But the women can happily love their male partners and pursue difficult careers without demanding any equivalent renunciation: Thérèse is a happy woman during their busy, undomesticated, egalitarian marriage. The text avoids any exploration of the causes of this imbalance by reiterating the arguments of natural predestination: 'the man supports the home and family and the wife abandons everything for her sovereign right – her true function, which is to live for her husband and her children' (p. 21), but the reader for whom this story had some personal resonance could hardly fail to notice the consistency with which one sex is revealed as dependent, the other as self-sufficient.

The strength of the feminist case is acknowledged in Yver's careful recuperation of words such as 'equality' and 'rights' into the discourse of female subordination. It also emerges in the weight she gives to her heroine's joy in her work. As a successful, married female novelist Yver was, of course, in a contradictory position as she argued for the exclusion of married women and mothers from public life. Even as she demonstrates the necessity for Thérèse to renounce her career, Yver lends conviction to the opposing argument, for in the passages which give voice to Thérèse's professional enthusiasm, focalization from the character's perspective gives way to direct narratorial comment which endorses Thérèse's justified pride in her competence. At the very moment in the narrative when Thérèse is realizing that to save her marriage she must give up medicine, Yver has her deal expertly with a badly burnt child:

> All emotion forgotten, the brows knit, calm and self-possessed, Thérèse examined the burns with her keen comprehensive glance. She summoned all her science and resources in view of the prompt action that was necessary to save the moaning, weeping child in her hands. (p. 285)

The narrator herself seems to share Thérèse's self-doubt at the point of decision:

> . . . was she not unfaithful to her duty? The woman-doctor beside the bedside of the woman-patient, was not that a great and precious role? . . . Was she right to desert the profession that afforded her such opportunities for doing good to her sex? (p. 325)

The novel's answer is a resounding 'Yes!', but the embattled tone of Yver's fiction is an implicit acknowledgement that the educational reforms and mild feminist movements of the period were experienced as a serious threat to established definitions of femininity.

#### GABRIELLE REVAL

It was precisely this challenge to established beliefs about gender that Yver's contemporary, Gabrielle Reval, celebrated in her series of novels about women in education. Reval herself studied at one of the first women's *Ecoles normales*, Sèvres, and wrote her first novel, *Les Sèvriennes*, both in fond memory of her time there and out of a desire to inform an ignorant public of the school's purpose and merits. The novel, according to Reval's obituary, was considered scandalous in its depiction of independent women, and became a major news story. Subsequent novels focused on different areas of female education: *Professeurs-femmes* (Women Teachers) in 1901; *Lycéennes* (Secondary School Girls) in 1902; *La Bachelière* (The [Female] Graduate) in 1910.

A culture which restricts women's lives to the domain of home and family tends to have as its central female narrative the love story, or romance. Sand's later writing, with its concern for social legitimacy, largely observes this pattern. Although Reval admired Sand greatly and acknowledged her influence, *Les Sèvriennes* largely refuses the structure of romance, for in place of a single heroine the novel follows the fortunes of a group of young women, and ii stead of love between a man and a woman the novel foregrounds female friendship. The central story line follows not the development of a relationship but the academic career of the students, culminating in their graduation to become qualified secondary teachers.

*Les Sèvriennes* radiates pleasure in the company of other women and in the satisfaction of intellectual curiosity. Women's education throughout the nineteenth century had been restricted by the theory of female inferiority and innate domesticity – a theory which operated both as a belief and as a policy. The new *Ecoles normales* provided a modified version of the rigorously philosophical training provided by the men's colleges, and indeed often employed the same professors to teach it. The young women in *Les Sèvriennes* are of different social backgrounds and temperaments, but have in common what Reval terms in her preface 'the history of poor but clever schoolgirls who hope to find in Education a means of making a living' (pp. vi–vii[7]). What they share, apart from relative poverty, is a passion for learning, a delight in being granted access to the most demanding and challenging ideas of the day in their reading and lectures: 'The Sèvriennes drank in his every word, words which revolutionized their habitual ways of thinking and opened up a new direction for thought' (p. 47). The college discourages excessive attention to appearance and mere learning by rote, encourages intellectual and moral independence and the goal of becoming 'upright, strong and intelligent women (p. 79), 'sure of their ability to earn a living honourably and freely' (p. 77). The group of friends, from the irreverently humorous Berthe to the single-minded Victoire, all thrive on this regime of hard work and mutual respect and affection. The novel clearly argues for women's education and employment as essential to dignity and happiness, but a connection is also traced between intellectual and sexual repression. If there is a central protagonist it is Marguerite Triel, author of the diary which forms part of the narrative, and final victor in the competitive graduation examinations. It is Marguerite who finds herself enabled, through the college's insistence on honesty rather than prudishness, to acknowledge both her own desires and the erotic element in art and literature.

Although in all these senses *Les Sèvriennes* is an affirmation of the value of the new colleges, it ignores neither the social isolation of such institutions nor the tenacity of belief in women's special and limited destiny. One of the women teachers warns her students: "'we are mocked and despised and attacked wherever *lycées* for girls are opened'" (p. 98), and vacations away from the college reveal to them the social difficulty of being a highly educated woman: "'I make men uneasy. They admire me because I'm clever but their admiration is . . . suspicious. . . . Men imagine we are too clever to be pure'" (p. 152) laments Marguerite.

This theme is woven into the narrative through the letters of an ex-Sèvrienne who is now teaching in a *lycée*, and whose enthusiastic proselytism is gradually destroyed by a hostile and suspicious society. Unsupported by a headmistress who is in league with the Catholic Church, accused of being 'a dangerous emancipator, a rebel and a nihilist' (p. 153) because she encourages independent thought in her pupils, Isabelle Marlotte becomes increasingly lonely and desperate, and finally commits suicide. The happy sisterhood of Sèvres is thus presented as the prelude to a solitary and difficult career.

It is perhaps not surprising, then, that the novel makes some concession to the romance form, and thus to the desirability for women of avoiding the difficult role of the spinster. Only heterosexual love is presented at all persuasively, for the one lesbian character is negatively characterized by intellectual inferiority, an unappealing and even sinister appearance, and an undignified refusal to accept rejection: 'No one in the cohort had any sympathy for her' (p. 14). But despite the emphasis on the joys of independence, intellectual freedom and sisterhood, a narrative thread of heterosexual romance weaves through the novel and plays an important part in the dénouement. Marguerite's closest friend, Charlotte, is engaged to an artist whose progressive opinions and emotional warmth endear him to Marguerite too. By a rather contrived piece of plotting, Reval has Charlotte die an early death and demand, on her deathbed, a promise that her friend and her fiancé will never marry. This allows the novel to conclude with a decision which is profoundly romantic and saves Marguerite from the fate of the lonely schoolteacher, but which at the same time may be read as an endorsement of the novel's less conventional values. Inspired by the teaching of the charismatic Principal of Sèvres and her insistence that

> these free beings, trained in solitude by a manly education, should know how to respect the law but where necessary should also have the courage to break it, when their conscience is no longer in accord with the laws of man (p. 229),

Marguerite gives up her career as a teacher not to *marry* Henri but to live with him outside marriage. The novel's defence of female independence is undermined by the defection of the most central character, yet reinforced by her flouting of the institution of marriage in the name of individual integrity and happiness.

## MARCELLE TINAYRE

The fiction of Marcelle Tinayre can be aligned neither with the anti-feminism of Yver nor with the anxious but sincere reformism of Reval. Tinayre's novels articulate in narrative form that mild and cautious feminism which appears to have predominated in France between 1870 and 1914. Certain reforms are demanded in the name of the equality of the sexes, but equality is not taken to conflict with the principle of ahistorical gender difference. Tinayre's achievement was to find for this world-view a wholly appropriate literary form. Her novels address a number of the real conditions and problems of her female readers' lives, and solve them, pleasurably, at the level of fantasy and without implying any serious challenge to existing institutions and ideologies. Tinayre appears to make the case for women's rights – and this in itself is important in a society which legislates for inequality – but she also pursues a reassuringly conservative agenda at a textual level.

Tinayre was a prolific and popular novelist whose career began in 1897 with the publication of *Avant l'amour*[8] (Before Love) and continued until her death in 1948. Highly regarded in the mainstream press, she came very close to being awarded the Legion of Honour in 1908, and was frequently ranked with Colette as one of the major French women novelists. Her public pronouncements on the nature and status of women were invariably reactionary ('Public glory, for a man, is a sort of sun which illuminates the whole of life. Woman has a different destiny, before being a woman writer she must be and remain a woman'[9]), but her first novel was criticized as 'pernicious' and 'perverse' for its frank treatment of female sexuality, and thematically her work shows a consistent preoccupation with women's right to education, with the injustice of the sexual double standard, and with the plight of the unmarried mother.

The novels written around the turn of the century mostly employ the basic romantic plot of single heroine, meeting with hero, elimination of obstacles and conclusion in marriage.[10] However, the heroines oppose what is presented as the social norm in that they refuse to see themselves as destined only for marriage and motherhood, and value their education (*Hellé*,1898[11]) and their ability to earn a living (Fanny in *La Maison du péché*[12] [The House of Sin, 1902] is a successful artist; Josyane in *La Rebelle*[13] [The Rebel, 1905] a journalist on a feminist newspaper). There is an explicit refusal of the assumption that, in a relationship, the man's needs and desires must prevail ('What strange ideal of love is proposed to woman? Why should she, rather than the man, sacrifice herself? [*Hellé*, p. 230]), and a defence of women's right to sexual desire is both articulated by the female protagonists ('I am no more guilty than a young man who, one stormy day, falls into the arms of a prostitute, yet my heart is torn with regret' [*Avant l'amour*, p. 80]) and implied by the positive characterization of women who have sexual relationships outside marriage (Fanny, Josyane). The injustice of the sexual double standard and of the stigma attached to illegitimacy are themes of both *Hellé* and *La Rebelle*.

This engagement with feminist concerns does not seriously affect the profound conservatism of the texts. Like most successful popular fiction, Tinayre's work operates within easily recognizable codes. It is easy to read because items of decor such as weather, light and location have straightforward metaphorical significance (a dark rainy day will almost certainly mean sadness for the heroine), because qualifying adjectives are standardized rather than unusual or demanding ('celestial love', 'supreme possession'), because the narratives are patterned to arouse and satisfy expectation predictably (when the heroine's fortunes can go no lower, we know the hero will appear). This reassuringly familiar formal structure leads the reader into a fictional world where values and gender identities are also familiar, because they are fundamentally those of patriarchy.

However educated she may be, however succesful at earning her own living, the goal and the nub of each heroine's story is the discovery of love – experienced, even where it happens more than once, as unique and eternal. In these novels female virginity is marked by a state of permanent sexual and emotional expectation, and widowhood returns the heroine to a similar state. The narratives begin by setting up a mood of anticipation. The very title of *Avant l'amour* (Before Love) is revelatory, and the young heroine is posed for the reader at windows, 'half-dressed', as the rest of the world sleeps, her 'soul enlarged by immense desires and suffering the torment of emptiness' (*Avant l'amour*, p. 63). Hellé, sharply distinguished from her contemporaries by her classical education and her independence, none the less finds the central question to be 'When will I meet him? By what mysterious sign will I know him?' (*Hellé*, p. 36). *La Rebelle* first shows Josyane walking down a Paris street, slim, lively and well-dressed, but the omniscient narrator rapidly inflects the description to set up the necessary expectations. She is displaying 'that air of defensive toughness, that air of freedom which reveals the emancipated woman or the woman without a husband – alone in the street, alone in life' (*La Rebelle*, p. 2).

Female desire is certainly asserted as a reality and defended against social censure, but desire is always legitimated and, indeed, generated for the female characters by the belief that they have found the object of their unique and absolute love. Josyane is 'forgiven' by the text (and ultimately by the hero, Noël) for her affair with Maurice, and for the illegitimate child of their union, but only because she sincerely believed that he was her one true love – whereas the narrator clearly condones Noël's keeping a mistress in an arrangement based on desire and mutual liking. Despite the rhetorical condemnation of double standards, and the creditable attempt to represent sexual experience as part of women's lives, there is really little equality of representation here.

Women are consistently marked out textually as the objects of desire rather than as subjects, by the use of an implicit or an explicit male focalizer. In *Avant l'amour* the first-person narration demands the use of mirror-scenes, or of a certain disingenuous posturing on the heroine's part, to ensure that the perspective of desire is male: 'Sometimes, at night, when the whole house slept I would suffocate in my narrow room. Half-naked, I would lean out of the window' (p. 20). When Josyane and Noël begin to desire each other, it is his perspective on her body which is given by the text: 'He contemplated . . . her bosom which swelled the muslin . . . her white, matte flesh which must be to the touch like that of flowers' (*La Rebelle*, p. 235). Male protagonists are described only in terms which signify their qualities of character and their suitability as competent, authoritative partners: Noël Delyle displays 'a sort of latent violence which he kept under control' (*La Rebelle*, p. 148); Etienne Chartrain has 'an admirable forehead, high and regular', 'an aquiline nose which emphasized his pride' (*La Rançon* [The Ransom, 1898], p. 16).

And this concession of the power of the gaze to man alone is consistent with the whole representation of gendered identity. The signifiers of authentic masculinity in Tinayre's novels are familiar still in romantic fiction: they are those of a society which attributes to the male the right to authority backed by physical strength. Tinayre's heroes are older than the heroines by as much as twenty years; they are big (Genesvrier in *Hellé* explicitly has 'the stature of a man of authority' [p. 80]), have piercing eyes (reinforcing the text's male focalization), and show signs of potential violence restrained by wisdom. It is the antiheroes, the men with whom the heroines mistakenly become infatuated, who are physically beautiful, like Maurice Clairmont in *Hellé* with his shiny black hair, bright blue eyes, 'the sort of virile beauty . . . no woman could look at coldly' (p. 60). The function of such characters is merely to act as foil to true heroic virtues, and to delay the inevitable dénouement of the plot.

The heroine, however emancipated in the text's initial stages, becomes the hero's complementary partner, malleable, submissive and other-directed: '"A woman is made to be protected, cared for and loved. Be a woman, without shame – be weak"' (*La Rebelle*, p. 234), Noël tells Josyane 'the rebel'. Initiative and independence are qualities valued in the heroine until she finds her Hero-Mentor

– at that point the nature of feminine virtue is transformed, and rewarded by marriage.

The novels discussed above were all published within the decade which ended the nineteenth century and began the twentieth. Their commercial and critical success arose from their combination of compelling narrative form and topicality: Yver, Reval and Tinayre all wrote fictions which discuss, imagine and explore the new possibilities for women opened up by the Third Republic's educational policies, by legal reform and by the emerging feminist movements. Although the three authors start from very different perspectives and values, their novels converge interestingly in the sense they give of a moral and political dilemma: in each, the urge towards change and redefinition of identity is countered by anxiety at the implications of rethinking gender.

Even in the novels of Colette Yver, an author who devoted her career to promoting anti-feminism, there is a strong sense of the attraction of new roles for women. Yver's young doctors, like Reval's student teachers and Tinayre's educated, emancipated heroines, enjoy the satisfaction of participating in intellectual debate, of acquiring prestigious skills and using them, of being recognized in their own right as thinkers and workers. The explicit theme of social injustice is, of course, absent in Yver's novels, but Reval and Tinayre make fiction work to condemn the social exclusion of the unmarried mother and the professional woman, the assumption that women's sexuality can be redeemed only by enclosure within monogamous marriage and motherhood, the devaluing of women's intellect and judgement.

Yet there is, equally, a sombre side to all these novels, including Reval's celebrations of educational opportunity. All the texts represent the difficulty of negotiating greater freedom, and the sense of what is at stake when domestic and personal happiness has been placed squarely in women's domain. Yver's cold, broken households and injured or dead children are the most extreme representations of this anxiety, but beyond the charmed and temporary interlude of the female community of students Reval etches in lonely women suffering from social ostracism to the point of suicide. Tinayre's robust, protective heroes are the reassuring, if reactionary, answer to the dilemma: her heroines end the novels warm and secure in their arms, assured of their own socially approved role at the heart of what, in this pleasurable fantasy world, is always a stable and loving household.

The fundamental narrative form employed by all three authors is the stereotypically feminine form of the romance. Yver's fiction deviates in the sense that her didactic intentions demand a plot that continues after the union of hero and heroine, but the structure of meeting, overcoming of obstacles and final happiness is none the less at work. Reval's more radical intentions determine an initial major departure from the structure of the love story, but it weaves its way back in an attempt to bring together moral independence and personal happiness. Tinayre follows most closely the form of the romance – Tinayre, who was the most popular and perhaps the closest of the three not only to the 'mainstream' feminist movements of the day, but also to all those women readers who did not identify themselves as feminists but were none the less aware of current debates as mingled threat and promise.

The work of Yver, Reval and Tinayre, like that of most of the 'glittering team' of women writers of their generation, is now uniformly out of print and lost to literary history. Yet their fiction, with its delineation of a precise historical moment, demonstrates how the popular novel has served as the site for women's reflection on the changing conditions of their lives, and for the negotiation of the meanings of femininity.

# 4
# Rachilde (1860–1953): Decadence, Misogyny and the Woman Writer

[P]ossibly the woman's situation has, more than the man's, been torn between respect for the established cultural world to which she aspires and her sense of the inequities that world imposes upon her.

(Germaine Brée, *Women Writers in France*, p.xi)

Legally, politically and economically, inferiority was an intrinsic part of the definition of womanhood still operative in France at the turn of the century. Although after Sand (and perhaps, to some extent, thanks to Sand) women writers became a less rare phenomenon, the positions women could adopt in relation to current social and literary conventions were limited. To imagine that a woman writing could place herself outside the dominant discourse and contest its very terms is utopian, and ignores the very real sense in which individuals are constructed by the culture in which they develop. Women, like men, came to writing equipped with knowledge of the language and genres currently available, and constrained by their own internalized sense of possible identities.

In the late nineteenth and early twentieth centuries, women could adopt a discourse which defined them within the acceptable role of the good mother, writing moral or orthodox texts which would not preclude some ambivalence of meaning. They could modify the terms of the heterosexual romance to introduce elements of female independence – or they could adopt a male subject position, write as honorary men, on the principle that to beat them was impossible, so one might as well try to join them. This, in effect, was the position taken up by Rachilde.

Rachilde was the pen name of Marguerite Emery, born in 1860, daughter of an illegitimate branch of an aristocratic family. Like George Sand, she had an exceptional education for a French girl of her class and era. Her father, whom she adored, clearly regretted the fact that she was not a boy, and brought her up partly as the son he never had. A solitary child, she was educated by a defrocked Jesuit tutor and self-educated through extensive and uncensored reading in her grandfather's library. Marguerite began to write early, and published stories and articles in the local paper while she was still in her teens. Unusually for a well-bred young woman of the time, she succeeded in establishing for herself an independent life in Paris, and, like George Sand some fifty years before, she regularly adopted men's clothing in order to move freely around the city. Under the name Rachilde she published, in 1884, the scandalous *Monsieur Vénus*, a novel whose portrayal of a cold sadistic heroine and her merciless destruction of a young male lover earned her a prosecution for obscenity. She married Alfred de Vallette, founding editor of the influential literary magazine *Mercure de France*, and entered the otherwise wholly male literary circle of the writers whose shared thematic and formal preoccupations are designated by the term 'Decadence'.

Rachilde wrote consistently within the terms and conventions of Decadence – a literary and visual aesthetic of the fin-de-siècle period characterized by intense melancholy, a preference for the artificial over the natural, and a degree of misogyny which heightens and almost parodies the gender ideology of late-nineteenth-century France. She was not a feminist – indeed, in 1928 she devoted a book to the elucidation of the question 'Why I am not a feminist'.[1] Her interest for feminist readers lies in the questions her writing poses: does her version of the Decadent position mimic perfectly the masculine discourse of her male contemporaries, or are there signs of the curiously untenable situation of a woman writing not only as a man, but as a misogynist? As a woman claiming the male prerogative of writing, or Gilbert and Gubar's pen as metaphorical penis,[2] how does Rachilde negotiate the gap between her assumed identity as masculine subject, and her lived identity as a woman defined as naturally inferior?

THE DECADENTS

The Decadents' exotically grim vision of their society can be seen as the response of a declining class to their exclusion from power.

Not all the Decadent writers were aristocrats by birth – though many, including Rachilde, were – but their rejection of the mediocrity of the bourgeois Republic, and their emphasis on the natural superiority of an elite, identify them with the class whose vestiges of power disappeared over the last decades of the nineteenth century. The Third Republic replaced Napoleon III's Empire after the Prussian defeat of France in 1870, and between the inauguration of the Republic and the end of the century economic and political power was consolidated in the hands of a capitalist, conservative bourgeoisie. The Republic's proclaimed ideals of Liberty, Equality, Fraternity were partially and selectively applied, and the most feared opposition to the regime came from the working class, whose perception of their own exclusion from prosperity and power led to the birth of the labour movement. The Decadents detested the bourgeois values of conformism and security, yet knew that their economic survival – and, indeed, their recognition as artists – depended on the ruling class they despised. Quite unable to identify with the alien and threatening power of the working class, they were placed uncomfortably between revolt and dependence, despising the uniformity of mass democracy yet lacking any viable counter-ideal.

Before examining Rachilde's fiction, it is crucial to identify the principal features of the fiction written by male Decadents. The task of this chapter will be to explore the extent to which the Decadent conventions are reproduced and mimicked in Rachilde's texts or, conversely, the extent to which these invite a different reading. The point at which potential contradictions most obviously occur is that of misogyny – and it is on this aspect of the Decadents' writing that I shall focus.

The Decadents' profound sense of alienation both from the dominant values of their society and from any viable form of opposition is very apparent in their fiction. Not only is the social world characterized as profoundly mediocre, inadequate to the aspirations of the artistic individual, but the natural world offers no solace: Nature is indifferent, or plainly malevolent. Following here in a long Judaeo-Christian tradition as well as echoing their precursor, Baudelaire ('Woman is natural, which is to say abominable'), the Decadents identified nature with woman – or, more specifically, with woman as a sexual being. For Huysmans, in the seminal

Decadent text *A Rebours*[3] (*Against the Grain*, 1884), the figure of Salome in Moréas's painting exemplifies female sexuality: 'the monstrous Beast, indifferent, irresponsible, unfeeling, poisoning all that approaches her, all that see her, all that she touches' (*A Rebours*, p. 86).

The figure of Eve the temptress or the *femme fatale*, a spectre which haunts nineteenth-century French male writing, is one of the central motifs of the Decadent text. In Catulle Mendès's *La Première Maitresse*[4] (The First Mistress, 1887), she lures the adolescent hero to her home and subjects him to a long, humiliating rape scene, the beginning of a sexual enslavement that will last for the rest of his life. In Barbey d'Aurevilly's *La Vengeance d'une Femme*[5] (A Woman's Revenge, 1874), she enacts her revenge on a cruel husband by becoming a prostitute and spreading venereal disease until she herself dies horribly. Despite the major differences between the literary and political philosophies of Naturalism and Decadence, there is a strong similarity between the latter's *femme fatale* mythology and that of Zola, whose eponymous heroine Nana (1880) is also a voraciously sexual woman whose promiscuity destroys all the men who desire her, and finally herself. The same figure had much wider currency as the Eve of Catholic demonology, the prostitute of the Republican moralists' discourse (frequently invoked, for example, as a reason for not giving women the vote). The ubiquity of the figure implies a real fear of the female sexuality so thoroughly repressed and silenced in late-nineteenth-century social and cultural practice.

If the sexual woman appears as a monster rather than a human being, she is not the only female monster let loose in the Decadent text. Active female desire for the male body is represented as monstrous, as threatening and sadistic, from Huysmans's seductive Salome dancing by the severed head of her victim, John the Baptist, to Mendès's ghoulish 'First Mistress'. But woman can also transgress by representing the tedium of the domestic, of responsibility, of that unelevated ordinariness that the Decadents associated with republican democracy, and rejected as unworthy of the exceptional individual. The noble and world-weary hero of Villiers de l'Isle-Adam's *L'Eve future*[6] (The Future Eve, 1886) recognizes the venal, prosaic spirit of the age in his mistress's failure to observe a feminine silence. He is aghast at the hideous discrepancy between Alicia's Venus-like beauty and her articulate, unromantic assessments of love and marriage. Her verbosity is unbearable to him, for women should by nature be silent: 'Venus should have nothing to do with thought. The goddess is veiled in stone and silence' (*L'Eve future*, p. 64).

In *The First Mistress* Mendès brings off the extraordinary feat of combining the two opposing figures of monstrous femininity, the sexual and the banal, the *femme fatale* and the ball and chain,[7] in a single character. Madame d'Arlement is an ogress, a voracious lover who sucks the life out of her young partners and descends, throughout the narrative, ever deeper into perversion and corruption. She also remains – apart from a spell in prison for murder which, in narrative terms, is briefly passed over – a conventionally minded bourgeoise, whose banality of thought and insistence on the need to make a good living kill the hero's artistic soul as surely as her sadistic sexuality destroys the innocence of his desire.

The pessimism of the Decadent world-view means that frequently these female representations of an evil fate end the narrative triumphant – but this does not prevent the texts from enacting a symbolic punishment. This punishment of the woman's sexual or domestic power is frequently enacted in the most sadistic terms, for the Decadents' repressed anger took the textual form of violent and macabre imagery. In Mendès's *The First Mistress*, the central female protagonist manipulates the hero to the end, but her sister functions as the text's scapegoat and is beaten, then finally strangled when she too becomes his sexual partner. *A Woman's Revenge* allows the heroine to wreak her vengeance only at the cost of a hideously slow and disfiguring death (a fate identical to that of Zola's Nana), and the same author's *A un Dîner d'athées* (The Atheists' Supper) culminates in the sealing of the promiscuous heroine's vagina by her enraged husband, in a grotesquely violent scene which prefigures Irigaray's suggestion that for man woman represents a terrifying hole which he must close in order to assuage his fear.[8]

This strain of sadistic imagery is echoed in *The Future Eve* in the apparently amputated female arm, entwined with a gold viper, which lies on the desk of the scientist Edison. In fact the arm is the first indicator of what is to be the novel's central Pygmalion theme: here the punishment of female pretensions is to be more complete than in the narratives of physical violence, for the female subject is to be destroyed in favour of man's own creation of the perfect partner. Edison's mastery of science has reached the point where he can create and animate human flesh. By constructing a female android in the likeness of his friend's beautiful but awkwardly assertive mistress, he bestows on him the ideal wife whose responses can be directly controlled by a touch of the hand, a pressure on her ring. Unlike most myths of this kind (Coppelia, Pygmalion, Pinocchio, Frankenstein), the android creature does not escape her creator's control and thus question the wisdom of man's playing god, but overcomes her lover's incredulity and is loved as the ideal woman. Although both she and her lover perish in a fire at the story's end, in the novel's terms this does not invalidate the experiment's success. Here the woman is not merely brutalized or killed but annihilated – fantasized as replaceable by man's total control of the material universe.

The annihilation of the female subject is also an affair of narrative form. It is not simply that the narrating voice in the Decadent text is, on the whole, an omniscient male voice, for this is the norm in nineteenth-century French fiction. It is also crucial to the characterization of woman as either *femme fatale* or ball and chain that she be focalized externally. A female point of view is rare in this fiction, even when a woman is the central figure in the narrative. *A Woman's Revenge*, for example, provides a rare case of female, first-person narration in a Decadent text, but the woman's narrative is contained within and mediated through the commentary of the male narrator.

The dominance of male discourse is still more apparent in those works structured as a dialogue or conversation for male voices. *The Future Eve* is written largely in the unusual form of a dialogue between the scientist Edison and his friend Lord Ewald, while Barbey d'Aurevilly favours the narrative recounted by one speaker to a group of male companions who question, applaud and comment on the tale (for example, *Le Rideau cramoisi* (The Scarlet Curtain), *Le Bonheur dans le crime* (Happiness in Crime), *The Atheists' Dinner*[9]). This has the effect of emphasizing the objectification of female protagonists and inviting the reader to adopt a male position, relayed by the listeners within the text. This is a similar device to that frequently used in mainstream narrative cinema in the twentieth century, where the spectator is positioned to view the female characters through a male gaze, relayed on the screen by an observing male protagonist.

## RACHILDE'S FICTION

Rachilde's writing adopts many of the forms and conventions of the Decadent text. The world she creates bears the hallmarks of Decadence: a lack of concern with mimetic realism, a morbid eroticism and the regular use of shocking and macabre imagery. Nature is hostile and always characterized in feminine terms: beyond the repressive but safe walls of a rational, masculine culture lies a violent and dangerous realm, exposure to which generally leads to death. This realm is signified in a variety of ways: in the story 'La Buveuse de Sang' ['The [female] Blood-Drinker') the central image of Nature's malevolence is the moon; in the novel *La Tour d'Amour* (The Tower of Love) it is the sea; in 'Mortis' flowers engulf and destroy human civilization. Each of these images is strongly identified with the feminine – by convention, by the feminine gender of the nouns moon, sea and flower in French and, as we shall see, by Rachilde's quite explicit textual foregrounding of the words' gendered connotations.

The figure of the *femme fatale* is also present: the lover of 'Monsieur Vénus', the female 'Juggler', the 'Marquise de Sade' all lead men to their doom and, moreover, without themselves achieving any power beyond the purely destructive. A reading of Rachilde's fiction confirms Jennifer Birkett's damning observation:

> Rachilde puts her creative imagination at the service of male masochistic fantasies, acting out the temporary triumph of the vengeful female and the humiliating overthrow of the male – subject to the reinstatement of paternal power in the last act.[10]

Yet reading the work of this curious woman who struggled free of the constricting roles available to young women, who recognized that she must dress as a man if she wanted social mobility, who refused to adopt the prescribed roles of dutiful daughter and selfless wife and mother, only to use her pen in the service of misogyny, it does not seem adequate simply to dismiss her as a collaborator with male supremacy. If one reads Rachilde with a deliberate degree of critical sympathy, it becomes apparent that there are contradictions in her texts which both set her apart from her male contemporaries and signify the difficulty of her position as a woman writer working within masculine forms. Such a reading does not open up her work to feminist meanings in the obvious sense: there is no positive hope there for reform or change, no assertion of women's rights and legitimate desires. But there are tensions apparent in both the autobiographical and the literary texts which are worthy of exploration. Rachilde's writing fixes, in violently memorable images, the repressions and constraints on women's lives at the end of the nineteenth century, and women's anger and frustration are also inscribed there.

With their vivid, brutal imagery and their emphasis on the fate of a central female protagonist, Rachilde's fictions in some ways resemble fairy stories. The best-known of these – 'Cinderella', 'The Sleeping Beauty', 'Snow White' – signify the inevitability of female submission – for there is no happy ending for a woman outside marriage – but also represent the anger generated, but effectively repressed, by patriarchal power. Their dominant message is a defeatist one: accept the authority of the King/Prince or be doomed; but when the wicked fairy wills her goddaughter to oblivion rather than a normal female destiny, when the stepmother dances herself to a furious death in the red-hot slippers, they express, beyond the bland happiness of the stories' conclusion, the anger of the defeated, and invite the reader/listener to question the sacrifices necessary to become queen. Rachilde's narratives similarly encode both resignation and revolt.

Rachilde's accounts of her own gender identity contain a curious contradiction. On the one hand she protests that she has no sympathy with feminists, that she accepts the natural difference in authority, power and role between men and women: 'my tendency to adopt a masculine style has never tempted me to claim rights which do not belong to me' (*Why I am not a feminist*, p. 6). She is always ready with the broad and conventional generalization about gender and class: women are like the working class, irrational, inconsistent, incapable of detachment (and thus presumably neither is fit to vote, though working-class men were already enfranchised). Yet interleaved with these deplorably anti-democratic and anti-feminist sentiments are passages which express a clear and painful awareness of the injustice of women's situation:

I have always regretted not being a man, not because I have
more esteem for the other half of humanity but because since
I was forced, by duty or by inclination, to live as a man and
carry life's heaviest burdens alone in my youth, it would have
been preferable to have at least the privileges of masculinity . . .
(*Why I am not a feminist*, p. 6)

She recalls with acerbic humour the behaviour demanded of the
well-bred young woman, and particularly the way she was required
to suppress all signs of self-assertion.

she must not drink wine or eat red meat . . . or show impatience.
. . . She must blow her nose without making a sound, wait to be
asked before giving her opinion . . . avoid looking at any part of
a man above his shoes . . . (*When I was young*,[11] pp. 12–13)

More poignantly, she recalls her most heartfelt wish as a child: 'I
ask the good Lord to change me into a boy because my parents will
never love me as long as I'm a girl' (*Why I am not a feminist*, p. 40).
This central and unresolved contradiction – acceptance of patriarchal power and female inferiority, together with a bitter sense of
injustice – can also be perceived in the tension between Rachilde's
mimicry of Decadent narrative forms and those differences which
constitute her specificity as a woman writer.

### THE *FEMME FATALE*: EVIL AND ITS MOTIVES

Rachilde's heroines are both destructive and self-destructive.
Raoule de Vénérande in *Monsieur Vénus*[12] (1884) escapes from
the empty world of her aunt's austere household, and the round
of suitors and social engagements, by taking a male 'mistress',
the beautiful Jacques, whom she sets up in a flat, uses and
brutalizes and finally, indirectly, kills. If the killing is indirect,
this is because it occurs in a duel which she engineers between
the gentle plebeian Jacques and a friend and suitor of her own
class, Raittolbe. Raittolbe, it could be said, reinstates the patriarchal
order by killing the feminized male who threatens it, and by thus
condemning Raoule to a life of seclusion centred on an eroticized
devotion to a mechanical model of Jacques, also – as Jennifer
Birkett points out – created by a male craftsman.

This pattern of a female revolt which takes only cruel and

individualist forms, and results in the heroine's destruction rather than her liberation, recurs in several texts. The 'Marquise de Sade', Mary Barbe, tortures and almost kills the innocent Paul and poisons her husband, ending the novel, however, unsatisfied and unfree, finding pleasure only in dreams of murder and in drinking the blood from the slaughterhouse which forms the novel's central motif. Basine in *Le Meneur de Louves*[13] (The Leader of (She)Wolves, 1905) escapes convent and marriage to live as a rebel, but ends the novel having repented and returned to the patriarchal order. In stories such as 'Les Vendanges de Sodome'[14] ('Sodom's Harvest', 1900), a woman's rebellion against exclusion from male society ends in her violent death at the hands of the male group.

The difference between these fictions and the doomed yet dangerous *femme fatale* of the male Decadents lies in the extent to which Rachilde contextualizes and motivates their revolt within the narratives. Even where the omniscient narrator defines her heroines as inherently evil – as with Mary Barbe, whose close-set eyes and unusually long thumbs are clearly indicators of malevolence[15] – the narrative sets in place intolerable conditions which explain – if not legitimize – the heroine's revolt. The sexual energy of Raoule de Vénérande is clearly set in opposition to the bleak austerity of her aunt's house and to the void of her life. Her perception of the men of her own class is one of

> brutality or impotence. . . . The brutal ones are infuriating, the impotent ones degrading, and they are all in such a rush for their own pleasure that they forget to give us, their victims, the only aphrodisiac that can make both us and them happy – love. (*Monsieur Vénus*, p. 93)

In the case of Mary Barbe (*La Marquise de Sade*) the childhood conditions which produce the heroine's cruelty and perversity are more explicitly established. Mary grows up between a sickly, self-indulgent mother and a brutal father who rejects her because she is not a boy. On the birth of a younger brother (a birth which kills the mother) Mary is further rejected, as all attention is turned to the male heir. On her father's death, she is grudgingly taken in by an old scientist uncle who again pays no attention to her because she is merely a girl. When she persuades him, by demonstrating her aptitude for scientific study, that she is worthy of interest, he combines his private tuition with what would now be termed sexual abuse. Mary is defined by the narrator as intrinsically evil, yet her desire to inflict pain on men and her inability to love are strongly motivated by the series of rejections and the abuse she suffers simply because she is born a girl.

The heroines' sadism, and their incapacity for love, are consistently linked in the narratives with their own impotent position as women. This connection is implicit rather than explicit, for Rachilde observes the surface conventions of the *femme fatale* myth, overtly attributing to her heroines a mysterious and innate capacity for evil. Yet Basine in *Le Meneur de Louves* is gang-raped early in the novel by a troop of her father's drunken soldiers, in a particularly nightmarish scene, then punished for her own humiliation by confinement to a convent. This context can hardly be divorced from her subsequent hostility to the male sex, and bloodthirsty enthusiasm for war. Eliante's refusal to reciprocate Léon's love or desire is surrounded by mystery in *La Jongleuse*[16] (The [Female] Juggler,1900), but in passages that sketch in Eliante's past, an explanation starts to appear. Uprooted from her native island by marriage to a depraved and physically repulsive man, she was then left widowed in an alien city. The relative autonomy of her life as a rich widow would be threatened by an amorous relationship; to become Léon's mistress would mean becoming, in her own words, 'like the others, a humble little errand girl trotting along behind the gentleman' (p. 198). Eliante is reduced to suicide as the only exit from an impossible situation.

In several texts the powerlessness of the woman is the corollary of the power of a brutal father figure – a figure both adored and feared, with an ambivalence typical of Rachilde's whole stance towards patriarchy. Rachilde characterizes her own father with precisely this ambivalence, focalizing him from the perspective of her adolescent self, observing him in uniform at the local army manoeuvres:

I loved my father with a strange love, unique and full of the terror which only a god both unknown and cruel could inspire. . . . [To me] he had neither age nor rank, nor any job other than that of killing wolves . . . wolves which after all were OUR BROTHERS, my mother's and mine, according to the legend.

I was frightened of the father I loved . . . (*When I was young*, pp. 74–6)

The father as the object of reverence and terror is central to Rachilde's work. In *La Marquise de Sade* Mary Barbe also reveres the father who ignores or beats her, and in a key scene at the beginning of the novel it is her perception of paternal power which triggers her revolt and her own will to destruction. As a child she is taken to the slaughterhouse to collect a cup of fresh blood, a remedy prescribed for her sick mother, but the adults lie to her and conceal the real function of the place. When she escapes their supervision and sees the killing of a bull she is traumatized, identifying with the victim ('she brought her hands up to her neck in an instinctive movement. She had felt there, to the very quick of her nerves, the blow which felled the huge animal' [p. 14]), and fainting. She comes round to find the huge, bristly face of the butcher bending gently over her, the compressed symbol of the ambivalence of paternal power and thus associated with all the other figures of brutal, and sometimes solicitous, male authority in the text.[17] In a sense the father in the story 'The Frog Killer' is equally ambivalent, for the child who focalizes the story both perceives him as a violent, dangerous figure – he kills the child's mother – and identifies with him furiously, anxious to be the father and not the dead, transgressive mother. In this instance, though, the resolution is simpler, for the child is male and thus can assume the father's power.

Mothers, by contrast, are ineffectual, absent or accomplices in male violence. There are only surrogate mothers in *Monsieur Vénus* and *La Jongleuse*, ageing aunts who play minor roles in the narrative and neither understand nor share the dreams of their nieces. The mother of the 'Marquise de Sade' is merely inadequate, dying to leave in her place a male child who will further exclude Mary from paternal affection. Similarly, the grandmother in 'La Buveuse de Sang' sends her young granddaughter out to suffer the consequences of her own sexuality, symbolized by the powerful, vampire-like moon. The negative representation of mother figures is both an important aspect of Rachilde's defeatism in the face of patriarchy – to be contrasted, for example, with the mother as source of alternative values in the work of her friend and contemporary, Colette – and can be read as an inscription of women's exclusion from power.

FEMALE VOICES

In the work of male Decadents, women are evil or prosaic because that is their nature. In Rachilde's fiction there is at least ambiguity: on the one hand there are indications of innate female malevolence; on the other the narrative supplies a conflicting account of female transgression motivated by oppression. This ambiguity is produced partly by an ambivalent narrative perspective. Whereas a female point of view is excluded from most Decadent texts, Rachilde employs both male and female focalization, thereby introducing two mutually contradictory views of the world.

Within the world-view of the male Decadents, women represent the sinister, even terrifying chaos that lies beyond reason and beyond the boundaries of the ego. Some of Rachilde's fictional works stage with exceptional clarity the male Oedipal drama and its possible outcome in misogyny. In Freud's scenario of gender acquisition, the male child first identifies with the mother, without a clear sense of the frontiers between his identity and hers. In order to become a human subject, however, he must separate, and in order to become a male subject he must recognize the mother's lack of the literal and symbolic phallus, reject identification with her, and identify instead with the father, whom he also fears as his rival and possible castrator. Nancy Chodorow[18] emphasizes the anxious fear of the feminine that can remain as a part of male psychology: mothers – and, by extension, all women – represent that formless realm that preceded the establishment of the individual self and of masculine identity. Both threatening and desirable, femininity is an area which must be distanced and controlled for fear of losing the fragile certainty of the male self.

Certain works by Rachilde produce striking representations of this drama. In the one-act play *L'Araignée de Cristal* (The Crystal Spider) two protagonists, mother and adult son, occupy the stage, which also contains a large looking-glass visible in the gloom. The son is in a state of morose anxiety, the mother solicitous. He is gradually led to recount the source of his withdrawal from social life and from women. One day during his childhood he found himself alone in an outhouse used to store the family's old furniture, and gazed at his own reflection in a tall mirror fixed to the wall. As he watched, his reflection was slowly blotted out from within the mirror by a silver 'spider' which began as a point of light and swelled to cover his face and finally 'decapitate' him. At that moment the mirror shattered and the source of the spider was revealed: the gardener was drilling a hole in the wall next door, and the tip of the drill had penetrated the wall and the mirror. Since then he has been able to face neither mirrors nor women. After this narration of the crucial episode the mother sends her 'cowardly' son to fetch lamps as night falls, and the audience hears the sound of a breaking mirror and the cry of a man whose throat is cut by falling glass.

In this play Rachilde's imagery anticipates that of Jacques Lacan, though with certain differences. In Lacan's version of the Oedipal drama, the mirror represents the first stage of separation from the mother, for by (mis)recognizing the self as that whole, visible being reflected in the mirror, the child takes a first step towards the acquisition of subjectivity – and towards the adoption of the 'I' position offered by language. In Rachilde's story, the boy's untroubled recognition of his own image seems to represent the stage prior to separation, when his sense of identity is still securely merged with that of the mother. In the play, mirrors are firmly associated with the maternal. It is only when the irresistibly phallic image of the drill protrudes through the mirror, shattering the boy's self-image, that he develops a fear of mirrors and women. The phallic Law forbids him to recognize himself in the maternal mirror. Thus the feminine becomes a realm of terror, threatening and sinister, until finally it destroys him. In texts like this one, which adopt a male point of view and subscribe to the Decadent fear of the feminine, there is none the less an uncannily lucid representation of the mechanisms that underlie misogyny.

The central image of *La Tour d'amour*[19] (The Tower of Love, 1899) also denotes a conflict between masculine identity and the threatening power of the feminine. Focalized and narrated by a male character, the young lighthouse-keeper Jean Maleux, this novel centres on the battle between the lighthouse – a phallic symbol if ever there was one, and representative of a male ability to control and master the natural world – and the sea, characterized as a deceitful and dangerous woman who on stormy days 'swelled and curved like a belly . . . opening her green thighs' (p. 122). The moon is also a symbol of the feminine, and in one particularly explicit passage struggles to dominate the light from the 'tower of love':

> It was a strange conflict between She, the great virgin, and He, the monster sprung from the darkness. . . . Little by little she devoured him, making him a part of her own light.
>
> They knew that what was happening was the work of an animal or of a dissolute woman – they could tell by the shadowy mouth which formed a slit in the lower part of her face. She has a wound there, a scar, lips which reopen each month and suck in the wills of men and the light of their reason . . . (p. 115).

*La Tour d'amour* is one of the most extreme examples of that part of Rachilde's writing which adopts a male perspective and represents the feminine as threatening, powerful and alien. The novel's narrative development endorses the central image of a struggle to impose order and control on a menacing universe: when Jean Maleux, half-crazed with loneliness and alcohol, stabs a prostitute to death and thus symbolically kills the feminine, he is never brought to justice but in a sense is rewarded by promotion to chief lighthouse-keeper. Indeed, not all the images of alien femininity depend on the intermediary of a male focalizer: 'La Buveuse de Sang' (The Blood-Drinker), for example, employs an external narrator to depict the moon as a female vampire which lives off women's blood. Raoule de Vénérande in *Monsieur Vénus*, Mary Barbe in *La Marquise de Sade* or Eliante in *La Jongleuse* are all perceived as monstrous and sinister figures at some points in the text by an external narrator. We might even add that they perceive themselves in this way, for they are all characters whose style of dress and behaviour is calculated to present to the world an image of the monstrous, the dangerous and the enigmatic.

A psychoanalytic explanation based on Rachilde's own childhood would be possible. It would demand consideration of her failure to negotiate the difficult process of separation and identification with the mother, her overidentification with the father rendered the more problematic by the fact that, as a girl, this could have no clear reward, her possible castration complex producing intense hostility to the mother. However, Rachilde's personal biography is of less interest than the broader issue of the position of the woman writer in a misogynist culture. At one level, Rachilde exemplifies the temptation to achieve acceptance as a writer by assuming a masculine perspective on the world – and carries it off so well that she produces texts infused with an intense and explicit fear of women.

At the same time the contradictions of her position are apparent in the fact that female voices do sound in Rachilde's texts, and from the female perspective women's lives no longer appear alien, enigmatic and threatening but, rather, restricted, frustrating and enclosed. Although Mary Barbe is a cruel and violent figure, we are also given access to her perceptions of the discrimination she suffers as a girl, and her wedding-night speech to her husband contains an astute analysis of her real socioeconomic position and a rejection of hypocrisy:

> If I'm accepting you without waiting for the handsome young gipsy I used to dream of, it is because I am determined to be free of the guardianship of my uncle. You represent freedom to me and therefore even if you were a thief I would accept you . . . I do not wish to be a mother because I wish neither to suffer nor to inflict suffering . . . (pp. 214–15)

Eliante, 'the Juggler', is largely focalized by Léon, so that her air of sinister mystery is maintained, but in certain passages the narration also adopts Eliante's perspective. Thus the reader learns that viewed from within, the heroine's mask of enigmatic evil is both deliberately produced and self-destructive: she perceives herself as 'the great actress, or the great victim of her own juggling act' (p. 197). Through the passages which adopt her perspective, it becomes apparent that Eliante's self-dramatization as *femme fatale* expresses her refusal to adopt the subservient role of wife or mistress, but her failure to invent any alternative.

The short story 'La Panthère' ('The She-Panther') offers a condensed illustration of Rachilde's ambivalence towards women's situation and the effect of this ambivalence on the female narrative voice. The panther is let loose among the Christians in the Roman arena for the amusement of the crowd. Because, unlike the human spectators, she is a beast who kills for meat and not for pleasure, she fails to grasp what is expected of her and feeds instead on the meat of a dead elephant lying in the arena. Brutalized and tortured by the disappointed humans, she is locked away and left to starve – but as she awaits death, dreaming of her native jungle, the daughter of the jailer takes pity on her and brings her meat. The panther leaps for her throat and kills her.

This story shifts between two narrative perspectives. One is that of the panther, an animal whose integrity is clearly greater than that of the bloodthirsty crowd, and whose suffering and compensatory dreams of the jungle encourage reader identification:

> In the distance, in tiered circles, a blur of pale forms emitted strange cries. . . . She gave a scornful mewing cry . . . and unhurried, seized by the curious desire to show them the gentleness of real wild animals, she settled down to feed on the tasty flesh of the huge elephant, disdaining human prey. (*Contes et nouvelles*, p. 218)

The other is an external perspective which emphasizes the panther's ferocious appearance, her air of a 'sinister virgin', and takes over at the story's close to recount the killing of the jailer's daughter: 'she watched her a moment with her phosphorescent eyes, now deep as an abyss, then with a single leap was at her throat and strangled her '(*Contes et nouvelles*, p. 225). Through the first perspective, the story identifies with the panther as victim and shows the irrational brutality of men's behaviour and the way in which this, in turn, brutalizes her. The second perspective refuses the panther innocence and integrity, and demonstrates that the crowd's perceptions of her as intrinsically savage and violent are justified. It is no accident that the panther is female, for this parallels closely Rachilde's ambivalent representation of women.

GENDER AND SUBVERSION

There is a fascination with power and the accoutrements of power in Decadent writing which raises the possibility of role reversal. The man who is victim of the *femme fatale* is in a sense feminized, like the young hero at the start of *The First Mistress*, or Des Esseintes in his imagined relationship with the female acrobat in Huysmans's *Against the Grain* – for true power is seen as masculine.

In the case of Rachilde, though, this goes further and becomes a regular narrative preoccupation. Her writing contains a number of role reversals and frequently displaces signifiers of gender. Jacques Silvert in *Monsieur Vénus* wears silk and lace, makes a living by weaving flowers, and is the object of a voyeur scene in which Raoule spies on him naked in the bath – all conventions associated with the feminine. Another male protagonist, Léon (*The Juggler*), experiences a feminine sense of 'lack', dreaming of Eliante as a phallic column of smoke and finding himself short of the 'revolver or pistol' needed to shoot her down. Conversely, heroines take on masculine signs and roles. Raoule wears men's clothing, refers to herself in the masculine form, and keeps Jacques as her 'mistress'. Mary Barbe visits her young lover in a garret apartment and abandons him she is when satisfied, displaying a 'masculine' cold-bloodedness and detachment quite opposed to his naive emotion. Basine in *The Leader of Wolves* cross-dresses and leads an army.

A preoccupation with the conventional signs of gender and with their attribution to the 'wrong' sex does not in itself produce a feminist meaning. It does, however, signify a questioning of the dominant ideology of late-nineteenth-century France which took gender to be a stable category linked inextricably to sex. Rachilde's heroines transgress the codes of female good behaviour by becoming scientists (Mary Barbe), rebel leaders (Basine in *The Leader of Wolves*), the dominant lovers of kept men (Raoule de Vénérande and Mary Barbe), and though their impropriety is punished and patriarchal power firmly reinstated, this does not entirely negate the texts' disturbance of gender identity.

The departure from the norms of gender representation is particularly apparent in the depiction of female desire. The dominant ideology of the late nineteenth century made the desiring subject male and woman the object of desire. Where the Decadents represent female desire, this is generally as an attribute of the evil and destructive *femme fatale*, which means that the taboo on active female sexuality is not only maintained but reinforced. Although we have seen that Rachilde's heroines too are monstrous and frequently 'fatal', some of them are also desiring subjects in a more positive sense. Raoule de Vénérande does destroy Jacques Silvert with her violent and cruel desires, but in the process she focalizes a most unusually sensual description of male nudity for a late-nineteenth-century text: 'It was worthy of the Callipyge Venus, that curve of the hips, the way the spine dipped to form a voluptuous plane then rose again into two firm, plump, adorable curves' (*Monsieur Vénus*, p. 59).

Eliante, 'la Jongleuse', neither destroys Léon nor accedes to his desire for her. Her sexual hunger is not merely the complement to male sexuality but seeks objects outside the impasse of heterosexual power relations. Léon is shocked and dismayed to observe her achieve orgasm in his presence but without his intervention, as she embraces a huge and graceful alabaster vase. Her words confirm his sense of exclusion: '"I despise the coupling of bodies, which destroys my strength. . . . For my flesh to be moved and to conceive of infinite pleasure, I have no need of a sex as the object of my love"' (pp. 49–50). Basine refuses the desire of Harog because the male violence she has suffered in the past has killed any possibility of her taking pleasure in heterosexual intercourse: '"Ah!", she said, "if you were not a man I would love you, for I don't find you at all displeasing, but I feel a disgust for all men, a nausea like the desire to vomit"' (*The Leader of Wolves*, p. 204). Women, in other words, are posited as actively desiring subjects (*Monsieur Vénus*), whose situation in relation to men may demand the transference of their desire from the male body to another object (*The Juggler*), or may indeed kill desire altogether (*The Leader of Wolves*). Both the focalization of the male body from the perspective of female desire, and the heroines' refusal of heterosexual relations, problematize the dominant assumptions of active-male, passive-female, and of women's natural position as complementary to male sexuality. It might be added that Rachilde's fiction divorces female sexuality from reproduction in a manner quite at odds with nineteenth-century views on the centrality of motherhood to female identity. It is the 'Marquise de Sade' who explicitly declares her refusal to be a mother on the terms available, but most of Rachilde's heroines refuse a necessary connection between sexual activity and maternity.

Two curious and ambivalent figures run through the novel *The Leader of Wolves*, figures which echo and amplify consistent themes in Rachilde's fiction. One is the lone wolf within the city walls on Christmas Day, come to disturb the feast, black against the white snow he later stains with the blood of his victims, disruptive to the peace and security of the citizens – but also, because much of the scene is focalized from his point of view, a hungry and rebellious creature with whose needs the reader may identify. Rachilde herself identifies wolves as creatures hated by her father and as 'our brothers, my mother's and mine' (*When I was young*, pp. 74–6), and the novel's title makes wolves female. The other is the skeletal figure of the nun who was walled up in a tiny cell years before the story begins, as a punishment for having attempted to escape the convent. When she makes her second and successful escape she joins the rebels, but she is a repulsively decayed shadow of her former self, crazy with anger and silence, capable only of destruction. Both wolf and nun must die for the novel's resolution to take place and for order to be restored.

Both of these figures – the one vibrantly, violently alive, the other inwardly destroyed by repression – resemble Rachilde's depictions of women. Her heroines threaten the city of men by their anger and their hunger, but either they are destroyed, or their bitterness turns inward and decays them from within. Their revolt achieves little because they aim only to have revenge by usurping the father's power to inflict pain and exercise domination, failing to contest the very nature of that power.

The violent, unsettling figures of repressed female anger, the voices of a possible revolt, none the less haunt Rachilde's texts. The explosive tension between their frustration and their respect for male power fuels the narratives and produces vivid images of Rachilde's own ambivalent position as a woman writer – torn between the desire to question gender roles and the desire to belong by perfectly mimicking the masculine text.

# 5
# From the Pillory to Sappho's Island: The Poetry of Renée Vivien

In a society materially and symbolically founded on the division of people into two unequal but complementary genders, the formation of heterosexual relationships is inevitably one of life's central narratives – indeed, for women, virtually the only narrative. Homosexuality becomes either literally unthinkable – so that, as Lilian Faderman has shown, women could engage in the most intimate and passionate relationships without fear or accusation of impropriety[1] – or homosexual relationships may be acknowledged in order to be defined as deviant, unnatural and threatening to the social order. One of the many strategies used to condemn and belittle the assertive woman was to define her as unnatural or monstrous. Thus George Sand's presumption in daring to dress and write like a man met with accusations of lesbianism: here was a woman whose desires, it was implied, placed her outside the ranks of authentic womanhood. Until the very end of the century, most literary representations of erotic love between women were penned by men, and charged with the mingled fascination and disapproval of the voyeur and the anger born of the fear of exclusion.

Baudelaire's *Femmes damnées* and 'Condemned poems', the latter banned by the Public Prosecutor after the 1857 publication of *Les Fleurs du mal*, are among the most representative and influential nineteenth-century texts on lesbian love. Fascinated by the mythical female community of Lesbos, the poet represents Sappho and her sisters as inspired and courageous –

De la réalité grand esprits contempteurs,
Chercheuses d'infini . . .

[Great spirits contemptuous of reality,
Seekers of the infinite . . .][2]

– for within the logic of his anti-bourgeois stance, the refusal of normality is positively valued. Baudelaire's female lovers, however, are also damned souls tormented by 'fièvres hurlantes' (clamouring fevers) and 'soifs inassouvies' (unsatisfied desires). The emphasis is almost entirely on physical desire, on the torment of desire frustrated yet the 'bitter sterility' of sexual pleasure (*Delphine et Hippolyte*). Baudelaire's lesbians have a certain tragic dignity, but they are doomed by the monstrous nature of their desires to endless suffering –

> Loin des peuples vivants, errantes, condamnées,
> A travers les déserts courez comme des loups;
>
> [Far from the living, wandering, doomed
> Across the deserts run like wolves;][3]

– a suffering which is finally both reassuring and erotically pleasing to the male poet/reader contemplating the 'stérile volupté' of 'hollow-eyed girl[s]' who 'Caressent les fruits mûrs de leur nubilité' [Caress the ripe fruits of their nubility].[4]

When the last decades of the century brought a resurgence of feminist activity and some minor advances in women's rights, the hostile depiction of the lesbian intensified. Zola stages a grimly sordid lesbian gathering in *Nana* (1880), filling his scene with fat, predatory older women, 'with bloated flesh hanging in puffy folds over their flaccid lips' (*Nana*, p. 257) and provocatively ingenuous girls, 'still [wearing] an innocent expression in spite of their immodest gestures' (p. 257). The presence of a young woman dressed as a man, and of a few male customers 'come to see the sight' (p. 258), complete the portrait of a lesbian underworld which both imitates and provides new pleasures for male sexuality.

Poets and artists, themselves often marginalized by the patriarchal status quo, were fascinated by lesbianism as a force which disturbed the reigning order, yet repelled by the notion of active female desire which excluded men. Where lesbianism was named and made visible, it tended to be explained away as a pathetic or ludicrous desire to emulate men, as in the case of Baudelaire's 'male' Sappho (in the poem 'Lesbos') and Zola's transvestite, or seen as an erotic spectacle for male consumption – within the literary text as well as in the brothels of the period. In both cases women who loved women connoted decadence and disorder.

Paris of the *belle époque* was none the less the scene of a flourishing, if marginal, lesbian community. Within that wealthy, cultured milieu centred on the *salons* and immortalized in Marcel Proust's *In Search of Lost Time*, there developed a network of lesbian relationships and gatherings. The *salon* of the expatriate American Natalie Barney was one of their principal meeting places, and Barney's clearly articulated and unapologetic celebration of lesbian love as the 'confirmation of woman's separateness and wholeness'[5] drew a clear connection between lesbianism and feminism. The network was composed both of committed, self-defined lesbians like Barney and of visitors to the lesbian scene: courtesans from the *demi-monde* of whom the most famous, Liane de Pougy, had a passionate affair with Barney and published a novel based on the relationship (*Idylle saphique*, 1901), and society women on temporary excursions outside conventional lives. The 'Amazons' were frowned upon in respectable circles, tolerated as a titillating sideshow in libertine circles, taken seriously by few outside their own number.

'Paris has always seemed to me the only city where you can live and express yourself as you please',[6] wrote Natalie Barney. The purpose of the lesbian community was not only to allow women to live their love and desire for each other, but also to encourage them to write. Barney's salon brought together a considerable number of the French women writers of the *belle époque* including Colette, Lucie Delarue-Mardrus, Anna de Noailles and Renée Vivien – as well as many expatriate and visiting American writers and some of the major French male artists of the period, among them homosexual writers such as André Gide and Jean Cocteau.

Of the lesbian writers who met in Barney's *salon* at the turn of the century, Renée Vivien was the most dedicated to the cause of writing poetry which would speak of love between women in a woman's voice. Her life was short and sad: born Pauline Tarn in London in 1877, she was educated partly in Paris and presented at court as a débutante in 1897, but succeeded in escaping her family and the almost inevitable destiny of marriage by setting up home independently in Paris in 1899. Her affair with Barney began in

1900 but was broken by violent disputes over Barney's principled refusal of fidelity, and interrupted by long separations. Vivien was anorexic, alcoholic and severely depressive. She died of alcohol poisoning at the age of thirty-one, having published ten poetry collections, a short novel and a collection of stories under the name 'Renée Vivien', as well as poems and prose under the name 'Paule Riversdale'.

The portrait Colette leaves of her in *The Pure and the Impure* conjures up a pretty, delicate woman, barricaded inside a dark, exotically furnished flat from which the external world was rigorously excluded, scarcely eating but secretly consuming large quantities of alcohol, in thrall to a mysterious 'She' who would suddenly demand her presence. Lacking the robust irreverence of a Colette or a Barney, Vivien had to construct defences against a hostile world rather than confront it in the light of day.

Her poetry also constructs defences against a society which defines the lesbian poet as monster, failure or spectacle for the male voyeur. The contemporary social world is banished from Vivien's poetry, and is only marginally more present in her prose narratives. The poems fall mainly into two categories: love poems addressed to a female lover, and evocations of Mytilène, the utopian community of women on the island of Lesbos in the time of Sappho (or Psappha, as Vivien names her). In the love poems, the material world is reduced to a single room in which the lovers meet and make love, or to a garden where nature functions primarily as reflection of the lover's beauty. The Mytilène poems, both spatially and temporally distanced from *belle époque* Paris, can abandon this enclosure and open on to a wider world of sea, sky and collective sisterhood.

THE PILLORY

'Intérieur' (p. 303[7]), published in 1906, typifies Vivien's representation of love as refuge from a hostile world. Addressed to the lover – 'O my Serenity' – the poem describes a state of sensual and emotional happiness which can be maintained only by the exclusion of society.

> Dans mon âme a fleuri le miracle des roses
> Pour le mettre à l'abri, tenons les portes closes.

[In my soul has flowered the miracle of roses
To shelter it safely let us keep the doors closed.][8]

The 'miracle of roses', composed of calm silence and the lover's
beauty, must be protected by closed doors and drawn curtains: the
words 'tenons les portes closes' ('let us keep the doors closed') form
the poem's refrain. If, within the room, all is a 'still garden' of warm
light, soft lamps and dancing fire, in which the lover's eyes and
hair can contain seasons and landscapes, this state of bliss is fragile
and constantly contrasted to the icy streets, poisonous gossip and
threatening hatred on the other side of the walls:

Tes cheveux sont plus beaux qu'une forêt d'automne,
Et ton art soucieux les tresse et les ordonne.

Oui, les chuchotements ont perdu leur venin,
Et la haine d'autrui n'est plus qu'un mal bénin.

[Your hair is lovelier than an autumn forest
Woven and ordered by your careful art.
Yes, the cruel whispers have lost their poison
And the hatred of others is now only a benign evil.]

The urban love poems represent mutual desire and tenderness not
as emotions which light up the surrounding world, but as treasures
to be defended against hostile others. They are indoor poems,
contained within defensive walls and boundaries, expressing a
consistent preference for twilight, evening and seclusion from
the outside world, for 'the dying day which fades gradually/The
fire, the enclosed intimacy of a room' ('Paroles à l'amie' ['Words
to a (Female) Friend'], p. 258). The city itself is rarely more than
a malign presence which threatens the lovers' retreat.

In those few poems which do evoke the material reality of the
city, urban images are rapidly absorbed into an imaginative universe
in which their function becomes figurative. 'Reflets d'ardoise'
('Lightplay on a Slate Roof', p. 177) describes the slate roofs of the
title, blue-grey and dampened by a 'sly drizzle' so that they reflect
the same blue-grey of the clouds. However, the descriptive note
of the first stanza is subordinated to the imperative 'Vois' ('See')
which opens the first line: the slate roofs are evoked as a prelude

to a comparison between their subtle, cool colouring and the eyes
of the poet's lover, the poem's addressee.

O mon divin Tourment, dans tes yeux bleus et gris
S'aiguise et se ternit le reflet de l'ardoise .

[O my divine Torment, in your blue-grey eyes
The slate's reflection is sharpened and dulled.]

The slate's qualities of colour and light are precisely delineated
less for purely descriptive purposes than in order to evoke, by
analogy, the elusive and uncompliant charm of the lover. In the
last stanza the slate roof is used figuratively in another sense, to
signify 'home':

Jamais, nous défendant de la foule narquoise,
Un toit n'abritera nos soupirs incompris . . .

[No roof will ever shelter our sighs
From the mocking crowd.]

Homeless, outcast, the lovers will never be protected from society's scorn.

Thus the material world of the city is largely absent from
Vivien's poetry or, if it is present, it is dissolved through the figurative use of language into an element in the poet's inner drama.

The exclusion of a society perceived as censorious and cruel
is a condition of happiness in Vivien's poetry. In certain poems
the threat of social opprobrium is realized and the drama of the
lesbian poet as object of abuse and ridicule is fully staged. 'Sur la
place publique' ('In the Public Square', pp. 264–5) is a nine-verse
narrative poem which tells the story of a fall from grace to despair.
The narrator lives at first in an Eden-like forest:

J'étais fervente et jeune et j'avais une harpe
Le monde se parait, suave et féminin.

I was fervent and young and I had a harp
The world adorned herself in smooth feminine beauty.]

In the third verse she leaves the pure happiness of the forest to
follow the crowd to the town, where she sings in the public square,
surrounded by the smell of dried fish, the cries of merchants and

the gibes of her audience, but lost in her music and oblivious to distraction. As night falls she sings on alone in the deserted square, but the poem ends not on a note of victory but on an image of creativity destroyed by the entry into the social world :

Je me mis à chanter sans témoins, pour la joie
De chanter, comme on fait lorsque l'amour vous fuit,
Lorsque l'espoir vous raille et que l'oubli vous broie,
La harpe se brisa sous mes mains, dans la nuit.

[I began to sing without witness, for the joy
Of singing, as one does when love escapes you,
When you are mocked by hope and broken by neglect,
The harp broke in my hands as night fell.]

'Le Pilori' (p. 300), a poem of nine rhyming couplets, offers a still more explicit image of public abuse and ridicule, for the narrator, condemned for an unnamed offence, is tied to the pillory, where men pelt her with mud, women laugh at her, and insults fall like 'whips of nettles'. Pride prevents her from weeping, but the last stanza emphasizes the lasting effect of her humiliation:

Je suis partie au gré des vents. Et depuis lors
Mon visage est pareil à la face des morts.

[I left to wander at the mercy of the winds. And since then
My face has been like the face of the dead.]

The most complex and interesting of these poems of public humiliation is 'Les Oripeaux' ('Cheap Finery', pp. 197–8) from the 1904 collection *La Vénus des aveugles* (Venus of the Blind). Here the 'I' of the poem is not the innocent artist of 'Sur la place publique', nor the pilloried victim of mob hostility, but herself painfully complicit in the exposure of her love as spectacle. She is a 'saltimbanque', a performer in a travelling circus, a charlatan who parades her desires and her art before the scornful crowd. To write love poetry as a lesbian is seen here not just as a brave act of sincerity but as unavoidable complicity in the subjection of women's sexuality to public prurience. The poet prostitutes her partner by offering her body to the public gaze:

Devant la foule aux remous de troupeau

. . .

De mes vers, pareils à des oripeaux
J'ai drapé follement tes membres d'arlequine.
Découvre à l'air des nuits tes seins prostitués

[Before the milling, herdlike crowd

. . .

With my verses, cheap finery,
I have draped your Harlequin limbs.
Bare to the night your prostituted breasts.]

The dilemma of the poet is beautifully rendered in the image of the passionate performer, caught between tender desire for her partner and need for the crowd's acclaim, presenting the loved body in the 'cheap finery' of verses and thus offering her own love as spectacle. 'O toi la danseuse ivre, ô moi la saltimbanque!' [O you the drunken dancer, and I the charlatan!] she addresses her mistress, and the poem ends by calling their performance 'Ce spectacle effronté de nos âmes publiques!' (This shameless spectacle of our public souls!)

Much of Vivien's poetry thus thematizes her own vulnerability before a world perceived as hostile and uncomprehending. In terms of form, most of her poems observe the rules and conventions of French versification with a fidelity which is perhaps also a defensive acknowledgement of outsider status. As a female, lesbian poet, Vivien was already doubly marginalized within an almost uniquely male and heterosexual French tradition, but she was also an English woman for whom French was a second language. Vivien studied French prosody with the writer Charles-Brun before and during the preparation of her first publications, and while her manipulation of rhythm and rhyme is fluent and effective, she uses the standard forms of ten- or twelve-syllable lines with regular rhyme-stopped endings far more than she risks formal experimentation.

Poets of the preceding generations, most famously Verlaine (1844–96) and Rimbaud (1854–91), as well as some of Vivien's contemporaries, had experimented with lines of different lengths and rhythms, with prose poems or poems where a powerful rhythm replaced rhyme as the primary formal device, with lexical shock effects such as the juxtaposition of formal and colloquial registers. In contrast Vivien's Alexandrines, regular patterns of rhyme and maintenance of a recognizably poetic register provide a defensive exterior for the semantic scandal of homosexual love. When the first collection, *Etudes et préludes* (Studies and Preludes), was published, the poet was named simply as R. Vivien. naturally it was assumed that the poems were written by a young man in praise of his mistress, and the feminine voice of the poet passed unnoticed couched, as it was, in familiar poetic forms.

The defensive exclusion of the wider social world, the representation of the poet's vulnerability which also takes the form of a certain formal cautiousness, suggest that the dominant representation of the lesbian as alien, doomed to ostracism and ridicule, had come to inform Vivien's sense of personal identity and her poetic imagination. In certain poems the lover is characterized as that same *femme fatale* who haunts the poetry of Baudelaire and the writing of the Decadents, including, as we have seen, that of Rachilde. The *femme fatale* is the negative image of the Good Woman: she is the menacing face of a femininity which escapes male authority, declares the autonomy of women's desires and threatens the patriarchal order. The woman writer, usurper of the pen/penis, always risked denunciation in these terms; indeed, Isabelle de Courtivron makes a convincing case for George Sand having been 'the very prototype for the exotic and satanic version of the *femme fatale* which dominates French art and literature from the 1830s on'.[9] As a writer and a lesbian, Vivien was doubly vulnerable to identification with this demonic figure.

In Vivien's poetry the *femme fatale* figures both the poet's fear of desire itself, since the desire for another woman means self-definition as pariah and alien, and her fear of loss and betrayal. The 'Amante aux cruels ongles longs' (lover with the long, cruel nails) ('Désir', p. 49) is compared to the sea in her dangerously seductive beauty: 'Tu m'attirais vers toi comme l'abîme et l'eau' [You drew me towards you like the abyss and like water] ('Naïade moderne' ['Modern Naiad'], p. 59), and to a poisonous yet beautiful snake in 'Ressemblance inquiétante' ('A Disturbing Likeness', p. 79), which ends by addressing the lover as 'Reptile and Goddess', to death itself:

Les tombeaux sont encore moins impur que ta couche
O Femme! je le sais mais j'ai soif de ta bouche.

[Graves are less impure than your bed
O Woman! I know this, yet I thirst for your mouth.]
('Lucidité', p. 54)

For the characterization of the lover as corrupt and dangerous means the devalorization of love and desire itself, and leads to the emphasis in many of the poems on the longing for death and oblivion. In some poems Vivien internalizes the *femme fatale* persona, not only representing the object of her desire as inherently evil but making the *femme fatale* herself the 'I' of the poem, representing the poet as a doomed wanderer for whom death would be a a welcome escape. One of the most vivid images of despair is that of the labyrinth: 'J 'erre au fond d'un cruel et savant labyrinthe . . .' [I wander deep in a cruel and knowing labyrinth] (Le Labyrinthe, p. 197). In this poem the 'grey ambiguity' of the maze of corridors is represented formally through a pattern of repeated and semi-repeated lines, the first line of each five-line stanza echoing in the fourth and a complex play of repetition producing a sense of entrapment. The labyrinth represents that side of Vivien's poetry which articulates the difficulty of speaking and desiring from the position of the 'damned woman'.

TOWARDS MYTILÈNE

There is another, more positive side to Vivien's writing which expresses resistance to the definition of lesbianism as deviant, represents the refusal of heterosexuality as a political gesture, and seeks new ways to articulate feminine desire. This affirmative voice coexists with the defensive tone of the outcast throughout her brief poetic career, gaining the ascendant in the collections which celebrate the female community on Lesbos (*Sapho*, 1903; *Les Kitharèdes*, 1904), in certain happy love poems and in the story collection *La Dame à la louve* ('The Lady with the She-Wolf', 1904).

'Eternelle vengeance' ('Eternal Vengeance', p. 50), which appeared in *Etudes et préludes* (1901), takes a biblical story which has always functioned as a cautionary tale of female duplicity, and reverses the meaning. When the hero Samson is captured by his enemies, his survival depends on concealing from them that the source of his strength lies in his long hair. It is the seductive Delilah who discovers and betrays his secret, demonstrating, in the Alfred de Vigny poem which typifies the dominant version of the story, that:

> Une lutte éternelle en tout temps, en tout lieu,
> Se livre sur la terre, en présence de Dieu,
> Entre la bonté d'Homme et la ruse de Femme,
> Car la femme est un être impur de corps et d'âme.

> [An eternal struggle in all times and places
> Is waged on earth, in the presence of God
> Between the goodness of Man and the guile of Woman
> For woman is a creature impure in body and soul.][10]

In Vivien's version Delilah rather than Samson is granted a voice, so that she may speak of her humiliation as the object of transitory male lust, describing herself as 'La fleur que l'on effeuille au festin du désir' [The flower stripped of petals at the banquet of desire]. The poem foregrounds Delilah's repulsion at the need to feign desire in response to 'the imperious sign of passing lovers', and thus motivates and justifies her anger. Her revenge becomes an act not of betrayal, but of resistance.

'Je pleure sur toi' ('I Weep for You', p. 276), published in 1906 and – according to Paul Lorenz[11] – addressed to Lucie Delarue-Mardrus on her marriage, identifies heterosexual relationships with intimate acceptance of submission, and female celibacy or homosexuality with freedom and dignity. The poem mourns the transformation of a 'daughter of the sea' who 'rode the crest of waves' into a docile wife reduced to the status of her husband's sexual and legal property . The sixth quatrain reads:

> L'époux montre aujourd'hui tes yeux, si méprisants
> Jadis, tes mains, ton col indifférent de cygne,
> Comme on montre ses blés, son jardin et sa vigne
> Aux admirations des amis complaisants.

[Today the husband displays your once disdainful eyes,
Your neck, indifferent like a swan's,
As one displays one's crops, one's garden and one's vine
To the admiration of obliging friends.]

The poem plays on the contrasting imagery of seascape and conjugal enclosure, making what is finally a political comment on the powerlessness of the married woman.

Masculine arrogance, supported by legal and economic power but felt most intimately in sexual behaviour, is the target of 'Je pleure sur toi' and of other poems such as 'Litanie de la haine' ('Litany of Hatred', 1903) –

Nous haïssons la face agressive des mâles

. . .

Nous haïssons le rut qui souille le désir

[We hate the aggressive face of men
We hate the rutting which defiles desire]

– a poem which envisages the outlawed status of lesbian women less as a source of suffering than as the prerequisite for revolt.


Many of the short stories collected in *La Dame à la louve* share a narrative structure which functions to stage, then ridicule, masculine arrogance. A male narrator expresses towards women a condescension born of unquestioned belief in male superiority, but the story proceeds to demonstrate the discrepancy between his comfortable assumptions about women and their irreducible reality. Thus the complacent traveller of the title story 'La Dame à la louve', who makes casual advances to the only female fellow-passenger on board the ship because 'the enforced chastity of these floating prisons exasperates my senses',[12] persistently reads all her refusals and rejections – including the snarling hostility of her pet wolf – as disguised expressions of attraction: 'I smiled without anxiety. We have to be patient with women, don't we? and never believe a word they say. When they tell you to go, you must always stay' (p. 9). His confidence is shaken only by the most dramatic of dénouements, for the ship sinks and the woman, rather than enter the lifeboat and thus abandon the she-wolf who is her true companion, floats away to sea with the wolf on a broken mast. The narrator's smug and deeply conventional tone struggles to encompass the woman's preference for a wild death over his company: 'But the cold, the slowness and fragility of that improvised craft, without sails or rudder, the fatigue, the weakness of women!' (p. 21). In other stories, virile heroes – cowboys, adventurers, in 'Trahison de la forêt' ('The Forest's Betrayal') a hunter known as 'The Forest Devil' because of his history of murder and rape – discover that their female companions cannot be depended on to applaud their exploits or to respond to sexual advances. The brothel Madame of 'La Chasteté paradoxale' ('Paradoxical Chastity') stabs the narrator rather than accept his advances, since despite her trade she herself is not for sale. The arrogant narrator is punished for ignoring the words of his wiser companion, who warns him that 'her profession must have inspired in her a hatred and disgust for men' (p. 105).

The eponymous queen of 'Le Voile de Vashti' ('Vashti's Veil') renounces her throne and her wealth for exile in the desert rather than obey her husband's order to appear unveiled before his male guests. Vashti's departing speech is an explicitly feminist call to arms. She accepts the possibility that she may die in the desert of hunger or solitude, but presents her choice as a gesture on behalf of all women:

> Since the revolt of Lilith I am the first free woman. My deed will be known by all women, and all those who are slaves in the homes of their husband or father will secretly envy me. Thinking of my glorious rebellion they will say 'Vashti renounced her queenship in order to be free'. (pp. 143–4)

In some of Vivien's work, then, there is an explicit and combative assertion that heterosexual relations are political – that is, that they bring into play structures of legal and economic power – and a refusal of the definition of femininity as submissive and male-directed. Although a significant element of her writing represents lesbian women in terms of Baudelairean exile and damnation, this more militant stance extends to attempts to represent women outside the terms of patriarchy. There is in Vivien's poetry both the articulation of a female tradition of revolt and a search for ways of representing the female body from a feminine perspective.

The story of Queen Vashti and the poem which celebrates Delilah's victory over Samson both suggest historical continuity in the oppression of women and indicate a tradition of female revolt. In the poem 'Souveraines' ('Queens', from *Evocations*, 1903) Vivien brings together a chorus of eleven women whose beauty brought them male desire and adulation but whose stories ended tragically. From Lilith (mythical figure of feminine evil) to Lady Jane Grey (whose persona Colette recalls Vivien adopting for a fancy-dress party), each woman tells her own story, ending in the refrain which echoes from verse to verse:

> . . . sur mon front d'amoureuse
> L'astre fatal de la Beauté.
> Je ne fus pas heureuse.

> [on my brow [was placed]
> The fatal star of Beauty/I was not happy.]
> ('Souveraines', pp. 113–16)

The poem's form is unusual and effective. The juxtaposition of famous women from myth and history emphasizes the dangerous fragility of that female power which is built on the ability to seduce and charm. The repetition of the refrain, with the contrasting lyricism of 'l'astre fatal de la beauté' and the bleak simplicity of 'Je ne fus pas heureuse', links the stories of women condemned to a tragic fate by their celebrated ability to inspire male desire. Yet despite the attempt to give a voice to these icons of female beauty, Vivien's poem does not go much beyond a plaintive picturing of their common plight, for apart from the recurring 'Je ne fus pas heureuse' the women's perspective is narcissistic, scarcely emerging from the familiar and highly visual myth that surrounds each of them. Cleopatra is mysterious –

> Je rayonnai. Je fus le sourire d'Isis,
> Insondable, illusoire et terrible comme elle.

> [I shone. I was the smile of Isis
> Unfathomable, illusory and terrible as she.] (p. 115)

– and Lady Jane Grey is touching and pathetic: 'Mon sourire d'enfant éclaira l'échafaud' [My childlike smile lit up the scaffold]

(p. 116). Even though they are granted their own voices, the women present an externally focalized vision of themselves, confirming – albeit sympathetically – the view of them as essentially figures in a male landscape.

Vivien's work often reveals the difficulty of writing against the grain of an androcentric culture. Even the search for a female genealogy founders on the power of patriarchal vision. It was by turning to the poetry of the Greek lesbian poet Sappho, who wrote in the seventh century BC, and to the female community which her poetry evokes, that Vivien was able to create an image of women, and specifically of lesbian women, freed from the defensive consciousness of public censure and from the salacious gaze of *fin-de-siècle* pornography. The sense of a female community, implied by 'Souveraines', is realized more fully in the poems which sing the beauty of Lesbos, or Mytilène.

In the collections *Sapho* (1903) and *Les Kitharèdes* (1904) Vivien translated parts of Sappho's poetry. This in itself was an act of reclamation of the work of an important female ancestor, a project also undertaken by Virginia Woolf who, like Vivien, had first to study Greek, since a classical education was a male prerogative at the beginning of the century.

When Vivien takes a fragment of Sappho's verse and writes poems which are part translation, part amplification of the original, a sort of poetic collaboration across time takes place, affirming the image of women as 'sisterly mirrors' which is at the heart of the poem 'Psappha revit' ('Psappha Lives Again').

The poems emphasize the interpenetration of past and present, a construction of time which suspends the linear chronology of history, with its scarcity of female figures:

Du fond de mon passé, je retourne vers toi,
Mytilène, à travers les siècles disparates.

[From the depths of my past, I return to you
Mytilène, across the disparate centuries]

writes Vivien, joyfully transcending the boundaries of individual biography in favour of a communal female history. The Lesbos to which she invites her lover in 'Vers Lesbos' ('Towards Lesbos') is both the island inhabited by Sappho and her companions, and the contemporary Lesbos which Vivien visited with Natalie Barney:

> Mytilène, parure et splendeur de la mer,
> Comme elle versatile et comme elle éternelle,
> Sois l'autel aujourd'hui des ivresses d'hier . . .

> [Mytilène, jewel and splendour of the sea
> Versatile and eternal like the sea
> Be the altar today for the ecstasies of yesterday.] (p. 265)

Spatially, too, Mytilène reverses the restrictive structures of Vivien's contemporary world – or, in Elyse Blankley's words, 'demands that [the] female lovers redefine the sexual politics of space that have dominated their lives'.[13] Where the world of the Parisian poems is enclosed, dark, protective of a private feminine sphere that would be disrupted by the harsh light of the male gaze,[14] the world of Mytilène is open, bright and colourful, characterized by a blurring of the frontiers between internal and external, indoors and outdoors. Only women live there, and the absence of men and of masculine culture means 'days without immodesty, fear or remorse' ('Psappha revit', p. 253). The lovers' bed is the beach; the 'miracle of roses', so carefully preserved from the light of day in 'Intérieur', becomes one element in a complex network of sensory and emotional pleasures:

> Quand, disposant leurs corps sur tes lits d'algues sèches,
> Les amantes jetaient des mots las et brisés,
> Tu mêlais tes odeurs de roses et de pêches
> Aux longs chuchotements qui suivent les baisers . . .

> [When, laying their bodies on your beds of dried seaweed
> The lovers would let slip tired, broken words
> You mingled your scents of roses and peaches
> With the long whisperings which follow kisses.]
> ('En Débarquant à Mytilène' ['Landing at Mytilène'], p. 249)

We have seen that much of Vivien's poetry articulates or struggles against a sense of having transgressed the laws and values of the community:

Et l'on a dit: 'Quelle est cette femme damnée
Que ronge sourdement la flamme de l'enfer?'

[And they said: 'Who is this accursed woman
Secretly consumed by the flames of Hell?']
('Paroles à l'amie', p. 259)

This produces both images of an embattled poet and her lover
defending their love from a hostile world, and a characterization
of the poet's self and that of her mistress as demonic and doomed
women. Love and desire become focused on a single partner, for
the lover is the sole ally, the sole source of warmth in a coldly
malevolent society, and her betrayal means complete isolation. This
desperate emphasis on the fidelity of the single lover is a feature of
Vivien's poetry and was the source of much of her suffering in her
relationship with the cheerfully polygamous Natalie Barney.

But in the Mytilène poems Vivien creates an alternative community stretching through space and time, a community in which she
is not an outsider but to which she belongs. The focus shifts from
the couple to the more inclusive 'Nous' ('we'): 'Et nous aimons
comme on aimait à Mytilène' [And we love as they loved in
Mytilène] ('Psappha revit', p. 253). The poems stage an imprecise
but plural number of female lovers whose desire and tenderness
extend beyond the one to the many:

Nous redisons ces mots de Psappha, quand nous sommes
Rêveuses sous un ciel illuminé d'argent:
'O belles, envers vous mon cœur n'est point changeante'
Celles que nous aimons ont méprisé les hommes.

[We repeat these words of Sappho, when we are
Dreaming beneath a silver-lit sky:
'O my beauties, towards you my heart is unchanging'
Those we love have rejected men] (Psappha revit, p. 253)

In her merging of individual identities within a plural female
pronoun ('Nous', 'Elles') to evoke a utopian community of
women, Vivien here looks forward sixty years to the work
of another French lesbian writer, Monique Wittig, whose 1969
*Les Guérillères* (The Female Warriors) imagines a band of female
warriors self-exiled from a society ruled by men.

To adopt the collective voice of an autonomous female community means to abandon the image of the lesbian poet as damned woman. It also precludes the representation of lesbianism as erotic scene, for the perspective becomes not that of the voyeur but that of the lovers themselves. Instead of Baudelaire's scorching passions and torrents of kisses (in the poem 'Lesbos', for example), there is a love both sensual and sisterly, both passionate and tender:

Et nous pouvons, quand la ceinture se dénoue,
Etre tout à la fois des amants et des soeurs.

[And when the girdle is untied
We can be both lovers and sisters.] ('Psappha revit', p. 253)

Desire and pleasure are articulated as experience rather than spectacle.

In Vivien's world love between women involves a constant play between sameness and difference. The sense of difference, the fascination with the lover as other, is articulated in descriptions of precise and desirable physical features: Vivien's love poems often address a woman whose hair is 'honey blonde', whose eyes are grey and whose body is white and generously curved. The pleasure of sameness – the sense of the lover as a 'sisterly mirror' ('Psappha revit', p. 252) – translates into a more original and particular style of representation of the female body. In Vivien's Mytilène poems, but also more generally in her love poetry, the lover's body is characterized by its reflective power. Hair, eyes, even clothing are not precisely defined but celebrated for their capacity to reflect and echo light, colour, the poet's imagination:

Tes cheveux irréels, aux reflets clairs et froids
Ont de pâles lueurs et des matités blondes;
Tes regards ont l'azur des éthers et des ondes;
Ta robe a le frisson des brises et des bois.

[Your unreal hair with its cold clear glints of light
Gleams pale, dull yellow
Your eyes are the azure of the air and the waves
Your dress quivers like the breeze and the forest.]
('Sonnet', p. 60)

Vivien's happier poetry is full of the play of light in the lover's eyes
and hair, of her body as mirror and echo of the natural world and
of the poet's emotion:

> Tu sembles écouter l'écho des harmonies
> Mortes; bleus de ce bleu de clartés infinies
> Tes yeux ont le reflet du ciel de Mytilène.
>
> [You seem to listen to the echo of dead
> Harmonies; blue with the blue of infinite light
> Your eyes reflect the sky of Mytilène.]
> ('Sonnet féminin' ['A Feminine Sonnet'], p. 87)

This marked emphasis on reflection and echo both corresponds
to the theme of female lovers as mutual mirrors, patterning and
enhancing each other's experience, and imagines the female body
as constantly changing and as permeable, open to the surrounding
world. In this Vivien prefigures some of the early work of Hélène
Cixous, who proposes a difference between the masculine sense
of bodily identity and the feminine. A masculine organization of
sensation around clearly demarcated parts of the body, and notably
the penis, would contrast with a feminine diffuseness of sensation. Cixous employs metaphors of 'diffusion', 'overflowing', and
describes the female body as 'an unlimited moving and changing
whole, a cosmos endlessly traversed by Eros, an immense astral
space'.[15] Vivien's 'corps à l'imprécis contour' ('body of uncertain contours', 'Algues marines' ['Seaweed'], p. 123), constantly
described in terms of the sea, the ebb and flow of waves, the
reflection of moonlight, presents the same emphasis on flux and on
a sexuality which permeates experience rather than being restricted
to the specifically genital event of arousal and satisfaction. Her
representation of women's bodies also strikingly prefigures the
writing of Luce Irigaray, for whom the unsettling, linguistically
unrepresentable nature of women within patriarchy arises precisely
from the fact that 'woman is neither closed nor open. Indefinite,
unfinished/in-finite, *form is never complete in her.*'[16]

Vivien's rare excursions into non-standard poetic forms produce
an interesting formal counterpart for her characterization of femininity in terms of permeable boundaries and flux. Some of the
poems in the collection *Sapho* are written in the metre of the

'Sapphic verse': three lines of eleven syllables followed by one
of five. To a reader accustomed to French prosody this reads as
an unfinished rhythm: the lines merge into each other and never
reach a conventionally satisfying conclusion:

> Je demeurerai vierge comme la neige
> Sereine, qui dort là-bas d'un blanc sommeil
> Qui dort pâlement, et que l'hiver protège
> Du brutal soleil.
>
> [I shall stay as virgin as the snow
> Serene snow, sleeping in white slumber
> Sleeping palely, protected by the winter
> From the brutal sun.]
> ('Je serai toujours vierge' ['I Shall Stay Forever Virgin'], p. 170)

The latter half of this study of Vivien's poetry has concentrated
on the most affirmative side of her poetry and prose – on the
more militant writing which sees the dilemma of the lesbian and
the woman writer in terms of sexual politics, and on the creation
of an imaginary, utopian female community which transcends
time, place and the normative power of established discourses on
gender. Vivien's story was not, however, a linear narrative leading
to a happy conclusion of literary transcendence, but a sad tale
illuminated by brief passages of hope. There were few Mytilène
poems in her last collections and Vivien effectively killed herself,
seeking a last desperate comfort in conversion to Catholicism.

The work itself continues to hold the two strands of Vivien's
writing in a tension that cannot be resolved. The voice of the
*femme fatale*, rarely allowed to speak for herself in men's writing,
here expresses the pain of imposed exile and exclusion, while
the collective voice of women in voluntary exile from a society
that condemns them sings of serenity and joy. The definition of
lesbianism in terms of decadence and disorder is transformed in the
Mytilène poems into lesbianism as innocence and serenity.

Although the real female community of *belle époque* Paris could
not save Vivien, it is worth reflecting briefly on the senses in which,
as a poet, she belongs within a network of women writers. Vivien
herself translated and revived the work of Psappho. As Pauline
Tarn, before the adoption of her pen name, Vivien sent her early

poems to Marcelle Tinayre, who encouraged her and followed her career, publishing an article in memory of the poet and in praise of the poetry in 1910.[17] Natalie Barney and Colette both left memorable portraits of Vivien. In 1935 Hélène de Zuylen de Nyevelt, Vivien's lover to whom several of the collections are dedicated, created a Prix Renée Vivien to be awarded annually to a woman poet. The jury included Rachilde, Marcelle Tinayre, Gérard d'Houville, Rosemonde Gérard, Myriam Harry and Hélène Vacaresco, all household names in the early part of the century and all vanished from the canon of French literature. Finally, Vivien's work looks forward across the century to feminist writers of the 'second wave' of feminism, writers such as Monique Wittig, Hélène Cixous and Luce Irigaray.

# PART II
## 1914–58

# 6
## Women in French Society 1914–58

WOMEN AND THE FIRST WORLD WAR
At the beginning of August 1914, the territorial and political rivalries dividing Europe into two hostile alliances finally exploded into war. France mobilized its armies on 2 August. Marcelle Tinayre rapidly provided her readers with a fictional reflection of their changed situation, her novel *La Veillée d'armes: le départ*[1] (*The Armed Vigil: The Departure*) appearing in 1915. Tinayre's representation of the impact of war on gender relations is characteristically idealized, but it is also prophetic.

Simone and François Davesnes begin the novel as a happy young married couple, their relationship based on intellectual and sexual compatibility. The outbreak of war not only separates them physically, as François must leave to join his regiment, but redefines and polarizes their roles as woman and man. Focalized increasingly through the eyes of admiring male characters, Simone is progressively transformed through the novel into a symbol of the nation, 'the perfect flower of the race, the rose of France' (p.115), in whose defence François realizes he is prepared to die. François – like the novel's other male characters, and despite his intense love for Simone – gradually withdraws from the company of women and seeks the virile comradeship of his fellow men. Just before his departure, François shares a meal with his wife and a male colleague: '[François] did not look at his wife; he was addressing his friend, spontaneously, because he too was a citizen and a soldier, and for the two of them words had the same meaning' (p. 182). Simone nobly accepts her own exclusion from comradeship with François, reflecting proudly that the man whom she loves and who has chosen her is 'a man!' (p. 281) whose duty is to fight, and that her own role is to love and suffer. In the description of their last night together, Tinayre implies the fulfilment of a patriotic duty to repopulate the nation: 'From these farewells a nation would be born' (p. 276), thus completing the definition of women's wartime role as icons of the nation and as mothers. 'First let them be silent!' exclaims one male character: '"No suffragette demonstrations! Women's duty in wartime consists of looking after the home, bringing up children, looking after the wounded. The rest is our business"' (p. 201).


Despite the persistence of a mythical view of the First World War as the scene of women's emancipation, the polarization of gender roles which Tinayre adeptly romanticizes in her novel predicts with some accuracy the real impact the 1914–18 war was to have on French society. In 1914 French feminists had every reason to be optimistic about their cause: although employment continued to be divided along traditional gender lines, 38 per cent of the labour force was female, and since 1907 the 20 per cent of married women in paid employment had legal control of their own wages. With improvements in women's education, pioneers were increasingly entering the male bastions of the professions. The right to vote seemed almost won, with 500,000 votes cast for women's suffrage in the referendum held in 1914 by *Le Journal*, and the Socialist Party now publicly supporting the cause.

But in many important senses the war halted this momentum. It is true that the mobilization of eight million French men, or 20.5 per cent of the population (as compared to 12.5 per cent in Britain),[2] led to women's entry into new sectors of employment such as heavy industry, munitions and transport, and that as a result female militancy increased and the gap between male and female pay narrowed in some sectors. It is true also that for the first time many women found themselves of necessity in the role of head of the family, and that there was an inevitable relaxation of the strict codes of behaviour that kept women confined to the private sphere. But, first, wartime changes in women's employment patterns and social behaviour should not be seen in isolation but read against existing prewar trends. Female employment had already begun to shift from the declining textile industry towards light engineering and the tertiary sector, and this, together with improved educational opportunities, had begun to undermine the public/private boundary. Second, in the longer term the experience of war in many ways weakened women's position on the labour market and lessened the possibility of challenging their subordination to male authority.[3]

Tinayre had read the mood of the times accurately. In 1914 the majority of French feminists suspended their campaign for the vote, confident that their cause was won and its satisfaction was merely delayed by war. They turned their energies to supporting the country in its struggle against Germany, victor of the last war in 1870 and widely perceived as – in Tinayre's words – 'iron-clad, brutal and cunning, pedantic and greedy' (p. 51).

The prewar feminist commitment to pacifism was abandoned; feminist newspapers were voluntarily closed down or, like *La Fronde* in 1914, resurrected 'not to claim the political rights of women, but to help them accomplish their social duties'.[4] An invitation to a 1915 international feminist congress for peace was rejected by the major French organizations, the Conseil National des Femmes Françaises (CNFF) and the Union Française pour le Suffrage des Femmes (UFSF), on the grounds that France was fighting a just, defensive war and it would be inappropriate for French women to meet with representatives of enemy countries. Only a handful of left-wing French feminists put the collective cause of women above that of the nation-state, and opposed the war. For most, national identity at a time of crisis took precedence over solidarity as a sex.

However, this demonstration of loyal citizenship failed to win the vote or, indeed, any significant extension of civil rights. All the other major nations involved in the 1914–18 war extended suffrage to women before 1920, but in France the bill for women's suffrage was passed in the Chamber of Deputies in May 1919 only to be first delayed, then finally, in 1922, rejected, by the Senate. The momentum built up in the years preceding the war by an active and vociferous suffrage movement[5] was stopped short by the hostilities. The war period refocused the emphasis on the collective good of the nation rather than on the rights of the individual, undermining women's arguments for their rights as citizens and repositioning them as mothers, wives and symbols of the nation, roles whose meaning depends on the centrality of a male perspective.

The war permitted a regrouping and strengthening of the

conservative male majority, and left women without even minimal citizenship on the grounds that – to take just one of
the fourteen anti-suffrage arguments advanced by the Senate
commission's report – 'Nature has given women 'a different
role than men . . . a primordial role' to attend to the incom-
parable grandeur of maternity and to the family, which is the
basis of French society'.[6] Nor did the war produce any radical improvement in women's situation in the labour market.
The sense that women had suddenly taken advantage of men's
absence to rush into paid employment was powerful at the
time, and has survived in popular images of World War I.
It was not completely without foundation: in the munitions
factories women workers numbered 15,000 by 1915 and almost
70,000 by 1917.[7] Railways and the métro, government min-
istries, banks, businesses and secondary education all replaced
absent males with female workers, thus placing women in unaccustomed and often highly visible jobs. But this redistribution
of female labour to new sectors in a sense only accelerated
a process that was already under way, and cannot be seen
simply as a great leap forward for equal opportunities. Women
in traditional sectors *lost* jobs before they, or others, gained
them – employment in textiles, for example, declined by 13
per cent for women between 1906 and 1921.[8] Working in
physically demanding jobs such as the munitions factories was
more likely to have been a brutal economic necessity in the
absence of the male breadwinner than a bid for liberation.
And as the war ended, the large-scale dismissal of women from
the workforce confirmed their status as merely a reserve army
of labour.

A contemporary commentator charted the alacrity with which
women were thrown out of work on the men's return, describing
thousands 'thrown onto the street almost immediately after the
Armistice, that is, before the end of November, some with a
few days' pay and others with nothing'.[9] Statistics of female
employment for the period encompassing the war confirm this:
39 per cent of the female population worked outside the home in
1906, 42.2 per cent in 1921, but by 1926 the figure had dropped
to 36.6 per cent.[10] Women constituted a smaller percentage of the
French workforce in 1926 than they had in 1911.[11]

THE POSTWAR BACKLASH

The postwar return to the home was accompanied by a propoganda campaign designed to put women back in their place in the broader, figurative sense of the phrase. Although the wartime changes in women's employment and rights were in reality very slight, they were sufficient to alarm conservative opinion, which exaggerated and condemned women's higher public profile, their adoption of new, less constricting styles of dress, their experience of authority and independence in the absence of fathers and husbands. Victor Margueritte's bestseller *La Garçonne* (1922, translated as *The Bachelor-Girl*) shocked and fascinated the nation with a heroine who claimed the right to sexual and economic freedom, and articulated widely shared fears when she observed: 'Since the war we have all become, more or less, *garçonnes*'.[12]

*Petit écho de la mode*, France's bestselling women's weekly, had spent the war years preaching women's ability – and, indeed, duty – to combine traditional feminine virtues with work outside the home. This encouragement ceased on the men's return:

> Many women . . . refuse to understand that, now the men are home, life will resume its normal pattern: that is, it will again be the job of the husband to provide for the family. However valuable the wife's work may seem, it will henceforth be merely an extra. (16 February 1919)

The popularity of *Petit écho de la mode*, which in 1928 was claiming sales of well over a million per week, suggests that the magazine did respond to the desires and preoccupations of many French women. The editorial team addressed their readers as wives and mothers who enjoyed an informed interest in fashion and domestic crafts, but also thought seriously about the meaning and purpose of their lives in a changing society. Impeccably conservative, but sensitive to its readers' anxieties, *Petit écho* acknowledged the difficulty of readjustment to a subordinate domestic role by redefining housewifery in heroic terms: 'The mistress of the house can set no limits to her labour. From morning till night, she is at the helm and must steer the ship that carries her happiness and fortune' (10 August 1919).

The practical problem of reconciling a female imperative to marriage and maternity with the demographic imbalance resulting from the death of 1,300,000 French men was also addressed. Young women must marry disabled ex-soldiers ('This is your duty, if you love France, then do not be a deserter!') and in the event of remaining single must devote themselves to the children of their more fortunate sisters: 'The role of girls unable to marry is clear and imperative: they must help to care for the children of others' (19 February 1919).

If women were reidentified with the home by a two-pronged campaign of compulsory dismissal and propaganda, this was partly because society's leaders recognized and sympathized with the returning soldiers' need to reassert their role as men. The media and literature of the 1920s reveal a *mal du siècle* resulting from the impossibility of reconciling prewar values with the horrific experience of the trenches. In the popular press this often took the form of inflated accounts of female emancipation, which served to express men's anxieties about their own reinsertion into the civilian world. There was a proliferation of male-authored articles on, for example, 'Modern Woman' (*L'Illustration*, 6 December 1924), 'The Place of Women in the French elite' (*L'Illustration,*, 28 November 1925), 'Controversy: does the emancipation of young women represent progress?' (*Le Progrès civique*, May–June 1925).

On the literary front, too, all the movements which have passed into literary history as significant were led by and composed of male writers, so that we are left with a much fuller literary record of men's responses to a perceived change in women than of how it felt to be a woman at a period of anti-feminist backlash. The success of female-authored novels such as Jeanne Galzy's *Les Allongés* (The Patients, 1922) and Princess Marthe Bibesco's *Catherine-Paris* (1927), is testimony to the continuing importance of the novel as a medium in which women could communicate an alternative view of gender relations, but their moment of glory was followed by long years out of print.[13]

Certain male writers such as André Gide, Jean Giraudoux, and the polemical popular novelist Victor Margueritte, implicitly or explicitly questioned male supremacy, but they were in the minority. The return to traditional values of a Barrès or a Maurras included a deeply conservative vision of gender roles; Surrealism glorified Woman and paid little attention to women. One literary current, exemplified by Montherlant and Drieu la Rochelle, represented the war as the occasion of a radical division between the masculine world of dignified, virile comradeship and the trivial, materialist 'country of women'.[14] Their protagonists play out their heroic masculinity in a degraded, peacetime world by seducing, abandoning, or raping women, particularly assertive women with pretensions to financial or intellectual independence.[15]

In Drieu's *Gilles*, published in 1939 but representing the full interwar period in terms of a crisis of masculinity, the eponymous hero's final disillusionment with the feminized peacetime world occurs when his pregnant mistress develops cancer of the womb and loses their child. Fear and dislike of the 'new woman' frequently involved accusations of sterility, of women rejecting or failing in their maternal role. Articles or letters attacking women's emancipation interpreted the fashion for slender, athletic figures as a refusal of fertility, and condemned

> this generation of bony, crop-headed, graceless women who make non-maternity their creed. They claim not to want to be mothers because they dare not admit that they are sterile – physically and emotionally. (letter to *Le Progrès civique*, 30 May 1925)

In interwar France, this cannot be read only as an expression of emotional fears of the loss of women's love and nurturing, but must also be seen to correspond to a specific social problem. Since the last quarter of the nineteenth century, the proportion of births to existing population had been lower in France than anywhere else in Europe, and the problem had been exacerbated by the war deaths of a considerable proportion of the male population. Convinced of the need to raise the birth rate, the postwar conservative government proposed and enacted legislation which outlawed not only the practice of abortion but also the dissemination of information about abortion or contraception. This repressive law had little positive effect, since the birth rate continued to decline from 219 children per 100 families in 1906, to 182 in 1926 and 180 in 1936.[16] Abortion, according to Theodore Zeldin, was reasonably estimated to have been 'as normal and frequent as childbirth' in the period between the wars in France.[17] What the law did mean was that most French women were dependent on the self-restraint and goodwill of their partners to avoid pregnancy through coitus interruptus or abstinence, and many of them underwent illegal – probably often unhygienic and painful – abortions. Despite the popular image of the skinny 'garçonne', too fond of her freedom for motherhood, sexually active women had little chance of controlling reproduction effectively.

The polemical debates around women's role in fact took place against a background of remarkably little change: at worst, women's situation regressed from the optimism of 1914; at best there was slow and limited progress. This was the case in education, where the gradual alignment of female with male education, begun in 1879, continued with the 1924 adoption of the same secondary syllabus for both sexes, resulting in the upgrading of the female *baccalauréat*. By 1929 over 50,000 French girls were continuing into state secondary education – still well under half the number of boys, but clearly a point on a steeply rising curve. In the universities female students had increased from a mere handful in 1889–90 to about 37 per cent of the student body by 1929–30, though if women had reached near-equivalence of numbers in arts subjects, they formed a tiny fraction of students in the more prestigious and career-orientated Law and Medicine faculties.[18]

Naturally, women also continued to work outside the home, despite the drop in numbers employed once the 'female demobilization' had taken place at the end of the war. Figures show a gradual decline in the numbers of women employed in the agricultural sector, both in absolute terms and as a proportion of all agricultural workers – a decline which would continue, apart from a brief reversal during the 'reconstruction' years after World War II, into the 1960s. In industry there was also a gradual decline from the high point in 1906, when women formed 34 per cent of the industrial workforce. By 1931 this had become 28.1 per cent, and by 1962 23.4 per cent. The tertiary sector, by contrast, continued to become feminized, with both absolute numbers and women as a proportion of the sector increasing gradually, though with some irregularities, towards the 45.7 per cent that would be reached in 1962. Women continued – and would continue – to be concentrated in the lowest-paid, inferior grades of clerical professions.

THE DEPRESSION

Women's participation in the labour force thus continued to be an economic necessity, acceptable provided that they received lower pay and occupied the less prestigious posts. With the Depression of the 1930s, however, the working woman became a handy scapegoat for governments embarrassed by the levels of unemployment. As the numbers of workers officially registered as unemployed rose from zero in 1929 to 260,000 in 1932 and 426,000 in 1935[19] (low in relation to Britain, Germany or the USA, and by comparison with figures in the 1980s and 1990s, but none the less experienced as catastrophic), the feminist press warned of a growing campaign against the employment of women.[20] The mainstream press ran articles which argued that to prohibit women from working would 'reduce unemployment, raise salaries, increase the birth rate, reduce infant mortality, improve family life' (Charles Richet: 'Woman's True Place', *Le Matin*, 5 November 1931), and that with women's return to the home:

> life will become what it was originally: girls will understand that they have their own mission in life which has nothing to do with gaining diplomas and becoming men's rivals. (Claude Montorge: 'Woman's True Mission', *L'Impartial*, December 1932)

The *Petit Parisien* published moral tales in which working wives lost their husbands' love by earning more than they, and *Petit écho de la mode* preached genteel resignation to hardship. All the arguments advanced for returning women to the home assumed that the vast majority of working women also had working husbands, whereas in fact half of the women employed in France in the 1930s were single, widowed or divorced – and many more were married to unemployed men.

Women's place in the labour market was further weakened by the Depression. Not only did they lose jobs and see their wages reduced, as did men – civil servants and teachers, for example, taking a 10 per cent salary cut in 1934 – but they were less likely to receive unemployment benefit on the often specious grounds that they should be supported by the male members of the family. In January 1932, for example, 89.1 per cent of unemployed French men received state benefits, but only 77.7 per cent of women.[21]

The shock of the economic crisis, together with the threat posed by small but violent fascist movements in France, encouraged the formation of an electoral alliance between the three centre–left and left parties: Radicals, Socialists and Communists. The Popular Front won the elections in 1936 and formed a government headed by the Socialist Léon Blum. Blum's government did not break the cycle whereby, throughout the interwar years, bills in favour of female suffrage were campaigned for by feminists, half-heartedly passed by the National Assembly, then thrown out by the Senate. The Popular Front did appoint the first three female members of government in France, even if they were relatively junior undersecretaries, and the social reforms introduced by Blum's government – notably workers' right to paid holidays and the forty-hour week – undoubtedly improved the quality of many women's lives. By 1937, though, the Popular Front had lost power, and only three years later the Third Republic itself was to end.

THE OCCUPATION

One of the many reasons given for refusing French women the right to vote was that women were under the influence of the Church and naturally conservative, so that they constituted a threat to the survival of the Republic. It was argued that women voters were responsible for the election of the right-wing Von Hindenburg in Germany in 1928, although the feminist newspaper *La Française* disproved this theory with statistical evidence. The rise of Nazism was also attributed to female suffrage, and used as a supplementary reason for refusing French women the vote: 'Is it wise to try feminist experiments just when the Germans are ruled by young men fervently bent on war?' (*L'Echo de Paris*, February 1935). In fact, when it came, the death of the Third Republic was an all-male affair. When the French were defeated and their country was occupied by Hitler's armies in June 1940, the National Assembly suspended the Constitution of 1875 and conferred all powers on the eighty-four-year-old hero of the 1914–18 war, Marshal Pétain. The Vichy government (based in Vichy because Paris was occupied) at first received widespread popular support, but they were to prove not only impotent to protect the French against the Nazi occupants, but also dangerously willing to collaborate with the Germans in their anti-semitic policies and their brutal repression of all opposition.

Pétain's government, composed of politicians from the conservative and extreme Right, blamed the defeat of France on the nation's decadence in the 1920s and 1930s, characterizing this period as one of excessive freedom, generalized hedonism and low moral standards, and aiming to replace a lax parliamentary regime with an authoritarian government which would oversee the return to traditional values: nationalism, obedience to authority, respect for the family. The motto of the Republic – Liberty, Equality, Fraternity – was immediately replaced by the more austere and bracing 'Work, Family, Fatherland'.

Central to Pétain's 'National Revolution' was the rebuilding of the French family on the traditional model of father as family head and wage-earner, mother at home and – since the birth rate had sunk still lower in the late 1930s – several children. Legislation in November 1940 suspended the employment of married women in the public sector and promised, within three months, the imposition of a percentage limit on the number of women employed in both public and private sectors. The wives of the huge numbers of French prisoners of war still captive in Germany (1.6 million in 1940, of whom 57 per cent were married[22]) were advised to 'act as if he were there. . . . Ask his advice, because he is still the Father and the Head'.[23]

The existing laws against abortion and contraception were tightened, a headline in the *Petit Journal* on 14 January 1942 approvingly reporting the imposition of harsher penalties for 'this crime which deprives France of many births each year'. Women found guilty of carrying out abortions could be sentenced to ten or twenty years' hard labour, or even to the guillotine, as was one poor woman convicted, in 1943, of performing twenty-six abortions. Women who conformed to the domestic and maternal ideal were rewarded: engaged girls received a state grant if they promised not to take paid employment; on the birth of her third child a mother received a 'carte de priorité' giving her priority status for rations and public services. The Vichyite press sang the praises of 'les belles familles françaises', describing the health and happiness of the twenty-one-year-old mother of seven (*Paris-Soir*, 2 February 1941) and gushing over the smallest members of families of fifteen or twenty children.

The fact of being a mother, or supporting other dependants

such as ageing parents, clearly did determine the situation of many women in a period of rationing, terrible shortages, and intensifying civil war, as the Resistance to the Nazis and to the collaborationist government developed. For the majority of women – as indeed for the majority of the population as a whole – the Occupation period was probably spent more in struggling to survive than in political activity.

Many women were, none the less, active in the Resistance, though historians' recognition of their importance has often been impeded by the emphasis on a uniquely military definition of resistance. Some women, generally those with minimal family responsibilities, did join the partisan combat troops of the Resistance, but far more used their domestic situation as a basis for Resistance activities such as hiding those on the run, supplying the guerrilla 'maquis' bases with provisions, providing communication points. Women working in administrative jobs passed on useful information or used the materials to hand to print Resistance literature. Women were often liaison agents, like Elsa Triolet and some of her fictional heroines, the traditional dissociation between femininity and political activism making them less liable to suspicion as they travelled between towns carrying vital information.

Thus women's resistance was, in a sense, often limited by domestic responsibilities, but also succeeded in exploiting or 'extend[ing] traditional feminine roles in the home and workplace'[24] in effective ways. The German and Vichy authorities certainly included the support and liaison activities outlined above in their definition of resistance, their brutal sanctions applying equally to the maquis fighters and to those who enabled, supported or concealed them.

THE LIBERATION AND THE FOURTH REPUBLIC

The liberation of France from four years of Nazi Occupation generated a euphoric will to create a just and equal society, a society that would be the antithesis of Vichy's hierarchical, authoritarian traditionalism. Although the provisional government was presided over by the autocratic Charles de Gaulle, leader of the London-based Free French throughout the war and thus in a sense the nation's saviour, the constituent assemblies were dominated by the Left and Centre – Communist and Socialist parties and the newly formed Christian Democratic Party, the Republican Popular Movement (MRP). Both the first draft Constitution (rejected by referendum in May 1946) and the Constitution endorsed by the electorate in October 1946 stressed the equality of men and, specifically, of women: 'The law guarantees to women rights equal to men's in all spheres' (Article 1).

The right to vote and to stand for office was finally, after seventy-five years of struggle, granted to women on 25 August 1944. The principle of equal pay for equal work was established by the Minister of Labour on 20 June 1946 and, in a direct reversal of Vichy policy, citizens of both sexes were ensured equal employment rights in the civil service. In the first general election at which women voted in October 1945, thirty-five women were elected out of 545 deputies, a proportion which, while small, was nevertheless to be the highest obtained in the thirteen years of the Fourth Republic.

However, although the Left's commitment to social equality extended, in principle, to women as individual citizens, neither Communist nor Socialist parties had ever demonstrated any commitment to rethinking the relations between the sexes, and in any case, political dominance rapidly passed from the Left towards the Centre and the Right, as the Cold War developed and de Gaulle rallied opposition to the new regime. From the outset there was some discrepancy between the official celebration of women's equality and the survival, within this discourse, of the same old assumptions about woman's essential identity as wife and mother whose interests could be subsumed under those of the patriarchal family. The preamble to the new Constitution guaranteed 'the conditions necessary to the development of the individual and the family' – but in the case of women there was frequently a contradiction between these two.

The new Constitution failed to alter the subordinate status of the married woman prescribed by the Napoleonic Code. A husband could still refuse his wife the right to employment or travel if he deemed these 'contrary to the interest of the family'.[25] The husband retained the title and the prerogatives of the 'chef de famille'.

The perceived need to raise the birth rate or, in de Gaulle's words, to produce 'twelve million bonny babies in twelve years' – continued to determine policies and discourses which defined women essentially as mothers. Pursuing policies begun by the Daladier government in 1939 and developed under Pétain, the government supplemented the policy of discouraging contraception (for there was no reform of the 1920 law) with that of providing incentives to reproduction. From July 1946 families with more than one child received state family allowances, tax reductions and other benefits proportionate to the number of children, grants to help with school expenses and a special allowance in the case of a non-working mother.

This policy of encouragement, in conjunction with the return of the prisoners of war and, perhaps, a national mood of optimism fuelled by economic expansion, did produce an increase in the birth rate, which rose by 20.6 per cent in 1946 and 21.3 per cent in 1947, and continued to rise throughout the 1950s. However, since allowances were paid to the head of the family, this system promoted and rewarded the dependence of the woman within the family. To refuse motherhood was both practically and emotionally difficult in a social climate which still depreciated single and childless women, but to combine independence and a real sense of equality with having children was virtually impossible.

The glorification of woman as mother and as the object of man's desire had long been a particularly marked feature of French culture. In the postwar period and the 1950s, the renewed emphasis on the birth rate harmonized nicely with advertising campaigns for the swarm of new domestic products appearing on the market, to produce a ubiquitous image of woman as happy modern housewife rearing her children with the aid of a benevolent technology. Since a study carried out in 1947 demonstrated that housework accounted for 45 billion hours' work per year, out of a total of 105 billion worked by the total population,[26] it is not surprising that machines and products which promised to make housework easier were eagerly welcomed – even if for many working-class women the new washing machines, for example, were of little use until the housing construction programmes of the 1950s and 1960s provided them with running water and electricity for the first time.

The housewife seen on the advertising posters was young, slim and elegant. Dior's New Look (1947) celebrated the end of wartime austerity by dressing women in long, full skirts; fashions emphasized an exaggeratedly feminine appearance rather than comfort or mobility, as tiny waists, jutting bosoms and high-heeled shoes came to create the ideal 1950s silhouette. France was engaged in reconstruction and modernization, and a major element in this process was the development of a consumer society on the American model. Advertising posters, the cinema, the appearance of new glossy women's magazines such as *Elle* (1945), all contributed to the pressure on women to be not just housewives and mothers but also beautiful and well-groomed, like the stars glimpsed 'at home' in the gossip press (such as *Jours de France*, founded in 1954), or the models in the advertisements for a growing range of beauty products.

Rapid economic expansion – industrial production increased by 85 per cent between 1950 and 1958[27] – changed French society profoundly. For women the impact of accelerated urbanization, technological development and consumerism was complex and contradictory. While manufacturers' need to target women as consumers further encouraged the representation of them as essentially mothers, housewives, and objects of desire, the return to full employment meant that women's position on the job market was strengthened and the growing tertiary sector continued to become feminized, at least in its more junior ranks. This in turn confirmed the need for a highly educated female workforce, and the percentage of female university students in France rose steadily from 32.7 per cent in 1945–46, to 34 per cent in 1950/51, 36.4 per cent in 1955–56 and 41.1 per cent by 1960–61.[28] Although an analysis of the figures by faculty reveals a fairly stable concentration of young women in the less prestigious Arts subjects, and a corresponding dominance of men in the faculties such as Law and Medicine which led to highly paid, high-status professions, the opportunity for more and more young women to enjoy the relative freedom and the intellectual challenge of university education was significant.

While the celebrated literary figures of postwar France were almost all male, and the theatre in particular continued to be dominated by male playwrights and directors, there were important exceptions to the rule. In the post-Liberation enthusiasm for the democratization of culture, the French theatre enjoyed a lively renewal in the 1940s and 1950s. New regional theatres were created with public funding, and young directors like Jean Vilar at the new Théâtre National Populaire (TNP) in Paris tried to put into practice the belief that theatre should be 'a public service in exactly the same way as gas, water and electricity'.[29] Central to these initiatives was a woman, Jeanne Laurent, who ran the Spectacles et musique department of the Ministry of Arts. It was Laurent who spearheaded the establishment of Centres Dramatiques Nationaux in the provinces, and who appointed Vilar to direct the TNP. Although she was removed from her post in the early 1950s, when opposition from privately funded theatres intensified, Laurent's work none the less helped to create the more experimental climate in which, two decades later, women would begin to find their voices on the French stage.

CONFLICTS OF IDENTITY

The postwar boom, with its emphasis on mass consumption, also in a sense created the teenager. The targeting of an audience of young consumers by the fashion, cosmetic and music industries no doubt increased the pressure on adolescent girls to conform to shifting norms of style and beauty, thus reinforcing that sense of being the object of the male gaze which Simone de Beauvoir analysed with prescient clarity in 1949 in *The Second Sex*.[30] But the existence of a culture which belonged specifically to their generation, and often shocked and repelled parents and elders, also opened up a margin of freedom to redefine feminine identity in opposition to traditional patterns. Brigitte Bardot – whose star status began with the 1957 film *And God Created Woman*, but whose sensual, sulky face had first been captured on the cover of *Elle* in 1948 – represented an ambivalent role model, half docile sex kitten, half assertive rebel claiming the right to take the sexual initiative. With Bardot the *jeune fille*, or unmarried girl, became sexualized not just as forbidden object of male lust, but as the subject of desire. As one teenage fan of Bardot, interviewed later in life, expressed it: 'sexuality was taboo, you just didn't talk about it – and B.B. was the explosion of all that was forbidden'.[31]

Two bestselling, female-authored books bear witness to the presence of conflicting models of female identity in France of the Fourth Republic.[32] Beauvoir's *The Second Sex* scandalized not only conservatives but also the male Left with her thorough and radical critique of male appropriation of subjecthood and consignment of women to the role of 'Other'. Critically reviewing representations of feminine identity in a wide range of fields, from the interpretation of biology to the works of renowned authors, Beauvoir's central thesis is that feminine identity is not a natural given but a human construction – constructed, moreover, against women's own interests. The book rejected marriage as an inherently flawed and unequal institution, and refuted the notion that maternity was women's natural goal. Beauvoir received a large number of letters from women who identified wholeheartedly with her arguments. She also found herself the object of bitter and widespread criticism which ranged from the Left's dismissive 'the problem of woman is a false problem' to François Mauriac's charge of pornography. The conditions for a radical feminist analysis of relations between the sexes were thus present, but there was also a powerful and broad-based opposition to such arguments which reacted – not with reasoned argument, but with outrage – to the articulation of what was still considered unthinkable.

Beauvoir's book is long, closely argued and full of learned references. Its audience was large, but almost certainly limited to the highly educated. In 1954 a much less demanding book hit the bestseller lists and remained there for the rest of the decade, selling four million copies by 1959. *Bonjour tristesse* was the début novel of the nineteen-year-old Françoise Sagan, and the author's youth certainly contributed to the publicity which greeted the novel and to the aura of scandal that surrounded it. *Bonjour tristesse* is the story of a still younger heroine, Cécile, who, at seventeen, lives with her widowed, playboy father and shares his hedonistic lifestyle. When this is threatened by the arrival of a potential mother figure for Cécile, as her father falls in love with Anne, a cultured, strong-minded woman of his own age, Cécile is torn between the attraction of being loved and cared for and fear for the loss of her freedom. She engineers the couple's break-up and, indirectly, the death of Anne.

The extreme popularity of this slight story can be attributed, at least in part, to its articulation of a conflict between two models of femininity: the one ordered, centred on the family, and channelling sexuality into the monogamous couple; the other still tentative and unclear but representing women without reference to family, and separating female sexuality from reproduction. Although Cécile ends the book unhappy and uncertain, the solution of the monogamous couple and that of the patriarchal family are implicitly rejected within the narrative. The young narrator's nice mixture of cynicism and intensity, and the novel's glamorous milieu and setting, were the immediate causes of its success, but *Bonjour tristesse* also owed its popularity to its accessible representation of a real and complex issue which was to be much more openly recognized and explored in the period after May 1968.

# 7
## Everyday Adventures, or What Makes Colette (1873–1954) a Feminine Writer

If we were to depend only on the available histories of French literature, we would believe that women wrote very little – or very little of any value – for the first sixty years of this century. To take just two examples, Jean Thoraval's *Les Grandes Étapes de la civilisation française* discusses forty-eight male writers for the period 1914 to 1960, but only two women (Colette and Beauvoir); and *Du surréalisme à l'empire de la critique*,[1] the post-1920 volume of a much more recent and on the whole admirably thorough history, devotes space to just sixteen women authors for 166 men.

This widely accepted view conflicts with the real numbers of women published and critically acclaimed at the time: in 1928 Jean Larnac recorded that between a quarter and a fifth of the membership of the Société des gens de lettres, or writers' professional association, was female (671 women out of a total membership of 3,077).[2] Colette's name was linked throughout her career to those of other women writers, generally in terms which suggested that they were her literary equals. Marcelle Tinayre, Anna de Noailles, Gérard d'Houville, Lucie Delarue-Mardrus, Colette Yver, Rachilde, Gyp, Gabrielle Reval – the 'glittering team' identified in Reval's 1938 obituary continued to publish in the interwar years, and they were joined by many younger women, of whom Elsa Triolet was one. Yet only two women writers have fully survived the selective and tendentious process of canon formation: Colette and Simone de Beauvoir. Although a study of French women's writing would be seriously incomplete without discussion of these two, it is important to read them in the knowledge that the majority of their contemporaries have disappeared from history.

As writers Colette and Beauvoir could scarcely be more different, but their survival both as literary 'stars' and as key figures for feminists may also be determined by what they have in common. Because each of their very considerable *œuvres* contained a significant element of autobiography, and because each led an unconventional life for a woman of her time, perception of them as authors became fused with an evaluation of them as women. Whether admired or condemned, they became important reference points in the ongoing struggle over the meaning and implications of gender difference.

But though each may appropriately be described as a feminist writer, they diverge in all manner of ways. Beauvoir was an intellectual in the French sense of the word – a Parisian, winner of the most prestigious academic prizes, politically committed and articulate in the defence of her beliefs. Colette, born thirty-five years earlier (in 1873), came from a rural, lower-middle-class background, and in terms of schooling went no further than the certificate awarded for an extended primary education. She became a professional writer by – as it were – marrying into the trade, for her first husband, Willy, made a living by subcontracting impoverished authors to write novels he published under his own name. Given the legal situation of married women at the turn of the century, his wife's labour came free. Separated from Willy, Colette wrote less out of the conviction that she had something to tell the world than out of the need to survive financially:

> The day when necessity put a pen in my hand and I was given a little money in return for the pages I had written, I understood that I should have to write slowly, submissively, each day . . . [3]

Colette's writing appeared as frequently in the popular press as between hard covers, most of her work having its first publication in article or serial form before becoming a book. She was read by schoolgirls for her sexual frankness, by older women for her practical wisdom, as much as by literary critics for her style. Although in *The Second Sex* Beauvoir cites Colette to exemplify positive representations of female adolescence, sexuality, and motherhood, she also distances herself from that lowbrow, cheerfully prosaic side of Colette that led her to combine a literary career with those of a music-hall dancer and a beautician, and to write as elegantly about food and fashion as about nature and the meaning of life. 'Colette', Beauvoir commented, 'is really very taken up with her little stories about love, housework, the washing and animals'.[4]

In some senses the parallels are closer between Colette and George Sand. Towards the end of her career, in *The Evening Star* (1946), Colette paid half-humorous tribute to her predecessor by bemoaning the speed and apparent ease with which Sand produced her enormous literary output, as compared to the time it had taken Colette herself to 'scribble some forty volumes of literature'. 'How the devil did George Sand manage!' she exclaims. 'That sturdy woman of letters found it possible to finish one novel and start another in the same hour. And she did not thereby lose either a lover or a puff of the narghile . . . '.[5] But this rueful praise of Sand in fact draws our attention to the similarities between two 'sturdy women of letters', for both Sand and Colette had prolific careers extending over half a century; both enjoyed passionate personal lives which scandalized their contemporaries and encouraged biographical readings of even the least subjective of their works; both became celebrities whose mythologized public selves retained elements of earlier scandals but incorporated these into more orthodox models of feminine identity – Sand as 'la bonne dame de Nohant' and Colette as 'notre grande Colette'.

In the context of this book, Colette's work forms an important meeting point for many of the women writers studied. Not only Sand but also Rachilde and Renée Vivien appear in her essays and memoirs, and she knew, read and was in turn read by Marcelle Tinayre, Gabrielle Réval and Colette Yver – apparently even being confused with the latter in the minds of some (surely none too attentive) readers.[6] As we have seen, Colette is an important reference point for Beauvoir in *The Second Sex*, and a quarter of a century later she is one of only two French women writers whom Hélène Cixous, on the whole dismissive of her French foremothers, acknowledges as a truly 'feminine' writer.[7]

Cixous does not explain this positive evaluation of Colette's writing, but the article in which it appears (in a footnote) does propose definitions of the feminine which can be seen to correspond to Colette's work. For Cixous, the radically *feminine* writer 'returns to the body', or writes of female bodily experience in ways which patriarchal culture has silenced and censored. One important aspect of Colette's originality lies precisely there.[8] Cixous also proposes as typical of the *feminine* text the determining presence of the mother–daughter bond, of that 'first music from the first voice of love which is alive in every woman'.[9] Here again, as I shall try to show, Colette's writing corresponds to Cixous's model. But before exploring the relationship between Colette's texts and theories of *écriture féminine*, I want to suggest another sense in which her writing is specifically and positively feminine.

From before the 1914–18 war, up to and beyond World War II, Colette was a widely read journalist and columnist, publishing across a range of newspapers and magazines. Her style was unusual, and involved the projection on to the public stage of a constructed version of her own life and personality. In Colette's journalism there is no attempt to conceal the mediation of an observing reporter, nor to produce the illusion of pure objectivity. The 'I' who addresses the reader is an important part of the scenario offered for her/his instruction and entertainment. Since it is a distinctly female 'I', Colette in effect ensured the regular presence of at least one, frequently irreverent feminine voice in a predominantly masculine medium.

Colette's journalism probably began well before the signature 'Colette Willy' ever appeared, for she collaborated, silently, in much of Willy's varied output, which included reviews and articles. After she left him, in 1906, writing became her major source of income, and a regular outlet for her pieces clearly offered the advantage of security. In between periods of freelancing, during which articles, essays and reviews appeared in several different publications, Colette had spells as a newspaper's regular columnist. Most of her fiction was serialized in the press before being published in book form, and much of the journalism was subsequently collected, edited and reappeared in volumes. In other words, the dividing line between Colette's 'literature' and her apparently more ephemeral writing is a fine one.

Between 1906 and 1912 Colette had published a series of articles about life in the music hall, written during her tours as a mime and dancer and narrated by an 'I' who shared the canny stoicism of her fellow performers, but also brought to bear on their situation the curious, lucid focus of the outsider.[10] Most of these articles were published in the daily *Le Matin*, whose chief editor, Henry de Jouvenel, became Colette's lover, and later her husband. The war journalism was also mostly published in *Le Matin*, then collected in the volume *Les Heures longues* (The Long Hours). The volume opens with Colette's account of the day war was declared, and the effect of the news on herself and her fellow civilians in Saint-Malo, where she had been holidaying. The meadows and coastline of Brittany become 'no more than scenery interposed between myself and reality: reality is Paris, Paris where lives the other half of myself' (II, 478[11]). Back in Paris, the articles continue to stage Colette's own experience with its combination of the typical – she worries about her husband at the Front, chronicles the effect of wartime conditions on her small daughter, nurses wounded soldiers in a military hospital – and the exceptional, for as a journalist Colette travels to the Front at Verdun, where Henry de Jouvenel was stationed, and is sent to report on wartime life in Allied Italy.

The theme which links the varied articles is that of human adaptability in the face of change and loss. Although she shows little concern with the causes of the war, or with apportioning blame for the suffering it causes, the writing does suggest that Colette sees her role as one of raising or maintaining morale. She does this not through rhetorical exhortation or glorification of the nation, but through an often humorous emphasis on the unpredictable versatility and will to survive and grow of human beings.

An elderly man left in Paris with the women and children, instead of deploring the loss of a virile role through age, discovers the pleasures of crocheting and female conversation, and makes his new craft an excuse for getting away from 'all those other tedious old duffers' (II, 486) at his club. This article also exemplifies that crossing of gender boundaries which is a persistent theme in Colette's work, and which reappears in the reports from Italy where a handsome young soldier makes an excellent job of modelling the new season's female fashions, his 'grey uniform disappearing beneath furs, flounced dresses, and even for a moment a gauzy pink petticoat' (II, 556).

Behind the lines at Verdun, civilians living under constant bombardment concentrate their energies on the issues over which they do have a degree of control, notably where the next meal is coming from, so that when the newly arrived Colette asks 'So what's new?' they tell her all about the state of rationing and the black market before finally realizing that she means the war: '"Oh! yes of course, the war. . . . Well, it's going . . . pretty well. Don't worry about it . . . "'(II, 491). In her descriptions of life in Verdun Colette herself emphasizes the visual beauty of the explosions, 'the shooting flowers of the rocket flares, bursting into the night' (II, 490), and the excitement of watching an aerial chase, so that the immediate sensory pleasure of perception takes precedence over the anxiety of danger.

Colette's first-person narrator, and the majority of her characters, share an instinctive strategy for survival: they shift attention from the life-threatening horror of war to those aspects of the situation still within their control, and to war's conceivably pleasurable side-effects. Colette's fictional friend Valentine, used in many a prewar article to represent an amiable but blinkered conventionality, is employed here as the foil for this strategy of displacement. Loving and dutiful, she writes every day to her husband in the trenches, trying hard to adopt an appropriately patriotic and serious tone. He objects that her letters full of the war 'make him feel as if he's married to Maréchal Joffre', and begs her to send him samples for the new bedroom carpet instead: 'That great stain between the cupboard and the window keeps me awake at night and I need to have my mind free for the battle' (II, 487).

Valentine's solemn adaptation to war conditions is echoed humorously in the articles devoted to Bel-Gazou, Colette's daughter, born in July 1913. Bel-Gazou has known only a world at war, and among her first words are 'Boom', 'gun' and 'soldier', the latter used imperiously to summon any passing man in uniform to her pram. By the age of three, the story of Little Red Riding Hood shocks her sense of the justice of rationing: 'She was taking a *galette* [cake] to her grandmother and she hadn't told the mayor? . . . The mayor would have said "Monsieur, I am requi . . . requi . . . requiquitioning that *galette* . . . "' (II, 572). The enthusiasm with which Bel-Gazou integrates rationing, instruments of war, and the disappearance of male relatives to the Front into her games and stories is touching but never sentimental, for her assimilation of whatever life brings contributes to a central theme of Colette's war articles: the human capacity to thrive on adversity through humour and invention.

A fellow writer, André Billy, described the articles collected in *The Long Hours* as 'a completely new form of journalism, a lyrical journalism . . . based on everyday encounters between the life of a woman, a mother, a female traveller, an artist, and the events of history'.[12] The specific femininity of Colette's perspective was foregrounded by *Le Figaro* in 1924, when they ran her articles weekly from April to October under the heading 'A Woman's Opinion'. Since Colette consistently refused, in articles or interviews, to express what are normally viewed as 'opinions',[13] this initiative presumably came from the paper's editors, but the column's point of view remained very much that outlined by Billy. Indeed, the volume in which the articles were republished was entitled 'Everyday Adventures' (*Aventures quotidiennes*, 1924).

The range of 'everyday adventures' is wide: *faits divers*, parliamentary elections, murder trials, cruelty to animals, the education of children, cinema, holidays in Brittany, the heat in Paris. The introduction of a state driving test in May 1924 is the occasion for Colette to present herself as a struggling but determined learner-driver, and to reflect on men's discomfiture faced with women drivers to whom they have not, as yet, formulated any standard response. A condescending 'You child! You poor child!' has been tacitly agreed upon as the right response to women's demand for the vote, but a woman behind the steering wheel 'still surprises man and leaves him uncertain. He hasn't had time to instigate a code of relations with this most recent female conqueror, nor to characterize her except in terms which mask lack of invention with invective' (III, 82).

The victory of the Left in the May 1924 elections produces a description of the crowd, gathered to hear the results, and this triggers memories of other crowds, notably in London in 1900 when the victory of Mafeking was announced. By situating herself, in memory, at some distance from her hotel, forced to make her way through an excited and aggressive male crowd, Colette views the scene from the perspective of a small, determined but vulnerable woman, a perspective reinforced by the glimpse of 'the tragic struggle, taking place in an archway, between a young girl and two or three men. Bruised, and sure that she would be more so, she did not cry out but fought as best she could with her fragile arms and her silent courage' (III, 90). Thus, despite

Colette's complete lack of interest in the suffragist movement, a report on an election which totally excludes women shifts to the themes of sexual aggression and female resistance.

Articles on education – for example, on the advantages and disadvantages of weekly boarding – stage Colette's own relationship with her daughter as a point of departure and as exemplification. Colette's attitude to children is unusual in its emphasis on discretion and respect for the child's autonomy. In 'Combats', she narrates a conversation with her daughter in the presence of a female visitor, acknowledging her own unspoken maternal request to perform for the audience and her daughter's generous acquiescence: 'I think my daughter very kind to have given the appropriate answers, out of respect or politeness' (III, 121). The incident leads on to a meditation on relationships between mothers and growing daughters, on the painful need for the mother to accept that her emotion will not always be reciprocated, and to respect 'the mystery of the loved one' (III, 123) despite her own 'inalienable pride as the giver of life' (III, 123).

Both in *Everyday Adventures* and elsewhere, Colette reported on murder trials, notably those of the mass murderers Landru (in 1921) and Weidmann (1939). A retrospective article on Landru, published in 1924, also includes reflections on the English murderer Patrick Mahon. Colette's representation of these men is neither sensational nor condemnatory, but concerned above all to go beyond their facile relegation to the category of 'monsters'. In each case she stresses their apparent normality in court, which in Landru's case gives him a certain superiority over the crowd of onlookers and the lawyers. Colette as observer finds herself with 'the scandalous impression that only one person in this court cares about propriety and knows how to behave: the man seated in the dock' (III, 746). Similarly Weidmann's 'physical dignity', 'measured words' and 'refusal of self-pity'[14] in court are such that Colette presents herself struggling against an inclination to sympathize for him.

Since all three men were murderers of women, it is hard at first to see in what sense Colette's perspective might be a feminine one. Her position as a woman seems to result, here as elsewhere, in a failure fully to identify with the moral and social laws which govern society, producing a marginalized and thus unconventional point of view. Whereas the more common angle on mass murderers emphasizes their sinister strangeness, what interests Colette is what connects the monstrous killer to the ordinary human being. The truly horrible criminal, she reflects, is the one who 'fills us with fear' not because he is bestial and strange, but because 'he is like us, he makes us aware of his resemblance to us'.[15] Beneath the social and moral laws by which we must live, Colette implies, lies another order in which the desire to 'deliver blood from its prison of flesh' (III, 85), 'the pleasure of killing, the charity of bestowing death like a caress' (III, 86) are as natural and as celebrated as other human desires.

The dignity she attributes to these multiple murderers resides in the fact that they are not just 'bestial or furious men who let themselves go under the influence of wine or temper', but the possessors of a 'terrible innocence' (III, 86), in whom persists an 'animality abolished elsewhere', visible in Landru's dark eye 'like the eye of a bird, bereft of language, tenderness or melancholy' (III, 85). The temptation to identify with their crimes to the point of condoning them must be resisted – 'From a human point of view, it is at the point of complicity with the beast that monstrosity begins, and the human point of view is right' (III, 86) – but though we must protect humanity from their violence, Colette implies, we do well to recognize in these criminals instinctive desires repressed, but not erased, by the social order. The dignified, amoral innocence of Colette's murderers links them to certain fictional characters, notably Chéri and Alain (in *The Cat*), for whom the process of socialization fails, and who remain locked in regressive desire to escape separation, individual consciousness and the social law.

By the time of the French defeat in 1940, Colette was sixty-seven years old and a celebrated personality in France. Her literary persona was woven from elements of her own biography, partially fictionalized constructions of that biography presented to the public both in her writing and in interviews, and the needs and desires of her readers. Colette played to the tension in French culture between the nostalgic idealization of a rural past, and the sense of national identity as sophisticated, urban, and intellectual. As Margaret Callender puts it, she:

seemed to have transcended some deep-rooted dialectic of the urban and the pastoral in the French consciousness by linking the energy and adaptability of the one to the conservatism and physicality of the other.[16]

In the articles published during the war years and collected in the volume *De ma fenêtre* (*From My Window*),[17] Colette draws on the folk wisdom she can claim to owe to her celebrated rural childhood, and on her city-dweller's self-possession gained through half a century of life in Paris, to produce a series of practical, humorous but also deeply serious exhortations to survive the material and emotional hardship of the Occupation.

Colette's evocation of a peasant sapience, grounded in a harmonious relationship with the natural world, had an immediate appeal in that it emphasized the continuity of national identity at a time when France was fragile and divided. To that extent it drew on the same sources as Pétain's deeply reactionary National Revolution, but Colette's use of folklore and memory does not idealize the past for conservative ends. The past is enlisted in the service of that ethic of adaptability, inventiveness, and resilience which is present throughout her work, and is – given women's domestic and maternal roles, which have to continue in times of crisis – a particularly feminine ethic. Colette herself assumes a largely female readership: "'Speak to us", they write to me – they are the women – "speak to us of pleasant things"' (LB, 165). And she does, while at the same time offering genuinely practical hints and remedies and a humour which refuses the conventional solemnity of patriotism.

The cold winter of 1941–42 and the shortages of fuel, food and clothing meant that Parisians suffered from chilblains: Colette recalls her mother's remedy of red rose petals infused in strong vinegar, but undercuts the romanticization of the peasant mother by also recommending the solution adopted by an 'elderly street-walker' of 'newspapers fixed round the legs by string gartering' (LB, 128–9). Austerity recipes abound – for boiled chestnuts, for 'a quickly made and substantial dessert' called *flognarde*, requiring minimal ingredients; and one reader, she tells us, has threatened to tax her five francs for every time she mentions swedes. The anecdote of the young girl incredulously reading a prewar recipe provides a comic illustration of the gap between present shortages and remembered abundance: "'Take eight or ten eggs . . . '" "From whom?" asks a young girl who does not laugh' (LB, 115). Courage, in Colette's writing, is not a grandly heroic virtue but a refusal to be cowed by adversity into relinquishing life's pleasures or abdicating personal dignity.[18] Even as she castigates her younger contemporaries for braving the cold with their 'uncovered ears and short gathered skirts' (LB, 187), she is clearly also paying tribute to their 'terrible rage to live' (LB, 202), and the articles are full of examples of this same affirmative spirit. Colette's fellow Parisians soon cease to respond to the sirens calling them to air-raid shelters, preferring to spend the curfewed nights together in a revival of the old village gatherings or *veillées*, during which, in conversation 'All the fine, imaginary, small coin of human life dances, changes, gleams, chinks . . .' (LB, 122). Parisians make do and mend, combing the flea markets for unlikely objects to replace the unobtainable, feeding the birds in the park despite their own shortages, demonstrating:

A clenched-teeth courage guid[ing] [the city's] population towards goals it will not and cannot abandon: to acquire the means of subsistence and to give each the share that will prevent him from dying. (LB, 135)

Throughout more than four decades of journalism, then, Colette maintained in the public medium of the mainstream press a voice that emphasized a woman's perspective, both in the sense that contemporary events and ideas were viewed in relation to women's lives, and in the sense that she wrote from a position outside normative masculine values and assumptions. It is hard to imagine Colette's male contemporaries dealing with problems of childcare, fashion, the difficulty of finding food and suitable underwear at times of shortage, alongside questions of patriotism and ethics. Colette also consistently questioned the nature of gender difference and rigid notions of what constituted feminine virtue, introducing, for example, into her portrayal of everyday Parisian courage the unlikely heroine of a Palais Royal streetwalker, whose dignity and diligence bear comparison with those of her more respectably employed compatriots, for she embroiders beautifully as she waits for clients, and refuses to be cowed by the unexplained aggression of her fellow prostitutes, attributing this, with a nice reversal of the convention of female dependence, to the fact that "'they're jealous. And with reason. Just think, I've no man in my life'" (LB, 203).

The unorthodox perspective and the recurring themes of the journalism are equally present in Colette's narrative fiction, including those stories and novels narrated in the third person and thus excluding the autobiographical voice. There, too, the world is consistently focalized through female eyes – or, notably in the case of the *Chéri* novels, through the eyes of a man who fails to assume his place in the masculine realm. There, too, normative assumptions about gendered identity and what constitutes human fulfilment are disturbed. *The Last of Cheri* (1926), for example, depicts the return of the soldiers from World War I and the industrious escapism of the early 1920s in terms of the drama of masculine subject formation. Chéri, already established, in the 1920 novel that bears his name, as Léa's physically beautiful but emotionally inarticulate young lover, has distinguished himself on the battlefield and is described by several characters as a 'warrior' (LC, 156–7[19]). He returns to a world of commercial opportunity and frenetic activity, personified by his friend Desmond, 'the tango merchant' who runs a successful nightclub, and by Chéri's wife and mother, now self-importantly active in hospital management and speculation in commodities.

Chéri, though, with whom the novel's sympathies firmly lie, lacks any will to 'manage people and things' (LC, 155), as Desmond puts it. The masculine eminence conferred by his wartime heroism contrasts sharply with his complete disinclination to reassume the role of head of the household, with his loss of all sexual desire, with his textual representation in terms of extreme and desirable physical beauty (despite his signs of weariness, the narrator observes 'youth perfectly preserved in the ravishing curve and full ripeness of his lips, the downiness of his nostrils, and the raven–black abundance of his hair' [LC, 176]). Chéri, who at the end of the first novel seemed to have made the difficult separation from the loving, maternal body of Léa, now discovers that he desires nothing other than the state of blissful dependence he enjoyed in her arms.

Chéri cannot live outside her embrace, but Léa has 'found her consolation – and what a disgrace that is!' (LC, 246) in the stoical acceptance of old age. In the earlier novel, *Chéri*, Léa's warm, capacious body, domestic skills and authoritative management of her lover's life had made her a maternal figure - though one in whom the maternal was so mingled with the erotic as to challenge the more usual separation of these female roles. Thus what Chéri wants is, in a sense, a return to infantile symbiosis with the mother, a return to the time before the harsh demands of severance and individualization. This desire is persuasively presented through Chéri's longing for the muted blue light of a shuttered bedroom, his repulsion for the stark, blinding whiteness of his wife Edmée's adult world, where the will to power masquerades as charity. Chéri finally retreats to what he fantasizes as a 'refuge, existing at some unknown point in space, but secret, small, warm' (LC, 226), and in this womblike space, surrounded by pictures of Léa as he loved her, he kills himself.

What distinguishes Chéri from most of his contemporaries is, in part, his relationship to time. While many of his fellow soldiers 'pine away in silence, solitude and frustration' (LC, 163) during the long periods of inactivity between the battles, Chéri is content with 'contemplative silence' and to brood over 'two or three ideas, over two or three persistent memories, as highly coloured as a child's' (LC, 163). Because he has not succeeded in separating, emotionally, from Léa, Chéri has no sense of possible progress in life, but remains content in a present enriched by the past . His sense of time runs less on a horizontal axis, directed towards the future, than on a vertical axis that runs from present to past.

The sympathy with which Chéri's plight is depicted does not mean that his failure to develop a viable life beyond Léa is endorsed. Chéri's immobilism is incompatible with living, and though Léa's graceless old age is painful to observe, the novel also implies admiration for her powers of adaptation. In the many texts which, like the journalism, stage a first-person 'Colette' narrator, a sense of time which is 'vertical' rather than 'horizontal' recurs, but here the relationship between past and present is reciprocal and creative rather than destructive. This model is present in the articles written under the Occupation, where the possibility of exploring the past in order to enrich a depleted present is founded on a model of time past as still fully existing and available to endless rediscovery. In *From My Window*, writing in a France growing thin on austerity, Colette evokes 'scenes of abundance' full of wine, cherries and peaches. Although this might be considered 'a rather mortifying exercise', she justifies it by the richness of pleasure to be found in memory itself: 'We are, most of us, too heedless of those insubstantial benefits with which our memory is overflowing' (LB, 177). Rediscovering among her recollections 'an escaped lizard under a pleasant disorder of meridional titbits, cicadas and sticky wasps' (LB, 177), Colette sets off on her 'magic carpet' to refind forgotten memories for her own pleasure and that of her readers.

AUTOBIOGRAPHICAL FICTIONS: *THE RAINY MOON*
Most of Colette's texts that can loosely be termed 'autobiographical' are founded on this model, in which the narrator's development of a viable subjectivity, and her establishment of an ethic of generous attentiveness to experience and to others, depend on the continuing presence of the past and its availability for further exploration, re-reading, rediscovery. The 'Colette' narrator appears, for example, in the novella *La Lune de pluie* (*The Rainy Moon*, 1940). Although she is unnamed throughout, the narrator shares with the author her profession as a writer working regularly for newspapers, and the presence in her past of a painfully broken marriage. The presence of two non-fictional characters, Colette's mother, Sido, and her close friend, Annie de Pène, confirm the element of autobiography.

The story begins as the narrator takes some handwritten pages of her work to a professional typist, Rosita Barberet, and realizes suddenly that Rosita's appartment is the very one she herself inhabited some years previously, at a very unhappy period of her life, during her gradual separation from a man she loved. Rosita has a younger sister, Délia, who at first appears only 'off-stage' but who, according to her sister, is 'in a sense, ill'. "'She has no disease," she said emphatically. "It's since she got married. It's changed her character"'(CSC, 356[20]). It is gradually revealed that Délia is separated from her husband, and suffering from his absence just as the narrator herself suffered, in the same rooms, some years before. The narrator's pain returns to her acutely through the agency of sense impressions: the feel in her hand of

the window-catch, which is shaped as a mermaid; the sight of
the little 'rainy moon', a reflection cast on the wall by light
refracted through the coarse glass of a windowpane. Although
a visit from Sido, and outings with her friend Annie de Pène,
distract her temporarily, she continues to visit the appartment and
Délia herself, both drawn to and irritated by the latter's apparently
passive, but intense, preoccupation with her own unhappiness.
Finally, 'Colette' learns that Délia is employing witchcraft to
bring about the death of the man she has lost, and the last
time the narrator sees her, after she has broken all connection
with the two women, Délia is dressed, significantly, as a widow.

*The Rainy Moon* observes the conventions of narrative fiction
to the extent that it introduces a central, fictional character,
poses the problem of her unrequited love, and leads the reader
to a dramatic dénouement in the glimpse of a Délia who has
apparently committed murder by witchcraft. But Délia's story is
refracted through, and ultimately secondary to that of the narrator
herself, a story which has no clear beginning or end, but represents
a period of intense reflection about emotional priorities and what
constitutes female integrity. The meditative aspect of the text and
the story proper are structurally linked by the multiple analogies
between the narrator and Delia, for memories triggered by the
scene of her forgotten pain are made more vibrant by the echoing
of her situation in that of the younger woman.

As in *From My Window*, the past recaptured through memory
has all the sensual texture and specificity of lived experience, and
carries a charge of joy even when the recollection is one of pain.

> Breaking with the present, retracing my steps, the sudden appa-
> rition of a new unpublished slice of the past is accompanied by
> a shock utterly unlike anything else and which I cannot lucidly
> describe. (CSC, 351)

As Colette explicitly acknowledges, this image of memory sur-
mounting the contingency of linear time is close to that of
Proust.[21] In Colette's model of the past, though, it is not only
what has been which is recaptured, but also what might have
been. The significance of Délia lies not just in her resemblance
to the narrator, but also in the fact that this obsessive, embittered
woman, whose energies are focused solely on a single, failed

relationship, is a threatening image of a self 'Colette' might have become.

The connection between the narrator and Délia is accentuated throughout the story. Not only do they share a situation and the place in which it is lived out, but the narrator has dreams in which 'I was now my real self, now identified with Délia' (CSC, 385), and in which it is she who murmurs sinister incantations to will the death of an absent lover. Although the recognition that the past is still alive produces a shock of pleasure, Délia herself represents the menace of a danger so narrowly avoided as still to have a certain potency. The narrator's fascination with that 'former self, that sad form stuck, like a petal between two pages, to the walls of an ill-starred refuge' (CSC, 367) is presented as an unhealthy temptation, an episode which is somehow sordid and frequently leaves the narrator exhausted and without energy for other activities.

The fact that Délia represents a negative version of the narrator's self is confirmed by the latter's disinclination to mention the episode to Sido, whose visit to her daughter occurs in the middle of the story. Sido belongs with the positive evocation of the past, with the continuing presence within the self of a rich fabric of accumulated perception and experience. When Sido is present she 'recall[s] [her daughter's] life to dignity and solicitude' (CSC, 372), both reminding her of the importance of her writing, and setting this within the context of a broader imperative to be attentive and open to life. '"Don't forget that you have only one gift," she used to say. "But what is one gift? One gift has never been enough for anyone"' (CSC, 373). Where Délia is young but locked into a bitter immobility, Sido's old age is active and curious: she arrives bearing gifts of home-made jam and 'the first roses in bud wrapped up in a damp handkerchief', and insists immediately on 'buying pansy seeds, hearing a comic opera and seeing a collection bequeathed to the Louvre' (CSC, 372).

Since in the story's present the narrator lives alone, apparently happily, and since a number of passages testify to her exuberant pleasure in that 'marvellous commonplace' (CSC, 366) beloved of Sido, she has already made the choice for Sido rather than Délia, but the temptation of a morbid and destructive obsession with suffering is still present. The other force working against this danger is that of friendship – for 'Colette' also escapes the 'temptation to be entrapped in this snare of resemblances' (CSC, 361) through her outings with Annie de Pène, outings which she describes with all the concrete detail of pleasures minutely savoured. Their cycling trips culminating in copious picnics constitute 'days in which work and sauntering and friendship played the major part, to the detriment of love', and these, with an ironic nod towards the predominance of love in her earlier works, she would 'very much like – late in life, it is true – ' to term 'the good days'. She also terms them 'merciful blanks', by analogy with those 'blanks that introduce space and order between the chapters of a book' (CSC, 354).

Colette thus privileges these periods lit by the happiness of friendship which free the senses to turn outwards, rather than training them, as passionate love does, in a single direction. The novella articulates a preference for the 'blanks' of contemplative, uneventful time over the drama of romance, a preference confirmed both by the narrator's decision to distance herself from Délia, and by the text's privileging of the narrator's self-discovery over Délia's love story. Here again, the horizontal model of time as a connected sequence of events driving forward to the future is less in evidence than a vertical model, in which the two-way relationship between past and present is the central focus. Horizontal time is the time of narrative, and here, as elsewhere in Colette's writing, the text's narrative thread is obscured and marginalized by the vertical axis of memory and reflection. The defeat of linear narrative is mirrored, too, with a touch of self-reflexive humour, in the subplot of the narrator's work as a writer. Although as the story begins she is contracted to write a 'serial novelette', every time she tries to 'introduce "action", swift adventure, and a touch of the sinister into it' (CSC, 355) she begins to loathe the project more, and eventually renounces it in favour of a less plot-driven mode of writing.

The significant role played by Sido in the establishment of the text's positive values echoes many other works by Colette, most famously *My Mother's House* (1922) and *Sido* (1929), both books composed of a series of brief lyrical evocations of a childhood presided over by the wise, irreverent and profoundly benevolent figure of Sido. The bond between mother and daughter resonates

throughout Colette's work – not only literally, in the frequent
staging of her own relationship with her mother, but also figuratively in the pervasive presence and thematic importance accorded
to characters and places associated with the maternal, of whom
Léa, in the *Chéri* novels, is just one. In this sense Colette's texts
clearly correspond to Cixous's criteria for a distinctively 'feminine'
writing.

But the model of temporality we have observed in a number
of very different Colette texts can equally well be linked to her
femininity as a writer. Jerry Aline Flieger draws attention to the
unusual form of Colette's autobiographical writing: whereas the
conventional form of the autobiography is that of the retrospective
*Bildungsroman*, which traces the individual's development towards
a fully formed self, Colette writes of her childhood and youth
through a multiplicity of 'autofictions', which can be placed on
a wide spectrum running between fiction and memoir. Flieger
suggests that the conventional structure of autobiography is more
appropriate to the 'voyage of achievement' of the male subject,
and that Colette's texts could more aptly be termed *Bildsroman* or
'picture novels' than *Bildungsroman*, for in them: 'rediscovery is not
the result of an extension of experience, and progress through time,
so much as it is a kind of vertical piling up of associations'.[22]

This association of horizontal temporality with the masculine,
and vertical temporality with the feminine, recalls Julia Kristeva's
1981 essay on 'Woman's Time'. Kristeva argues that female
subjectivity – at least, as historically constituted in Western
culture – tends to 'retain repetition and eternity from among
the multiple modalities of time known through the histories of
civilisations'. Women's subjectivity, Kristeva suggests, retains a
connection with 'cycles, gestation, the eternal recurrence of a
biological rhythm which conforms to that of nature', imposing a
temporality whose 'regularity and unison with what is experienced
as extrasubjective time, cosmic time, occasion vertiginous visions
and unnameable *jouissance*'.[23] Whereas the first stage or generation
of modern feminism 'aspired to gain a place in linear time as the
time of project and history', fighting for the vote, for political and
social participation and the right to a historical role, the second
phase – which Kristeva identifies with the post-1968 movement
– tends, rather, to refuse linear temporality and to emphasize the

'specificity of female psychology and its symbolic realisations'.[24] In this sense Colette has more in common with a later generation of women writers than with Beauvoir, whose work is very much concerned with the insertion of women into history.[25]

FICTIONAL AUTOBIOGRAPHY: *BREAK OF DAY* AND *THE EVENING STAR*
The autobiographical voice which characterizes Colette's journalism echoes in the implied values and focus of her third-person narrators, plays an intra-diegetic role in a number of stories and novels, and reappears centre-stage in some of her most innovative texts. *Break of Day* (1928), for example, and *The Evening Star* (1946), are both books which defy classification within existing literary genres. In each, the primary narrative time is that of the writing itself, so that the narrative ends as the narrator completes her text. In *La Naissance du jour* (*Break of Day*), 'Colette' is in her fifties and spending the summer in Provence at her house, La Treille Muscate. The text is peopled by Colette's real-life friends and fellow artists, but diverges from factual reality both by excluding the presence of Maurice Goudeket, with whom Colette was engaged in a passionate affair, and by including two fictional characters, Valère Vial and Hélène Clément. Vial is a handsome neighbour, some twenty years 'Colette''s junior, who falls in love with her and is refused, and Clément is a young artist who, in her turn, loves Vial. In *L'Etoile Vesper* (*The Evening Star*) Colette is in her seventies, immobilized by arthritis, and writing from her 'divan-raft' close to the window overlooking the Palais-Royal gardens. The present here is inhabited by Maurice, Colette's third husband, and by a regular stream of friends and visitors.

Those features which make Colette's voice distinctly feminine are all strongly present here. The foregrounding of women's life experience is a key element of each text: it is in *The Evening Star* that Colette gives the fullest account of her pregnancy and the birth of her daughter, and *Break of Day* is in one sense a book about the climacteric, or change of life, since it deals with a time of mid-life transition in which the centrality of sexual love fades and the question of female identity is differently posed. Both texts view the world from an unorthodox angle, ignoring or deliberately subverting dominant values. Although each text celebrates heterosexual love and motherhood, each also firmly refuses to accord to these experiences the privileged status they are assumed to enjoy in a woman's life and identity. Recalling the pervasive presence of sexual love in her life and literature, and tempted by Vial's desire, the narrator of *Break of Day* none the less reflects, in a provocative reversal of received wisdom on female priorities, that

> Love, one of the great commonplaces of existence, is slowly leaving mine. The maternal instinct is another great common-place. Once we've left these behind, we find that all the rest is gay and varied, and that there is plenty of it. (BD, 18[26])

And though she writes lyrically of the 'state of pride, of banal magnificence which I savoured in ripening my fruit' (ES, 133), and warmly of her new-born daughter's 'assembly of marvels' (ES, 135), the narrator of *The Evening Star* also celebrates her own failure to have become fully absorbed by maternity: 'Beneath the still young woman that I was, an old boy of forty saw to the wellbeing of a possibly precious part of myself' (ES, 138). The implication of Colette's writing is that whilst this 'precious part of the self' can be nurtured by the experience of sexual love and motherhood, these other-directed female roles also constitute a danger against which the self must be defended. In *Break of Day*, the conflict is played out between the narrator's inclination towards a life of contemplation, memory and writing, a choice identified with Sido, and her lingering desire for the drama of erotic love, represented mainly by Vial. It is here that Kristeva's alternative models of temporality again provide a useful lens for reading. While Sido's ethic of openness, curiosity and a sense of connection with the past generates the majority of the text, which mingles reminiscence and reflection, there is also the linear narrative of Vial's desire and disappointment, which appears to struggle for the narrator's attention. Despite the narrator's mock-serious injunctions to herself and to the reader, Vial is repeatedly edged out of the story by perception of the beauty of the world – 'We were saying, then, that Vial . . . / How beautiful the night is, once again!' (BD, 63) – or by meditations on his place in a broader vision of self-fulfilment:

> Yes, let's get back to Vial. . . . So here – at a time of life when I accept only the flower of any pleasure and the best of whatever

is best, since I no longer demand anything – here is a fruit out of season . . . (BD, 64–5)

The love story, classically feminine form of the linear narrative, conflicts with and is defeated by the text's alternative, vertical structure, that of the layered accumulation of often disparate but associated images, brought together by the processes of memory, observation and reflection.

It is in these texts, too, that Kristeva's association of cyclical time with feminine subjectivity becomes most relevant to Colette's writing. The profound optimism of Colette's world, and its absence of any tragic sense of mortality, rest on a sense of time as cyclically recurring rather than as leading inexorably towards death. In these texts an ending is always also a beginning. The narrator of *The Evening Star* is immobilized by arthritis and knows full well that 'from here I can see the end of the road' (ES, 144), but her travels through a 'cosy jumble of crumpled souvenirs' (ES, 65) take place against the coming of spring to the gardens outside her window, and the evening star that gives the book its title also rises in the morning. Furthermore, the lifetime of memories and wisdom evoked in the book are not condemned to erasure by death, but weave together to form the text itself – a text, moreover, which through its comparison to that more widespread form of female creativity, the tapestry, becomes an image of all those signs and traces we leave in the world which mean our passage is inscribed in time: 'My memories are written in blue foliage, in pink lilac, in varicoloured marguerites' (ES, 143).

In *Break of Day*, images of cyclical time are everywhere. Sido, long dead at the time of the book's composition, is reborn in her daughter's memory and in her text. Sido is consistently associated with the dawn, both by the preference for this time of day that she shares with her daughter ('My mother climbed too, mounting ceaselessly up the ladder of the hours, trying to possess the beginning of the beginning. I know what this particular intoxication is like' [BD, 26]), and by the fact that in French the metaphor for dawn, 'la naissance du jour' ('the birth of day'), is closely linked to the metaphor for giving birth, 'donner le jour' ('to give day'). *Break of Day* ends as dawn breaks, and the narrator's 'decline' into age is clearly represented as a new beginning.

Colette situates the individual within a continuum of growth, death and rebirth which is both natural and specifically human, for it implies not just acceptance of the inevitable but also a positive ethic of creative adaptation. Kristeva's association of this sense of temporality, which she characterizes as feminine, with an experience of 'unison with . . . extrasubjective time, cosmic time' occasioning 'vertiginous visions and unnameable *jouissance*',[27] corresponds precisely to the joyful tone that pervades much of *Break of Day*. The narrator's discovery that the return to the mother is also the way forward is expressed in passages of intensely lyrical imagery, culminating in the text's final, jubilant images of dispersal and radiating movement: 'spindrift, meteors, an open and unending book, a cluster of grapes, a ship, an oasis . . . ' (BD, 143).

The painful memory of Sido's death is swept away by the memory of her last letter, with its affirmatives and indications of an ecstasy irreducible to normal language:

> Two pencilled sheets have on them nothing more than apparently joyful signs, arrows emerging from an embryo word, little rays, 'yes, yes' together, and a single 'she danced', very clear. (BD, 142)

The model of time as structured by the cycle rather than the straight line, in which the 'road back' to the past can also represent the way forward, also determines the form of Colette's writing. Rather than a set of chronological memoirs, or a straightforward 'story of my life', her autobiography takes the form of a series of loops back into the past, each loop re-created in the light of the narrator's present. For half a century, with a nice disregard for the usual hierarchies that separate the serious from what she termed the 'marvellous commonplace', her public voice mingled ironic and irreverent social commentary, practical advice, and a movingly lyrical wisdom. Her originality, and her representations of a woman's life which is both typical and subversively unorthodox, can appropriately be termed, in the most positive sense, feminine.

# 8
## Simone de Beauvoir (1908–86) and The Second Sex

Like George Sand a century before her, Simone de Beauvoir was a 'miraculée', an apparently miraculous exception among the women of her generation. Despite the social and educational disadvantages of her sex, Beauvoir succeeded on men's terms: achieving the very highest educational qualifications, becoming famous as a philosopher and writer, joining that intellectual elite who enjoy a unique degree of attention and respect in France. Like Sand, she was politically committed and active in the struggle against the inequalities and tyrannies of her age. Both women recognized the liberation of their sex as a part of this struggle, though both have also been accused of some ambivalence about that female identity which constantly threatened to undermine their hardwon legitimacy as members of a privileged group.

Whereas Sand's entry into a male world of journalism and authorship owed a lot to accidents of birth – for her education and upbringing were most unusual – Beauvoir's background was inauspicious for a future feminist intellectual. Born in 1908 to a middle-class Parisian family, she attended a private Catholic school for girls, where the emphasis was more on forming virtuous and accomplished young ladies than on turning out scholars. It was Beauvoir's exceptional intellect and her passionate determination, combined with a decline in the family fortunes that determined the need for its daughters to have a profession, which took her on to the *baccalauréat*, then to the Sorbonne, and so to the highly prestigious *agrégation* in philosophy.

Beauvoir had decided on teaching as a career, and considered the possibility of attending the women's *Ecole normale* at Sèvres (see Part I, Chapter 3 above). If she did not go to Sèvres, this was first because the students there had to commit themselves to teaching in the state sector, and Beauvoir's Catholic mother was still resisting the prospect of her daughter entering that godless domain; and secondly because the women of Sèvres could not sit for the philosophy *agrégation*, since this was not a subject taught in girls' *lycées*. The Sorbonne was the alternative, though Beauvoir's mother insisted that she do the majority of her studying at Catholic institutes, which prepared Catholic students for the Sorbonne exams without exposing them to the moral dangers of student life.

Toril Moi points out that when Beauvoir sat the rigorous *agrégation* exams in 1929, she had been studying philosophy for only three years.[1] She had not had the advantage of several years' training at the Ecole Normale Supérieure, the country's top institution of higher education attended by her male contemporaries, including Jean-Paul Sartre, whom she met during her studies. Sartre came first in the 1929 philosophy *agrégation*. Beauvoir, three years younger, with four fewer years' study of philosophy behind her, came second. Women had been allowed to take the whole range of the *agrégations* alongside men only since 1924.

Beauvoir went on to become a teacher, then a writer of fiction, theatre, philosophical and political essays and a multivolumed autobiography which chronicles the intellectual and emotional itinerary not only of a remarkable woman but also of an era. She maintained a close and unconventional relationship with Sartre, refusing monogamy, marriage and motherhood and thus providing a public model of an alternative way of living as a woman. In the early 1970s, in her sixties, she welcomed the second-wave Women's Movement, and campaigned and wrote with the generation that one study refers to as 'The Daughters of Beauvoir'.[2] Her life and work have been extensively written about from a feminist perspective, particularly in some excellent recent studies (see Bibliography), and I am not going to undertake a broad study of her work here. Instead, I want to devote this chapter to what is probably Beauvoir's most influential and most original work, her much-praised and much-maligned study of women's situation in mid-twentieth-century Western society: *The Second Sex*.

*The Second Sex*, published in France in 1949 and in English translation in 1953,[3] is a founding text of modern feminism and has inspired many of the women writers who followed Beauvoir,

not only in France but all over the world. It is also a book that
has had a direct personal impact on many women's lives. Its power
seems to derive first from the fact that it provided a vocabulary in
which to talk seriously about issues till then relegated to the domain
of the personal and the trivial. In the words of the American
poet and novelist Marge Piercy: 'if things have no names all
you can do is feel a sense of uneasiness . . . instead of being an
issue it's your own problem'.[4] By discussing women's everyday
experience, from menstruation to housework, as a subject that
merited intellectual analysis, Beauvoir allowed women to identify
what felt like personal failings as aspects of a collective and political
dilemma. 'It was as if someone had come into the room and said
it's all right to feel what you're feeling',[5] comments a woman who
read the book in 1979, as a young full-time mother suffering
from depression and severe social isolation, and was enabled by
its encouragement to change the direction of her life.

Since the book generated a great deal of publicity about the
author, and was later often read alongside Beauvoir's fiction and
autobiography, it also offered an inspiring alternative model of how
a woman's life could be lived. Beauvoir's life seemed to represent
'a way of life in which a woman had chosen to remain committed
to her own work, her own politics, retained her sense of integrity
without giving up her life as a woman'.[6] This problematic fusion
of personal fulfilment and 'life as a woman' is central to the lives
and works of the earlier writers discussed above, and would be at
the heart of the new feminist movement some twenty years later.

The story of the genesis of *The Second Sex*, which Beauvoir
recounts in the third volume of her memoirs, *Force of Circumstance*,
is revealing in a number of ways. By 1946 she had published five
books which had been largely well received and reviewed, and
completed her essay on the ethical implications of existentialism,
the philosophy she had forged with Sartre.[7] She felt inclined to
write something more personal, 'about myself', and realized that
in order to do so she would have to consider what the fact of
being born a woman had meant in her life. At first her verdict was
dismissive – 'For me,' she said to Sartre, 'it just hasn't counted.'
But further reflection led her to a revelation which constituted
the founding moment of Beauvoir's feminism: 'This world was
a masculine world, my childhood had been nourished by myths

forged by men, and I hadn't reacted to them in at all the same way I should have done if I had been a boy.'[8] Abandoning the autobiographical project in favour of a study of women's situation, Beauvoir set off for the National Library to research the topic as thoroughly as possible, thus echoing Virginia Woolf's investigative trips to the British Museum Reading Room in *A Room of One's Own*,[9] published twenty years previously.

Beauvoir's initial sense that her femaleness had counted for almost nothing in her personal development demonstrates the subtle power of ideology to conceal and naturalize inequalities. The educational and social disadvantages of her situation as compared, for example, to that of Sartre had simply not struck her, even though while he had been a student at the country's most highly reputed secondary schools and universities, she had been taught by teachers neither trained nor inclined to develop critical female intellects; and even though while he was acquiring the social skills and confidence of one free to move in a variety of social circles, she was scarcely able to leave the house unchaperoned.

But beyond this, it also demonstrates the understandable disinclination of an individual who has achieved entry into the elite to question that elite's *doxa* or its unspoken, fundamental values. The French intellectual tradition – and in particular that group of mid-century writers and philosophers associated with existentialism – emphasized the sovereign freedom of the individual mind to grasp, understand and hence act upon the world, and minimized the power of material and social circumstances to shape and constrain individual consciousness. For Beauvoir to insist on the role of gender in determining or limiting her own development would have been a denial of that voluntarist individualism with which she had so fully (and successfully) identified. To undertake a study of women's situation meant a critical shift in the way Beauvoir viewed the relationship between individual freedom and material and cultural circumstance.

Before discussing specific themes and issues raised by *The Second Sex*, it will be useful both to outline the existentialist premises from which Beauvoir begins, and to give an idea of the scope and structure of the whole work. The word 'existentialism' refers to that philosophy's refusal of the idea of an essential human nature and to its insistence, instead, that humans determine their own being and values by their freely chosen actions in the world. Existence, for Beauvoir as for Sartre, precedes essence, and it is impossible to justify one's choices by reference to an intrinsic human tendency towards any particular form of behaviour.

Human existence is complicated by a fundamental duality: whereas all that is non-human exists solely in the mode of the *in-itself* [*en-soi*], unconsciously present in the world, human beings also have consciousness and thus exist *for-themselves* [*pour-soi*]. Whether I like it or not, I am present in the world and subject to the perceptions of others, but I am also consciousness, aware of myself and of the world around me. This can produce a conflict or tension, for others' perceptions of me do not necessarily coincide with my self-consciousness; thus they may be perceived as hostile. Viewed, interpreted and judged by others, the self takes on a consistency and fixity incompatible with the freedom constantly to determine my being by freely chosen acts. The existentialist model of intersubjective relations is a conflictual one, each subject anxious to assert their own sovereignty as consciousness, and equally anxious not to be objectified as the *in-itself* by another subject. Authentic relationships can be achieved only on the condition that each subject recognize and respect the free subjectivity of the other.

The difficulty of reconciling the two modes of being, however, can also be resolved in less ethically respectable ways. Human beings suffer from the temptation to abdicate freedom and to valorize their own existence through the perceptions of another, or through the mode which Sartre terms *for-others*. The existentialist sin − though such moral vocabulary is really quite out of place in a philosophy that eschews deities and absolute values − is *bad faith*, escape from freedom, or acting not out of personal conviction but in order to achieve the desired image in the eyes of others. Being *for-oneself*, as sovereign consciousness, is associated with the assumption of freedom in existentialist thought, and is thus a positive category; whereas being *for-others* denotes the uncomfortable fact of our involuntary material existence and subjection to the perceptions of other people. To validate the self in this way is a form of self-objectification, of self-definition as primarily *en-soi*, and thus tends to connote passivity, a failure of freedom, the opposite of existentialist virtue.

This philosophy determines Beauvoir's point of departure in studying women. The model of warring subjectivities is extended from the individual to the collective: 'when two human categories are together, each aspires to impose its sovereignty upon the other' (p. 93). Because of their physical disadvantage as the sex which bears children, Beauvoir argues, women lost the fight at the very beginning of history, and have since been constructed economically, socially, politically and culturally as man's 'Other', or the 'second sex'. Equally consonant with existentialist philosophy is Beauvoir's refusal of any notion of a feminine nature or an intrinsic feminine essence. Although the book will study how women think and act, and will thus assume that they are significantly different from men, this difference will be viewed not as natural and eternal but rather as historical and open to change. Although Beauvoir asks 'What is a woman?', the verb 'to be', as the introduction explains, 'must be rightly understood here; it is in bad faith to give it a static value when it really has the dynamic Hegelian sense of "to have become"' (p. 24).

In order to understand how women have become the 'second sex', and what it means to live as a secondary being, Beauvoir examines what appears to be the 'given' in women's condition from the point of view of biology, psychoanalysis and historical materialism, then reviews women's history from the earliest known period to the present, concluding Volume 1 with a critical analysis of the myths which make up the ideology of gender. In Volume 2 (published a few months after Volume 1) she studies female development from childhood to old age, explores the forms of *bad faith* which are particularly female temptations, and looks optimistically towards the future in a conclusion entitled 'Towards Liberation'.

One of the book's radical dimensions is its close consideration of the female body, and of sexuality. To write explicitly about women's anatomy and bodily functions was both novel and shocking in 1949, and when François Mauriac commented acidly that after he had read *The Second Sex* Beauvoir's vagina 'no longer held any secrets for him',[10] his deliberate and uncharacteristic vulgarity expressed a widely shared masculine outrage at the book's sexual frankness. Women were generally dissuaded, by an unwritten but powerful taboo, from writing or speaking in public about their own bodies. The importance of patrilineal heredity under patriarchy had led to the identification of female virtue with sexual modesty. Moreover, as Beauvoir's book so cogently revealed, the female body had become the metaphorical site of men's dreams and fears almost to the exclusion of its material reality, and the precise delineation of anatomy and physical experience from a woman's own perspective undercut the myths. Earlier women writers had, in different ways, addressed the issues of the reproductive cycle and sexuality, but even Colette, for all her disruption of the conventions of gender, dealt with menstruation, the menopause and the mechanics of sexual intercourse through allusion rather than directly. By the very act of treating the subject seriously and openly, as well as through the arguments she advanced, Beauvoir became 'the first thinker in France to explicitly politicize sexuality'.[11]

The importance of *The Second Sex* as a pivotal text of contemporary feminism is widely acknowledged, but Beauvoir's treatment of female sexuality and reproduction has also been much criticized by feminists of the post-1968 period. In the book's discussion of these areas, there is a tension between two lines of argument, both arising from Beauvoir's existentialist premises. On the positive side, existentialism refuses the status of the 'natural' to what are in fact social and personal choices, so that aspects of women's lives which were still, in 1949, largely accepted as natural disadvantages were now redefined as the results of human agency, and thus open to change. On the other hand, existentialism is in itself a gendered philosophy which privileges the masculine, and thus produces some curious contradictions when it is used as the conceptual framework for a feminist analysis of women's situation.

Beauvoir's existentialist model of reality is a positive one for feminism, then, in that it makes the significance of biological difference depend wholly on social context:

[W]henever the physiological fact (for instance muscular inferiority) takes on meaning, this meaning is at once seen as dependent on a whole context; the 'weakness' is revealed as such only in the light of the ends man proposes, the instruments he has available, and the laws he establishes. (p. 67)

Thus women are the 'weaker' sex only within a specific social and economic framework, and it is shown that the meaning of biology depends on social ideologies and practices – a liberating philosophy not only for women but for any social group disadvantaged by physical difference.

The same refusal of essentialism leads Beauvoir to argue against what Adrienne Rich, thirty years on, was to term 'compulsory heterosexuality'.[12] In her section on 'The Lesbian', Beauvoir reverses the standard argument which defines women as naturally heterosexual and lesbians as deviant. If eroticism has its origins in infantile sensuality, she argues, then 'the female body is for her [the woman], as for the male, an object of desire', and 'if nature is to be invoked, one can say all women are naturally homosexual' (p. 427). Since sexual orientation can no more be reduced to instinct than can any other human activity, a complex interplay of motivations will lead many women to desire male partners, but Beauvoir presents female homosexuality as in many ways the more comprehensible choice. Lesbian relationships do not only avoid domination by a male partner; by remaining outside the power structures which frame heterosexuality, they offer the freedom to explore and interchange a variety of roles. Citing Colette's lesbian couple Claudine and Rézi in *Claudine Married*, as well as the poetry of Renée Vivien, Beauvoir attributes to lesbian relationships an equality and a plurality of possibilities which the heterosexual couple, constrained by fixed gender roles, can rarely match:

> They can enjoy their love in a state of equality. Because the partners are homologous, basically alike, all kinds of combinations, transpositions, exchanges, *comédies* are possible. Their relations become balanced according to the psychological tendencies of each of the two friends and in accordance with the total situation. (p. 439)

The refusal to justify or condemn human behaviour by reference to *nature* also underpins the impassioned critique of the reproductive politics of postwar France, with which Beauvoir opens her section on 'The Mother'. That women should be expected to have and raise children in order to repopulate the nation deeply offends Beauvoir's sense of the individual's right to self-fulfilment. That contraception and abortion should remain illegal, on the grounds that it is 'natural' as well as desirable for women to be mothers, is anathema to her both as existentialist and as feminist. While the law forbids women to choose their maternity freely, motherhood can rarely coincide with a woman's aspiration as a free subject. The result, she argues, is unhappy women, frustrated and oppressive mothers, and unwanted children.

Beauvoir's insistence that the meaning of biological facts and processes is socially constructed extends, in some parts of *The Second Sex*, to a recognition of the way in which language can shape fact in accordance with ideology. Thus she begins the chapter on 'The Data of Biology' with a caustic analysis of the way in which the fertilization of the ovum by the sperm was normally represented. The egg was said to 'wait motionless', 'its compact mass, sealed up within itself, evok[ing] darkness and inward repose' (p. 44); while the sperm, 'free, slender, agile', was granted the active role, its 'rational activity measurable in terms of time and space' (p. 44). Beauvoir rewrites this narrative of mysterious feminine passivity brought to life by masculine dynamism, this time as a fusion of two 'interrelated dynamic aspects of life', 'both suppressed in bearing a new whole' (p. 45). The scientific accuracy of her description is of much less importance than her demonstration of the way language can construct reality in deeply tendentious ways.

Yet it is precisely this linguistic loading of the dice of which parts of *The Second Sex* stand accused, and particularly in relation to sexuality and reproduction. Existentialist values are structured on a series of binary oppositions – with terms logically or metaphorically associated with the free consciousness, the *for-itself*, on the positive side, and all that derives from immanence, or being *in-itself*, on the negative. Thus activity, progression, linearity, transparency are positive terms, whereas passivity, immobility, circularity, opaqueness are negative. Whatever escapes conscious knowledge and control is suspect, for it opposes transcendence by anchoring the subject in a reality that denies his (her) freedom. To feminists of the post-'68 'second wave', for whom sexual politics means rethinking phallocentric visions of the world, existentialist values as outlined above immediately spell out privileging of the masculine and devaluation of the feminine. Much of Sartre's writing confirms this equation between gender and value. In his novel *The Age of Reason*, for example, the most powerful image of entrapment in immanence is the stuffy pink room in which Marcelle, the hero's pregnant mistress, seems to sit immobile, passively nourishing the invisible foetus whose conception was involuntary, and whose existence threatens Mathieu's freedom .

Beauvoir's fiction, frequently narrated or focalized from a woman's perspective,[13] shows a less rigid apportionment of positive and negative value to masculine and feminine characters. None the less, her novels and memoirs share the same repugnance for what escapes consciousness, and display an intense disgust for the involuntary processes of the body – from unwanted pregnancy, vividly dramatized in the abortion scene in *The Blood of Others*,[14] to ageing, a central issue for Anne in *The Mandarins*,[15] as for Beauvoir herself in *Force of Circumstance*. I have discussed above the reasons why, as the only woman member of a male elite, Beauvoir might understandably have internalized the values of what reads now as a very gendered world-view, and there were no doubt also psychoemotional reasons, equally dissociable from a gendered context, which led Beauvoir to identify firmly with masculine rather than feminine, father rather than mother.[16] In *The Second Sex*, existentialist values produce a devaluation of female sexuality and of women's reproductive cycle which goes well beyond a political critique of sexual and reproductive politics in 1949.

According to Beauvoir's account of history, it was women's biology – the fact that they were 'biologically destined for the repetition of Life' (p. 96), while their menfolk were 'transcending Life through Existence' (p. 96) – which first established male supremacy. All aspects of women's biology connected to reproduction are thus negatively evaluated. At puberty, the young girl's desire for freedom and transcendence comes into conflict with her reproductive capacity: 'Not without resistance does the body of woman permit the species to take over; and this struggle is weakening and dangerous' (p. 59). The menstrual cycle is truly a 'curse', 'a burden, and a useless one from the point of view of the individual' (p. 60). Beauvoir's language registers her distaste for the body's escape from the control of consciousness – 'the bloody mass trickles out as the menstrual flow' (p. 60) – and her sense of a violent invasion of the self by a form of life which is indifferent to the individual's will:

[I]t is during her periods that [the woman] feels her body most painfully as an obscure, alien thing; it is, indeed, the prey of a stubborn and foreign life that each month constructs and then tears down a cradle within it. (p. 61)

While in a society that devalues women the onset of menstruation may very well be experienced as a further obstacle to freedom, this account seems to relate less to a historically specific situation than to menstruation as such. Existentialism allows for no conceivable pleasure in the cyclical, or in change which is independent of individual will.

Beauvoir's account of heterosexual initiation is equally negative, and displays a surprising disregard for the linguistic construction of reality, which we have seen elsewhere to be the explicit object of her critique. Here again, women (though not men) are the prey of the species: the irrelevance of the clitoris, and hence of women's orgasm, to the act of coition excluding them from that combination of 'service to the species' with 'personal enjoyment' which ensures that 'the man's body retains its integrity' (p. 393).

The key passage which describes intercourse (pp. 406–7) opens with a clear assertion that the superiority of masculine sexuality is socially constructed rather than biologically determined – 'Woman is thoroughly indoctrinated with common notions that endow masculine passion with splendour and make a shameful abdication of feminine sex feeling' (p. 406) – but the sentence, rather than ending there, concludes by contradicting itself: 'woman's intimate experience confirms the fact of this asymmetry', and the passage will indeed imply that the male role in coition has a dignity quite lacking in that of the female. Whereas Beauvoir had refused to read the sperm as the active, dynamic partner in fertilization, she seems to have no such problem with the penis:

The sex organ of a man is simple and neat as a finger; it is readily visible and often exhibited to comrades with proud rivalry; but the feminine sex organ is mysterious even to the woman herself, concealed, mucous and humid, as it is (p. 406).

Here the visible, external penis is endowed, despite the frequently involuntary nature of erection, with the subject's intentionality: it expresses the man's free desire. The female genitals, on the other hand, are negatively valorized as unknown, unseen, unwilled by the female subject. Similarly, physical manifestations of desire are evaluated very differently: the male 'getting stiff' is 'an active operation', but the female 'getting wet' is 'humiliating', making the body:

> no longer an organism . . . under control of the brain and expressive of a conscious subject, but rather a vessel, a container, composed of inert matter and the plaything of capricious mechanical forces. (p. 407)

This valorization of the singular, the visible, the linear, as opposed to what is concealed and spatially less definable, is deeply rooted in Western culture. Almost thirty years on, Luce Irigaray was to demonstrate the hegemony of 'the visual, and of the discrimination and individualization of form' which made women's sexual organs 'represent *the horror of nothing to see*'.[17] But this unconsciously gendered vision is particularly acute in existentialism, which consistently represents freedom in terms of phallic masculine imagery, the constraints of an absurd universe in terms of feminine enclosure and humidity. As Carol Ascher puts it: 'the physiology of female sexuality . . . seems to determine oppression for heterosexual women.'[18]

Like menstruation, which signifies the body's capacity for maternity, pregnancy and childbirth are viewed in terms of a conflict between species and individual subject. Sickness in pregnancy is 'the revolt of the organism against the invading species' (p. 62); childbirth cannot be read as properly creative because it is not the work of conscious intention but, rather, a 'strange kind of creation which is accomplished in a contingent and passive manner' (p. 513). As a defence of women's right to choose their maternities, and an attack on the limitation of female creativity to their maternal role, this is an important element in Beauvoir's feminist project. Her expressed admiration for Colette's account of her own active, busy pregnancy, 'typical of all those women who bear their condition valiantly because they are not absorbed in it' (p. 519), supports the case for women to remain in employment and public life when they have children. Yet Beauvoir's negative account of maternity implies that the very fact of childbearing is hard to reconcile with human freedom – that its difficulties must be overcome in the pursuit of individual transcendence, rather than its specific pleasures enjoyed as part of the human experience.

Since women's reproductive cycle, from puberty to mother-hood, is seen in terms of the invasion of the individual by the species, the menopause should logically represent a release. Beauvoir recognizes that the experience is less simple: in the course of their adult life, most women's sense of identity becomes partially dependent on their sense of themselves as sexually attractive, or as mothers – roles which are threatened or ended by ageing. Also, the society of which Beauvoir writes is a society which offers few viable roles to older women; though the acceptance of advancing age represents a liberation from many of the 'chains' of women's lives, the older woman still has to find something to do with her freedom: 'she must maintain a place on earth' (p. 595).

But though she insists, from time to time, that the problem is one of a sexist society, Beauvoir stresses the loss and pain of female ageing to the extent that here again women seem doomed by nature to an extra share of unhappiness. There could scarcely be a greater contrast on this point than that between Beauvoir and Colette. Beauvoir asserts that 'whereas man grows old gradually, woman is suddenly deprived of her femininity' (p.587), that 'long before the eventual mutilation, woman is haunted by the horror of growing old' (p. 587); that 'when the first hints come of that fated and irreversible process which is to destroy the whole edifice built up during puberty, [the woman] feels the fatal touch of death itself' (p. 588). In *Break of Day*, published in 1928, Colette had written movingly of a woman on the brink of old age who, while briefly mourning the ending of a life in which erotic love had figured large, welcomes the freedom to explore all that love and maternity exclude.[19]

Colette's conclusion – that ageing frees women from some of the specifically female constraints on their lives – ought logically to be that of Beauvoir. But Beauvoir, in line with her existentialist model of the world, is as horrified by the involuntary ageing of the body as she is by its other signs of non-conscious change. There is no more radical denial of the autonomy of the subject than death, and Beauvoir reads the menopause as a first sign of death. She also assumes that the ageing female body must cease to be an object of male desire, which – while quite possibly true in the social context she describes – also seems to be an internalization of a male-centred view of sexuality much more radically deconstructed by Colette.

In *The Second Sex*, then, the female body is experienced as inferior because of women's second-class social, economic and cultural status: on one level the problem of female sexuality and of reproduction is one of situation, not nature, and existentialist theory provides a useful methodology for feminist politics. But in its valorization of qualities anatomically and symbolically associated with the masculine, existentialism condemns women's anatomy and biology to the status of an obstacle to be overcome in the pursuit of full humanity, implicitly identified with masculinity. Despite her astute analysis, in some sections of the book, of the interplay between ideology and the construction of knowledge, Beauvoir's identification with the values and world-view of her male peers seems to preclude any more positive evaluation of the female body – whereas Colette, whose lack of education and intellectual capital ensured that she never achieved legitimacy on male terms, was able to pursue a much more subversive agenda in terms of bodily representations.

We must now consider how Beauvoir's analysis of sexuality and reproduction relates to the rest of her project in *The Second Sex*, and to what extent her overvalorization of the masculine works against the book's feminist meaning, a meaning so clearly inspirational for the majority of its women readers.

In her account of women's relationship with their own bodies, Beauvoir emphasizes one aspect which is unequivocally the consequence of cultural situation rather than biological disadvantage. In patriarchal societies, women's bodies connote what Laura Mulvey has named 'to-be-looked-at-ness';[20] they are assumed to be objects of visual and erotic interest to men. Constantly on display, in existentialist terms the female body is situated, more definitively than the male, as the object of another's gaze, as *in-itself*. While Beauvoir's account of the girl's experience of menstruation as an alien force is open to question, her analysis of the recognition, at puberty, that the body 'with which the girl has identified' will now be 'apprehended as flesh' (p. 333) is compelling, and crucial to the demonstration of how women are constructed as man's 'Other':

> The young girl feels that her body is getting away from her, it is no longer the straightforward expression of her individuality; it becomes foreign to her; and at the same time she becomes for others a thing: on the street men follow her with their eyes and comment on her anatomy. (p. 333)

This sense of being the object of the gaze, being defined and evaluated in terms of the desires and needs of another, remains central to women's self-perception, and is sustained and developed by the ideological structures which Beauvoir brilliantly dissects in her section on 'Myths'. We have seen that according to Beauvoir's existentialist model of intersubjective relations, 'each separate conscious being aspires to set himself up alone as sovereign subject' (p. 171) by possessing the other as object, as *in-itself*. Men's success in establishing their own sovereignty has placed women in the role of man's 'Other'. 'Defined exclusively in her relation to man' (p. 174), woman becomes the embodiment of male dreams and fears, ideals and anxieties, to the virtual exclusion of her own subjectivity: 'Women do not set themselves up as Subject and hence have erected no virile myth in which their projects are reflected . . .' (p. 174). Feminine myths, therefore, abound, and nations, virtues, institutions, all tend to be personified as female:

> Man feminizes the ideal he sets up before him as the essential Other, because woman is the material representation of alterity; that is why almost all allegories, in language as in pictorial representation, are women. (p. 211)

Female figures people the collective imagination – not as themselves, but as representations of men's ideals and terrors – and these mythical personae, in turn, shape and constrain the behaviour and self-image of real women. From Eve to the Virgin Mary, from Muses to mothers-in-law, Beauvoir explores the powerful representations of positive and negative femininity produced by male imaginations and forming a lens through which women are perceived and judged.

Prefiguring an important section of Kate Millett's *Sexual Politics*

(1969) and much 1970s 'Images of Women' criticism, Beauvoir also addresses the mythologisation of women in the the work of five male authors: Montherlant, D.H. Lawrence, Claudel, Breton and Stendhal. She enacts a sharp and telling critique of Montherlant's ethics, as articulated through his representation of gender ('Montherlant's works, like his life, admit of only *one* consciousness' [p. 240]), and demonstrates in each author, with the exception of the admirably non-essentialist Stendhal, the attribution of subjectivity to the male and secondary, subordinate ontological status to women. Her analysis of the problem posed by Breton's poetry is exemplary. Breton does not belittle women but idealizes them: in his work, woman is the force that can save humanity. But, Beauvoir points out, to say that woman *is* truth, beauty, or love is to say nothing about woman herself as seeker after truth, as poet, as lover – as subject:

> But one would like to know if for her also love is key to the world and revelation of beauty. Will she find that beauty in her lover, or in her own image? . . . She is poetry in essence, directly – that is to say, for a man; we are not told whether she is poetry for herself also. (p. 267)

It is because women find themselves so comprehensively defined as man's 'Other' that their temptation to avoid the responsibility of freedom takes particular forms. Beauvoir argues in *The Second Sex*, and demonstrates compellingly in her fiction, that in a world where women are required to be dependent and ornamental, the way is open for them to take flight from freedom by founding their identity in the approval of others. Perhaps the most widespread temptation is to centre one's life in romantic love: Beauvoir shows that since most women are condemned to economic and social dependence on a husband, their best hope of redeeming some glamour or glory for their lives is to convince themselves that they have been chosen by an exceptional man: 'She chooses to desire her enslavement so ardently that it will seem to her the expression of her liberty' (p. 653). By making a hero of the man she loves, the 'amoureuse' (woman in love) can see her own life and person as unique and wonderful; rather than create a life through a series of choices, she depends on his approval and desire to give her worth. Like Paule in Beauvoir's novel *Les Mandarins*, she may then become tyrannical, for she has invested so much both in the heroic status of her partner and in his love for her that she cannot bear any sign of his human imperfection, or any change in their relationship. Beauvoir thus analyses characteristically feminine forms of *bad faith* with a combination of criticism and sympathy, showing that they are the consequence of situation rather than nature, but also emphasizing their ethical and practical inadequacy as recipes for human happiness.

Beauvoir rejects heterosexual love as a sufficient project to give meaning to a life – not only because romantic love has long been used to camouflage and justify women's subordination, but also because the 'woman in love' founds her existence more on being than on doing, on what she is rather than what she does. As in her representation of sexuality, underpinning Beauvoir's model of reality is a clear valorization of active progressive movement over passive stillness or, for example, contemplative inactivity. This has led to the accusation, by feminist critics who are none the less fundamentally in sympathy with Beauvoir's project, that she proposes only a masculine model of self-realisation. For Jean Leighton, in *The Second Sex* 'the traditional masculine virtues are regarded frankly as the only true human qualities and values'[21]. Mary Evans objects that 'De Beauvoir's answer to the "woman question" was the adoption by women of male habits and values.'[22] Toril Moi foregrounds the 'rather repetitive set of phallic metaphors' used by Beauvoir and Sartre to 'illustrate their theory of freedom and transcendence',[23] and demonstrates that 'the basic image of the project remains male erection and ejaculation', so that 'Repetitive, circular, cyclical, erratic or random modes of activity . . . can never hope to be classified as authentically transcendent.'[24]

There is no doubt that the goals Beauvoir proposes for women are those which Western, patriarchal societies have been proposing to male individuals since the beginnings of industrialization: self-determination, mobility, employment unencumbered by the demands of dependants, personal autonomy. Liberation can be achieved only if women minimize their physical disadvantage by effective use of contraception, and become financially independent through paid employment: 'It is through gainful employment that woman has traversed most of the distance that separated her from the male; and nothing else can guarantee her liberty in practice'

(p. 689). There is very little question of rethinking masculinity and its goals: women must accede as completely and rapidly as possible to a lifestyle hitherto available only to men. Just as in sexuality the masculine model of goal-orientated action was seen as more fully human than the less visible, more diffuse pattern of feminine pleasure, so here a conventionally masculine lifestyle is seen to embody an enviable freedom.

Contemporary feminist criticisms of Beauvoir's account are grounded in a different model of liberation. In her existentialist narrative, difference was constructed and maintained by men's biological advantage, which allowed them to claim for themselves the specifically human attributes of subjecthood and transcendence, and to relegate women to the place of the 'Other' and to immanence. The emancipation of women thus means the assertion of their equal right to and capacity for activities and attributes identified as masculine. Post-1968 feminism has tended to challenge the values of conventional masculinity, asking to what extent women want to share in a culture of individualism, competitiveness, aggression and control. Many contemporary feminists would share Beauvoir's rejection of the notion of intrinsic or natural gender difference, but would none the less claim that for historical reasons women have developed counter-values of co-operation, respect for the natural world, tolerance and a less 'either/or' model of reality which are worth promoting.

There are two points to make here in defence of *The Second Sex* and its major significance as a feminist text. One is that in 1949 there was every reason to avoid any concession to the theory of natural gender difference, since this theory had always been a euphemism for women's inferiority and was still being used to justify oppressive policies, in particular the prohibition of contraception and abortion. Like earlier feminists who campaigned for women's right to education, employment and civic status, Beauvoir emphasizes women's similarity to men in order to attack the model of sexual difference which confines them to the domestic world, to immobility and enclosure.

Secondly, although it is true that in its totality *The Second Sex* glamorizes rather than deconstructs masculinity, Beauvoir's respect for the dominant masculine culture is often laced with scepticism. Implicit throughout her critique of women's oppression is an attack on male self-importance, and this develops in some passages into the argument that women, by virtue of their historical exclusion from public life and from roles of authority, have maintained a healthy cynicism and capacity for subversive thought. Masculine reasoning, she argues, is often erected on a series of fixed premisses whose arbitrary nature remains unquestioned. While an educated man may succeed in winning logical arguments against a female opponent, she will remain profoundly unconvinced – both because her experience makes her unwilling to believe that there is any 'fixed truth', any 'principle of constant identity' (p. 624), and because she knows the masculine world itself to be mendacious: in its claims to respect liberty and equality, for example, and in the gap between public and private sexual moralities.

Because they identify less with official rhetoric and values, Beauvoir suggests, women are less likely to be taken in by them: 'Man's enterprises are at once projects and evasions: he lets himself be smothered by his career and his "front"; he often becomes self-important, serious' (p. 636), whereas women's domestic lives, limited as they are, have at least the virtue of remaining 'concrete'. Beauvoir even acknowledges here that the absence of an absorbing, future-directed project can permit an enriching degree of curiosity and contemplation: the woman isolated by domestic responsibilities 'experiences more passionately, more movingly, the reality in which she is submerged than does the individual absorbed in an ambition or a profession'; 'she declines to be fooled by man's mystifications, seeing the contingent, absurd, unnecessary inverse of the imposing structure built by males' (p. 637). These arguments are carefully premissed on women's historical situation, not on their nature, but they suggest that women's access to masculine institutions might bring to bear a critical perspective and a different set of priorities which will transform the dominant culture rather than merely permit women to join it. Beauvoir's work has a strong utopian dynamic, which explains the enthusiasm with which she greeted and was accepted by the post-1968 wave of feminism – with the exception of those feminists committed to a politics of radical gender difference.

In a historical chapter on 'Patriarchal Times and Classical Antiquity', Beauvoir recalls a scene glimpsed in a Tunisian village, where the situation of women had remained unchanged for centuries. In a subterranean cave, four women squatted, one old and physically devastated by age and the harshness of her life, two younger and carrying children, though already disfigured, and one 'young idol magnificently decked out in silk, gold and silver'. Outside this 'kingdom of immanence, womb and tomb' which was the wives' domain, she passed the husband they shared, 'dressed in white, well groomed, smiling, sunny', returning from the marketplace, part of that 'vast universe to which he belonged' (p. 116). As a successful intellectual and writer, Beauvoir enjoyed an exceptional degree of access to that open, sunny world where decisions are made and action is taken: she wrote to assert the right of those enclosed and silent women to leave the cave and discover that wider universe. It is not surprising that the white-clad figure of the free, adventurous but secure male should be touched with the poetry of envious desire. For the tensions in Beauvoir's work arise from the insecurity of her own position as a woman whose legitimacy depended, as Toril Moi demonstrates, on 'identifi[cation] with a set of values which contributed to her own marginalization'.[25] Twenty years before the beginning of the contemporary Women's Movement, *The Second Sex* made a major contribution to the creation of a climate in which those values could be seriously challenged.

# 9
## *Elsa Triolet (1896–1970):*
## *Stories of Exile and Resistance*

Elsa Triolet is now best remembered in French literary history for
her eyes. In the war poetry of her husband, Louis Aragon, Elsa is
the Muse who provides inspiration not only for the poet but also
for all those who would resist the Nazi invader. Her eyes hold
within them a world worth fighting for, and signify the hope of
victory:

> Il advint qu'un beau soir l'univers se brisa
> Sur des récifs que les naufrageurs enflammèrent
> Moi je voyais briller au-dessus de la mer
> Les yeux d'Elsa, les yeux d'Elsa, les yeux d'Elsa.
>
> [It happened that one fine evening the universe broke apart
> Crashed on to reefs lit by the fires of wreckers
> I saw shining over the sea
> Elsa's eyes Elsa's eyes Elsa's eyes.][1]

Elsa's eyes formed the title not only of a poem but also of the
volume in which it appeared. *Les Yeux d'Elsa* was published and
circulated by the underground Resistance press, and has remained
one of the best-known works of Resistance poetry.

It is virtually impossible to imagine a reversal of roles here –
that is, that Triolet might have made of Aragon's eyes a symbol
of hope for France and for the defeat of Nazism. As the woman
loved by a patriotic poet, Triolet could appropriately fill the role
of Muse and represent the enduring spirit of a country always
personified as feminine, 'la France', despite the fact that she herself
was Russian. As a writer, however, she suffered from the same
double illegitimacy as Renée Vivien before her – as a woman in
a literary culture still predominantly male, and as a foreigner in a
language not her own.

None the less, although Aragon's name is now the better known, Triolet herself was a prolific and respected writer. She was a major literary and political figure on the French Left, author of twenty-seven books, mostly fiction but also including biographies, translations and essays. Elsa Kagan was born in Moscow in 1896, the younger daughter of Russian Jewish intellectuals. In the years leading up to the Russian Revolution she became involved in Moscow's artistic avant-garde, among them the poet Mayakovsky, who became the lover of Elsa's sister Lili. In 1917 she married a French officer, André Triolet, and left Russia for Tahiti, where their ill-matched marriage ended after two years. Triolet (she was to keep the name for the rest of her life) then moved for a time to Berlin, where there was a considerable Russian community in exile, and thence to Paris in the mid 1920s. During the Berlin years she published three semi-autobiographical works in Russian, but their pessimistic tone was not well received in a country where celebration of the new order was beginning to be imposed as the sole aim of art.

In Paris in 1928 Triolet met the Surrealist poet Louis Aragon, and entered a relationship which was to last for the rest of her life. Aragon was one of a group of poets and artists whose response to the horrors of World War I was initially to attack all orthodox systems of value and belief as mere masks for life's absurdity. Out of this movement, Dadaism, grew Surrealism, with its more affirmative theory of the primacy of the imagination, and its exploration of techniques which could provide access to the irrational and the marvellous. Surrealism demanded a radical rethinking of the boundaries between reality and dream, between the rational mind and the unconscious, and thus implied a challenge to prevailing hierarchies of value and codes of behaviour. By the late 1920s the Surrealists, led by the poet André Breton, were aware of the need to define their own relationship with what they saw as the other major revolutionary force of the age, Communism.

The Surrealists' will to dissent stopped short of a rethinking of gender roles. As they were an all-male group, their poetry cast women in the conventional role of Muse or object of desire, but never implied that they might be fellow artists and rebels. In Breton's poetry women are magical intermediaries between man and the surreal, as in the 1931 poem in the form of a litany to 'Ma femme' (ambiguously 'my woman' or 'my wife'), in which each part of the woman's body is qualified by disparate images, producing that shock of unexpected juxtaposition which was crucial to the Surrealist project but also, incidentally, denying the poem's subject any intimation of subjectivity:

> Ma femme au sexe d'algue et de bonbons anciens
> Ma femme au sexe de miroir
> . . .
> Ma femme aux yeux de savane
> Ma femme aux yeux d'eau pour boire en prison
>
> [My woman with a sex of seaweed and old sweets
> My woman with a sex like a mirror
> . . .
> My woman with savannah eyes
> My woman with eyes of water to drink in prison.][2]

The only member of the group to show any awareness of the discrepancy between the Surrealists' radical philosophy and their conservative sexual politics was Aragon, whose own illegitimacy and bisexuality gave him a less conventional angle on sexual identity. When the group conducted an 'Enquiry into Sexuality' in 1929, only Aragon pointed out that the entire debate had excluded women's point of view and assumed the primacy of masculine desire: 'The validity of all that has been said seems to me to be partly invalidated by the predominance of a masculine viewpoint.'[3] When Breton took an instant dislike to Aragon's new lover, and Elsa Triolet reciprocated both personally and with some scepticism about the Surrealists' political credentials, Aragon began to distance himself from the group. He broke with Surrealism and joined the Communist Party, accompanying Triolet on a trip to Moscow in 1930 during which he denounced Surrealism as the art form of a *petit-bourgeois* elite responding blindly to the contradictions of capitalism. Aragon would remain in the Party for the rest of his life; Triolet never became a member, but actively supported the Communist cause until her death in 1970.

During the 1930s Triolet and Aragon were in the mainstream of French intellectual life, sharing the stage with André Malraux as

French delegates to the Congress of the Union of Soviet Writers in Moscow in 1934, working with André Gide, Malraux and other leading intellectuals in the Association of Revolutionary Artists and Writers. As Stalin's censorship intensified, it was becoming increasingly difficult to have work published in the USSR, and in the mid 1930s Triolet began to write in French. Her first novel, *Bonsoir, Thérèse*, was published in 1938 and favourably reviewed by the left-wing press.

Triolet and Aragon married shortly before war broke out. Since Aragon was conscripted, the couple were separated during the 'phoney war', but once the German army invaded France they fled South to the unoccupied zone. As Communist sympathizers they were regarded as potential traitors from August 1939, when Stalin and Hitler signed the Nazi–Soviet pact and French Communists faced an uncomfortable division of loyalties. Once the Nazis were in France and Pétain's right-wing government was in place, to be a Communist was to be marked out as a potential subversive. Triolet was also Jewish. When the Nazis invaded the Free Zone in November 1942, the couple went underground and worked for the Resistance for the rest of the war. For Elsa Triolet, resistance meant a number of different activities: writing and editing the clandestine *Lettres françaises*, to which Camus, Sartre and Mauriac also contributed and whose first editor, Jacques Decour, had been arrested carrying the first edition and executed; publishing stories in Vercors's *Editions de Minuit*; acting as a courier maintaining communications between the groups of Maquis; providing support for escaped Russian prisoners of war. In 1944, the Occupation over, Triolet was awarded the prestigious Prix Goncourt for a collection of Resistance stories, *A Fine of Two Hundred Francs*.

Although she had lived under threat of capture and death, and often in wretched material conditions, the Resistance had provided Triolet with a sense of belonging and purpose, banishing that sense of exile and alienation she had often felt in France. After the war, the feeling of participating in a collective struggle against evil ended, and was succeeded by more difficult ethical and political choices. Triolet's work of this period reveals some bitterness about the rapid reinstatement of collaborators and the retrospective belittlement of the Communists' contribution to Resistance. At the same time, evidence was emerging of the brutally totalitarian nature of Stalinism in the USSR. Triolet and Aragon remained loyal to the Party, despite the accumulating evidence that the homeland of democratic socialism shared some of the worst features of fascist regimes.[4]

Triolet's writing, though, shows no sign of subordination to political aims. Unlike Aragon, she made no attempt at all to follow the Party line on socialist realism. While she took part in the important political campaigns of the 1950s, heading marches against the atom bomb, demonstrating against NATO, the Korean War and the execution of the Rosenbergs, becoming a leading member of the left-wing National Council of Writers and of the Communist women's organization, she was writing novels which address political issues only obliquely, and often seem to have their thematic centre elsewhere. In 1957 *The Monument*, which defends the integrity of the artist against the Party's imperative to make art socially useful, was given a hostile reception by the Communist Left. As a political activist, Triolet's failure to speak out against Stalinism is perhaps open to criticism, but as a writer her integrity remained uncompromised.

STORIES OF EXILE

In Triolet's fiction, narrators and heroes rarely enjoy the certainty of active commitment to a political cause. Her protagonists are typically rootless, mobile and solitary, often exiled from the place or person whom they identify with home. The opening of *Bonsoir, Thérèse* introduces a perspective and a mood which inform much of Triolet's work. The anonymous narrator finds herself in the middle of a prototypically French country scene: church bell ringing, Gallic weathercock on the church roof outlined against a blue sky, village priest at his parishioners' table, talking of Joan of Arc. The narrator acknowledges her own foreignness with mild and self-derisory humour: 'I landed in this scene like a hair in the soup' (p. 7[5]). Her arrival here has resulted not from deliberate choice, but from a causality she fails to understand or control: 'One day you stayed too long in the café, or walked instead of taking the tramway, and now your life continues all askew . . .' (p. 7). Homesick and resigned, she dreams of the past and observes the present with the fascination and detachment of a stranger: 'When one is alone and a foreigner one can observe people and things well, observe them endlessly' (p. 12).

From this first work on, Triolet's fictional world is inhabited and often narrated by characters who are outsiders: foreigners, political refugees, itinerants, individuals separated from family and possessions. While the position of the outsider can provide a vantage point for observation, and an avoidance of what one hero terms the 'ready-cooked'[6] nature of a life determined by nation and family, it also generates a powerful desire to belong. 'You don't know how lucky you are', Alberto, a Spanish political refugee, tells his French friend in *Le Rendez-vous des étrangers* (The Foreigners' Meeting Place, 1956), 'to be born and to die in the same place!' (p. 7).

Triolet's own situation was in several ways that of an outsider and an exile. She was an expatriate Russian in France who, despite her strong Communist sympathies, no longer felt that she had a home in a Russia radically altered since her departure in 1917. She was Jewish, in a country with a long tradition of anti-Semitism, then under a regime that persecuted and massacred Jews. She was a Communist, in a society where the majority viewed Communists with deep suspicion. But, as earlier critics have also recognized, the sense of exile in Triolet's work is also gendered. 'The life of which she writes is dominated by a deep *malaise*,' wrote the Communist novelist Paul Nizan, in a review of *Bonsoir, Thérèse*, 'that of the [female] foreigner in Paris, that of the woman alone – and finally that of women.'[7] Jacques Madaule finds Triolet's gender central to all of her writing:

> A woman author is more or less marked by her sex. Elsa Triolet is extremely so. There is not a line of her writing which could have been written by a man. The way she views everything, and in the first place herself, is essentially feminine.[8]

Although Triolet's fiction contains male protagonists who are, in a variety of senses, exiled, the insecurity and marginality of the Triolet heroine is always in part a function of her sex. In the early, pre-Resistance fiction, Triolet's female characters are economically and emotionally vulnerable, lacking any stable sense of social identity unless this be gained, provisionally, through dependence on a man.

*Bonsoir, Thérèse* accentuates the shared and gendered nature of women's situation through its unusual narrative technique. Although it is presented as a 'novel', the book is in fact composed of a prologue, five short stories, and an epilogue, narrated by female voices which are markedly similar, since each narrator is female, young, and living alone in temporary accommodation, but also sufficiently different in tone and circumstance to throw doubt on the presence of a single, unifying narrative voice. The text is held together by the echoes and parallels between the situations of the characters, and by the device of one narrator's quest for the 'Thérèse' of the title.

The narrator of the central story, the story which gives the book its title, hears on the radio the words 'Bonsoir, Thérèse', and makes of the greeting's unknown addressee a mythical everywoman, whom she seeks in memory and imagination among women old and young, happy and unhappy, from elegant bourgeoises to prostitutes, asking of each: 'Was that Thérèse?'. The story concludes provisionally with a dream-like passage in which the search for Thérèse becomes the search for herself: 'She smiles, I see two pointed teeth. I know that beauty spot. She wears her hair like me. She has my perfume. "Bonsoir, Thérèse". It is my voice that replies' (p. 96).

With the next story, the identity of Thérèse passes to Anne Favart, who shoots the man she loves when she discovers the discrepancy between his private tenderness and his criminal activities in a right-wing cause. Anne's story in the newspapers fascinates the narrator, both because it is exceptional and because the experience of betrayal and solitude forms a link between Anne and other women: 'The story of the woman with the diamond who is not like other women and whose fate is exceptionally tragic is none the less a standard story. . . . Anne, my sister Anne . . .' (p. 97). Thereafter the identity of Thérèse passes to a series of women evoked in the Epilogue: a murderess, a woman arrested for vagrancy, a girl whose marriage plans are wrecked by an overcautious family, and finally an old woman who dies alone of hunger and neglect – stories linked by social exclusion and loneliness. The book ends on the words 'Bonsoir, Thérèse'. The passing of the name from one woman to another both accentuates their shared situation and signifies the uncertainty of female identity.

The women of *Bonsoir, Thérèse* enjoy only the most tenuous sense of a social identity, and live, for the most part, on the margins, in temporary accommodation, short of money, and under the threat of harassment and violence. The first narrator has been casually rejected by her husband and exiled to grim lodgings in an unfamiliar town, where she fills long empty days with dreams and memories. Her solitude is echoed in that of subsequent narrators: 'When you are alone, nothing comes between you and the horizon' (p. 79); her economic insecurity is reflected in that of the young woman glimpsed in a restaurant, dining in the company of an affluent man, 'a recent acquaintance': 'She would have liked to casually leave some food on her plate, but when you're eating for the past week and the next week . . .' (p. 85). As she eats, her companion 'complacently' observes her 'young, firm skin' (p. 85), quietly assured of the rights conferred by his affluence. Women's vulnerability is markedly sexual in *Bonsoir, Thérèse*, particularly in the third story, 'Seeking a Name for a Perfume'. The narrator works for a perfume company, and has been set the task of finding an original name for a new product. As she travels on the métro, she mentally pursues word-associations, but is constantly distracted by a fellow-traveller who tries to draw her into conversation, then follows her in the street. This leads in turn to memories of harassment: 'Like to have some fun with me, Mademoiselle?' (p. 67), an experience which she generalizes to the whole 'compact crowd' of women 'hurrying towards mysterious goals' and crossing the paths of 'men who are not in a hurry, and who murmur things in your ear' (p. 67). The sense of quiet menace is heightened by the detail of specific encounters: the man with 'his trousers all wrinkled between his legs' (p. 67) and the drunken passer-by who suddenly struck her hard across the calves with a walking stick ('What could I do? I sobbed all the way along the street . . . ' [p. 68]).

The muted bitterness that emerges from these episodes of rejection and sexual menace connects them to the book's positive representations of female violence. The book contains three female killers, each of them in some way celebrated rather than censured in the text. In 'Seeking a Name for a Perfume', it is humour that prevents the reader from feeling revulsion at a woman's (unexplained) decapitation of her lover. In a scene that neatly integrates the comic and the macabre, the presence of her lover's head in the murderess's shopping basket is revealed when blood drips on to a fellow passenger's knees, but the red splashes and the woman's cry – 'My lover's head!' – at last provide the narrator with inspiration for her perfume brand-name: 'Poppy heads!'. In 'The Woman with the Diamond', Anne Favart's shooting of her lover is both explained and legitimated by the preceding narrative, so that the reader's sympathies are with the killer. Violette Nozières – who, like Anne, haunts the narrator's imagination and is celebrated as a 'tender criminal' (p. 155) – was the heroine of a real-life *fait divers* in 1930s France, the daughter of an apparently respectable family who poisoned her parents. Condemned in the press as a 'monster' and an example of the morally degenerate 'modern girl',[9] Nozières figures here as another dramatic image of a woman whose violent act expresses a collective sense of alienation and anger: 'What could she possibly fear now, what evil could still befall her? She has made her journey to the end of the night. The judge doesn't even know there is a night . . .' (p. 159).

What connects the women of *Bonsoir, Thérèse* and many of Triolet's subsequent heroines is the fact that they live outside the institutions of marriage, home and family which would provisionally legitimize their existence as women and integrate them into society. In the 1930s, high rates of unemployment and the perceived need to raise the birth rate had led to an increasing emphasis in the press and in political discourse on women's maternal and domestic role. Under the Vichy government, what had been uncoordinated expressions of opinion gained the status of official ideology. Motherhood was publicly rewarded, abortion was criminalized, and the single or childless woman became a potential emblem of that decadent and selfish past which Vichy held responsible for France's defeat. Both in the prewar *Bonsoir, Thérèse* and in the stories in *Mille regrets* (A Thousand Regrets), published in 1942, the isolation of Triolet's heroines arises in part from public disapproval of their way of life.

The narrator of the first story in *Mille regrets*, separated from her lover by the defeat and invasion of 1940, and struggling to survive on her last few francs in Nice, reflects that 'There is no age at which a woman is allowed to live alone' (p. 11[10]): 'A woman on her own is always suspect. People think it just isn't done, that a family is obligatory. I don't know how to apologize for such bad form . . .' (p. 18). Charlotte, narrator of 'Le Destin personnel' ('Personal Destiny' in the volume *Mille regrets*), begins the story in the winter of 1940–41 sharing her Paris apartment with her mother, her brother-in-law, and his wife and child. The domestic discomforts this entails range from permanently damp towels and washing soaking in the bathroom, to sleeping on the hard sofa, but as a childless woman whose husband is a prisoner of war Charlotte is assumed to be willing to sacrifice herself. 'I have no children', she comments wryly. 'A woman without children is a monster, a sort of hermaphrodite' (p. 172).

Triolet's female protagonists are thus exiled not only in the sense that they are separated from whatever they perceive as home – be it country, family or lover – but also because as women, particularly single and childless women, they are internal exiles, excluded from full membership of the community. Michel, hero of Triolet's picaresque portrayal of the interwar period, *The White Horse* (1943), is also in many senses an exile, lacking family, national identity, and any sense of a collectively shared past and future. Yet his status as a single man, attractive to women, represents for Michel a form of freedom, for it allows him to move from place to place and job to job, and to be fed, cared for and loved by a series of female partners. In the case of female characters, we have seen that to be desirable can intensify solitude by creating the fear of sexual violence or exploitation. Conversely, female youth and beauty can also provide a provisional form of legitimacy, a social capital which can earn male protection and admiration, hence material security and a recognized identity. But where Michel's beauty merely gives an added dimension to his social mobility, single female characters depend on the fragile asset of their looks and youth to preserve both material and emotional security. Thus in Triolet's early fiction there is a terrible fear of female ageing.

In *Bonsoir, Thérèse* and *Mille regrets*, to age means to be doomed for ever to the invisibility and social exclusion of the woman who can no longer provoke desire. Women conceal the signs of age behind cosmetic masks: 'lashes stiffly laden with mascara, too pale foundation and a dark-red mouth almost black against the white skin' (BT, p. 85). The narrator of 'Mille regrets' fears that she has already lost her youth and become invisible:

When I was young and penniless, I had the luxury of my youth.
I could, for example, choose any man I wanted. . . . . . .

And, then, I don't know how or when, but the current was
no longer there. There was no longer anything passing between
the world and me. I feel like a shadow among the living – not
a ghost yet, but a shadow. (pp. 34–5)

Although she discovers that the lover she believed dead is on his
way to find her, she kills herself, unable to bear the thought that his
first look at her might reveal her loss of beauty. Neither wives nor
mothers, Triolet's early heroines can maintain their fragile sense of
identity only through the certainty that they are physically worthy
of desire.

The fiction is haunted by spectres of lonely and eccentric old
women who have neither an economic nor a social role to play,
but exist on the margins of society. In *Bonsoir, Thérèse*, it is the
'poor, ugly, old' pair of women who can always be seen at the
fashionable Dôme café in Paris with their permed, bleached hair
and velvet neck ribbons, greeted by all and talked to by none:

One gave some sort of private lessons, the other did some
drawing. They sat there with a coffee in front of them and
avidly searched the room with their eyes. And when they did
manage to catch someone it was terrible . . .

I used to say: 'I'm like them, I shall be like those women'.
(p. 83)

The rich old lady at the hotel glimpsed in 'The Woman with
the Diamond' is a more nightmarish figure. Entering the text
at the height of Anne Favart's passionate, tender relationship
with Jean, she implies the fragility of that happiness, and the
transience of the physical beauty with which feminine identity
is so closely identified. Her fashionable clothes sit absurdly on a
bent old body, her face is horribly scarred from a failed attempt
at cosmetic surgery, she is dependent on the care of paid servants.
In the epilogue to *Bonsoir, Thérèse* an unnamed woman – clearly
linked to Anne Favart both by their deep-blue eyes and by their
sable coats – ages until her skull can be seen beneath a scalp 'like
an old wedding glove yellowed in a drawer' (p. 168). She dies
of hunger and poverty in an empty rented room. The simile of

the wedding glove links her, too, to the old woman in 'Mille regrets', who parades along the seafront dressed, like Dickens's Miss Havisham, in her ancient bridal clothes and a tattered veil. In 'Notebooks Buried under a Peach Tree' the village madwoman stalks the countryside screaming obscenities at passers-by, in a permanent rage at the infidelities of her dead husband and her own abandonment.

STORIES OF RESISTANCE

The exile's dream of belonging is a powerful theme throughout Triolet's work. Between the 1930s and 1950s the state of exile was shared by many on the Left: the cast of her novels includes political refugees from Hitler's Germany and Franco's Spain, and victims of the McCarthy era in the USA. Michel Vigault, in *The White Horse* (1943), which Triolet called 'the most autobiographical of my novels', wanders between countries and relationships in search of a past and a future which will give his life meaning. In *Le Rendez-vous des étrangers* (1956) the anxiety of dispossession, shared by political refugees and stateless persons, is contrasted with the warm bustle of life in the extended Grammont clan, rooted for generations in the same small French provincial town.

The state of exile, composed of nostalgia for a real or imagined home and a sense of exclusion from the society one lives in, is intensified in the case of those characters who are not only foreigners but also women, like the narrator of *Bonsoir, Thérèse*, and Olga in the postwar *Le Rendez-vous des étrangers*. But the insecurity and uncertainty of belonging engendered by exile also characterize many of the women protagonists who are French by birth. Unless they are legitimized by marriage and motherhood, like the female members of the Grammont clan, women have only a tenuous place in the social structure – the precariousness of their position signified variously in the novels by their lack of financial resources, their provisional accommodation, their social isolation and their clinging on, to the point of madness, to the signifiers of an acceptable femininity. It is in Triolet's Resistance fiction that women find a surer sense of identity and belonging. From her first publication in French, *Bonsoir, Thérèse*, Triolet had always to some extent balanced the themes of isolation and exclusion against those of community and solidarity. Despite the thematic emphasis on solitude and exile, there are indications in *Bonsoir, Thérèse* of a collective dilemma, which could unite the dispossessed in a community of opposition. We have already seen that across the book as a whole, at a textual level, the narrator's reflections and the analogies between the many female stories develop an implied ethos of female solidarity. The second story, 'Paris qui rêve' ('Paris Dreaming'), is the most explicitly political, if the least concerned with gender, for the narrator recounts the brutal police repression of a workers' demonstration in Paris, shifting the emphasis from the narratorial 'I' to the scene and event observed, so that the spotlight falls directly on the affluent and complacent city, protected by mounted police in black steel helmets – 'Cast-iron men, with cast-iron brains and steel bullets . . . ' (p. 49) – opposed to the demonstrators who are charged and batoned into silence, but regroup to rescue their own: 'A man all alone in the deserted street clutches his head in both hands. . . . The blood flows from a great wound on his forehead. But the shadows return: "Comrades!"' (p. 49).

The cause of the demonstration is unspecified and the narrator's sympathies are implied rather than stated, largely through the contrast between images of cold brutality and voices of fraternity. Yet this story has implications for the meaning of the book as a whole, for it specifies that the society which marginalizes or destroys the different incarnations of 'Thérèse' is a society founded on the defence of class as well as gender privilege, and that collective resistance, if not always successful, is possible.

In the texts written under the Occupation, the polarity between isolation and communal resistance becomes – not surprisingly – more marked and more central, and the choice for or against resistance to the Nazis becomes a clear indicator of a character's ethical status. In the story 'Henri Castellat' (in *Mille regrets*), the moral inadequacy of the central character takes the form of a refusal of commitment which is emotional, aesthetic and finally political. Castellat's failure to reach outside himself sufficiently to risk the words 'I love you', or to commit himself by writing, predetermine his political stance when he is faced with war against Nazi Germany: he deserts his compatriots and opts instead for a career move to the United States. The story's conclusion is voiced by the woman he failed to love, who declares him 'Too cowardly to love, too cowardly to create, too cowardly to defend his skin except by running away' (p. 34). Conversely, the heroic status of Michel Vigault in *The White Horse* is confirmed by his death on the battlefield during the Nazi invasion of France, and by his composition of a marching song which, it is implied, will become a Resistance anthem.

As in other fiction which deals with this period – for example, Simone de Beauvoir's *The Blood of Others*, or Jean-Paul Sartre's trilogy *The Roads to Freedom* – the war and Occupation simplify ethical and political dilemmas, and permit a neat closure of narratives through the protagonists' choice of Resistance, a choice which often neatly unifies the personal and the political.

For Triolet's protagonists, joining the Resistance frequently means exchanging the isolation of exile for the community of a common struggle. As the eponymous hero of the story ironically entitled 'The Private Life of Alexis Slavsky, Painter'[11] discovers, under the Occupation it is no longer possible to maintain a distinction between one's personal destiny and political events. History enters Alexis's life by forcing him to leave Paris and go into hiding to escape the anti-Semitic policies of the Nazis – for Alexis has a Jewish grandmother. In a series of rented houses and rooms, Alexis tries to re-create his inner world in his paintings, but history will not be excluded. Acquaintances are arrested and executed, the apartment he shares with his wife is searched by the Vichy police. Alexis can no longer see private houses as defences against the world outside:

> He gazed at the houses in mortal anguish; these fortresses of privacy were no more inviolable than the shells of snails. They were as open to the winds as those half-demolished houses into which everyone can look and see the wallpaper and the lay-out of the rooms. (p. 101)

Alexis is gradually drawn into the orbit of the Resistance, discovering both the joy of comradeship and renewed inspiration for his painting.

In the case of female protagonists, the Resistance provides a community in whose aims and activities women can fully share. The normal rules of intersex relations are modified or suspended, and Triolet's Resistance heroines are markedly different from their pre-Resistance sisters. Juliette Noël, in 'Les Amants d'Avignon' ('The Lovers of Avignon', 1943), superficially shares the character-istics of Triolet's women in exile, for she is single, poor, frequently condemned to find temporary and uncomfortable accommodation. But Juliette is working for the Resistance, and is thus a member of a beleaguered but committed and purposeful community. Triolet gives her a secure home to return to between her travels, and a family composed of an elderly aunt and an adopted child, himself orphaned by the Spanish Civil War but saved from solitude by Juliette. On her journeys through France, carrying information between Resistance groups, Juliette is often cold and tired, but she is not isolated, for she shares fully in the muted chorus of dissent that underlies apparent obedience to the German forces and the Vichy state, and she knows that she forms part of a mutually supportive network of Resistance.

Louise, protagonist in 'The Private Life of Alexis Slavsky, Painter' and narrator of the following story, 'Notebooks Buried under a Peach Tree',[12] is also a Resister who superficially resembles Triolet's prewar heroines. Like the first narrator of *Bonsoir, Thérèse*, she has Triolet's own past of a Russian childhood and adolescence; she has lived alone in foreign cities, nostalgic for the 'landscape loved in childhood [which] speaks the true language of the heart' (p. 199); war has separated her from the man she loved. Yet from the perspective of involvement in the struggle against oppression, France becomes not just a land of exile but an alternative home-land. Louise remembers the glorious landscapes of her past:

> And then I look at the landscape before my eyes, sucked bare as a fishbone by the winter, the light mist in the thin poplars . . . and almost feel ashamed of the splendours that stuff my head, as though I had come into this village decked out in velvet and satin, ostrich plumes. (p. 199)

Although Louise is captured and – the reader must assume – killed at the end of the story, it is a far less bleak ending than that of *Bonsoir, Thérèse* or 'Mille regrets'. Louise's life has had a purpose and contributed to a cause, and her voice survives in the notebooks she has buried under a peach tree, to be retrieved and read by Jean, whom she loved, and by Alexis Slavsky, whom she desired.

In his own story, Alexis Slavsky is drawn into the Resistance through his friendship for and attraction towards Louise. Her first-person narrative in the 'Notebooks' is thus connected to the preceding story, and finds an admiring and affectionate first reader in Alexis. This reduces the lonely singularity of the first person which characterized Triolet's earlier writing. Indeed, unlike the stories of exile, the texts which foreground resistance tend to employ third-person narration, laying the emphasis less on subjectivity than on action and relationship. Although the use of free indirect style allows for the representation of protagonists' characteristic vision and discourse, the third person also permits the articulation of a primary form of solidarity, that between narrator and character, for Juliette Noël, Alexis Slavsky and the hero of *The White Horse* (1943) are all treated affectionately by a narrator who is clearly in sympathy with their values.

In the title story of the collection *A Fine of Two Hundred Francs*, this solidarity is further marked by the merging of the narrator's voice into the collective voice of the community engaged in Resistance. The story is set in the last days of the Occupation, just before the Normandy landings, and begins: 'Everything's in a terrible mess: railways, the minds of men, and food supplies . . . ', the paragraph ending with a revealing first-person plural 'Those who fight, and those who help the fighters, and those who tremble – all of us are waiting' (p. 262).

In a village in an unspecified part of France, the radio in the bistro, tuned to the BBC, transmits the coded call to action: 'A fine of two hundred francs for the first rip'. The village, led by the local Maquis, throws itself into preparation for the Allies' arrival, receiving parachute drops of officers and material, stacking and preparing weapons, the whole population – with the exception of those who have collaborated and who are excluded from the occasion – happy and excited. The narration employs a collective free indirect style, attributing sensations and sentiments to the community as a whole, as in the moment where the parachutes float down:

> Suddenly black spots appeared, like the spots that float before your eyes when your liver is out of order . . . still they floated there, lower and lower, closer and closer. They were just overhead, they would fall on you! (p. 176)

The mood is broken by the news that the Germans are marching on the village in force. The devastation of the village, the murder of its inhabitants and rape of girls and women, is rendered the more horrible by its contrast with the shared optimism of the preceding scene, and by the narrative perspective that places the reader within the destroyed community.

There is little marking of gender in such stories. Participation in the Resistance challenges essentialist definitions of gender identity in more than one way. First, the struggle demands strengths and skills excluded by traditional concepts of the feminine. Triolet's work emphasizes prewar assumptions about the incompatibility between femininity and politics. Anne Favart (the 'Femme aux diamants' in *Bonsoir, Thérèse*) is slow to realize that she cannot tolerate her lover's ranting condemnations of Jews and Communists, and that her own integrity is at stake in the choice between acceptance or refusal of his views, because she has internalized the dissociation between women and political values: 'When it comes to the things newspapers are concerned with, women generally don't think anything at all at first – then they start to have the same opinion as their men' (p. 40). When, in the prewar France of *Personne ne m'aime*[13] (No one Loves Me, 1946), Anne-Marie discovers that her friend Jenny is actively engaged in politics, she is shocked and repeatedly distances herself from this 'unnatural' behaviour: 'I don't understand anything about it, I never think about politics. It's not a matter for women' (p. 35). But when they choose to resist, at the risk of their lives, Triolet's heroines actively demonstrate that politics *is* a matter for women.

Juliette Noël is carefully established in the opening chapter of 'The Lovers of Avignon'[14] as a conventionally feminine woman, 'as alluring as a typist in a film', with her 'silken hair, long lashes, and a kind of natural elegance in her close-fitting pullover, her very short skirt, and very high heels' (p. 7). The narrative then shifts abruptly to a freezing, rat-infested ruin of a farmhouse where Juliette has slept during her travels as a Resistance courier, and from where she sets off on long journeys to carry messages and seek new contacts to extend the underground network. Tough, astute and committed, Juliette's character belies the implications of her appearance. In *Personne ne m'aime*, Anne-Marie's acceptance of the apolitical nature of femininity is implicitly contrasted with her courage and conviction, once the necessity of Resistance is accepted. Drawn into the Communist Resistance partly through Jenny's friends, Anne-Marie accepts and continues the political mission which she has failed to understand during her friend's lifetime.

The assumption that women were by nature apolitical and fragile could be exploited by using their femininity to divert suspicion. Clandestine activity made use of femininity as a form of disguise, divorcing the signifiers of gender from the identity to which they conventionally refer. Juliette is an effective courier because her glamorous appearance dissociates her from the world of sabotage and struggle, so that when she enters a hotel with a man, even the Gestapo are willing to believe that the clandestine rendezvous was sexual, not political – an error which allows both her own escape and that of her contact. To save the life of a young comrade arrested by the Vichyite police, Anne-Marie puts on a hat and 'her most ladylike air' (p. 192), and goes to visit the local Prefect, brother of her dead friend Jenny but now an enthusiastic collaborationist. Anne-Marie's beauty, together with her faultless playing of her prewar persona, allow her to ask for the boy's release without arousing any suspicion of her motives. In 'Notebooks Buried under a Peach Tree' Louise employs a similar strategy, concealing her Resistance activities behind a 'curtain of lies' (p. 221) composed of elegant clothes and an apparently frivolous lifestyle.

The involvement of women in Resistance activity alters the terms of their relationship with men. In the texts written or set in the pre-Occupation period, all love stories end in failure or death, as if women's marginal status precluded a lasting emotional and sexual alliance. Of the women in *Bonsoir, Thérèse*, only Anne Favart becomes involved in a passionate and mutual relationship with a man, but this only intensifies the pain of her disillusionment. Each of the stories in the volume *Mille regrets* – published in 1942 but containing no reference to Resistance – foregrounds loss and betrayal: two end in the suicide of unhappy women, one in the female narrator's attempted murder of an unfaithful partner, the fourth – 'Henri Castellat' – with the condemnation of Castellat's cowardice and moral impotence by the woman who loved him. The Resistance stories, by suspending women's exile, introduce the possibility of love without betrayal, even though, ironically, the mobile and precarious lives of the protagonists preclude sustained relationships.

Louise, narrator of 'Notebooks Buried under a Peach Tree', loses Jean only because he is arrested and imprisoned, his fidelity being signified to the reader after her death by his recuperation of the title's notebooks. In *Personne ne m'aime*, Anne-Marie's only experience of intense love and desire occurs at the height of her involvement in Resistance activities, and ends not with betrayal or desertion by her lover but with his death in combat.

The narrative which centres most clearly on love, as the title suggests, is 'The Lovers of Avignon'. Juliette arrives in Avignon on Christmas Eve, to warn the local Resistance that six Avignon railwaymen are about to be arrested. In place of the dreary cold of most of her journeys, she finds herself in front of a roaring fire in the ancestral home of Célestin, leader of the local Maquis, whose romantic appearance – he has 'the head of an archangel, sombre, fallen' (p. 35) – and lyrical monologue on Avignon as a city of love lend the episode the perfection of fantasy. Juliette proposes a game: '"Let's pretend we're lovers. . . . The way we used to play at visiting, or going to the doctor. Everything is *as if*, you know –"' (p. 35). As the couple wander through Avignon on a 'white and starry' Christmas Day, with church bells ringing, a series of non-intentional verb forms ('they found themselves', 'they were caught up in') intensifies the sense of a dream unfolding. Even the grim walls of the prison cell in the old Fort bear inscriptions that signify the presence of past lovers, and the reality of the Occupation is forgotten in an interlude of intense and timeless happiness: 'The air, the stone, the sun, the grass underfoot, the wind, didn't even try to appear innocuous. They asserted their magic power, which caught and held these two' (p. 38). The interlude ends after they have eaten Célestin's 'most treasured stores' of food, in this period of shortages, and danced to the radio 'madly, foolishly gay' (p. 38), when a message comes that Célestin must return to his group, and Juliette sets off again on the cold, crowded night trains. The sound of German boots marching through the streets reasserts the reality of place and time. Avignon ceases to be Célestin's 'holy, satanic town, dedicated to miracles and sorcery' (p. 34) or the narrator's 'high-walled city, reaching towards heaven' (p. 37), and becomes an occupied city: the words 'Avignon was a German town . . . ' (p. 45) close this section of the story.

The relationship between Juliette and Célestin ends almost

before it has begun – not because of rejection or betrayal, but because of external constraints which are equally real to each partner. If the entire episode is cast in the style of dream or fantasy, this is both because the material conditions of life in the Resistance render relationships practically impossible, and because the narration of the love affair as fantasy emphasizes the incompatibility between loving relationships and the harsh regime of the Occupation. In the story, the Occupying forces and their French collaborators are represented by the grim anonymity of marching boots, the constant threat of brutality, the sinister Gestapo agents who try to use Juliette to capture Célestin. The existing order is clearly antithetical to the aspirations to love and freedom contained in the Juliette/Célestin meeting.

For all its unreality and enforced brevity, though, the relationship has qualities which the pre-Resistance texts exclude. Triolet insistently maintains Juliette as an ordinary *petite bourgeoise* of her time, whose cultural reference points are the songs of Edith Piaf and the films of Gary Cooper and Charles Boyer, and whose place of refuge, after the abrupt ending of her story with Célestin, is the cinema. The class difference between herself and the patrician Célestin, though, is erased by their equality as combatants in the same struggle, just as gender inequalities are minimized by the exceptional circumstances. Paradoxically, the specific situation of the Resistance makes love between men and women possible, even as it demands a degree of commitment incompatible with the pursuit of personal happiness.

After the war, however, inequalities suspended in the struggle against a common enemy return, and in Triolet's fiction the aftermath of victory is bleak. Célestin, hero of 'The Lovers of Avignon', reappears in the 1947 novel *Les Fantômes armés*,[15] and it is he who voices most clearly the mood of the whole book: "'You know as I do that the show is over. None of what we dreamed will happen. . . . We have given the best of ourselves for nothing'" (p. 64). Célestin himself, though, is now part of the problem. The alliance between the Gaullist nationalists of the Centre and Right, and the Communist Resistance, with its working-class base, soon broke down after the Liberation, and in *Les Fantômes armés* the patrician Célestin is part of a right-wing conspiracy to overthrow the Fourth Republic, and of a much wider backlash against the

Communists, whose patriotism is rapidly forgotten in fear of the threat they pose to the economic and social order. Heroes of the Communist Maquis are charged with 'crimes' committed as part of the Resistance struggle, and imprisoned, and one major strand of the plot concerns Anne-Marie's campaign to release her ex-comrades. Her affair with Célestin fails to develop into love partly because she sees him as her political enemy.

In a scene that retraces the central sequence of 'The Lovers of Avignon', Anne-Marie and Célestin wander through the city, but this time the magic is absent. Célestin and Juliette were united by their common struggle, their emotions intensified by the fragility of the moment. Célestin and Anne-Marie are separated by class, by political convictions, and by his possessiveness, for the relationship ends after Célestin attempts to keep Anne-Marie sequestered, against her will, at his country house. Along with the re-establishment of class and political boundaries, assumptions about the nature and capacities of women re-emerge after the relative equality of the Resistance. Yves de Fonterolles, a young Gaullist captain at the Liberation and now deeply suspicious of Communism, finds it hard to believe that the elegant Anne-Marie could have been an active member of the Resistance: 'Strange, the idea that this woman with her jewels and perfume, her shiny hair and slim waist, did "things" in the maquis . . .' (p. 81). He also finds the idea distasteful: '"I don't like Amazons or female adventurers"' (p. 85).

Those Triolet heroines who took part in Resistance are changed by it, in the sense that they are no longer financially, emotionally or politically subordinate. The middle-aged Anne-Marie of *Les Fantômes armés* (1947), like Olga in *Le Rendez-vous des étrangers*[16] (1956), lives on her earnings (she is a photographer), takes the initiative in sexual encounters, and shows no anxiety about the ageing process. Triolet also has this previously apolitical character assert women's political rights and responsibilities, in an angry response to a friend's declaration of indifference to her newly won right to vote:

'Women', said Anne-Marie, red-faced, 'have borne the brunt of the Occupation for five years . . ., they've shivered in queues and carried guns in their bodices and pamphlets in

their babies' prams. . . . The men come back and start telling
them what a great soldier Pétain was! And you don't want to
vote!' (pp. 167–8)

To this extent Resistance breeds resistance, and Triolet's postwar
heroines emerge from their author's and their own wartime
experience with a strengthened sense of identity. Yet women
return to the place of the exile within the texts, connected
to the society they live in neither by family, nor by durable
relationships, nor by any permanent residence, and marked by
a powerful sense of estrangement which empties the world of
meaning:

She had tried all the usual answers, she'd taken a lover, she'd
worked, she'd tried to become interested in the happiness or
unhappiness of mankind. And they must have been the right
answers, they must have worked – if only you could feel some
love for love, for work, for humanity. (p. 325)

Thus Anne-Marie reviews her unsuccessful attempts to achieve
social integration through love, through work or through political
commitment. Olga, Russian by birth and thus doubly an exile, was
also a heroine of the Resistance, but finds the return to peace
equally painful:

At the moment when others were emerging from the night and
shadows, she was going – or rather, returning – further into the
darkness.
    She had returned to a life alone and without love. (p. 125)

This emphasis on postwar alienation is in part Triolet's articulation
of the disillusionment of the Left, as dreams forged in the struggle
against Nazism faded into the Cold War and, in France, Resistance
idealism was replaced by technocracy, consumerism and the
reinstatement of the Right. But within the logic of Triolet's
work it can also be argued that the return to exile is a metaphor
for the situation of women. In the fiction, the brief intensity of
the Occupation years suspends women's inferior, marginal status.
They return to a peacetime world more assured of their right to
political and social equality, but uncertain that participation in the
political process or in employment can confer the legitimacy they

lack, or provide the figurative home of which they feel themselves dispossessed.

In Triolet's subsequent fiction, which is wide-ranging in theme and form, female protagonists continue to have a fragile and tenuous sense of where they belong in society. Martine, for example, heroine of *Roses à crédit*[17] (1959), starts the novel as 'Martine-lost-in-the-woods' and embraces the role of female consumer with such obsessive passion that she destroys the emotional and social security she has built, and ends the novel returned to the forest, beyond the city walls, where she dies alone.

I have argued that exile is one of the central themes and metaphors of Triolet's fiction, particularly of those texts written or set in the pre- and postwar period. The state of exile brings together all those who, in the mid twentieth century, were dispossessed of their homelands by the victories of political regimes they opposed. It also stands, metaphorically, for the situation of women, internal exiles in a society which offers them no place of their own, but only a provisional legitimacy conferred by male desire or by the role of wife and mother.

Resistance, too, functions both as a historical event represented within the plot, often serving to resolve the dilemmas of exile, and as an image of the state of belonging which is precisely what exile negates. Triolet's heroines do not emerge from their author's experience of Resistance, and in many cases their own, into a brave new world where the dreams forged during the struggle are realized, although they do have a strengthened sense of identity which partially withstands the return to isolation. Structurally, women continue to occupy the place of the exile in Triolet's postwar texts, their connection to the social order remaining tenuous. The idea of solidarity between women is less an element of plot than it is present at a textual level, through narrative sympathy and the elaboration within and between texts of a shared female story. Exile and resistance work as the twin polarities of the Triolet texts discussed here, and provide a compelling metaphor for the situation of women in mid-twentieth-century France.

# PART III
## 1958–94

# 10
# Women in French Society 1958–94

In the century that separated the short-lived Second Republic
(1848–51) from the birth of the Fifth Republic in 1958, French
women had progressed from a position of total legal and civil
incapacity to one of partial, if often merely theoretical, equality.
Where feminist demands converged with what governments
perceived as the country's broader interests, rights had been
extended to women: access to education, the right to vote and
to a degree of economic independence within marriage. The Fifth
Republic replaced the Fourth when Charles de Gaulle, invited
back to power by a regime in crisis over the Algerian war, made
it a condition of his acceptance that he be allowed to draw up a
new, more presidential Constitution. The new Republic was to
be the scene of radical and widespread feminist campaigns and
achievements, so that in 1994 the feminist writer Elisabeth Badinter
could argue that French women had 'nothing left to demand from
a legal point of view'. In France, she went on, women were now
equipped with 'an arsenal of very powerful egalitarian laws in all the
relevant areas'.[1]

Equality before the law, however, is far from synonymous with
effective social equality, and the story of French women under the
Fifth Republic is not only one of legal victories. That configuration
of gender which is, at least in part, specific to French culture
continued to shape debates and conflicts over women's lives.
French anti-feminism had always shown a particularly intense
allegiance to the theory of fundamental sexual difference. As
we have seen, feminism has often been resisted in France on
the grounds of the need to respect and maintain the distinct and
complementary nature of masculinity and femininity, for each of
these elements has its separate part to play in the delineation of a
specifically French national identity. Apart from the straightforward
defence of patriarchal interests, the anxiety over difference seemed

to be fuelled both by a concern for the survival of 'Frenchness' and by fear that women's abandonment of traditionally feminine roles would mean the loss of all those human qualities assigned to the female sex. This latter fear, as my analysis of women's writing has shown, motivated not only phallocentric opposition to feminism but also, in some instances, women's own reservations about feminist goals.

The 1970s and 1980s were the scene not only of a continuing struggle between feminists and the defenders of a version of gender difference indistinguishable from male supremacy, but also of a conflict between two diverging tendencies within feminism itself. One (minority) current of feminism has declared indifference to the struggle for equality within existing society – that is, to mini-mizing the differences which disadvantage women – and shifted its ground to the promotion of a model of radical sexual difference, demanding that women explore and celebrate a femininity which patriarchy has repressed and silenced. This tension – at times an outright conflict – over different concepts of what constitutes the liberation of women is complex and by no means reducible to a simple binary opposition. Its presence will shape and inform this third part of the book.


In Christiane Rochefort's wonderfully satirical *Les Stances à Sophie* (Stanzas to Sophie), the heroine, Céline, confronts the problem of difference. In marrying the deeply conformist young executive Philippe, Céline finds herself in an intimate confrontation with the hegemonic values of 1960s French society. One of Philippe's favourite tactics, in what rapidly becomes the war between them, is to define Céline authoritatively as 'a woman': 'You drink too much for a woman',[2] and 'I know what is best in you – the fact that you are a woman'.[3] It is imperative, the novel makes clear, that Céline extricate herself from this definition, whose function is to police her behaviour and exclude her from the pleasures and rights assigned to men. On the other hand, Philippe's masculine world of mindless economic expansion (he works for the State Planning Department), fast cars and the pursuit of status hardly invites any desire for inclusion, and Céline's identity as a woman must be defined by opposition, not emulation. She must refuse to be 'a woman', but also insist on being 'a woman'. Céline's dilemma, the resolution of which makes up the narrative, provides an image for the situation of contemporary feminists – and particularly French feminists.

WOMEN IN DE GAULLE'S REPUBLIC

Despite France's rapid economic expansion in the 1950s, the Fourth Republic suffered from severe political instability, and failed to find a coherent policy when it was faced with crisis in Algeria. Fear that the French government might negotiate the colony's independence with the nationalist guerrilla FLN (Front de Libération Nationale) led to insurrection by right-wing French Algerians, and it was to solve this crisis that de Gaulle, who had withdrawn from political life, was voted back in to power on 1 June 1958. De Gaulle thus reappeared on the political stage in the role of heroic saviour, the father who had once before known best and salvaged the nation's honour. The new Constitution strengthened his own role as President, a shift of power reinforced in 1962 when, having successfully ended the war by negotiating Algeria's independence, de Gaulle had the French ratify by referendum the system of presidential election by universal suffrage. His style continued to be that of the wise father/husband, a masculine figure of authority, often seen in military uniform, controlling and guiding a beloved, feminine nation towards the path he knew to be right: he described himself as 'Head of State and the Guide of France',[4] and after his death in 1970 France was described by more than one commentator as a 'widow'. The Father whose Law is implicit in all patriarchal societies was in a sense made flesh in de Gaulle.

Economic expansion continued in the early years of the new Republic, the rise in productivity peaking in 1967–8 with an increase of 10.4 per cent.[5] Of the six EEC countries, France had the highest rate of economic growth. A system of central economic planning determined national priorities for redevelopment, with the emphasis in the 1950s on taking industry to the regions and improving housing. Car ownership rocketed, until by 1973 63 per cent of French families owned a vehicle. Since posts in middle management doubled between 1954 and 1975,[6] this was the era of the 'jeune cadre' or young executive, the well-educated, smartly dressed young manager, dedicated to efficiency, progress and his own self-advancement, beloved of the advertisers and satirized by Christiane Rochefort in the handsome but obnoxious character of Philippe Aignan, antihero of *Les Stances à Sophie*. Philippe, who represents the dominant values of a regime and an era, appropriately ends the novel as a Right-Wing Majority candidate for the National Assembly.

The wife or sister of the 'jeune cadre' was unlikely to be engaged in a similarly dynamic career, or to be on her way to Parliament. Although the most anachronistic aspects of the Napoleonic Code were finally ended by the 1965 law which gave married women the right to practise a profession or open a bank account without their husband's consent, and although girls took increasing advantage of educational opportunities so that by 1968 there were almost as many girls as boys passing the *baccalauréat* and going on to university,[7] the decade preceding 1968 still offered very different lives for men and women.

The 1920 anti-contraception law remained in force until 1967, when the *loi Neuwirth* finally made it legal to provide or obtain contraception under certain strictly regulated conditions. Pronatalist propaganda continued to encourage women to have large families, and the high postwar birth rate began to fall gradually only in the 1960s. If cars and leisure pursuits were the masculine face of the consumer society, household gadgets and beauty products were women's share, and 1960s advertising presented technology's 'liberation' of women from household chores as a chance for them to do more shopping and devote more time to achieving a properly feminine elegance.[8]

In the USA and Britain, 1960s rock 'n' roll was chiefly performed by male idols and consumed by adoring girls, but there were figures like Janis Joplin, Joan Baez, even Marianne Faithfull, who were a part of the sexual excitement and social rebellion rock represented. In France rock was softened to 'yé-yé', and the cute mini-skirts and bland lyrics of a Sheila or a Sylvie Vartan lacked even the ambivalent sexiness of Bardot in the 1950s.

The percentage of the female population reckoned to be economically active had been in decline in France since after the First World War, and reached its nadir in 1962 (27.6 per cent) before beginning a slow return to the level of 1906 (36 per cent, reached again in the early 1980s).[9] And the structure of employment followed the familiar pattern of the pyramid, with women concentrated at the base and increasingly scarce as status and pay improved: in the private sector in 1968 women formed 1 per cent of senior management but 60 per cent of semi-skilled office workers.[10] In politics, by 1958 the 42 women elected to the National Assembly in 1946 were reduced to 8, and the number of female Senators had shrunk from 19 to 6.

As Claire Duchen demonstrates convincingly in *Women's Rights and Women's Lives in France 1944–1968*, feminism did not disappear in the first ten years of the Fifth Republic, but – Beauvoir's *The Second Sex* notwithstanding – the identification of female virtues and aspirations with home and motherhood still went largely unchallenged. Women's groups, female sections of political parties and trade unions, on the whole restricted their demands to the reform of the marriage laws and the liberalization of legislation on abortion and contraception.[11]

MAY 1968

The heroes and villains of the May '68 rebellion were all male, from the student leaders who led the great marches through Paris (Daniel Cohn-Bendit, Jacques Sauvageot, Alain Geismar) to the politicians of both government and opposition who resisted this challenge to the fundamental structures and values of French society. But many women took part in the demonstrations, occupations and debates that filled those weeks, and from this brief period of imaginative contestation a renewed feminist movement was to emerge.

The causes, events and significance of May '68, including its relevance for French feminism, have been amply explored elsewhere.[12] Factors which contributed to the mood of angry protest ranged from outrage at American policies in Vietnam to frustration with the inadequate conditions in French universities. The Algerian war had already demonstrated the division between the established parties of the Left in France, including the Communist Party, and their more radical youth and student wings. While the official Left kept its options open, the student groups demonstrated unconditional support for the Algerian liberation army, and protested against French repression. It was an act of protest against the Vietnam War, and the arrest of the activist concerned, which led to a protest meeting at Nanterre University and the formation of the 'March 22nd group', which was to feature prominently in subsequent events.

At the same time, students were frustrated in their everyday lives by the overcrowding, rigid power structures and unimaginative pedagogy of French higher education. Since Beauvoir's era, when a small (and largely male) student elite inhabited a quaintly Bohemian Latin quarter and were taught by the most respected intellectuals of the day, student numbers had rocketed, and neither material infrastructure nor teaching techniques had kept pace with the change. In 1930–31, the year after Beauvoir completed her *agrégation*, there were 78,324 students in French universities, of whom 21 per cent were women. By 1946 the numbers had risen to 123,000 , and by 1968, with the postwar baby boom generation now of university age, to 514,000, of whom almost half were women. The new campuses, like Nanterre, built outside Paris to accommodate the overspill, were bleak and badly equipped. One of the students' recurring complaints was over the issue of sexual repression, for regulations kept male and female students in strictly segregated halls of residence. Refusal of the social policing of sexual desire was an important strand in the May protests, though it was initially cast in essentially male terms, as a slogan scrawled on the walls of the Institut d'Etudes Politiques demonstrates: 'Girls: don't drive men to alienation! Offer yourselves to the Revolution!'[13]

The phenomenon now simply referred to as 'May '68' escalated from student protests and demonstrations concerning both university reform and wider political issues, through the anger generated by brutal police repression, to a nationwide period of strikes, occupations and passionate discussion. Students took over the Sorbonne and moved in to live as a huge, democratically organized community dedicated to rethinking society from first principles; workers occupied factories, despite the cautious reluctance of their unions; the employees of the state-controlled broadcasting service struck in protest against censorship; a 'literary commando' of writers (including Beauvoir, Nathalie Sarraute and Marguerite Duras) took over the offices of the Union of Writers and declared it 'open to all those who believed that the practice of literature is indissolubly linked with the present revolutionary process'.[14] Slogans were everywhere, the most memorable disputing the authority of reason and mocking the solemnity of standard political discourse:

Imagination in power.

I'm a Marxist – Groucho tendency.

Opposition was thus not limited to demands for practical, economic or legal reform, but directed against the symbolic violence of rigid hierarchical structures, censorship of the media, the cultural imperialism of the ruling class.

These weeks of turmoil, which ended with de Gaulle's victory in the elections he called at the end of June, raised questions which had a particular resonance for women. How could communities be organized without hierarchies of power? (The Sorbonne's student Soviet elected a new committee every night to avoid the creation of an elite.) If culture was to be democratized, whose voices needed to be heard? What did the liberation of sexual desire mean in practice (and *whose* desire)? If the personal was political, and vice versa, what did this mean for relationships? Yet during the events themselves, assumptions about gender seem to have remained undisturbed for the majority. Patrick Searle and Maureen McConville, English journalists who covered the events and rapidly turned them into a book, display what reads now as a strikingly ingenuous sexism in their account of female students' roles in the occupied Sorbonne: 'Girls, often with more staying power and fervour than boys, typed, cut stencils, cooked, looked after children in the nursery, made beds in the improvised communal dormitories.'[15]

The male Leftists of May fought colonialist oppression, class oppression, even the psychological and sexual oppression exercised by the traditional family. Cast in the role of liberators, they rarely recognized their own position as members of a dominant and oppressive group. But in occasional meetings during the May period, women were beginning to turn the critical analysis of everyday power structures towards their own situation. Two women set up a stand in the Sorbonne courtyard, and distributed leaflets pointing out that despite women's equal participation in demonstrations, committees, fighting the riot police on the barricades, 'in the immense debate that has now begun across the country, no voice has been raised to declare that changing relations between men also means changing relations between men and women'.[16] A meeting on 'Women and Revolution', organized by the same pair (Anne Zelensky and Jacqueline Feldman), attracted a large and enthusiastic audience.

The MLF (Mouvement de Libération des Femmes) grew out of the great May debates, in which politics became not just a matter of elections, parties and policies but also of everyday interactions, language and culture. The existence of a 'Women's Liberation Movement' in the United States provided an enabling sense of international solidarity, but within France itself the post-'68 feminists found it hard to situate themselves within a wider tradition of female revolt. One account of the beginnings of the movement describes the young women of the MLF as 'motherless orphans; the bastard daughters of noble fathers and non-existent mothers – or mothers they would not wish to claim';[17] and while I hope I have demonstrated that there was no lack of feminist foremothers for the 1960s generation, the androcentric nature of both the school and university curriculum, and of the canonical version of French culture, meant that the MLF probably did feel themselves to be 'motherless'. Radical thinkers and activists like Séverine or Nelly Roussel, tackling the politics of sexuality long before the First World War, had more or less disappeared from history; George Sand had been reduced to the author of tame pastoral folktales, and Colette to a grand old dame who wrote passages on nature for anthologies. Even *The Second Sex* is scarcely mentioned in the early days of the movement. When the new feminists sought their roots, they went right back to the 1871 Paris Commune; a poster for a 1971 demonstration explicitly linked the current struggle to that of the previous century, when the Communardes had 'taken arms to defend a city which had at last become their own . . . begun to speak, to denounce their own oppression and the resignation of their men'.[18] The continuity between earlier-twentieth-century feminism and the MLF seems to have gone unrecognized – partly, no doubt, as Claire Duchen suggests, because of the 'sweeping gesture of starting afresh common to revolutionary movements',[19] partly because of the absence or misrepresentation of women in available histories, partly because of the real differences in theory and strategy between the MLF and previous generations. None the less, some feminists who could be seen as important precursors crossed the generational boundary: Simone de Beauvoir (born 1908) and Christiane Rochefort (born 1917) were both soon active in a movement largely composed of post-'45 'baby-boomers'.

From the start, the MLF placed the emphasis not on formal equality within the existing system but on contesting the hegemony of a masculinist culture, and opposing the ubiquitous belittlement and silencing of women. As in the USA and elsewhere, women-only consciousness-raising groups were an important aspect of the early movement, but so, equally, were high-profile public activities. The deliberate and provocative theatricality of early MLF events was politically significant, for the identification of femininity with modesty and eagerness to please was an important element in the ideology they opposed. The demonstration usually cited as the founding moment of the MLF took place on 26 August 1970, when a group of women (including Rochefort) scandalized the solemn crowd gathered for the annual laying of wreaths on the tomb of the Unknown Soldier by displaying banners which read 'Even more unknown than the unknown soldier – his wife', and 'One man in two is a woman'.

Posters for women-only events appropriated negative female stereotypes and used them triumphantly. One advertised a 'Wild festival of women – a witches' ball';[20] another represented the Statue of Liberty, pregnant and holding aloft the MLF symbol, calling women to a march for the legalization of abortion. Women voiced their demands and their protests in meetings, demonstrations and in the rapidly growing number of feminist publications, which began with 'Le Torchon brûle' (The Burning Rag) in 1971. From December 1973 Simone de Beauvoir and a feminist collective published an 'Everyday sexism' column in the monthly *Les Temps modernes*, inviting readers to send in examples of offensively sexist texts for inclusion and commentary, and thus popularizing the concept of verbal discrimination against women by giving it a name. Critical analysis of masculinist culture ran alongside the diffusion of women's voices. The des femmes publishing group began in 1973 and opened their first bookshop

– selling only female-authored texts – in Paris in 1974. Women film-makers formed their own organization, Musidora, in 1973, and from 1979 there was to be an annual Women's Film Festival.

If one major strand of the movement was concerned with cultural representations, exploding assumptions both by critique and by the production of a feminist counterculture, the other centred on women's reappropriation of their own bodies. Associations such as the MFPF (French Family Planning Movement) had campaigned for reform of the laws banning contraception and abortion throughout the 1960s, and the 1967 *loi Neuwirth* had legalized the sale of contraceptive devices under carefully controlled conditions and at the consumer's own expense. The post-'68 movement radicalized both demands and tactics, and one of the first MLF events to receive wide publicity was the publication of the Manifesto for abortion rights in the *Nouvel Observateur* in 1971. Three hundred and forty-three women, including many well-known names (for example, Beauvoir, Rochefort, Catherine Deneuve) publicly declared that they had undergone illegal abortions, challenging the state to prosecute them and demanding that women have access to contraception and to free, safe, early abortions when needed.

The campaign for women's right to choose or refuse motherhood was one of the central dynamics of the early MLF. In 1972 the lawyer Gisèle Halimi defended a group of women charged with procuring an abortion for a sixteen-year-old rape victim, the daughter of one of the defendants, and women surrounded the courtroom at Bobigny to demonstrate their solidarity. The mild penalties imposed betrayed the embarrassment of the judges. Out of the 'Bobigny affair' grew the pro-abortion group Choisir (Choice), and in 1973 the MLAC (Movement for Freedom of Abortion and Contraception) began to set up centres in major towns in which early abortions were illegally performed by the suction technique, and advice and information on contraception were provided. When in 1974, under the more 'modernist' presidency of Giscard d'Estaing, Simone Veil as Minister of Health carried through a hostile Parliament a bill legalizing abortion, the way had been thoroughly prepared by feminist campaigning. Nor was this campaigning over, for it was not until the 1980s, with the appearance of the Ministry for Women's Rights under the

Socialist government, that the reimbursement of abortion by the Social Security was finally obtained.

The struggle for every woman's right to choose free, safe prevention and termination of pregnancy was based on one of the movement's central demands: that women should retrieve the definition and control of their own bodies after centuries of subjection to male-defined goals and fantasies. Like their sisters elsewhere, French feminists set up refuges for women suffering domestic violence, thus defining their situation in terms of a collective, political issue rather than in those of personal misfortune. In 1972 an event entitled 'Days of denunciation of crimes against women' brought feminists together to analyse and denounce all forms of male violence against women, and the often inadequate response of the law. Lesbian feminists argued that heterosexuality was inseparable from oppression under patriarchy, and that only the political choice for women-only relationships could make liberation possible.

In 1975 prostitutes began a series of strikes and occupations in several French cities, protesting against the financial hardship and police harassment that resulted from their contradictory status in law. Since 1945 prostitutes had no longer been obliged to register with the police, but the state mingled censure with its acceptance of their trade by subjecting them to heavy fines for public disorder offences, if they were were caught soliciting, and by prosecuting anyone with whom they shared accommodation for living off immoral earnings. The prostitutes' protest represented another facet of women's angry recognition that their sexuality was defined in terms of male needs and fantasies, and policed by male authorities.

FEMINISM AND POLITICS

Post-'68 feminism politicized areas of life hitherto regarded as merely personal. The movement was less interested in politics in the conventional sense of the word. Many MLF feminists came from leftist groups for whom the corruption of the bourgeois state was axiomatic, and the very low numbers of women in political life could be interpreted as proof that the state was run not only in the interests of the dominant class but also in the interests of the male sex. An MLF poster displayed during the parliamentary elections of 1973 encouraged abstention:

We are women – we do not vote
We do not give our votes
To those who have power over us . . .
We are unrepresentable.[21]

A letter from a group of feminists to Le Monde in 1977 explained that they refused to vote because 'the struggle against the roots of women's oppression, the patriarchal family, isn't taken into account by any existing political party'.[22] The belief that gender inequality was simply not addressed by existing parties – and, indeed, that they subscribed (consciously or unconsciously) to a system founded on male supremacy – alienated feminists from the political institutions their foremothers had fought hard to enter.

None the less many women, convinced that sex and class wars went hand in hand, maintained their membership of Left parties alongside their participation in the MLF. Women in the French Communist Party produced a critique of the Party's traditionalist position on gender, under the title 'The Party laid bare by its women', and, when it was refused by the Party's own paper, published it in Le Monde (12 June 1978). In the Socialist Party, feminists attempted to form a 'current' or formally constituted group within the Party, but were voted down at the Party Congress in 1979.[23] They also produced their own magazine, Mignonnes allons voir sous la rose, a title which wittily alludes to a well-known sixteenth-century love sonnet, but replaces the poet's amorous invitation to his mistress with an exhortation to women to examine the meaning, for them, of the Socialist Party's symbolic red rose. Feminists also struggled within the more marginal far-Left parties to extend analysis and campaigns to the question of gender, and Huguette Bouchardeau of the PSU (Parti Socialiste Unifié) stood for the Presidency in 1981 with a manifesto that was clearly feminist. Bouchardeau argued that 'political parties exist and we won't be able to change that fact for some time to come. . . . If we want these instruments of power to help women instead of burying them, we have to be there, present'.[24]

There is no doubt that the visibility of the feminist movement had an impact on the thinking of even conservative political parties. Concepts such as sexism, the 'liberation' of women (with its implication of a prior imprisonment), contraception as a basic human right, permeated the national consciousness even where such ideas were contested, and made parties aware of the need at least to appear to take their female electorate seriously. Under the presidency of Giscard d'Estaing (1974–81), a politician who based his campaign on a liberal, modernizing – if fundamentally conservative – agenda, there was the first creation of a government post specifically for women's issues. The journalist Françoise Giroud was appointed Secretary of State for 'Women's Condition', her brief to identify factors which prevented women's access to employment and participation in public life, and to advise on solutions. Her department lacked any viable budget and was limited to an advisory role, but it set a precedent. Although Giroud was dropped in a 1976 Cabinet reshuffle, the minor and largely ineffectual post of 'Delegate Concerned with Women's Condition' continued to acknowledge the existence of women's problems. When the elections of 1981 brought in a Socialist President, François Mitterrand, and a Socialist majority in the National Assembly, the 'delegation' was upgraded to the more militantly named Ministry for Women's Rights.

In its first flush of idealism, before the grim reality of the economic situation led to a retreat from radical policies, the new Socialist government enacted a number of measures which were favourable to women. The 10 per cent increase in the minimum wage affected far more women than men, given the gendered inequality of wage levels.[25] The 25 per cent rise in family and housing allowances also benefited many women on low incomes. These improvements resulted from the Left's general commitment to reducing social inequality. But the Ministry for Women's Rights – in fact initially entitled 'for the Rights of Woman', in acknowledgement, perhaps, of the fact that the Republican 'Rights of Man' had failed to include women – had a budget and a mission actively to improve women's lot.

The Minister, Yvette Roudy, began with a national publicity campaign on contraception, on the grounds that the legal right to contraception (won in 1967 and 1974) had remained theoretical because of a lack of clear information on how and where it could be obtained. The feminist film director Agnès Varda was enlisted to make a series of publicity films for television, and Roudy discovered that mixture of 'classic anti-feminism and virulent political and cultural hostility'[26] with which each of her initiatives would be greeted. The Ministry then proceeded to a bill to make abortion reimbursable by the Social Security, like any other form of medical treatment, and succeeded despite the combined efforts of what Roudy describes as 'Catholic fundamentalists, traditional machos and the classical Right'.[27] The 1983 law on equality at work not only made it illegal to discrimate on grounds of sex in recruitment, training or promotion, but also required medium-sized and large firms to produce an annual report, assessing the degree of equality between men and women in their workforce and setting out measures planned to redress the (almost inevitable) imbalance. Although the practical effects of this legislation seem to have been limited – owing to the law's own shortcomings as well as to a lack of political will in subsequent governments – its emphasis, not just on equality of opportunity but also on positive measures to achieve equality in practice, was surely progressive.

The bill which provoked the most outrage was the failed Anti-Sexism Bill of 1983. The League for Women's Rights, with which Beauvoir worked, had already drafted such a bill in 1973 at the time of the 'Everyday sexism' column in *Les Temps modernes*. Based on the existing law against racism, its aim was to outlaw public representations of women which 'could be considered as a provocation to hatred or contempt of women, or violence against them'.[28] The targets were the ubiquitous advertising posters, magazine covers and television images which represented women as passively desirable bodies, or parts of bodies, offered to the male gaze as available and inviting, and thus helping to legitimate male aggression.

The loudest voices raised in protest against the bill thus came from the media and advertising industries. In the name of artistic and sexual freedom, they attacked Roudy as an 'Ayatollah', as a puritanical defender of censorship, as 'Auntie Yvette', a misguided old dear incapable of understanding the pleasure of erotic images. In the campaign against the bill, anti-sexism was thus conflated with anti-sex, and feminism ridiculed as outdated and irrelevant to a younger generation of women confident enough to recognize and enjoy the 'shadowy side' of sexuality, 'based on power and violence'.[29] The passion with which the media resisted any restriction on their use of the female body signified the crucial role it played in French marketing strategies and, in Roudy's view, in a particularly Gallic form of 'machismo'. The well-orchestrated campaign of opposition to the bill was successful: although the Cabinet had adopted it, it was dropped before it reached Parliament.

One of the terms used to ridicule Roudy by her opponents was 'Madame la Ministresse'. The feminine form of words designating positions of status or authority are frequently slightly absurd in French, conjuring up images of frivolous women playing at the role; or they denote the wife of the male figure of authority, as in 'Madame l'ambassadrice'. This leaves those few women who do achieve senior rank with a choice between becoming an honorary man ('Madame le ministre', where the role of minister remains masculine) or sounding silly. Roudy addressed this problem, and associated vexed questions of how to represent gender in a highly gendered language, by setting up a Committee on Terminology, chaired by the feminist writer Benoîte Groult. The Committee's recommendations, however, were circulated to ministers without any legal requirement that they be put into effect – and, moreover, on the very day in 1986 when the Left lost their majority in the National Assembly.[30]

MODELS OF DIFFERENCE

Yvette Roudy had never been part of the MLF – indeed, in 1979 she had opposed the move by feminists within the Socialist Party to found a feminist faction – and the sympathy with which feminists viewed the Ministry was tinged with suspicion. None the less, her initiatives were broadly in line with the aims of many feminist women, and the Anti-Sexist Bill, for example, was the result of collaboration with the League for Women's Rights, whose co-founder, Anne Zélensky, had been one of the two organizers of the first women's meeting in the occupied Sorbonne in 1968. The Ministry's priorities and strategies implied a view of women's situation which was broadly that of the majority of feminists: the differences between men's and women's situation were almost entirely to women's disadvantage; these differences were grounded in material inequalities, but also maintained and aggravated by the ideological superstructure of patriarchy which legitimated male authority and women's subordination. Thus it was crucial to make material changes, by improving women's conditions of employment and their control over pregnancy and maternity, but also to intervene in cultural practices, from language to visual imagery, disturbing the consensual view of gender.

Within the Women's Movement, this definition of sexual difference as primarily a relationship of inequality, which feminism aims to eradicate, did not preclude some desire to celebrate what is specifically and uniquely female. Although the emphasis in the early days of the MLF was mostly on avoiding unwanted maternity, motherhood was part of most women's lives, and there were soon attempts to separate the physical and emotional joys of childbearing from the social subordination of mothers. The 1975 book *Les Femmes s'entêtent* (whose title, spoken aloud, produces a play on words between 'Women refuse to take no for an answer' and 'Headless women' [*sans tête*]) has a section on maternity collectively written by a group of feminist mothers, and significantly placed in the chapter entitled 'Desires and Deliria'. Recognizing that so far the movement has 'concentrated its energies on the refusal of the child, because it refused to see women as merely functional', the text then takes the form of several subjective accounts of motherhood which mingle condemnation of medical and social context with lyrical reflections on the joy of bearing and loving children. Aware that they are in danger of sounding heretical, the text's authors parry criticism from more orthodox sisters by emphasizing the revolutionary potential of motherhood: 'if women really want to find pleasure [the French verb 'jouir' has an erotic charge which is hard to translate] in childbearing they will start to make enormous, uncompromising demands of this society'.[31]

For most feminists, working and talking with other women in the movement led to a new appreciation of 'feminine' culture. But the really urgent task was not so much to explore this positive side of difference as to improve the lives of the majority of women by campaigning for better pay and opportunities, for free and available contraception and abortion, for better childcare and against sexist discrimination in all its forms. One group of women's liberationists, however, refused to call themselves feminists because for them the term 'feminism' signified pragmatic reformism, merely an attempt to join the ruling sex on its own terms:

The bourgeois order, capitalism, phallocentrism are all quite
ready to integrate as many feminists as they need to. Since
women will thus become men, there will simply be rather
more men

Antoinette Fouque wrote.[32]

Fouque and the other members of the Psych et Po (Psychanalyse
et Politique) group, owners of the women-only bookshop and
publishing company des femmes, argued that rather than seek to
minimize inequalities within the existing economic and political
system, women must concentrate on exploring that femininity
which had been repressed and misrepresented by patriarchy. For
them, patriarchy's crime was less to have constructed sexual
difference as a justification for inequality than to have repressed
the feminine virtually out of existence. Rediscovery of the
feminine self meant living in separatist communities, undergoing
psychoanalysis, getting in touch with the body – and writing. The
'pro-difference' group made their opposition to what they termed
'feminism' very public, and in 1979, in a decidedly unsisterly
move, hijacked the name 'MLF' and registered this as their own
company title. Their tactics were thus divisive, and their defence of
difference was also perceived by many feminists as perilously close
to a reinstatement of biological essentialism. There was a significant
split in the French movement over the issue of difference.

The same issue in a sense underlay the split between radical
lesbians and other feminists in the Questions féministes collective in
1980, even though both groups agreed on their rejection of Psych
et Po's version of difference. The radical lesbians argued that by
removing themselves from heterosexual relationships and adopting
political lesbianism, women could extricate themselves from the
sex-class of 'women' as defined under patriarchy and determine
their own identity. The most politically advanced feminists would
thus be concerned less with fighting inequality within a society
composed of women and men than with 'transfer[ring] all our
creative powers, both intellectual and emotional, to women',[33]
a move which is strategically close to that of the Psych et Po
group and similarly assumes a fundamental, rather than socially
constructed, difference between the sexes. Those who opposed
this view both disputed the idea that it was possible to cease to

be positioned as a member of one's sex or class by an act of will, and argued for the need to accept the reality of most women's lives, intricately bound up as they are with the lives of men, rather than pursue a separatist path neither accessible nor desirable to the majority.

Conflicting models of difference will be used to structure the chapters below, but the aim will not be to present two distinct and opposed positions – rather, to show that within writing, at least, the two models frequently overlap and intersect. Françoise Picq, a feminist activist and academic who has lived through the history of the MLF since its earliest days, finds retrospectively that within the movement, too, the opposing currents were often held in a creative tension rather than locked into conflict. Defining the two approaches as, on the one hand, a Beauvoirian emphasis ('One is not born a woman . . . ') on difference as 'socially produced', and on the other an insistence on 'seeking to bring about the advent of a femininity repressed by the dominant society', she argues that it was essential not to choose between the two, as binary logic would normally demand, but to maintain 'the contradictory character of the goal set, even if that goal is a distant one'. The coexistence of these mutually opposed versions of difference she terms 'a necessary utopia'.[34]

WOMEN'S WRITING

The Women's Liberation Movement was accompanied – and to some extent preceded – by an increase in the numbers of female-authored texts published in France. Not all women writers engaged directly with questions of sexual politics – for example, Nathalie Sarraute, whose experimentation with new forms of psychological realism made her one of most celebrated of the 'New Novelists', was (and is) only obliquely concerned with gender – but even in the years preceding the birth of the MLF, much writing by women did display a new note of explicit militancy. Christiane Rochefort's pre-1968 novels employed satire combined with a bleak lyricism to attack assumptions about gender and sexuality. Violette Leduc's powerfully erotic novel of lesbian adolescence *La Bâtarde – An Autobiography* appeared in 1964, prefaced and praised by Beauvoir. Claire Etcherelli's *Elise ou la vraie vie* (*Elise or the Real Life*, 1967) used the form of the love story to explore relationships between different forms of oppression: that of workers on the production line, that of women, and that of North African immigrant workers. Marie Cardinal, whose later work clearly engages with the themes and practices of feminist writing, published her first novel, *Ecoutez la mer* (Listen to the Sea) in 1962, and Benoîte Groult – later co-editor of the feminist *F-Magazine* (founded in 1978) and author of the feminist essay *Ainsi soit-elle* (May She Be So – 'Ainsi soit-il' in French is the equivalent of 'Amen' – 1975) – co-authored several women-centred novels in the 1960s with her sister Flora.

The publicity that surrounded the early days of the MLF, the appearance of feminist publishing companies and of feminist 'lists' sponsored by mainstream publishers, all helped to create a climate that encouraged women to write, and there are far more important and influential texts published in this period than can be discussed here. Some of the most radical and imaginative critiques of heterosexual orthodoxy, for example, were produced by Monique Wittig: *Les Guérillères* (The She-Warriors, 1969) evokes a band of women rebels whose rejection of an androcentric society extends to a feminization of language itself. With *Le Corps lesbien* (*The Lesbian Body*, 1973), *Brouillon pour un dictionnaire des amantes* (*Lesbian Peoples: Material for a Dictionary*, 1976) and *Virgile, non* (*Across the Acheron*, 1985), Wittig pursued her project 'to create a lesbian language, in which the categories of sex are abolished . . ., to appropriate all cultural symbolic systems, to make them a tool for the abolition of gender itself'.[35]

In the theatre, women continued to form only a small minority of playwrights and directors, but here too the confidence and the opportunities generated by the Women's Movement produced a degree of change. Most accounts of theatre under the Fifth Republic cite only two or three women playwrights among the great and the famous: Françoise Sagan's plays, while more light comedies of manners than major drama, were consistently success-ful throughout the 1960s and 1970s; Sarraute's minimalist theatre of the 1970s was generally admired; and Duras's plays, particularly from 1965 with productions of *Le Square* and *La Musica*, are as original and disturbing as are her novels and films, so that Harold Hobson, in his 1978 *French Theatre since 1830*, could declare her: 'of all the dramatists . . . since . . . Beckett and Pinter . . . the most arresting, the most haunting and the most important' (p. 248).

Successful women playwrights thus remain something of a rarity, though not so scarce as in the earlier periods. The writing of plays, though, is only one mode of theatrical creation. As we have seen, the 1950s were a period of decentralization and democratization of the French theatre, and one result of this was to shift the emphasis in part from playwrights to directors, and to the collaborative creation of plays by troops of actors. May 1968, with its refusal of hierarchies and authority, reinforced this preference for shared modes of production, and for a theatre that was explicitly political.

The Théâtre du Soleil (Theatre of the Sun), founded under that name in 1964, was one of the most successful of the theatre companies whose political beliefs determined not only the themes of their plays but also the collective, egalitarian methods by which they wrote and produced, and shared out any profits. The troupe's central creative force was the director Ariane Mnouchkine, whose name became nationally and internationally known with Soleil's highly successful productions of two plays about the French Revolution: *1789* (in 1970–71) and *1793* (1972–73). The company based their plays on improvisation, and challenged the normally passive role of the spectators by having them move around the theatre from scene to scene and participate in the action, 'sweeping everyone along in a common celebration of the overthrow of tyranny'.[36]

This sort of theatre, with its refusal of hierarchies within the company and its commitment not only to entertain but also to raise the consciousness of the spectators, clearly shared some of the goals and strategies of the Women's Movement. It was perhaps not surprising, then, that Mnouchkine and the Théâtre du Soleil went on to collaborate with Hélène Cixous in the production of several of her plays, beginning with *L'Histoire terrible mais inachevée de Norodom Sihanouk Roi du Cambodge* (The Terrible but Unfinished Story of Norodom Sihanouk, King of Cambodia) in 1985 and *L'Indiade* in 1987. Cixous's 'historical' theatre does not address feminist issues directly, but deals with historical moments, such as those of struggles against colonial power, which foreground the problem of 'sustain[ing] otherness'[37] in the face of oppression – a theme which connects Cixous's feminist writing with her other concerns as an artist.

The 1970s and 1980s also saw a considerable amount of feminist theatre, often performed in 'fringe' theatres or at festivals, but demonstrating that women had gained much freer access to the stage. Celita Lamar, in her 1991 book *Our Voices, Our Selves: Women Writing for the French Theatre*, argues that 'the 1970s were perhaps the first time in French theatre that the world was truly being seen through the eyes of women' (pp. xiii–xiv), and traces through a wide variety of plays written, and generally directed and performed by women, the recurrence of certain themes and motifs: mothers and daughters, strategies of resistance to oppression, women and power. The 1989 Bicentennial of the Revolution was the occasion of several female-authored plays exploring the impact of 1789 on the women of France. Lamar's study suggests that the period of women's virtual exclusion from the French theatre (except as actresses) is ending, and that women playwrights are using the stage to say publicly (to borrow and adapt the words of Cixous): 'I [was] not the one who [was] dumb. I [was] silenced by your inability to hear'.[38]

THE MYTH OF POST-FEMINISM

The Ministry for Women's Rights disappeared with the return to power of a right-wing majority in 1986. When the Socialists regained their majority in 1988, they did not reinstate the Ministry but reduced it to a more junior department headed by a 'Secretary of State for Women's Rights'. During the 1980s and 1990s, the term 'feminist' has fallen into further disrepute in France, tending to evoke outdated images either of prim suffragists or of the generation known as 'sixty-eighters'. There is renewed evidence of that persistent conviction that the French enjoy a special relationship between the sexes, premissed not on inequality but on an appreciation of difference. Elisabeth Badinter, in the 1994 article quoted at the beginning of this chapter, explains that, unlike in the the USA or Germany, French feminists have nothing to be angry about because in terms of legal reforms they have achieved all their goals, and because sexual relations in France are experienced in terms of shared sensuality rather than power:

[In the USA and Germany] any indication that they are attracted to a man [in French 'la coquetterie féminine'] is felt by women

to be an admission of defeat; masculine seduction is felt by
men to be an expression of their desire to dominate. It's
astounding: what to us is a game, one of life's pleasures,
something profoundly natural, seems to them to be a threat
to equality! . . . American and German women are light years
away from French women.[39]

Although feminist work at grass-roots level continues – for
example running the refuges for victims of domestic violence
established in the early 1970s, maintaining feminist demands within
trade unions and political parties – and although feminist studies
have established a toehold in some universities, French feminism
has thus had a low profile over the past decade. Despite the
very real victories of recent decades, there is little evidence
that this is because French women have achieved full equality.
Thirty-four out of the 577 Deputies in the National Assembly
are women, and the number of women ministers in a Cabinet
has never risen above four. Because of resistance from some
doctors, and the marginalization of abortion centres within the
health service, two-thirds of abortions are still performed privately.
In the workplace, though they form 44 per cent of the working
population and a greater proportion of graduates than men, women
account for less than 10 per cent of management posts in two out
of three French firms. They are much more likely than their male
counterparts to be unemployed. More than twice as many rapes
were declared to the police in 1992 than a decade previously
(though this may also indicate something positive about women's
belief that they will be taken seriously), and Antoinette Fouques's
'Observatory of Misogyny' reported in 1992 that there were two
million cases of violence against women every day.[40]
    French culture remains a predominantly masculine sphere. Of
the thirty-one major literary prizes awarded in France between
1985 and the end of the decade, six went to women, and as we
have seen, it is still relatively rare to find a major commercial
and critical success in the theatre authored by a woman. The
film industry gives few prizes to women directors; Agnès Varda
in the 1960s, Marguerite Duras in the 1970s, and Coline Serreau
in the 1980s being among the rare exceptions. A review of French
Thought in 1993, published in the influential and left-of-centre

*Nouvel Observateur*,[41] named eighteen important contemporary intellectuals – of whom not a single one was a woman, and this despite the international reputations of writers such as Hélène Cixous, Julia Kristeva, Luce Irigaray or Michèle Le Doeuff.

Feminism thus continues to be both necessary and – beneath the surface – present in France. Edith Cresson's brief spell as France's first woman Prime Minister, in the summer of 1991, revealed much about the difficulties for a woman of achieving and holding political office. The media, predictably, showed as much interest in her appearance as in her policies, and represented her very much as Mitterrand's protégée rather than a career politician in her own right, *L'Express* describing the President as her 'Pygmalion' and her 'master'.[42] Cresson herself, having previously believed that women enjoyed equal opportunity within politics, emerged from the experience convinced that 'the only model of power acceptable amongst the political class is a masculine model. . . . Those who do not fit the norm, and notably women, are eliminated'.[43] In the early 1990s, a cross-party movement called simply 'Parity' emerged, linked to other European women's organizations which share the goal of achieving 50 per cent female representation at all levels of political life. As the daughters and granddaughters of immigrants from France's ex-colonies confront the difficulty of reconciling two cultures, they have begun to develop new and different types of feminist association.

But it is perhaps in writing that feminism has remained most creative and vibrant in France. Throughout more than three decades of the Fifth Republic, French women's writing has been prolific, innovative and immensely varied. The feminist debates and campaigns that emerged after May '68 were in part prefigured by the literature of the previous decade, and their implications were explored, imagined and put into practice in the writing that followed. Much more than in the earlier periods studied, women's writing under the Fifth Republic is an essential part of the story of feminism.

# 11
## Ecriture féminine:
## The Theory of a Feminine Writing

In her polemical, passionate essay 'The Laugh of the Medusa'(1975), Hélène Cixous coined the phrase *écriture féminine* to designate a writing that emerges from and celebrates the specific nature of women's sexuality, thought and imagination. Although Cixous attributes the practice of 'feminine' writing to certain male, as well as female, authors, the essay has the exhortatory tone of a manifesto, calling on women to invent a new language that would break through the repressive, censoring codes of a phallocentric culture. The concept of such a writing had begun to develop within the Psych et Po group (discussed in Chapter 10), and the idea of a gendered writing informed the publishing policy of their company, des femmes; but it also emerged separately, and with different emphases, in the work of a number of French feminist writers in the early 1970s. The aim of this chapter will be to explore and evaluate the theory of a 'feminine' writing, based as it is on the celebration rather than the contestation of sexual difference. In the next chapter I then want to consider, with reference to texts by Chantal Chawaf and Marguerite Duras, how far the concept of *écriture féminine* provides a productive strategy for feminist writing and reading.

In non-Francophone countries, the French exponents of a 'feminine' writing have tended to be treated as a group, even though the work of writers such as Hélène Cixous (born 1937), Luce Irigaray (born 193?), Julia Kristeva (born 1941) and Annie Leclerc is in fact grounded in different disciplines, highly individual and still developing over time. The aims and constraints of this chapter will mean that I too emphasize the points of connection between Cixous and Annie Leclerc, both of whom have explicitly defined and practised a writing of difference, and Irigaray and Kristeva, whose work has important implications for a definition of *écriture féminine*, and that I thus run the risk of underplaying their specificity as writers. While it is necessary to be aware of this, the main concern here is to identify a new vision of female identity and of gendered writing which emerged from the work of several French feminist writers in the 1970s, and continues to have wide currency. Excellent feminist studies of individual writers already exist, and are listed in the Bibliography.

THE INTELLECTUAL CONTEXT

Theories of feminine writing differed from earlier forms of feminism both in their emphasis on language as the key factor in women's oppression, and in their insistence that women's liberation meant not merely the claim to equality but the assertion of sexual difference. This new vision did not suddenly emerge unheralded from the creative chaos of May 1968; in a number of ways its roots can be traced to the intellectual climate of the preceding decades. In *The Second Sex*, Beauvoir had already harnessed to the feminist cause the Hegelian notion of the dominant subject who defines himself by reference to the Other, repository of his fears and dreams. This model of human relations was further developed by Michel Foucault in the 1960s, forming part of the period's broad theoretical concern with the way power is established and maintained through the symbolic relations of language, culture and ideology. Language was widely theorized as a system which constructed meanings, rather than simply codifying and communicating experience, a view present in the earlier, but still influential, linguistic theory of Ferdinand de Saussure, in the works of the philosopher Jacques Derrida, and in those of the critic and cultural theorist Roland Barthes.[1] Freudian theory, as interpreted in the 1960s and 1970s by Jacques Lacan, made the child's entry into language the point at which s/he acquired a fully gendered identity, and posited language as a system in which the phallus represents the most privileged signifier, and in which woman is designated only and always in relation to man.

The 'New Novel' authors of the 1950s and 1960s popularized the view that literature's power to alter mentalities depends less on theme than on form. Nathalie Sarraute, Alain Robbe-Grillet and Michel Butor each expounded and put into literary practice the theory that the realist narrative had become inherently conservative, and that only radically experimental forms of writing could contribute to cultural and even to political change. With Barthes, the literary text was not only politicized but also eroticized: Barthes's notion of the reader's response to the open-ended, multilayered, experimental text as one of *'jouissance'* has distinctly sexual connotations, and makes reading a bodily experience.[2] All these theories, with their shared emphasis on the primary role of language – and, by extension, literature – in both the construction of subjectivity and the distribution of power, provided a context for the development of new feminist theories of sexual difference and the role of women's writing.

A further significant context is provided by the French national tradition of emphasizing women's difference from men. Throughout the period under study here, and to a greater extent than other Western European nations, France had valorized sexual difference as a principle essential not only to social order but also to a pleasurable and interesting existence. The Napoleonic Code built the difference between male and female rights and functions into the state's legal framework, where it remained, its gradual replacement by the principle of equality beginning only well over a century later. The legal emancipation of women did little to reduce the emphasis on gender difference: that cliché of the music-hall Frenchman, 'Vive la différence!', encapsulates the importance that French culture attributes to the distinction between the sexes.

Michèle Sarde points out that many of the characteristics cherished as aspects of French national identity depend upon the separate but complementary mythologies of French masculinity and femininity. *La Française*, as celebrated by French men and imagined abroad, is characterized by a sartorial elegance that matches the intellectual elegance of French (masculine) culture, by a sexiness that is also a tribute to the seductive virility of the French man, by her skill in managing the domestic side of life, and particularly the quintessentially French domain of cooking. The feminist writer Marie Cardinal argues that in France, to a much greater extent than in the United States, for example, it is impossible for a woman to be considered a successful human being without reference to the gendered criteria of physical beauty and its related attributes:

Can you think of one physically unattractive woman who's managed to make her voice heard in France? . . . It's beauty that determines a woman's value in France, and beneath the beauty there's supposed to be a good lay, a good cook, mother, wife, nurse, seamstress, washerwoman, etc.[3]

Sarde detects a fundamental anxiety in French culture about the possible disappearance of a gender difference in which so much is invested: 'France was, and perhaps still is, a "feminolatrous"[4] society, in which the fear of a shortage of femininity resembles the terror of food shortages in wartime.'[5] Even Beauvoir, as Sarde rightly says, felt obliged to reassure her readers that if the inequalities of current gender relations were abolished, life would not necessarily take on the monotonous uniformity of a world without difference:

The reciprocity of their relations will not do away with the miracles – desire, possession, love, dream, adventure – worked by the division of human beings into two separate categories; and the words that move us – giving, conquering, uniting – will not lose their meaning.[6]

It was perhaps not by chance that a feminist revalorization of sexual difference began in France, where sexual difference had long been seen as the foundation not only of a properly ordered society but also of life's richness.

THEORIES OF DIFFERENCE

None the less, the starting point for the new feminist theories was a rejection of the dominant, androcentric version of sexual difference. The essays 'The Laugh of the Medusa' and 'Sorties', published by Hélène Cixous in the early 1970s, are simultaneously polemical arguments in favour of 'feminine writing' and exemplifications of its style, but they also operate a vibrant critique of patriarchal, binary models of reality. By juxtaposing opposing pairs of words:

Activity/Passivity
Sun/Moon
Culture/Nature
Day/Night,[7]

Cixous demonstrates that in every case the more positive term (Activity, Sun, Culture, Day) is aligned with the masculine, the negative term with the feminine, and that thus there is 'always the same metaphor: we follow it, it carries us, beneath all its figures, wherever discourse is organized' (HCR, p. 37). In an argument close to Beauvoir's model of the male subject and his female 'Other', Cixous asserts that 'woman has always functioned "within" the discourse of man, a signifier that has always referred back to the opposite signifier'.[8]

Irigaray's critique of the Freudian reduction of female desire to 'penis envy' similarly emphasizes the definition of women in terms of male needs and fears: 'If woman had desires other than "penis envy", this would call into question the unity, the uniqueness, the simplicity of the mirror charged with sending man's image back to him – albeit inverted.[9] This, however, is where Cixous and Irigaray depart from Beauvoir, for rather than deducing from the negative role allotted to women that the theory of natural sexual difference is politically dangerous, they conclude that the androcentric version of difference has concealed the real nature of femininity. Because our whole culture has been built on the repression of the feminine, neutralized into a mere foil for the masculine, its re-emergence as a positive value has explosive potential. To relinquish any claim to a specifically feminine identity, to settle simply for equality on masculine terms, thus becomes a form of surrender which Irigaray, in a text published in 1990, dramatically describes as genocide:

> The human species is divided into *two genders* which ensure its production and reproduction. To wish to get rid of sexual difference is to call for a genocide more radical than any form of destruction that has ever been seen in History.[10]

Although they refuse what Cixous terms 'sexual opposition' – that is, the definition of woman only as the negative to man's positive – they posit the existence of an authentic femininity as yet unsymbolized and scarcely known, but rich with the revolutionary power of the long-repressed.

None of the writers discussed here would dispute the necessity for women to work together to campaign, for example, for civil and reproductive rights. In *To Live the Orange*, for example, Cixous's meditation on language and its relationship to the substantiality of things, is interrupted by a phone call from a support group formed to campaign for women in Iran. Cixous moves from meditation and writing to political action: 'there is a time for letting things struggling with indifference give themselves to be heard. There is a time for the heart-rending call of an Iran. One doesn't resound without the other.' (HCR, p. 89). None the less, for Cixous as for the other theorists of difference, the main site of struggle has to be language and the philosophy implicit in language. What interests them is the symbolizing system which underlies and maintains patriarchy by determining (and restricting) both men and women's vision of the world:

> Philosophy is constructed on the premise of women's abase-
> ment. . . . What would happen to logocentrism, to the great
> philosophical systems, to the order of the world in general if
> the rock upon which they founded this church should crumble?
> ('Sorties' [1975], HCR, pp. 39–40)

or in the words of Annie Leclerc, in her 1974 text *Parole de femme*: 'Nothing exists that has not been made by man – not thought, not language, not words. . . . We have to make everything anew'.[11]

If everything is to be made anew, if the rock is to crumble, then women must write for themselves and contest the hegemonic version of what constitutes their identity as women. Since this writing will contest language itself, assumed as it is to be the vehicle of patriarchal philosophy, it will necessarily be wildly experimental and disruptive in form.[12] And one of the major sources of this formal innovation will be the material foundation of sexual difference – that is, the body.

WRITING THE BODY

*Ecriture féminine* is also referred to by the phrase 'writing the body', and the apparent naivety of proposing a direct relationship between anatomy and literary style has often been criticized. The theory is in fact more complex and more qualified, and Cixous in particular asserts, even in the early polemical texts, that there is no direct causal link between biological sex and capacity for writing outside patriarchal norms. Although 'nearly the entire history of writing . . . has been one with the phallocentric tradition', she argues, there have been male 'failures', writers (such as James Joyce,

Jean Genet) who have escaped the 'enormous machine' and written differently. Cixous attributes her own capacity to write partly to this inheritance: 'if it weren't for them, I wouldn't be writing (I-woman, escapee)' (LM, p. 337). Conversely, she dismisses the vast majority of her female predecessors as writers whose 'workmanship is in no way different from male writing' (LM, p. 336). Anatomical sex is not taken simply to determine the production of 'masculine' or 'feminine' writing.

There is, however, a degree of contradiction here, for Cixous, like Irigaray and Leclerc, also argues that physical sexual difference affects the subject's way of relating to the world and to others, and predisposes towards a particular mode of writing. First, the nature of male and female sexuality is seen as constitutive of different 'economies', or mental and emotional structures which govern thought and exchange with others. The masculine economy is related to the central role of the penis in sexual pleasure, and thus tends to be organized hierarchically and on the linear model of erection, ejaculation and detumescence, and the fact that under patriarchy the phallus signifies authority leads to a valorization of anything which is literally or figuratively phallic: centralized, authoritative, linear: 'Let masculine sexuality gravitate around the penis, engendering this centralized body (political anatomy) under the party dictatorship . . .' (HCR, p. 44). Female sexuality, on the other hand, is conceived as more diffuse and open-ended because it involves several erotic zones, rather than a single organ, and multiple orgasms rather than a single climax:

> [T]he geography of her pleasure is far more diversified, more multiple in its differences, more complex, more subtle, than is commonly imagined – in an imaginary rather too narrowly focused on sameness.[13]

Again by a process of analogy, these characteristics of women's sexuality are projected on to their mode of relating to others, which is said to be less hierarchical and less self-centred than that of men. Where man expends himself, both sexually and in a broader sense, in order to recuperate a profit (pleasure, acknowledgement of his power), woman is seen to have a more open, less calculated and self-interested relationship both to sexual partners and to the world in general: 'If there is a self proper to woman, paradoxically it is her capacity to depropriate herself without self-interest; endless body; without "end", without principal parts . . .' (HCR, p. 44).

The second aspect of the body evoked in this differential characterization of masculine and feminine economies is maternity. Both sexes experience relationship with the mother. In Lacan's reading of Freud, a model which forms the basis of *écriture féminine* theories, it is when the infant experiences loss of blissful fusion with the mother, and needs to express desire for her, that s/he begins to enter language. Language is thus associated with lack, and desire, but it is also associated with the entry of the Father or the Social Order into the mother–infant relationship. The entry into language is won, in a sense, at the cost of the maternal: acquiring language means losing the mother. Because the female infant cannot identify with the Father, the Phallus, the positive term of the linguistic order, Cixous, Irigaray and Kristeva suggest that in her the traces of the pre-linguistic time of fusion with the mother may remain more strongly present. This link with the maternal is represented as a source of subversive power, as access to an order which preceded and contests the authority of patriarchal language:

> In women there is always more or less of the mother who makes everything all right, who nourishes, and who stands up against separation, a force that will not be cut off but will knock the wind out of the codes. (LM, p. 339)

As daughter, then, the woman writer potentially has greater access to what Kristeva calls the 'semiotic',[14] that mode of meaning and communication preceding language and charged with the scarcely conceivable pleasure of fusion with the mother. Woman's own capacity to be a mother also appears in the theory of 'writing the body', although the objection that this represents a return to the oppressive glorification of the maternal role is carefully countered by the insistence that what matters is the capacity for, rather than the act of, conceiving and bearing a child:

> Either you want a kid or you don't – *that's your business.*
> . . . Oral drive, anal drive, vocal drive – all these drives are our strengths, and among them is the gestation drive – just like the desire to write: a desire to live self from

within, a desire for the swollen belly, for language, for blood. (LM, p. 346)

The significance of maternity centres on the unique nature of the relationship between mother and child, in which the mother gives life and nurtures, without self-diminishment, and with the aim not of appropriating the child but of allowing it to become another person: '[G]iving birth is neither losing nor increasing. It's adding to life an other' (LM, p. 346). In dialogue with the biologist Hélène Rouch, Irigaray makes a case for the relationship between mother and foetus to be seen as an ideal model for human relations, in which both the self and the other are respected through the 'negotiating' function of the placenta: 'The placental economy is therefore an organized economy, one not in a state of fusion, which respects the one and the other . . . .' [15]

Both women's sexuality, and their roles in reproduction, are thus read as the foundation for a specific way of relating to the world and others. For those women who can break down the internalized defences of the learnt culture, this can also lead to a dynamically different type of writing, that *écriture féminine* for which Cixous claims, in the early, manifesto-style texts, the power to 'produce far more radical effects of political and social change than some might like to think' (LM, p. 339), to 'smash everything, . . . shatter the framework of institutions, . . . blow up the law' (LM, p. 344). I want now to examine more closely what the characteristics of such a writing are claimed to be, then to review a number of objections to the 'feminism of difference' and its implications for literature. This will enable me, in Chapter 12, to sketch a reading of some texts which might qualify as *écriture féminine*, with reference both to the theory's own criteria and to the reservations I will have outlined.

WHAT CONSTITUTES *ÉCRITURE FÉMININE?*

Like the New Novelists – with whom there is a certain overlap, since Marguerite Duras has been claimed both as a New Novelist and as a (perhaps involuntary) practitioner of 'feminine writing', and Nathalie Sarraute's work is centrally concerned with finding ways to articulate what language reduces and conceals – the theorists of difference have situated the revolutionary power of the text at the level of form rather than theme. The linear narratives of realism, like the ordered, rational and discursive style of philosophy, are read as metaphors for masculinity, whereas the less ordered and centralized nature of female sexuality is said to correspond to less rigid structures. There is thus a privileging of disorder at various levels: the feminine text will avoid the pattern of opening, development, climax and subsidence into the calm of closure, which parallels masculine sexuality, and tends to proceed by association rather than logic or chronology, 'punctur[ing] the system of couples and opposition . . . overthrow[ing] successiveness, connection' (LM, p. 344). This will mean that such texts, read from a conventional perspective, will appear incoherent, that 'her' language will 'set off in all directions leaving "him" unable to discern the coherence of any meaning.'.[16]

In terms of structure, the point on which all the theorists discussed here agree most closely is that of temporality – that is, that feminine writing employs a model of time which is quite unlike that found in the majority of masculine texts. We have already seen, in Chapter 7 on Colette, that Kristeva characterizes women's sense of time in terms of 'cycles, gestation, the eternal recurrence of a biological rhythm which conforms to that of nature',[17] and that this pattern does indeed correspond to both the narrative structures and the imagery of Colette's texts. In *Je, tu, nous* (1990), Irigaray argues against the model of ageing as a straightforwardly linear process, 'a matter of growing old from an accumulation of years, and from increasing organic waste and decay',[18] demonstrating that most women's lives are structured by processes such as pregnancy, mothering, even (she argues) the menopause, in which time passing also means growth and development:

> A woman experiences menstruation, her periods, as continuously related to cosmic time, to the moon, the sun, the tides, and the seasons. [. . . And] menopause marks another stage in the becoming of a female body and spirit . . . [19]

Annie Leclerc makes a similar point in relation to men's linear view of time, relating this to the structure of male sexuality: 'Their eyes, their pulse neglect the seasons. All they see is History, they can only fight for History. Their sex grows erect, stretches, ejaculates and falls back' (PF, p. 59). But her own body 'returns to itself through a cycle of metamorphoses. Its perception of time is circular, though never closed or repetitive.' (PF, p. 58). Thus *écriture féminine* will disrupt the order of the masculine text, but beneath its apparent incoherence may display a different type of order, based on the cycle rather than the straight line.

The refusal to impose the order of reason or linear chronology on the text is paralleled, at the level of the textual voice, by an avoidance of any tone of impersonal authority. The 'I' of *écriture féminine* is often subjective and passionate, as in the Cixous essays and Annie Leclerc's *Parole de femme*,[20] but refuses to 'master' its own text. As Cixous puts it: 'her language does not contain, it carries; it does not hold back, it makes possible' (LM, p. 345).

This rather obscure formulation seems to me to mean two different things. On the one hand it refers to a vertical relationship between the text and the writer's most fundamental drives, memories and emotions, those repressed by standard discourse, which we may equate with Kristeva's 'semiotic' or with Cixous's 'what-comes-before-language' (HCR, p. 44). The feminine text will be rhythmic, musical, sensual, shaped by intense sensory experience which, by its very nature, is normally excluded from language. But the attempt to enable rather than dominate the text also seems to have a 'horizontal' meaning, connecting the self to the world beyond by allowing language itself a certain free play. Cixous describes writing as 'from this chorus of songs of the whole of time, making a new song stream forth' (HCR, p. xxi), which suggests the acceptance and incorporation of the rich associations which words accumulate through time. The aim is to avoid the tendency of language to reduce, to 'seize and mean' (*To Live the Orange*, HCR, p. 84), and, rather, to emulate what Cixous defines as truly feminine writers 'who speak to watch over and save, not to catch, with voices almost invisible, attentive and precise like virtuoso fingers . . . ' (HCR, p. 84)

On a formal level, then, *écriture féminine* seems to signify disruption of orthodox structures, cyclical patterning, a voice that is sensual, musical and passionate but self-effacing before the rich associative power of words. Although theme is rarely mentioned in theories of a 'writing of difference', which insist above all on the need to dislocate patriarchal language itself, they do contain clear implications as to what the privileged themes of such a writing might be. Since the first texts deliberately to practise such writing were simultaneously polemical arguments in its favour, writing itself is clearly one primary theme. Much of Cixous's work, which ranges from essays to literary criticism, fiction and theatre, deals with, even as it performs, the act of writing as a woman, as do the texts of Annie Leclerc. Irigaray, too, has done a considerable amount of work on language and 'all the strategies for erasing the feminine as the subject of discourse',[21] including those of grammatical rules and the gendering of nouns in French, questions which have a particular relevance for women writers.

The other themes which emerge as central to a feminine writing are those which the androcentric bias of most literature has excluded, notably women's experience of their own bodies and relationships with each other. *Parole de femme* not only argues that the female body can be the source of a renewal of language, but enacts this process by struggling against the gaps and the bias of existing words to describe menstruation, (hetero)sexual intercourse, childbirth. The text foregrounds the difficulty of articulating what has always been excluded from representation: advertisements for tampons promise the material equivalent of that concealment of the smell, sight and feel of menstrual blood effected by language, and Leclerc coins the verb 'to tampaxify' (*tampaxiser*) to signify this process: 'But do you realize what a struggle it is to speak of this blood?' (PF, p. 50).

To speak of sexual intercourse in a woman's voice poses similar problems, for the available words equate the male role with conquest and possession, the female with passivity and self-abandonment. Leclerc designates the experience by an 'X', explaining in parentheses:

> (I seek, but can't find, a word which just happens to be missing: neither coitus, brutal and technical, nor love, prudish and religious, nor screwing, jokey and aggressive – so what can I say? Where is the word to describe our bodies together?) (PF, p. 70)

Childbirth, too, has been 'stolen', represented in terms of pain and sacrifice rather than power and creativity, and Leclerc devotes long passages to a rewriting of the experience of giving birth from the perspective of the mother.

Both Cixous and Irigaray also deal with the problem of symbolizing the body in a language that situates the woman as subject, for 'female sexuality has always been conceptualized on the basis of masculine parameters'.[22] And the absence, in Western culture, of any symbolization of relationships between women, and particularly between mother and daughter, is one of Irigaray's central themes, to the extent that a 1987 essay recommends that as one practical move to overcome this: 'in all homes and public places, attractive images (not involving advertising) of the mother–daughter couple should be displayed'.[23] The representation of the female body, and of mother–daughter relationships, can therefore be assumed to characterize feminine writing.

OBJECTIONS

These theories of sexual difference, and of its implications for what a truly feminine writing is and should be, can be – and have been – challenged in a number of ways from a feminist perspective. First of all, when feminists had struggled for centuries against the disempowering theory of a femininity that was naturally self-sacrificing, intuitive and emotional, it was disturbing to find qualities very similar to these being claimed in the name of women's liberation. Colette Guillaumin, writing in *Questions féministes* in 1979, argued caustically that the femininity defended in the name of revolutionary difference corresponded precisely to the femininity foisted on women by their economic and political subordination, and that a feminism of 'difference' was thus most unlikely to meet with any opposition from the defenders of patriarchy. Strategically caricaturing the pro-difference definition of the feminine as 'attention to others, patience, sensitivity, the gift for making, and enjoyment of, jams, etc.'[24] she argues that the first priority of feminism must be material rather than symbolic oppression, for 'there is no maternal tenderness without childcare, no jam without domestic relations'.[25] To celebrate a model of femininity so close to that used to justify women's subordination is, she insists, a 'politically disastrous idea'.[26] The argument could be extended to the literary sphere, for the characteristics of *écriture féminine* are in many ways close to the emotionalism, irrationality, and emphasis on nature and maternity traditionally attributed to writing by women.

The idea of the body as source of a new writing also invited criticism. The theory assumes that beyond the repression and distortion internalized through a phallocentric language, there exists a bodily reality to which a woman can gain access, and which can then generate the radical text. Attractive as this idea is, many feminists have disputed whether in fact the body can be an unmediated source of self-knowledge, for surely sexuality, like maternity, 'is not a natural given but rather is the consequence of social interactions, among people and among signs'.[27] The theory of 'writing the body' seems both to ignore the very real differences of race, class, sexuality and culture that divide women, making their experience of their own bodies various and plural, and to idealize women's sexual pleasure as an inherently liberating force. Ann Rosalind Jones, making a broadly sympathetic but judiciously critical case for *écriture féminine*, offers a nice corrective to this idealization:

> All in all, at this point in history, most of us perceive our bodies through a jumpy, contradictory mesh of hoary sexual symbolizations and political counter-response. It is possible to argue that the French feminists make of the female body too unproblematic, pleasurable and totalized an entity.[28]

To these now widely-articulated critiques I would like to add a further point. Despite the care with which Cixous, in particular, avoids making a causal link between the attributes of 'femininity' and biological sex, there is in the whole *écriture féminine* argument a strong tendency to identify women with a cluster of positive values, and to demonize masculinity as the repository of all that (at least from a post-'68, broadly Left perspective) is negative. If 'femininity' produces, by analogy with women's sexual and maternal natures, texts that are open-ended, non-controlling, explosively original, sensual and generous, the 'masculine' text, by parallel analogy, is rigidly structured, closed and masterful, cerebral, linear and self-regarding. Not only does this produce (despite frequent disclaimers) a somewhat essentialist and idealized view of 'authentic' female identity,[29] and refuse any consideration of potentially positive aspects of the 'masculine', it also excludes the vast majority of female-authored texts from a properly feminist canon. On this model, women who have written within established literary forms, produced conventionally structured narratives, or adopted the voice of an authoritative narrator are condemned to Cixous's category of those 'whose workmanship is in no way different from male writing' (LM, p. 336). Since much of this book is devoted to demonstrating how women writers have used a wide range of orthodox and unorthodox literary forms to dispute, inflect, negotiate and reimagine female identity, this definition of what constitutes 'feminine' writing is clearly, in my terms, unduly restrictive.

These objections matter, and I think it is important that we resist being swept along uncritically by the powerful and appealing metaphors of generous maternal bodies and revolutionary *jouissance*. They do not, however, invalidate the whole project of imagining a feminine reworking of language and literary form that would allow the production of new meanings. Any attempt by feminists to contest existing social and cultural forms demands the definition of alternative values initially identified with women, and thus 'feminine'. The problem of pre-existing definitions of gender cannot be completely avoided; as Margaret Whitford puts it in her lucidly sympathetic study of Irigaray's work: 'the problem with a feminism of difference is that women's difference has always been used against them'.[30] *Ecriture féminine* attempts the difficult task of reclaiming otherness while refusing the hierarchical binary logic of patriarchal thought.

Despite the reservations outlined above, then, the concept of a writing of difference has opened up new perspectives on the relationship between sex, gender and literature. To rethink the value of qualities conventionally assigned to women, to identify the gaps and silences in language which exclude women's experience, to contest linguistic and cultural forms which implicitly support a world-view in which women are marginalized – these are all politically fruitful aims which make the concept of *écriture féminine* a potentially productive mode of reading and writing women's texts. Chapter 12 will explore *écriture féminine* as a writing strategy in the work of Chantal Chawaf, and as a critical lens through which to read a text by Duras – the only French twentieth-century woman writer, apart from Colette, whom Cixous considers to have 'inscribed femininity' (LM, p. 349).

# 12
## Defining a Feminine Writing: Chantal Chawaf (born 1943) and Marguerite Duras (born 1914)

> Write! writing is for you, you are for you; your body is yours, take it. . . .
> I write woman, woman must write woman.
> (Hélène Cixous: 'The Laugh of the Medusa', p. 325)

The theory of *écriture féminine* was in part a call to take up the pen, an exhortation to women to write radically, differently – to 'write woman'. Apart from Cixous herself, the French woman writer whose texts perhaps most clearly respond to this call – indeed, whose earliest work anticipated Cixousian theory – is Chantal Chawaf.

Chawaf published her first work of fiction with Editions des femmes in 1974, and was involved at the beginning of her career with the Psych et Po strand of French feminism. Having published almost a book a year since then, she has maintained the desire to produce writing 'aimed more at the body than at being read' which would 'give words to what had none before, . . . allow parts of ourselves which have never spoken to speak'.[1] For Chawaf, 'to write as a woman is to write [with] the body'.[2] Her theories of writing and stated aims as a writer clearly align her with the aims of *écriture féminine*, and her texts provide a particularly rich example of what a writing of feminine difference can be.

The 1976 text *Blé de semences* (Seeds of the Corn)[3] is centrally concerned with a daughter's conflicting but equally vital needs to identify with and separate from the mother, as she makes the transition to adult womanhood. This is a fictional world with scarcely a trace of mimetic realism. The narrative could be read as the dream/thoughts of the girl briefly evoked early in the book, living in 'anguished complicity' with her mother in an apartment, but this anchoring in contemporary reality soon disappears, and the text is almost wholly set in a figurative, mythical land, outside historical time and place.

Narrated by a girl on the threshold of maturity, the book immerses the reader in the warm, nourishing, tactile domain of the maternal, ruled over by the Mother/Queen, but inhabited too by a host of secondary mother figures, characterized as half cattle, half human. In a women-only, pastoral community, lives are devoted uniquely to the cultivation, preparation and consumption of food; collectively the women nourish the girl with rich, creamy foods, keep her warm, teach her their skills, massage her flesh with cream. She is merged into their close, loving, earthy existence, where all energy is expended on the maintenance and reproduction of the body. Even the dead body feeds back into the nourishment of the tribe, for skulls and shoulder bones serve as dishes and plates.

Enclosed in this hyperbolically maternal world, the daughter is torn between a sense of belonging and a need to escape:

> There is this house which keeps me here through its art of making milk so creamy, through all the memories which link me to my Queen. . . . And there is this desire to escape, this desire as strong as my resistance. (BS, p. 21)

Her ambivalence informs the narration: thus the descriptions associated with food are both richly sensual – the smell of new-baked bread and cake, the scent of 'cream cheese, dung, fresh cream and autumn harvest' (p. 19), or the Milk Nurse's 'plump breasts like boned chickens that the milk fills like creamy dough' (p. 14) – and nauseating, as when the cycle of eating and excretion is condensed until the narrator, overfed on fat-rich foods, fills her mouth and at the same time feels 'something warm and slimy beginning to come out of my anus and slip stickily down my legs' (p. 60). The repulsion extends in some passages to the female, maternal body, signifier of enclosure, fusion, earthbound passivity:

> [The Queen] asks the Milk Mother to sponge me. And sweating, the Mother of Milk and curds, flabby and soft, stops

moulding her fat udders of cheese with a soup-ladle and brings her swollen, flaccid flesh closer to me . . . (p. 63)

The Queen herself is described both as a beautiful, mobile goddess of plenty, 'girded with sheaves of corn on which hang onions and snailshells' (pp. 18–19), 'lighter than mist' (p. 22), and as a part of the stifling, malodorous world that must be escaped: 'There are moments when I can really take no more, when I have to get away even from the Queen with her smell of curdled soup and menstrual blood' (p. 38).

The stifled and yearning, yet secure and loved, narrator's conflicting desires to leave and to stay form the core of the narrative, and produce a prose which, as Fallaize says, 'is "felt" by the reader as much as read'.[4] Chawaf's writing both foregrounds the question of women's relationship to the maternal body, and exemplifies the sensual materiality of writing which all the theorists of *écriture féminine* suggest is a particularly feminine form of creative expression, made possible by the survival of the 'semiotic' or pre-linguistic modes of signification, and repressed into silence by patriarchal rationalism. However, though Chawaf's text powerfully conveys the sensuous pleasure of closeness to the mother, it also establishes the necessity of separation and escape. The question is: escape to what? If the alternative to a secure but formless and immanent world, characterized as feminine, is the more controlled and transcendent order of the masculine, then we seem to have remained within a familiar patriarchal scenario in which, as Valerie Hannagan puts it in her article on Chawaf, the daughter can gain access to a freer, wider world, but 'only as her *father*'s daughter'.[5]

*Blé de semences* seems at first to correspond to this clear demarcation of gendered spheres. The world beyond the domain of the mothers is characterized as a masculine world: the town which rises beyond their farthest cornfields is dominated by 'the Chief's farm' (p. 26), and separation from the mothers is connected with the girl's desire for a man, for 'a fiancé who would be boundless, so that I would not fear leaving life on earth for life on the sun, and being consumed there' (p. 24). The female world seems to be characterized as regressive, as incompatible with entry into adulthood, citizenship, and sexual maturity; the male world –

which a woman can enter only as a bride – promises excitement and sexual pleasure.

But Chawaf's writing also undermines this neat opposition. First, she employs an 'ironic strategy . . . which explodes myths by exaggerating them',[6] to make it clear that the glamour of the masculine is essentially a function of the girl's desire. The book's opening passage is a splendidly lyrical, and surely parodic, apostrophe to all that desire, informed by myth, attributes to masculinity: 'Bulls! Honeyed sperm! Lover! God! Heaven! Fire of the universe! Father! Light! Future son! Body of the Sun!' (p. 7). The passage which enumerates all the wonderful things the girl has heard about the golden-haired boy, whom she seeks from village to village, is similarly poised between poetry and humour:

> They told me that . . . when he loves you, there flows from him a thick substance that procures more spasms of pleasure than a rose bush has roses in the spring or the magic apple tree has apples or the fire-breathing dragon has testicles. (pp. 12–13)

The sensual qualities of the masculine body, viewed from a perspective of desire, are present here as in many later passages, but the gentle note of parody situates the attraction of men not in the innately transcendent power of the phallus, but in the girl's heterosexual longings.

In fact separation from the mothers is not finally determined by desire for or the intervention of men. In the figure of the Queen, the maternal order becomes more complex, and the nurturing of the daughter is an attempt not simply to imprison her in immanence but, rather, to prepare her for separation. The text frequently associates the male figures of the world outside with the golden light of the sun – traditionally a masculine symbol – but the Queen, too, is linked to the sun, which 'comes to join her, unites with her' (p. 21), 'mingles with the locks of her hair' (p. 92), lights up her beauty until the daughter too 'feels herself transfigured, melting into the sparkling light of day' (p. 92). Transcendence is thus also possible within the women's domain.

And the Queen does not try to prevent her daughter's departure, anxious only that she should be adequately prepared: 'I'm not holding you back. . . . You can leave. . . . Will you have taken enough food from my body?' (pp. 44–5). The daughter herself, though not yet able to leave, recognizes quite early in the text that the mother's gift goes beyond physical nourishment, and that to separate physically does not mean to lose the mother completely: 'You are my mother, you are all the love my flesh possesses, and you will welcome me everywhere when I have left you' (p. 44). At the book's conclusion, the mother sends her daughter into the world with a clear injunction to carry with her the values of the feminine realm: 'Your role will never be to destroy but to protect, to conserve, to save, to create, that is what the warm hollow of my hands will help you to do' (p. 119), and to remember that leaving the mother does not necessarily mean entering a relationship with a male partner but, rather, finding herself:

> – There may be someone at the edge of the forest, the Queen warned me, someone waiting for you, to support you and help you; but don't count on that: there may be no one but yourself. . . .
>
> What did it matter? I was ready to seek . . . , I was ready to cross all limits and frontiers . . . (p. 121)

Separation and entry into a wider, demanding but exciting world does not, in the end, mean deserting the mother when the phallic law intervenes but, rather, developing in accordance with the mother's values and internalizing her love. In this sense, Chawaf's Queen is reminiscent of Colette's Sido.

In a prose which is innovatory and radically sensual, the text explores the female domain of bodily experience, reproduction and the conflicting drives towards fusion and separation in the mother–daughter bond. Yet Chawaf avoids a self-enclosed pre-occupation with the female body as creative source, and obeys Cixous's other imperatives to 'fly in language and make it fly', to 'blaze *her* trail in the Symbolic' ('The Laugh of the Medusa', pp. 343–4; original emphasis). The narrator's jubilant entry into the public domain of men, cities, sexual relationships and adventure, at the close of the text, suggests that the dominant Symbolic Order is to be to be neither ignored nor feared, but explored and contested in the name of values strongly associated with the feminine.

READING DURAS

Marguerite Duras, unlike Chawaf, is not an intentional practitioner of *écriture féminine*, but a writer whose highly original style has frequently attracted the adjective 'feminine'. Adèle King finds that 'Of all twentieth century French women writers, it is Marguerite Duras who is most often cited as an example of a feminine author',[7] and cites, too, her own experiment of asking conference audiences to identify the sex of several contemporary authors from the evidence of a single passage. Only Duras was confidently recognized as a woman writer.

Born in 1914, Duras began to publish in the 1940s, at first loosely observing the conventions of realism. *Moderato Cantabile*, a novel published in 1958, marked a turn towards a more experimental and less mimetic style, which caused Duras to be linked for a time to the anti-realist New Novel movement. Since then, over the last three decades, Duras's unconventional and often enigmatic texts have ranged across prose fiction, autobiography, theatre and cinema. Duras was thus already a prolific and highly regarded author long before the theory of *écriture féminine* first appeared, but the correspondence between her writing practices and the definitions of the 'feminine' produced by Cixous and others led to attempts, particularly in the 1970s, to claim her for the cause of a contestatory, profoundly different feminine writing. Cixous herself, in the famous footnote to 'Laugh of the Medusa', named Duras as one of the two French women writers of the twentieth century who had written 'as women'; and Marcelle Marini, in *Territoires du féminin* (1977), discussed Duras in these terms at much greater length.

Duras herself has remained ambivalent on the point. In 1974 the publication of *Les Parleuses*, a text in the form of a transcribed dialogue,[8] shows Xavière Gauthier encouraging a slightly reluctant Duras to define her work in terms of *écriture féminine*. Gauthier, for example, argues that Duras's books immediately betray the sex of their author because they never follow:

> the model of masculine sexuality, with arousal, satisfaction, then it's all over and then it starts again. It isn't like that for women and men must be quite lost in your books because there's a very strong tension, which is never satisfied . . . [9]

Duras seems at first to have some difficulty grasping Gauthier's point, then she allows this interpretation, but without endorsing it: 'You can say whatever you like about it, you know, take from it what you will'. Elsewhere, Duras has made statements which seem to adopt the language and vision of the theorists of difference – for example:

> Women have been in darkness for centuries. . . . And when they write, they translate this darkness. . . . Men don't translate. They begin from a theoretical platform that is already in place, already elaborated.[10]

The question I would like to pose here, though, has less to do with Duras's own self-definition as an author – which in any case is notoriously changeable – than with with the meaning of the word 'feminine' when applied to a text. Duras's writing does carry an emotional charge, an unexpected, subversive energy that one is tempted to call 'feminine'; like Adèle King's conference audience, most readers seem to identify her texts as female-authored with a certain confidence. How far does the 'femininity' of her texts correspond to the concept of feminine writing produced by post-'68 French theorists? How far do her texts exemplify the features attributed to *écriture féminine*, and to what extent do we need to go outside such a definition in order to articulate what is gendered in the Duras text?

There is no doubt that in many ways Duras does produce a writing close to that advocated by Cixous and Leclerc, implied by Irigaray and Kristeva. Most of her texts, like *Détruire, dit-elle* (Destroy, she said), published in 1969 and written under the influence of the 'Events' in which Duras was very much involved, display only the slightest of narrative lines, conclude not with a resolution but with the opening of a new cycle of movement, are told by an elliptical and uncertain narrative voice, and both formally and thematically foreground the interplay of fusion and separation in relationships with others, particularly relationships between women. The dynamic force in her work, as the title of *Détruire, dit-elle* suggests, tends to be a female character – not because she stages feminist heroines, as might a more realist text, but because feminine desire often resists the conventional forms of feminine satisfaction, and leads to strange and passionate quests which frequently drive the narratives. Thus in *Détruire, dit-elle*,

Alissa, loved and desired by the two central male protagonists, appears to desire above all a closer identification with Elisabeth, who thus becomes the focus of the quest to be undertaken by Alissa and the two men as the novel ends. In *Le Ravissement de Lol V. Stein* (The Ravishing of Lol Stein), Lol's restless desire can find satisfaction only in watching, through the hotel window, as the friend with whom her own identity is partially merged makes love with Jacques Hold, who in turn desires Lol. In terms of conventional narrative expectations, Duras's novels display a disorder, an absence of clear imposition of meaning, an attribution of disruptive power to female protagonists, which could be claimed as 'feminine'.

The text that I want to explore in greater depth, however, is a considerably later work, and one which has the distinction of maintaining both a distinctly female perspective and a formally demanding style, while achieving the status of a major bestseller. The complexity and obscurity of many texts which correspond to theories of sexual/textual difference tend to limit their readership. Duras has generally managed to appeal to a wide readership, but with her autobiographical novel *The Lover*[11] she not only won the Prix Goncourt (in 1984) but also sold a million and a half copies in France alone over the next two years.[12] *The Lover* postdates the 1970s enthusiasm for situating Duras within *écriture féminine*, but it shares many of the thematic and formal features common to her texts, and its popularity means that if it does 'put woman into the text', and thus carry the subversive power Cixous attributes to such writing, we can assume that its disruptive effects touched a considerable number of readers.

*The Lover* is set in French Indochina, later Vietnam, and centres on the passionate affair between the fifteen-year-old daughter of a widowed white schoolmistress, and a rich young Chinese man some ten years her senior. Despite the fact that it recounts the narrator's girlhood from the perspective of her maturity, the narrative structure of *The Lover* is anything but linear and chronological, recalling instead the more complex temporality designated by Kristeva, but also by Irigaray and Leclerc, as characteristically feminine. The text begins with Duras (for the narrator shares the author's biography and persona) 'already old' (p. 7), though female ageing is immediately marked not as a decline but as a progression by the words of an unnamed male observer: 'Rather than your face as a young woman, I prefer your face as it is now. Ravaged' (p. 7). The face, with its marks of past experience, forms the transition to narration of the past – for which, however, the narrator adopts the present tense: 'So, I'm fifteen and a half. It's on a ferry crossing the Mekong river' (p. 8). Thereafter the text weaves between a present suffused with the emotion of the past, and a past in which the present was already implicit: 'Now I see that when I was very young, eighteen, fifteen, I already had a face that foretold the one acquired through drink in middle age' (p. 12).

As in Colette's writing, there is a marked absence here of the tragic model of time, of what one critic calls the 'rationalist, patriarchal model' of 'life as an inevitable linear progression of birth through to death'.[13] Rather, again as with Colette, the past has no one fixed form but remains available to be re-explored and re-created, a fact emphasized both by the use of a present-tense narration for the past, and by the textual reminders of the presence of an older, narrating self who not only retrieves but also shapes and reinvents her memories: 'This particular day I must be wearing the famous pair of gold lamé high heels. I can't see any others I could have been wearing, so I'm wearing them' (p. 15). Duras had already told the story of her girlhood, of her mother and brothers and the Chinese lover, notably in *The Sea Wall* (1950), but here the same events form a different set of images: 'The story of my life doesn't exist. Does not exist. There's never any centre to it. No path, no line.' (p. 11).

An autobiographical narrative might be expected to adopt a single and authoritative voice, in that the 'I' has uniquely privileged access to and control over her/his own story. Yet Duras undermines this structure in *The Lover* by representing her past self in both the first and the third persons, the latter signifying in some cases a distance between the present self and that of the fifteen-year-old girl, and in others focalization from the perspective of one of the other characters, notably the girl's mother or the lover of the title. Thus the initial 'I' that designates the girl on the ferry, crossing the Mekong river on her way to her boarding school in Saigon, becomes 'the girl in the felt hat' (p. 25), as she is viewed both by critical fellow-members of the French expatriate community and by the wealthy Chinese man who desires her.

Focalized by the mother, she is often 'la petite' – the child, or the little one. The sense of a confidently whole subjectivity is disturbed by these shifts in perspective: the self is always also an other, and the narrator claims no single, authoritative perspective on the meaning of her life.

Focalization through the mother's eyes is just one aspect of the centrality of mother–daughter relationships in the text. Although the story of The Lover is structured around the affair between the fifteen-year-old Duras and her gentle, passionate Chinese lover, her intense and ambivalent relationship with her mother is of at least equal importance. This crystallizes, in particular, around the daughter's sexuality, for the mother is, on the one hand, she who enables and defends her daughter – providing for her the delightfully unsuitable, erotically androgynous outfit in which she is first desired, composed of a hand-me-down low-cut silk dress, a leather belt, a wide-brimmed man's hat, and gold lamé high-heeled shoes: 'She not only accepts this buffoonery, this unseemliness, she, sober as a widow, dressed in dark colours like an unfrocked nun, she not only accepts it, she likes it' (p. 28).

This unorthodox endorsement of her daughter's desires extends to permission to return as late as she wishes to her boarding school, thus to spend nights with her lover. Yet at the same time this is the mother who locks her daughter up, screams that 'her daughter's a prostitute, she's going to throw her out . . . ' (pp. 62–3), and keeps her deepest love for her violent first-born son, the 'child-killer of the night' (p. 10). The characterization of the mother as bordering on madness both represents her dilemma, as a widow whose position in a patriarchal, colonial society is at best marginal and at worst untenable, and allows Duras to stage the conflicting emotions between mother and daughter with particular clarity. For the girl, the mother is both 'my mother, my love' and 'the beast' (p. 26). The Lover dramatizes the daughter's conflicting desires for a loving identification with the mother, and for a separation from her which is both inevitable for the daughter to grow, and represents recognition of the mother's own partial alliance with a society that refuses women the position of subject of desire.

For the theme of sexual desire and that of the mother are closely connected. In The Lover, as in so many of Duras's works, desire takes a triangular form, requiring the mediation of a third party.

The episode in which the girl and the Chinese man first make love, in the Chinese quarter of Cholon, is enclosed between two passages about the mother, but also traversed by images of her – both in the girl's conversation with her lover, and in her imagination: 'The image of the woman in darned stockings has crossed the room' (p. 43). The mother, significantly, 'never knew pleasure' (p. 43) ('*jouissance*' in the French, thus in the sense of sexual pleasure); and here, as in the passage where the daughter, moved by the mother's 'sweet, slightly mocking smile . . . almost told her about Cholon' (p. 98), there is evidence of a wish to bring the mother into the circuit of desire. The narrator's friend, Hélène Lagonelle, is also closely associated with desire for the lover:

> I'd like to give Hélène Lagonelle to the man who does that to me, so he may do it in turn to her. I want it to happen in my presence. . . . It's via Hélène Lagonelle's body, through it, that the ultimate pleasure would pass from him to me. (p. 79)

Adèle King suggests that 'the imitative desire of Duras's heroines seems finally to be an attempt to share the erotic experience with the maternal figure',[14] and this corresponds precisely to what seems to be happening in *The Lover*. In the text, the force of the narrator's desire for her lover is closely connected with her ambivalent desire to refind a fusion with the mother that would give joy to both of them, and to escape the mother by transgressing the law she upholds.

The novel's other focus of desire is writing, for the narrator's younger self intends to become a writer, in a move that again is both identified with the mother, who prizes education and is 'jealous' of her daughter's creativity (p. 26), and opposes her, for the mother's ambition for her daughter is a higher degree in mathematics. Writing, like desire, is powerfully associated with water in *The Lover*. The river Mekong, early in the narrative, has a 'current so strong it could carry everything away – rocks, a cathedral, a city. There's a storm blowing inside the water' (p. 14), an image which echoes forward to the 'torrent, the force of desire' (p. 47) which the narrator is about to experience, but also stands as an image of the text itself, with its ability to bear along everything from memories to dreams, places to emotions, in a structure linked by association and close to Cixous's 'language [that] does not contain [but] carries, does not hold back, [but] makes possible' (p. 345). It is the crossing of the sea, at the end of the book, that will take the narrator to a new life in which writing will be possible.

Water imagery is central to the triangular link between desire, the mother and writing. Water is constantly associated with the lover, who first appears on the ferry across the Mekong, who bathes the girl in cool water from jars, and with whom pleasure is compared to 'the sea, formless, simply beyond compare' (p. 42). The mother is also connected to water, for her rare moments of exuberant happiness occur when she washes out the house with buckets of it: 'And everyone thinks, and so does she, that you can be happy here in this house suddenly transmogrified into a pond, a water-meadow, a ford, a beach' (p. 66). In the use of water to signify extreme happiness and pleasure, and a rare sense of closeness to the mother, there is an implicit evocation, too, of the amniotic fluid of the womb.

The 'entre-femmes' or 'among women' which Irigaray finds it crucial to symbolize is present not only in the mother–daughter relationship but also in the network of female figures throughout the text. Most share the status of exiles or outsiders (in a recurring image of women's marginality which recalls the fiction of Triolet); from the Lady whose lover killed himself, and who resembles the narrator in that both are 'doomed to discredit because of the kind of body they have, caressed by lovers, kissed by their lips' (p. 95), to Marie-Claude Carpenter and Betty Fernandez, who live in Paris during the war – one, perhaps, a Resister, the other a Collaborator, but both foreign, exiled, isolated. There is also the Madwoman of Vinh Long who, like the Lady, appears in many of Duras's narratives, and whose madness connects her to the mother.

This reappearance of characters from one Duras text to another constitutes a kind of intertextuality which brings us back to the senses in which *The Lover* is structurally a 'feminine' text. The same scenes, episodes and protagonists constantly recur across Duras's corpus of work, not only between texts but also between genres, so that a different version of the 'story' of *The Lover* is also told in *The Sea Wall* (1950) and *L'Amant de la Chine du nord* (The Lover from Northern China, 1991), and the story of the 'Lady' and of the mad beggar-woman can be found again and again in fiction, theatre and films. Thus Duras's stories 'can never end, but only evolve',[15] negating the linear model of narrative in which stories have a definitive form, and reach an ending.

Finally, the pleasure of reading *The Lover* undoubtedly derives in part from the sensual, musical qualities of the text. Duras's characteristic syntax connects the elements of a sentence not by the use of grammatical constructions expressing relationships of sequence, causality or concession but, rather, by simple commas which both create a sense of an enigmatic world, irreducible to a single explanation, and lend a poetic rhythm closer to the signifying systems of poetry than to the traditional prose of fiction. The passage in which the girl and the Chinese lover first make love illustrates this:

> She doesn't look him in the face. Doesn't look at all. She touches him. Touches the softness of his sex, his skin, caresses his goldenness, the strange novelty. He moans, weeps. In dreadful love. (p. 42)

Repetition of verbs, elliptical absence of narrative explanation (why does he weep? Why is love 'dreadful'?), rhythmic function of the commas – all contribute to a reading experience in which the sensory outweighs the cerebral. This is not the apocalyptic writing of manifesto texts such as 'The Laugh of the Medusa', but it has many of the features which these texts celebrate as feminine: inscription of the body, breaking of the 'thread' of syntax, a moving musicality.

Reading Duras from the perspective of *écriture féminine* theory, then, does help to clarify what is original, feminine and femin*ist* about her text – for despite the reservations of French theorists of difference about the word 'feminism', their writing strongly implies that the radically feminine text will be by its very nature feminist, in the sense that it will challenge the structures of thought that support patriarchy. *The Lover*'s non-linear model of time, positioning of the self as both subject and Other, dislocation of rational syntax and closed meaning, all contribute to the articulation of a vision which is not unique to women but certainly undermines that authoritative patriarchal culture founded on women's marginalization. Thematically and formally, *The Lover* privileges areas of female experience silenced, masked or misrepresented throughout most of French literature – 'surpassing', as Cixous puts it, 'the discourse that regulates the phallocentric system' ('The Laugh of the Medusa', p. 340).

There are, however, aspects of Duras's text which seem to me to contribute to its femininity/feminism, and of which a reading performed solely through the lens of *écriture féminine* fails to take account. The exceptional commercial success of *The Lover* is due not only to the fact that it won the Prix Goncourt but also to the fact that it is significantly less enigmatic and difficult than most later Duras texts, and has a strong element of surface realism. The book has an identifiable and exotic setting (1930s Saigon), tells a story of sexual initiation and interracial love that belongs within a recognizable genre, and is apparently narrated by Duras herself, a well-known figure in France. This realist aspect of the text is not irrelevant to the book's feminist meanings. The physical characterization of the title's 'Lover', for example, contributes to the destabilizing of categories of gender and also, perhaps, questions the ethnocentricity of standard depictions of masculine beauty. He is both intensely desirable and soft-skinned, hairless, his body 'thin, lacking in strength, in muscle . . . weak, probably a helpless prey to insult, vulnerable' (p. 42).

Characterization and plot play interestingly on notions of otherness that include but go beyond the gender divide. The girl's poverty and low status as a woman are countered by the fact that she is a member of the dominant French community. Conversely, the lover's status as a rich, young male is cancelled out by his position as a Chinese man in a French colony, so that the girl's family treat him with scorn, and a marriage between them is socially unthinkable. So the narrator's self-designation in both the first and the third person not only serves to represent the self as Other, and thus undercut the narrator's authority, but also attributes to one condemned to the role of Other, in a colonial society, the position of focalizer, and hence of subject. When Duras writes: 'He breathes her in, the child, his eyes shut he breathes in her breath, the warm air coming out of her' (p. 105), it is 'the lover from Cholon' who is the subject of perception and desire.

Narrative technique, characterization and diegesis, or plot, all merit analysis in the course of a feminist reading of the text. The three come together in *The Lover*'s representation of the female protagonist as not only loved, but herself a lover — as not only object, therefore, but also subject. The text opens with the narrator focalized as object of the male gaze, as a man she does not know praises the beauty of her ageing face, but her fifteen-year-old self then becomes, consistently, the source and the agent of desire. *The Lover* breaks what are still quite powerful taboos in its representation of adolescent female sexuality, for the girl initiates the relationship and defines its terms: 'She says: I'd rather you didn't love me. But if you do, I'd like you to do as you usually do with women' (p. 41). From their first encounter she knows that 'she was attracted to him. It depended on her alone' (p. 41), and her desire for his body determines the duration of their relationship. When she leaves him, it is to make the journey across the sea to France, where she will become a writer, thus subject of her text.

The case of Chantal Chawaf demonstrates that as a writing strategy, *écriture féminine* can, at best, be powerful and effective. As a reading strategy, it is also productive in the quest to define what constitutes the 'feminine' text, but it can also lead to a restricted reading. In focusing only on the most formally disruptive aspects of a text as properly 'feminine', it can disregard more established signifying processes which operate in the majority of fictional texts and for most contemporary readers. This supports Susan Sellers's contention that feminist critics need to aim at an 'alliance between the two perspectives' – between *écriture féminine*'s 'relentless questioning of the processes through which we symbolize, order and understand ourselves, the world and others', and 'Anglo-American concerns with content'[16] and, one might add, with the signifying techniques of realism.

# 13
# Feminism and Realism:
# Christiane Rochefort (born 1917) and
# Annie Ernaux (born 1940)

The implication of *écriture féminine* theory is that language itself – and, by extension, all conventional literary form – is structured on a phallocentric model that relegates women to the margins. From this perspective, to address the issue of women's oppression referentially, within orthodox syntax and genre, is to fall into the trap of reformism, believing that a system founded on the repression of the feminine can be patched up from within.

We have seen, though, that the model of language and gender difference implied here can be – and has been – disputed by other feminists, who are no less committed to the need for radical cultural change. In the period from 1958 to the present – and despite a tendency outside France, since the 1970s, to identify French feminism solely with *écriture féminine* – many French women writers have continued to use the medium of narrative realism to critique and challenge patriarchal culture, in terms which in some respects overlap with the preoccupations of the celebrants of feminine difference.

Realism is a widely used word which carries accumulated layers of meaning. Here it is used to refer not to the nineteenth-century literary movement but, rather (though historical and contemporary meanings are clearly connected), to the most familiar and pervasive form of modern fiction. Realism represents society in terms of individual lives, in a recognizable, plausible manner that mimics documentary accounts of lived experience. The reader is encouraged to suspend disbelief and engage, intellectually and emotionally, with the characters as they live through the action. Because it reproduces a known social world, encourages identification, shapes meaning (at best) subtly while appearing simply to describe and recount, realism has always been used to explore and criticize contemporary institutions and values. The elasticity of the form means that although, historically, the univocal authority of the narrator, the comfortable assumption of the transparency of language, the tendency of realist plots to close with order neatly re-established, have all supported the view that realism is the patriarchal literary form *par excellence*, in fact all these features can be modified to more subversive ends. In France, Marcelle Tinayre, Gabrielle Réval, Simone de Beauvoir, Elsa Triolet, even Colette have all used modified forms of realism for ends that can broadly be described as feminist.

In English-speaking countries, contemporary feminist writers – for example in England Margaret Drabble, Doris Lessing, Fay Weldon; in Canada and the USA Margaret Atwood, Marilyn French, Toni Morrison, Marge Piercy, Alice Walker – have used and reshaped narrative realism, often in combination with or alongside the genres of fantasy (Weldon, Atwood, Morrison), science fiction (Lessing, Piercy) and satire (Weldon). For all these writers, realist narrative has accommodated the critical examination of gender politics, including in some cases that of the problem of language itself. In this respect, and in the not unrelated fact of their appeal to a wide, predominantly female readership,[1] Christiane Rochefort and Annie Ernaux have more in common with many Anglophone women authors than with the writers designated 'French feminists', though their work also reveals a significant convergence of interests with the latter group.

Rochefort is of an earlier generation than Ernaux, and is the more explicitly feminist writer. Born in 1917, she was over forty when the success of her first novel, *Le Repos du guerrier* (Warrior's Rest, 1958), began a literary career which to date (1995) has produced nine novels and three volumes of non-fictional writing. The novels fall into two main categories: the utopian/dystopian texts set in an imaginary past or future, in which contemporary conflicts are projected on to the wide screen of fantasy, and those written in the mode of satirical social realism and set in contemporary France. All her writing is fuelled by a spirit of militant opposition to the dominant values of her society, and by the belief that writing has a political function:

I like literature that's in revolt, that resists, that looks at things in
a clear light and says 'I'm not falling for your tricks'. . . . Anger
is one of the constants in my work – it has to be, simply because
there are numerous reasons to be angry.[2]

Rochefort's anger is wide-ranging: although the sexual and
social oppression of women is one of her primary targets – as
her involvement in the early campaigns of the MLF would lead
us to expect – this is represented as one integral element of the
entire socioeconomic order of the developed world, which reduces
people to economic units, the natural world to raw material for
profit, sexual pleasure to an incentive to conform. Rochefort's
image of contemporary Western society is close to that of Annie
Leclerc – 'This stupid, military world which smells rotten and is on
its way to ruin' (*Parole de femme*, p. 9) – and her tactics, as the critical
chronicler of such a world, recall those proposed by Leclerc: 'We
must simply deflate man's values by puncturing them with ridicule'
(*Parole de femme*, p. 15).

Annie Ernaux, born more than twenty years later (1940),
published her first novel, *Les Armoires vides* (*Cleaned Out*), in
1974, and has published six more books to date. Ernaux is less
inclined than Rochefort to situate her work within the aims
and traditions of feminism, emphasizing, rather, the range of
determinants that operate in the process of writing, of which
gender is only one: 'There are so many things that come into
it – the men/women dimension counts for no more than the
rest.'[3] But in her part-autobiographical representations of growing
up in 1940s and 1950s France, and of the ideological forces that
construct subjectivity, Ernaux foregrounds both class and gender,
and the complex interplay between the two. When, speaking of *La
Place* (*Positions*, 1983), she explains: 'Through my father, I had the
impression that I was also speaking for other people, [for] all those
who are still *beneath literature* and of whom so little is said',[4] Ernaux
is referring to the exclusion from literature of those with low social
and educational status, but there is also in her texts a consistent
preoccupation with the difficulty of articulating women's reality
within an androcentric culture. Women, too, are in many senses
'beneath literature'.

Rochefort and Ernaux are very different writers. Rochefort's political values openly inform her texts, which at times employ a form of heightened, satirical realism to attack their targets through ridicule. Ernaux's style is more sober, and the wider resonance of her personal stories is more subtly conveyed. Coming to writing after 1968, Ernaux designates the body and sexual experience more explicitly than Rochefort, despite a shared emphasis on female desire and its social repression. Both thematically, though, and in their use of realist techniques, the two authors have a great deal in common, and a study of three novels – two by Rochefort, one by Ernaux – will demonstrate both the foregrounding, in each writer, of themes which are central to mid-twentieth-century feminism, and the effective deployment of realism in feminist writing.

The texts are Rochefort's *Les Petits enfants du siècle*[5] (Children of the Century, 1961) and *Les Stances à Sophie*[6] (Stanzas to Sophie, 1963), and Ernaux's *La Femme gelée*[7] (The Frozen Woman, 1981). Each recounts the apprenticeship of a female protagonist who is also the narrator, and whose story is representative of a particular class and generation of French women. Each is firmly anchored in a precise spatial and temporal setting.

For *Les Petits enfants du siècle*, this is the world of the new high-rise housing developments, built outside Paris to rehouse inner-city slum-dwellers as part of the Fourth Republic's programme of modernization.[8] Narrated by Josyane, eldest daughter of one of the 'familles nombreuses' encouraged by postwar pro-natalist policies, *Les Petits enfants* evokes a world in which social conformity is imposed through a system of incentives – more children mean higher allowances, thus greater spending power – and threats, for if the family fail to make docile, productive citizens of their children, police, army or asylum will take over. The novel represents the domestic policies of the French state as a form of symbolic violence, disguised as benevolent modernization. Meanwhile, the boys' war games, and news of the death of a young conscript from the estate, sketch in, in the background, the overt violence of the war to maintain French control in Algeria.

*Les Stances à Sophie* is also set in the late 1950s or early 1960s, but in the world of the Parisian bourgeoisie. The novel attacks the complacent authority and belief in Progress of the ruling class, and in particular, through the story of Céline's experience of a bourgeois marriage, the construction of middle-class women as consumers, domestic managers, and supports for the masculine ego. Ernaux's novel *La Femme gelée*, published two decades later, also looks back to the 1950s. The spatial setting is the provincial France of the Rouen area and later Annecy, and the cultural location that of the awkward frontier between working class and middle class, inhabited by a narrator whose education forces her inexorably to desert the former in favour of the latter. Siobhàn McIlvanney's observation that Ernaux's writing is 'firmly anchor[ed]' in a 'mimetic framework' by the 'plethora of realist information'[9] holds equally true for Rochefort: references to places, reading material, types of car, fashions, school examinations, state policies and allowances situate each of these texts firmly in a specifically located 'real' world.

NOVELS OF APPRENTICESHIP
Each of these novels could be described as a novel of apprenticeship: Rochefort's Josyane and Céline, and Ernaux's unnamed narrator, each retrace, in the first person, a learning process that confronts their open-ended desires and ambitions with their society's definition of what a woman may be. Although the social milieu depicted is very different in each case, and although Rochefort's brand of realism tends much more towards the satirical, the novels occupy similar thematic territory in that they each represent pre-1968 French society in terms of the roles and identities it offers to a young, female narrator. Both from Rochefort's perspective, contemporary with the period of the narratives, and in Ernaux's post-'68 reconstruction, marriage and motherhood loom large as the central reference point of women's lives in 1950s France.

Each heroine chooses to marry a man whom she likes and desires, in the hope that this will lead to a life of happy companionship and to a social legitimacy which it is hard to acquire in any other way. The reality, though, is shown to be different: whatever the personal relationship between the couple, marriage is a social institution whose inequalities are deeply enshrined in practice, and immensely difficult to overturn. The assumption that women are naturally responsible for housework and childcare, that men are breadwinners and heads of the household, and that men's freedom and comfort matter more, prove in each case to shape the relationship once the couple are married. In *Les Stances à Sophie*, Céline is seduced into marriage by Philippe's good looks and persuasive rhetoric, but then finds herself trapped in a life of economic dependence, household management, and obligatory – hence joyless – sex. In *La Femme gelée*, the narrator's egalitarian relationship' with a fellow student fails to survive the marriage service. The plot of *Les Petits enfants du siècle* ends before the wedding day, but the pregnant Josyane's romantic optimism about her future has a hollow ring, set against the narrative's otherwise grim portrayal of women's lives.

Feminist writing has often functioned throughout the nine-teenth and twentieth centuries as a counter-text to romance, representing marriage as ending, not beginning, as alienation, not fulfilment.[10] The inheritance of the same conflicts over marriage, from one generation of women to the next, is signified within these novels by the presence of mother figures, omens of their daughters' possible destinies. In *Les Petits enfants du siècle*, Josyane's worn-out, dull-witted mother seems the very reverse of her critical, lively daughter, but a photograph of her before the children, astride a motorbike, 'long-haired, her flared skirt spread out, laughing' (p. 30), reveals that the dull, vacant woman Josyane has always known is the relic of a girl who resembled her.

In Rochefort's *Les Stances à Sophie* and Ernaux's *La Femme gelée*, the mother figure who embodies all that the narrator fears for her future is in fact a mother-in-law, whose name – thus whose identity – marriage will oblige the narrator to share. Both Madame Aignan (*Les Stances à Sophie*) and the mother-in-law of Ernaux's 'frozen woman' represent orthodox models of 'good' femininity: they have devoted their lives to the upkeep of their homes and the care of husbands and children. They both subscribe wholeheartedly to the philosophy of natural gender difference, and prize the authoritarian, demanding behaviour of husbands and sons as signs of their masculinity, deriving some reflected glory from the men they serve. Thus Madame Aignan cherishes her son's bossiness: 'Even when he was tiny, you should have seen him giving his orders!' (p. 74), and the more subtly drawn mother-in-law of *La Femme gelée* half-conceals her pride behind mock exasperation: 'Men! They're not always easy, are they?' (p. 136).

Ernaux's character, the bright, busy but self-effacing housewife, epitomizes the model of middle-class womanhood which both attracts and horrifies the narrator. The attraction lies in the warmth of social approval that surrounds her: 'everyone admired her, sons, daughter-in-law . . ., it didn't occur to anyone that she could have lived differently' (p. 136). But this approval is bought at the cost of abdication of the self: the older woman has given up education, career, and any aspiration to an identity defined beyond husband and sons. The irritation she inspires in the narrator comes in part from the fact that her story offers a threatening premonition of her own future, as marriage and motherhood make it increasingly difficult to pursue studies and career: "'I did a degree in Natural Sciences, you know, I even did a little teaching but then I met your father-in-law and the children came along, three and all boys, you can imagine!'" (p. 135). Here, as in *Les Stances à Sophie*, the mother-in-law represents all that her son's wife will be coerced and persuaded to become, and all that the novels imply she must avoid.

WOMEN AS CONSUMERS

The incompatibility between marriage and female self-fulfilment is thus a cross-generational theme, but these realist novels also situate the theme within a specific historical moment. The inter-connection between women's domestic role and the development of a consumer economy in 1950s and 1960s France figures in each novel.[11] As technology (at least in theory) reduces the manual labour and time required to maintain a family, and as production increases and diversifies, a married woman's role becomes increasingly that of consumer, invited by advertisers to express her personality and her care for the family by careful selection from the range of domestic aids, prepared food, and other home-centred goods.

Rochefort's representation of the consumer society displays the mechanisms beneath the mythology. The women on Josyane's housing estate are understandably attracted by the prospect of acquiring labour-saving devices, but their only way of gaining the money to do so is by having another child to increase their entitlement to state benefits, which in turn means more work. Thus the economy is kept turning and the pool of future consumers is increased, but at the cost of women's time and women's bodies

– Josyane's mother is already physically 'worn-out' after the birth of four children (p. 8) and goes on to have eight more. The function of consumer goods in locking women into a vicious circle of childbearing and domestic labour reinforces the irony of the teenage Josyane's optimism at the end, as she rejoices that the bonus payable on the birth of her first child will help to pay for the expensive crib glimpsed, and coveted, in the shops.

In *Les Stances à Sophie*, Céline's cynical friend Julia deftly summarizes the role allotted to the bourgeois wife: '"You've got nothing to do with his stupid work. You're his wife not his colleague. There's only one thing you've got to bother about: that he earns the cash and you spend it all"' (pp. 74–5). But even this freedom has its limits. Céline discovers the illusory nature of the consumer's choice when her request for household items in the colours and sizes she wants are met with: 'But we haven't got those, Madame. There's no demand. But aren't I demanding it? No, it's not that: there's no demand, therefore if I demand it I don't exist' (p. 57). Invited to use consumption as a form of self-expression by the range of colours and styles proposed, the female consumer in fact finds that her choice (and thus the self she expresses) is predetermined within firm limits.

Consumption operates, too, to place the emphasis on the unique individuality of the private home, hence on the need to invest labour in 'keeping it nice'. In this sense it is one strand in the web of pressures that turn a relationship based on liking and desire into a domestic arrangement predicated on the woman's labour. Ernaux's narrator and her husband, the latter now promoted from student to young executive, spend their first disposable income on furnishing their new flat, with care, as befits young intellectuals, to mark their distance from the ideology of consumerism: 'Of course we know happiness can't be found in owning things, we've done all that stuff about the difference between being and having, and Marcuse; things are just alienating shit' (p. 152). Acquiring things with a detached sense of irony, however, has exactly the same effect as acquiring them innocently: 'once you've got your own furniture that cost an arm and a leg, and got you into debt, how can you not "look after" them, how can you let the dust collect on them . . .' (p. 153). The moment of purchase is an important one in the narrator's downward slide towards the dull resignation of the conclusion.

LANGUAGE, OPPRESSION AND RESISTANCE

Within the mode of realism, Rochefort and Ernaux address the key issues of language and sexuality, also foregrounded in a different way by the theory and textual practice of *écriture féminine*. For Rochefort, too, language is to be regarded with caution and mistrust, as the medium of the dominant ideology that shapes and determines thought itself: 'as long as we use [language] without examining it, without taking it apart, we express the dominant order even when we are loudly and clearly expressing opposition to that order'.[12] But for Rochefort, the specificity of women's relationship to language depends not on the deep structures of language itself, nor on bodily difference, but on women's different *situation*: 'We have neither the same History nor the same culture. Nor the same experience. How could we have the same way of thinking, or the same style?'[13]

Whereas for *écriture féminine* the work of the feminine text is to find new linguistic forms to articulate a female sexuality, and a female imagination, unsymbolized by existing language, Rochefort's model is more optimistic about the adaptability of the language we have. The realist narratives of both Rochefort and Ernaux 'take language apart' in specific social contexts, showing how it works to shape and limit consciousness, but they also appropriate language and narrative form in order to articulate the world from a woman's perspective. In each of the novels under discussion here, language is the most intimate form of oppression, but it is also shown to be a crucial and viable medium of everyday resistance.

In *Les Petits enfants du siècle*, the conversation of adults is observed, with sardonic candour, by the adolescent Josyane, particularly during a low-budget summer holiday which brings several families together in a rural guesthouse and subjects them to unaccustomed leisure. The adults make conversation, expressing as personal opinion those ready-made clichés which serve the existing order by justifying their joyless lives and deflecting any impulse to revolt. The women compare numbers of children, and reflect on the inevitable suffering of their sex: '"You bring them into the world, and then . . . " "That's life, for us women."' (PES, p. 71). The men – the 'progenitors', in Josyane's mocking term – compete to demonstrate their virility through their knowledge of wine, 'dirty stories' and cars. The sexes unite to intone the platitudes of resignation which disguise boredom as pleasure and privilege: 'Well at least we're getting a good rest' (pp. 61, 62, 75). What keeps the men going is their sense of identity as providers and heads of the household, a self-image bolstered by their display of knowledge, and metaphorically sexual power, in the verbal combat over cars and other 'masculine' subjects. For the women, it is above all the discourse of romance that disguises limited horizons and lives of unpaid domestic labour. The conversation in the guesthouse is intercut with the plot of the novel Josyane is reading: a poor orphan girl is seduced and made pregnant by a rich aristocrat, but is revealed after many adventures to be the true heiress to the château, whereupon the duke marries her. The device of interweaving the discourse of masculine self-assertion with that of popular romance neatly ironizes both, but the function of the language of romance is also a serious theme in the book.

Josyane's mother and sister devour endless picture romances of the 'Oh my darling don't leave me I can't live without you' (p. 144) kind, to Josyane's disgust. But the novel's sharply ironic ending has Josyane, hitherto the reader's faithfully lucid ally in the text, herself adopt romantic discourse as she falls in love and enters what the novel has shown to be the inexorable cycle of marriage, multiple motherhood and domestic subordination – a common and collective fate, idealized as a unique and ecstatic personal destiny. All Josyane's dissatisfaction and well-motivated – if muddled – feelings of revolt are safely recuperated by the ideology of romance:

. . . we'd always known somewhere deep inside that something was missing, without knowing that it was Each Other. That's why I'd so often been sad, cried with no reason, gone round in circles not knowing what to do with myself . . . (p. 151)

In *Les Stances à Sophie* too, platitudes masquerading as personal opinion circulate to maintain belief in the wisdom of unlimited economic expansion, a market-led economy, and the division of labour by class and gender. Thus the leftish, libertarian Céline,

seduced by Philippe's physical charms and sexual skill into marrying an archetypal son of the bourgeoisie, finds herself with a
mother-in-law who declares with equal fervour that mass car
ownership is a tribute to the democratic nature of capitalism
('Even our cleaning lady's husband's got one' [SàS, p. 63]), and
that it is a sign of the fecklessness of the working class ('They
haven't even got enough to eat. . . . They feed their children on
potatoes but they've got to have their car . . .' [p. 63]). In this
novel the protagonists are the beneficiaries rather than the victims
of the system, so that the fervour with which they articulate even
the most contradictory clichés of 'common sense' is fuelled not just
by blinkered conformism but also by self-interest.

Playing the part of the perfect hostess, Céline relieves the tedium
by observing, with detached precision, the linguistic behaviour of
Philippe's colleagues and friends. What interests her is:

> not what they say (which is never the slightest, *slightest* bit
> interesting) but how they say it. The rhythm and the sound.
> . . . And what is remarkable is that once they've started off
> with 'In *my* opinion', they repeat word for word something
> they've pinched from elsewhere, content, syntax, vocabulary,
> the lot. (p. 103)

The culture of individualism, central to the consumer economy,
is displayed as a myth: those who, by necessity or choice, have
accepted the system can speak only within the discourse it allows,
and thus endlessly recirculate the same statements.

Philippe initially ensnares Céline, too, in this linguistic trap
by posing rhetorical questions based on the assumptions of the
dominant value system:

> Where does this lifestyle get you? (p. 9)

> Are you really happy like this? (p. 12)

> Why do you try to stifle what is best in you? [i.e. the fact that
> she is a woman] (p. 19)

Only by refusing the terms of the questions – disputing the model
of life as investment and return, questioning the definition of both
happiness and 'being a woman' – could Céline escape, and as
her wiser, retrospective narrating self notes, at that point in her

relations with Philippe, sexual attraction is powerful enough to blur lucidity.

If language is so intimate and effective a form of oppression, then it will clearly also be a site of resistance. Rochefort's rebels, those characters with whom the novels invite the reader to identify, are often those who display some form of linguistic non-conformity. Josyane has an early passion for grammatical analysis which prefigures her critical awareness of the language of her parents. Her brother Nicolas, her chief ally in the family, refuses to speak at all until he is two and a half, then enters language with the irreverent phrase 'Con maman', a more vulgar and almost rhyming equivalent of 'Mummy stupid' (PES, p. 36). Josyane's twin brothers, whose probable lack of consanginuity with the family (there was a mix-up in the hospital) is a positive sign in the novel's terms, are given to both linguistic vulgarity and wordplay, which irritate adults and their thuggish, macho brother Patrick: '"Patrick nous les casse, Pa-trick-noulékass, Pakass nous les trique"' (Patrick pisses us off – Pa-trick-us-off-pisses – Patpiss off us tick [p. 59]). Guido, the Italian immigrant worker who provides Josyane's only brief glimpse of a more generous, pleasurable world, speaks French with a slightly halting simplicity that excludes the commonplace. It is both ironic and appropriate that Josyane's final capitulation should be signified most clearly by a linguistic switch from irreverent candour to vapid sentimentality.

In the more optimistic conclusion to *Les Stances à Sophie* , Céline's self-liberation is doubly linguistic. First, she rejects the censorship of language imposed by Philippe, who found her frequent use of expletives such as 'merde!' (shit) unbecoming in a woman and inappropriate to his social milieu. The whole novel is Céline's retrospective account of her own mistaken attempt to keep Philippe on his terms, and of her return to lucidity. Céline-the-character reclaims the right to a verbal vulgarity that is in itself a rejection of codes of feminine propriety, and Céline-the-narrator mingles registers in a style that refuses the hierarchical division between 'literary' and 'popular' language, as in the passage on the beauty of the moon in Italy: 'And the olive leaves that the moon turns silver, the little bright bits that move. I love. I love. I love.The sky at night drives me crazy' (p. 181).

Secondly, Céline begins to recognize and question the implications of certain grammatical and semantic codes. For example, as
in the extract just quoted, she frees the verb 'to love' from the
grammatical requirement that it have an object. From Philippe's
first declaration that he loves the 'real her', a phrase which
excludes her 'way of life, social milieu, friends, habits, clothes,
hairstyle, language, taste and ideas' (p. 12), romantic love in
the novel has signified the desire to appropriate and control
the other. When Céline starts to come alive again, after a
period of alienation as 'Madame Philippe Aignan', she returns
to her earlier intuition that the verb 'to love' might not be
restricted to the transitive form ('Does it really need someone
as object?' [p. 24]). Loving need not imply a single other as
object, nor yearn inevitably towards the reciprocity of 'to love
each other', but can designate a state of joyful appreciation that
is intransitive, and hence unrestricted. Céline's refusal to obey
the norms of grammar here signifies her estrangement from the
orthodox concept of the couple.

This estrangement extends, during her final months with
Philippe, to an explicit attempt to analyse and classify the
linguistic differences between them, through the compilation of
a 'Célino–Philippian Dictionary', also known as the 'Dictionary
of Neo-Bourgeois Semantics'. This exercise permits both narrator
and novel to explore the semantic slipperiness of words, particularly
of words which are ideologically charged.

It is the word 'love' that has brought Philippe and Céline
together, for Céline values 'love', and is susceptible to the
argument: 'if you really love me, couldn't you do this, which
makes me happy, rather than that, which doesn't?' (p. 9). But
as *Les Petits enfants du siècle* shows, romantic love is also a myth
with a political function, for it conflates the pleasure of desire
and heightened emotion and the social imperative to become a
housekeeper and mother. For Céline, true love means 'acceptance
and contemplation of an Other, as he is, and without expecting
that your love be returned' (p. 188), but her 'Dictionary of
Neo-Bourgeois Semantics' shows that Philippe's definition is quite
different: 'Love. – A: for a woman; total devotion to domestic
service including night duty. B: for a man; enjoying this state of
affairs' (p. 188). Since it was semantic confusion that led to their

marriage, it is Céline's rigorous linguistic analysis that enables her to return to independence.

On Rochefort's model then, language is not inherently, structurally masculine, but it encodes the values and meanings which support the ruling ideology. Dissent can be articulated, but this demands the critical examination and deliberate transgression of prevailing linguistic conventions. Ernaux's unnamed narrator, the eponymous 'Frozen Woman', also discovers that language shapes and determines experience, even against the grain of initial perception. Ernaux's text, like Rochefort's, reveals the function of language in the construction of restrictive gender roles, but also demonstrates the possibility of expressing what the dominant language distorts or leaves unsaid.

In Ernaux's novel, the education system and the Catholic Church play a particularly significant role in the transmission of class and gender ideologies. As a very small girl, Ernaux's narrator learns from direct observation that sex does not determine a particular type of behaviour or personality. Her mother, who runs the shop side of their small business, is 'a woman who battles against everything, the suppliers and the debtors, the blocked gutter in the road and the bigwigs who are always trying to ruin us' (p. 15/p. 79[14]), while her father, 'a soft-spoken gentle dreamer of a man' (p. 15/p. 79), looks after the café but also most of the housework and cooking, and the everyday needs of his small daughter. Her aunts are tough, loud, cheerfully undomesticated women: 'no proud housewives, . . . always out of the house, brought up from the age of twelve to work like men' (p. 15/ p. 78). Going to school, however, means learning to read and write the correct grammatical form of the French language and internalizing, along with these, the officially sanctioned view of what constitutes social normality. The opening section of the novel juxtaposes the child's lived reality with the received version of family relations, the women she knows – 'all loudmouths with bodies that had not been kept in order' (p. 9/p. 75) – with the reading books' 'fragile women full of grace, angels of the hearth with a gentle touch'(p.9/p.75); the maternal 'whirlwind of strength' (p. 15/p. 79) and gentle, ever-present father, with 'In the mornings daddy-goes-to-work, mummy-stays-at-home, she-does-the-housework, she-makes-a-wonderful-meal' (p. 16/p. 79).

Although the narrator's sense of having betrayed her parents finally has more to do with class than with gender, the feeling of shame she develops at 'not being the child of normal parents' also contributes to her sense of guilt. She rejects their pragmatic and flexible division of roles along with their way of speaking: these parents contravene the grammar of acceptable gender relations.

## LANGUAGE AND SEXUALITY

Since, in *The Frozen Woman*, the narrator's upbringing provides her with sufficient love, freedom and encouragement to endow her with a positive self-image, she starts out with no sense of the disadvantage of being a girl. She and her girlfriends from the neighbourhood explore their bodies, and secretly examine and compare genitals. Despite the absence of any word to designate the female genitalia which does not imply shame – her mother's 'quat'sous' ('twopence') makes the child think of 'dessous'(underneath) and 'souillé' (soiled), and hence connotes 'Dirty, to be kept hidden' (p. 40) – the girls do not perceive themselves as lacking something, having 'only the "nothing" which, though I didn't know it yet, the boys would attribute to us' (p. 42). They are fascinated but unimpressed by the boys' 'titites' ('willies'), despite the latters' being endorsed by a variety of possible signifiers ('baisette', 'zézette', 'la machine' [p. 43]), in marked contrast to the girls' 'it'. Linguistic disadvantage does not initially stop the narrator from experiencing her body as the source of present well-being and future excitement: puberty, menstruation, intercourse, all are envisaged as 'glories', aspects of that 'glorious body I'd have in the future. . . . Travelling and making love, at ten years old I could think of nothing more wonderful' (p. 46).

Women's 'lack' is thus clearly presented as a social construction determined not by the nature of language itself, for a positive sense of the body long survives entry into language, but by particular and powerful linguistic practices. In decreeing that women 'haven't got one', language privileges the phallus and defines the non-phallic as simply non-existent. It is possible, within existing language, to assert the opposite, but the notion of a 'lack' carries the weight of social consensus in a society that assumes man as the norm, and the phallus as the signifier of authority. The narrator soon recognizes a disjuncture between her own confident sense of identity and the language learnt outside the home. Her Catholic school teaches its female pupils that 'the body is dirty and intelligence a sin' (p. 56), presenting the virgin martyrs and the 'stainless' Virgin Mary as the ideal of womanhood, but in the boys' school 'they're taught to be leaders and the holy fathers think having balls counts for something, *duas habet*'[15] (p. 56).

Because women 'lack' the phallus, they are assumed to lack sexual desire, creativity, and the right to authority. Thus the narrator's initial curiosity and desire for sexual experience with boys is soon restrained by the discovery of the linguistic and behavioural constraints on female sexuality. Even to use 'vulgar' language is to risk being labelled a 'slut': linguistic and sexual propriety are assumed to be closely connected. To manifest outright desire, or availability, is to relinquish the chance of attracting the 'right' boys: accept the rules 'or else loneliness' (p. 116). In a society where contraception is illegal, the unmarried mother is stigmatized, and only male sexuality is supposed to get 'out of control'; the woman's role is to keep sex within appropriate boundaries. Her desire must be expressed, and experienced, as 'giving in':

> A boy has the freedom to desire, not you my girl, resist, that's the code. . . . Every pleasure was called a defeat for me and a victory for him. Living the discovery of another person in terms of giving in. I hadn't foreseen that, and it wasn't much fun. (p. 96)

Literally, then, 'having balls' signifies the right to express and experience desire. The ten-year-old girl's happy sense of the promise of a glorious sexual future culminates instead in 'a body constantly under surveillance' (p. 68). The metaphorical meanings of 'having balls' are equally powerful: having suc-ceeded in gaining access to university, the narrator discovers that intellect and creativity are also the prerogative of the owner of the phallus. 'Literary creation is like ejaculation' (p. 108); 'a hundred times over I hear writing compared to the activity of the penis' (p. 108). In a moment of exasperation her new husband betrays the limits of his commitment to sexual equality: 'You're not a man – there's still a difference, you know, when

you can piss in the sink standing up then we'll see . . .'
(p. 133).


Both Rochefort and Ernaux depict a society in which the legal and
political equality of women has done little to alter a culture that
identifies sexual energy, power and creativity with the masculine.
Writing five years before May 1968, Rochefort indicates the
sources of the anger that was to fuel the MLF; Ernaux, looking
back from the 1980s, traces the potency of a model of sexual
difference that would be exposed, challenged and ridiculed by
post-1968 feminism, but which had already (the novel implies)
quietly stifled the aspirations of generations of women, and which
would not be definitively defeated on the barricades. In all three
novels the assertion of feminine desire, and the reclaiming of
language, are closely interwoven and central to women's resistance
to a phallocentric culture.

Rochefort is categorical about the subversive power of desire
throughout her work. 'There is nothing more instructive than
pleasure' (*Archaos*, p. 144[16]) is the guiding principle of Archaos, an
exuberantly 'soixante-huitarde' ('May '68 style') Utopia founded
on the abolition of property, authority, and law, and on belief in
the beneficial power of good sex for everyone. Outside Utopia,
though, desire and its satisfaction are not instructive and enriching
in all circumstances, for they have been harnessed to the cause of
Order and Progress, twin principles of patriarchy in Rochefort's
world. Heterosexual, monogamous desire clearly smooths wom-
en's path into marriage, an institution shown to be detrimental
to their health and freedom, and neither Josyane nor Céline's
lovemaking with their respective Philippes could be described
as liberating. Positive sexual experience in Rochefort's novels
includes tenderness and generosity towards the sexual partner,
but never demands reciprocal fidelity, nor focuses solely on the
body of the lover, opening instead on to a feeling of intense vitality
and communion with a wider, extra-social world.

Thus Josyane's ineffectual but (in the novel's terms) well-judged
attempts to escape the limits of her destiny centre on moments
of intense sexual pleasure, procured by 'getting laid by anyone,
anywhere' (PES, p. 143), but memorable less for the body of the

lover than for the sense of communion with a natural world that
negates the oppressive order of the everyday:

> Night blurs everything. Disorder and darkness. How is it that
> when I think back I always see above my head the sky and the
> trees, and never the face of the boy who must have been there
> . . . (PES, p. 143)

Conversely, Céline's regulated, conjugal couplings with the
Philippe for whom she once lusted put an end to her desire,
and to the sense of vital well-being this procures. Madame Philippe
Aignan 'has nothing between her legs' (SàS, p. 110), and this process
of castration is reversed only when she rediscovers desire with her
friend Julia. Desire between women provides an effective riposte
to Philippe's reduction of sex to the assertion of phallic power, and
returns to Céline the capacity to feel pleasure. Julia is followed by
Fabrizio, Thomas and Stéphanie, and by a renewed sensitivity to
the natural world and to music. It is this rediscovered curiosity and
appetite for life, triggered by the return of sexual desire, that leads
to Céline's critique of language, thus to her rebellion and the book's
happy ending.

Desire, then, is seen as a vital part of feeling whole, and
as an impulse constrained and diminished by the language and
institutions of a patriarchal culture. Writing which asserts and
explores female desire, as these novels do, and displays the
mechanisms of repression, plays its part in the process of feminist
reclamation of both sexuality and language. In *La Femme gelée*, the
role of literature in the formation of a gendered identity forms one
strand of the narrative. The narrator's positive sense of bodily
identity as a child, and her happy anticipation of womanhood, is
matched and reinforced by her sense of unlimited access to the
world through reading. Despite her own very limited education,
it is the mother who introduces her daughter to the pleasure of
reading, who shares with her *Jane Eyre* and *Gone With the Wind* and
whole series of romantic fiction, who buys her books as delightful
and mildly transgressive treats ('Just like at the cake shop, choosing
between meringues and almond slices, the same appetite and the
same feeling that perhaps we shouldn't really' [FG, p. 25]). Books
are thus initially women's domain for the narrator, and despite the
derision with which even her father treats 'women's novels', the

daughter adores her mother's ability to choose exciting fiction over household chores: 'I remember the books she encouraged me to read as an opening on to the world' (p. 27).

Like 'having my periods, and making love' (p. 25), the other grown-up pleasures the girl looks forward to, adult reading turns out to be a disappointment. The school reading books, with their graceful housewife mummies and awe-inspiring daddies, are a better indication of what was to come. With the one exception of Beauvoir, whose *Second Sex* provides a brief echo of childhood optimism, she meets only male authors and male heroes on the syllabus at school and university. Like most of her generation, the narrator is initially delighted to have access to high culture, and only too willing to believe that 'the question of what to do with one's life has no sex, nor has the answer' (p. 94). But the choice of career, the meaning of marriage, the significance of having children all turn out to be profoundly determined by sex, while canonical literature confers interest and human dignity only on the masculine experience. Camus's 'Myth of Sisyphus' dignifies the absurdity of the human condition, but in an image comically ill-matched to the banality of housework:

> Sisyphus endlessly rolling his rock back up the hill, what an image – a man on a mountain, outlined against the sky; a woman in a kitchen putting butter in a frying pan three hundred and sixty-five days a year, neither beautiful nor absurd, just life. (p. 155)

Not only do childcare and housework leave the narrator with minimal time for reading, even when this becomes an essential part of her job as a teacher, but the frustration and even the joy of these activities are beneath the attention of 'serious' literature.

Using the techniques of realism to situate their stories in a precise historical setting, each of these texts addresses the problem of women's reclamation of language and sexuality in a profoundly androcentric culture. By articulating the problem, they also contribute to its solution, for all three novels bring 'subliterary' female experiences into the domain of serious literature, producing compelling critiques of the process of repression, but also implied or realized models of resistance. Rochefort and Ernaux write women's stories into the literary memory of mid-twentieth-century France, and through the defeat of Josyane and of 'the frozen woman', as through the self-liberation of Céline, they demonstrate the importance for women of possessing a language and literature that can symbolize, and thus validate, their experiences and identities as women.

# 14
## An Open Conclusion:
## Women's Writing Now

A patriarchal society is a society structured by 'power relations in which women's interests are subordinated to those of men', and characterized by a discourse in which 'the nature and social role of women are defined in relation to a norm which is male'.[1] In nineteenth-century France, as the gradual process of industrialization accentuated the gendered separation of spheres, men defined their own roles in terms of production, decision-making, political and domestic authority, and attributed to women a natural propensity for domestic labour and management, and for the nurturing, affective side of life, relegated to the private domain. To women, also, fell the task of representing those ideals in whose name the creation of wealth and the pursuit of power were justified: the Nation, the Republic, Freedom, French Culture – Paris is still a city rich in semi-nude female statues eloquently symbolizing the regions, the virtues and the conquests of France. Their abundant marble curves also signify another female role: that of embodying and celebrating male desire.

Sexual difference is strongly marked in French culture. Inscribed in law for most of the last two centuries, accentuated by a set of symbols that have identified women with State and Nation but excluded them from citizenship, the significance of gender has deep historical roots. And despite the pronounced tendency to celebrate the feminine, and to represent French women as the incarnation of all that is best about 'Frenchness', women have always been the artefacts rather than the creators of culture. When, as we have seen, in *The Newly Born Woman* (1975), Cixous spelled out a series of binary oppositions which structure thought, few readers had (or indeed, have) any difficulty in allocating the terms to the masculine or the feminine side:

Activity/Passivity
Sun/Moon
Culture/Nature
Day/Night . . .
Form, convex, step, advance, semen, progress
Matter, concave, ground – where steps are taken, holding – and
dumping – ground.[2]

The division of human qualities and activities by gender, and the
consistent identification of the masculine with the positive term,
create problems both for feminism and for women writing. While
power, authority and the right to a public voice are so powerfully
marked as masculine, integration into the existing political and
cultural system means denying solidarity with the devalorized
feminine. Status is conferred by the Father, not the Mother, and
to admit to being the Mother's daughter, made in her likeness,
threatens the already fragile situation of the emancipated woman.

For women, access to the public world has often demanded a
literal or figurative transvestism. Sand's male narrators represent, in
the text, her assumption of the authority of the writer. Rachilde
adopts a literary genre which is overtly misogynist. Beauvoir,
in the very act of deconstructing the discourse of patriarchy,
reproduces the phallocentric view of human sexuality, and of
what constitutes human achievement, which is so deeply etched
into language and culture. To be considered a 'woman's writer' is
still suspect: even today, many French women writers fiercely deny
writing particularly *as* a woman or *for* women.[3]

The alternative to integration on patriarchy's terms, though,
is the acceptance of marginality. On the one hand, this may
mean agreement to remain within the limited sphere allotted to
women. Around the turn of the century, popular women novelists
expressed the anxiety that full emancipation would lead to the
abandonment of the altruistic, nurturing relationships identified
with the feminine, and thus resolved their narratives by the
heroine's return to romantic love, the home and motherhood.
On the other hand, women can reject the assimilationist model
of feminism in the name of a more radical challenge to patriarchy,
choosing to stay 'on the margins' in order to develop an alternative
philosophy based on their feminine difference. Renée Vivien's

poetry, for example, not only deplores the social exclusion of lesbian women, but also represents their separation from mainstream
culture as a source of creative freedom.

George Sand's later fiction, with its combination of unconventional heroines and conventional narrative resolutions, goes some
way towards redefining feminine difference as strength. Sand also
evokes the figure of the good Mother as a possible alternative
source of authority. In this she looks forward to Colette, whose
social commentary draws its originality and humour from an
unusually feminine perspective, and whose writing makes the
maternal figure the source of wisdom, creativity and – specifically
– writing. Colette, in turn, prefigures Cixous, with her powerful
image of the mother's milk as ink: the woman writing 'always has
within her at least a little of that good mother's milk. She writes in
white ink.'.[4] The chain extends further: in Chawaf, the mother is
a nurturing figure not only in the material, bodily sense, but also in
her capacity to give her daughter the strength to leave the maternal
world, to separate and seek her own path. Ernaux's mother figure,
too, in *The Frozen Woman*, bestows on her daughter a positive
sense of self-worth, and her first introduction to the pleasure of
the written word.

The recurring figure of the good mother, who is not merely
associated with the safety of the womb and childhood, but is
the source of adult freedom and creativity, is thus one of the
threads that can be traced through the work of several of the
writers studied. Women's writing – a category encompassing an
immense range of historical contexts as well as a great variety of
individual authors – can usefully be seen through the metaphor
of embroidery, an art form long associated with women, and
employed by Colette in *The Evening Star* as an analogy for the act
of writing. Seen thus, it is best envisaged not as a neat, completed
pattern, which would permit a once-and-for-all definition of what
constitutes its specific femininity, but as an unfinished tapestry with
an irregular but discernible design, through which can be traced
recurring colours, textures and motifs.

One such motif is the narrative of female apprenticeship –
or, in Beauvoir's formulation, of how 'one is not born, but
becomes a woman'. From Sand in the mid nineteenth century to
Ernaux writing in the 1980s, this narrative observes a very similar

structure: girls learn to repress their desire for pleasure, adventure and exploration, acquire the skills and attributes that will assure them acceptance as women, accept the inevitability of marriage, despite the unequal power relation that this contract implies, and conclude the story either angry and frustrated, or having reinvested their realistically whittled-down desires and ambitions in marriage and motherhood. Thus Sand's Fadette and Brulette learn how to please and to be less self-assertive, hence how to make satisfactory brides; while Rachilde's Mary Barbe accepts her marriage in a spirit of cynical self-preservation. Rochefort's Josyane turns her inevitable fate into a glorious destiny through the language of romance; while Ernaux's 'frozen woman' ends the novel bereft of her early dreams and numbly contemplating a future without desire or freedom.

The narrative of romance, then, in which two lovers meet and negotiate the perils of separation and misunderstanding before reaching the happy ending of a permanent union, is frequently subverted or reversed in women's writing. The marriage that traditionally closes the romance is more likely to close down the heroine's hopes of freedom or happiness – or to constitute, as with Colette, a diversion from the real concerns of the text. None the less, until relatively recently, life outside marriage presented the problem of viable alternatives, and another recurring figure in the writing of this period is that of the exile, the single woman who is an outsider and finds neither home nor role in the society she inhabits. Sand's Lélia, who precedes the period under study here by fifteen years, was a precursor of these female exiles. Rachilde's restless, angry heroines reject women's traditional destinies and find no alternatives, ending the narratives in embittered solitude or in death. Vivien's wanderers are mocked and pilloried, or retreat into secret, enclosed spaces far from the public gaze. Triolet's work is haunted by the solitary and often literally homeless outsider, whose short-lived experience of community in the Resistance ends, ironically, with the Liberation of France. The figure of the exile, however, fades as women's economic survival and social opportunities cease to depend so uniquely on marriage – thanks to their increased participation in both education and employment.

Patriarchal constructions of gender also underlie the occasional appearance of another figure of the exile: the male refugee from the masculine role. Sand's Sylvain (*The Country Waif*) and Joseph (*The Bagpipers*) are casualties of a ruthless system of gender differentiation that demands separation, emotional autonomy and physical courage of all male children. Colette's Chéri is their heir, and his story, like theirs, can end only in death. There is perhaps an echo of the male exile, too, in Duras's 'Lover', the gentle and passionate man caught between cultures, whose obsessive love for the narrator ends only with his life.

Writing by women frequently poses the problem of how to put the body into words. When Zola's Nana appears on her stage, the focus of the breathless desire of a whole audience, she highlights the difficulty of representing the body from a woman's perspective.[5] The female body is so overlaid with images rooted in centuries of an androcentric culture that its reclamation is immensely problematic. Until well into the twentieth century, powerful taboos also operated which discouraged women from writing explicitly about the body, female or male. Sand maintains a discreet distance from the body; Tinayre observes the prevailing conventions by turning the narrative's 'close-ups' on to the female body in erotic scenes, so that her heroes are spared the indignity of subjection to the female gaze. Rachilde, on the other hand, begins to undermine the convention of male subject and female object with sensual, precise descriptions of 'Monsieur Vénus', and Colette consistently represents her heroes from the affectionate, sensual and irreverent perspective of desire – also bringing the female body into a different focus by making her heroines the subjects of their desires, and the curious, proprietorial observers of their own bodies. Beauvoir shocked the nation with the explicit discussion of sexuality and bodily functions in *The Second Sex*, but it is since the 1970s, with the feminist movement's emphasis on the politics of reproduction, the prominence of lesbian feminism and the decensoring of the erotic in general, that women's writing has explicitly named and textualized the female body – making it, in the case of *écriture féminine*, the basis of a new aesthetics.

Arguments that ground a feminine world-view and a feminine aesthetics in women's biology cannot fail to remind us of the essentialist doctrines long used to prove women's inferiority. Yet the case for a connection between bodily and textual difference can be persuasive: among the writers studied here, there is certainly a recurring, though by no means uniform, preference for the cyclical and circular model of time over the linear. This can be related to biology, in that women's lives are patterned by the menstrual cycle and men's are not; and to sexual pleasure, in that male orgasm is more structured towards a single climax. However, this difference is equally related to women's different historical experience, for while men have been following their stories of separation from the mother, self-definition through education and work, towards the pinnacle of their adult prime and on into decline, women have been negotiating a combination of separation and identification with the mother, pursuing lives far more intertwined with those of others, in which the opportunity for self-definition may come much later – after the years of childrearing, for example.

Sand's narratives are not plot-driven to the same extent as those of her male contemporaries (Balzac and Zola in particular), but meander often towards a predictable conclusion, the interest of the narrative lying elsewhere. Colette's aesthetic is very markedly a non-linear one, for the circle, the spiral, the incorporation of the past into the present are central to almost all her work – and Duras displays many of the same features, weaving past with present so that the narrative is held together not by the drive towards resolution and closure, but by other, more complex patterns.

A final thread is that of the fairytale. As a form of narrative that was originally oral, fairytales have always been told by women as well as men, and their plots deal with women's lives and deaths. Sand's pastorals have a fairytale edge to them – being located outside contemporary time and place, they permit the imagining of relationships which defy the laws of the real: idyllic unions between mothers and sons, the triumph of love over economic and social inequality. Rachilde's grim stories reproduce the darker side of fairytales, colourfully expressing the anger of defeated women as the King's power is re-established in order for closure to take place. Chawaf's unlocated, timeless world of female nurturing, magnificently desirable heroes, and the heroine's quest for a happiness which is not the traditional one of marriage reworks familiar elements of fairytale myth.

Myth and fairytale are strongly present in much contemporary writing by French women. Sylvie Germain, winner of several literary prizes in the 1980s, creates a world grounded in historical reality but rich with the figurative, supernatural qualities of legend in *Le Livre des nuits* (The Book of Nights, 1985[6]) and its sequel, *Nuit d'ambre* (Night of Amber). Pierrette Fleutiaux won the 1985 Goncourt de la nouvelle (Goncourt Prize for the Short Story) with *Métamorphoses de la reine* (The Queen's Metamorphoses[7]), a collection of fairytales retold with wicked humour and serious intent. In Fleutiaux's versions, the reversal of roles and the modification of plots reveal the power relations that determined narrative outcomes in the classic tales: when Snow White's seven dwarves are replaced by seven female giants, and the refugee from the palace is not Snow White but her stepmother, then the happy ending depends not on marriage to the Prince but on contesting the power of the King. A vegetarian Ogress gives a very different slant to the story of Jack and the Beanstalk. Fleutiaux's incisive humour is both a critique of age-old but still powerful ideologies, and a pleasurable imagining of happier alternatives.

The location of stories outside realist time and place, and the archetypal simplicity of the narratives, also connect Marie Redonnet's texts with the fairy story. Redonnet has published two plays and several novels, the most recent of which, *Nevermore*, appeared in 1994. *Rose Mélie Rose*,[8] the third novel in a trilogy published between 1985 and 1987, exemplifies Redonnet's recurring themes and style of writing, its simple but powerful images achieving the resonance of myth.

Mélie, the narrator, reaches her twelfth birthday as the book opens. She has lived, since her birth, by the waterfalls above and far away from the town, cared for by her adoptive mother, Rose, who discovered her, newborn, in the cave by the river's source. Mélie's birthday coincides with the death of Rose, with her first menstruation and her departure, alone, to the port, capital of the increasingly depopulated island on which the story is set. The twelve chapters take Mélie through sexual initiation, a rapid education and employment in the town hall, marriage and pregnancy. At the end, after the departure of her husband, Yem, Mélie returns alone to the cave by the waterfalls, to give birth to a new Rose. Leaving to her daughter the Book of Legends inherited from the mother Rose, enriched by the twelve photos which mark each stage of Mélie's own initiation, and the jewels that were Yem's wedding gift, Mélie abandons the baby, to be found and cared for in her turn by a new mother, and goes back down the mountain to die by the sea.

Redonnet's fictional world is both highly original and strangely familiar. As with Colette and Chawaf, it is a matrilinear world, in which wisdom, values and symbolic wealth are handed down from the good mother Rose, to Mélie, to Rose and – the alternating pattern of names suggests – on through a limitless chain of mothers and daughters. The fluid boundaries between the identities of individual women are signified both by the echoing names, as Mélie also meets her own namesake in the town, and by Mélie's uncertainty about the validity of her own reflection. The older Mélie has a painting, at first believed to be a portrait of Rose in her youth: 'If I look for long at Mélie's picture and at myself in the mirror, I end by getting them all confused. It's the same with names. Sometimes I no longer know who is Mélie' (p. 94). Despite its ending with Mélie's imminent death, the story closes on a note of hope for the future, for the return to the cave, and the bathing of the baby at the river's source, presage a childhood as happy as Mélie's own for the new daughter, and all Mélie's acquired wealth of love and knowledge is present in the gifts left to Rose.

The cave of birth and death is set significantly away from the structured, largely masculine order of the town – a town, moreover, which is gradually dying, reclaimed by the forest, the water of the lagoon, and the superior power of the mainland. The town is full of symbols of decay: gradually all administrative authority, and even the island's cultural heritage, kept in the museum, are transferred to the mysterious mainland. Mélie's acquaintances die one by one, and in the lagoon the hull of a wrecked ship gradually sinks. Yem, the book's hero, is associated with Mélie's world not only through her love for him, but also through the fact that his boat bears the name of the same Fairy Queen who figures in the Book of Legends. Yem neither dies with the town nor goes to the mainland, but sets off to sea to seek a legendary channel, appearing. as Elizabeth Fallaize suggests, 'in his own way, to be making the impossible return to the mother, in a parallel journey to that of Mélie'.[9] If the 'return to the mother' is associated with death, it is also associated with life – both because it takes Yem and

Mélie away from the dying town, and because it leads to the birth of Rose.

*Rose Mélie Rose* resembles a condensed, lyrical version of the narrative of female apprenticeship, though with an ending that is neither resignation nor revolt. It echoes the cyclical structure of many Colette texts, as well as that location of positive values in the mother observed in the work of Colette, Cixous, Chawaf and Ernaux.

Contemporary France is a multicultural community, in which debates over the meaning of gender now have the added dimension of cultural and religious differences. A generation of young women, whose parents were immigrants from the French ex-colonies of North Africa, have grown up in France, been through the same educational system and acquired all the same cultural reference points as their peers, while they are aware, too, of a very different cultural heritage. Second-generation French North Africans are known as 'Beurs', a word based on the 'verlan' (a slang which reverses syllables) version of 'Arabe'. The feminization of this word in its diminutive form gives 'beurette' – a word often used in the media to designate young 'beur' women.

The voices of the 'beurettes' are beginning to be heard in literature, and two novels over the last eight years have had a particular impact: *Georgette!*[10] (1986), by Farida Belghoul – who is also a film director – and the more explicitly entitled *Ils disent que je suis une beurette*[11] (1993) by Soraya Nini. The novels have certain features in common: first-person narration by young female narrators, thematic emphasis on the conflict between on the one hand the authority of French culture, represented by school and teachers, and on the other that of the father at home; a focus on language and reading as the sites of this conflict. They are also very different. Nini's novel, marketed as a semi-autobiographical account of the author's struggle against the racism of French society and the prejudices of her family, seems to aim directly at a liberal French readership. Indeed, the novel opens with the arrival of a television team at the narrator's housing estate, and their invitation to her to be their guide as they make their documentary. The programme is never broadcast, but the episode frames the novel within the expectations and the curiosity of a French spectator.[12] Belghoul's novel, on the other hand, plunges the reader into the consciousness of an imaginative, strong-minded seven-year-old, and presents a much more complex picture of the cultural tensions she negotiates.

*Beurette* clearly resembles Rochefort's *Les Petits enfants du siècle*, an earlier novel of female apprenticeship, also set on a rundown housing estate and told by a narrator whose conventional parents, macho brother and too-numerous siblings restrict her life unbearably. Samia is twelve as the novel opens, and the victim of occasionally explicit, verbal racism, though more damaged by the less conscious and overt racism that allows her to underachieve at school and end up in the vocational stream, for girls destined to be sales assistants or domestic workers. Meanwhile, at home, the traditionalist culture of her parents and brother leads to violent conflicts with Samia's eldest sister, who eventually runs away from home to gain her freedom. Samia is also the victim of brutal assaults by the brother, who defends his own masculine privileges, and the family 'honour', by enforcing the strict seclusion of his sisters outside school hours.

Although the mother is characterized with a degree of sympathy, both she and the father correspond in many ways to Western stereotypes of the immigrant: the father is permanently out of work on grounds of ill-health, yet never available to fulfil any fatherly role other than that of imposing his authority; both parents are incapable of understanding their daughters' frustration at the restrictions imposed on them; neither seems capable of acquiring any understanding of the culture in which they now live. Paradoxically, it is in the characters of the two Algerian aunts who make lengthy, separate visits to the family that Nini portrays attempts by adults to understand and facilitate the negotiation between cultural traditions. Overall, though, the narrative is unequivocal: Samia gains freedom and happiness thanks to a French education and to the acquisition of qualifications that will allow her to make a living and leave the family.

Language and literature are crucial to this process. Secret communication between Samia and her sisters is often important if they are to protect each other from the wrath of parents and of the brother they name the 'KGB'. Their invention of a secret code, the 'S language' composed of 'verlan', contemporary slang and elements of English, allows them to communicate between themselves without being understood by the others: 'We just wanted to keep our spirit safe, hold on to our own story . . . – it was our thing, our girls' secret' (pp. 111–12). A sympathetic and inspiring teacher introduces Samia to reading, and she devours Beauvoir, Sagan, 'books in which women had the most important role, or those that talked about oppressed peoples' (p. 119). Thanks to the same teacher, she manages to start training as a youth worker. School becomes 'my only gateway out of all this and into freedom' (p. 118).

Thus Samia relives, though with a happier ending, the drama of Rochefort's Josyane, with the oppressive power of French state policy in the 1960s replaced by that of a traditionalist North African, Islamic culture. Despite its indictment of racism, the novel appears to endorse the image of 1990s France as a modern, egalitarian society, in which patriarchal politics survive only in the backward culture of the immigrant community. The liberation of women is identified here with complete integration into the dominant culture, and with the renunciation of difference.

In *Georgette!*, the home culture and the school culture also conflict, but value is distributed much less simply. The father embarrasses his daughter by failing to understand the importance of having the right pencil, by writing in Arabic in her new exercise book, and thus starting at the wrong end: 'His rotten writing's just scribble. Back to front writing doesn't exist! . . . I'm dishonoured for life. My mother will kill herself. My brother will go mad' (p. 58). He seems to her quite mad at times – as do most of the adults who surround her – though Belghoul uses the little girl's incomprehension to signal indirectly the racism from which the father suffers at work. Understanding only the surface meaning of her father's words, the narrator finds his reaction to the foreman's apparent invitation to take a holiday strange: 'The boss says to him "If you don't like it, clear off home then!" . . . And instead of shaking his hand, he wants to strangle him! (p. 34). But the father is also a warm, generous presence, the dispenser of cakes and pastries to guests, the source of a rich, mellow singing voice: 'Even a lion, if I had one, would go to sleep in heaven listening to him' (p. 34). The mother, too, is sometimes embarrassing, arriving late to pick up the children from the crèche, for example, because she got lost on the métro and someone maliciously gave her the wrong directions. The narrator's brother, a little older, interprets the teacher's polite remark about the mother's bright, ethnic dress as patronizing or sarcastic, but the little girl defends her mother passionately: 'Mummy's beautiful in her lovely dress' (p. 100). Yet as a woman who has neither education nor any recognized role or status in French society, the mother cannot provide her daughter with any model that merges the feminine with the desirable – if alien – public world.

The female schoolteacher, on the other hand, fails as a role model because her view of the world excludes the narrator's home culture. Seen through the eyes of the little girl, the teacher's assumptions about North African families appear both offensive and inappropriate, and the narrator's unvoiced indignation is shared by the reader. The teacher is, at one level, well-intentioned, and determined to persuade her mute pupil to benefit from the education on offer. But she assumes that the problem is a violent father – 'I know that over there men hit their wives and children like animals' (p. 121) – and that as the daughter of a working-class immigrant family, the little girl must be suffering from poverty and neglect. 'Worse than a loonie', opines the narrator and, with a nice reference to French cultural eccentricities, 'that raving madwoman is a cannibal. She eats frogs and she eats me, right to the marrow' (p. 130).

*Georgette!* is not, to the same extent as *Beurette*, a novel of apprenticeship, for its timescale is short, its narrative minimal and composed of episodes whose status, as event or as fantasy, is sometimes unclear. The plot revolves, in a sense, around the question of whether it is the (female) teacher or the father who has authority over language: learning to read and write with the teacher is immensely difficult, as Belghoul intimates through the child-narrator's recurring images of deep, treacherous inkwells, but the father seems to have writing back to front. Neither school nor home has the monopoly of sense or virtue, and the novel ends on the image of drowning in an inkwell, the problem of language and authority unresolved.

Given the strong dynamic towards homogeneity in French Republican culture, Beur women writers have to deal twice over with the problem of difference. In a France which defines itself as 'one and indivisible', equality is achieved through integration and the erasure of difference, and otherness is ignored or equated with inferiority. Women's otherness has been celebrated, but the rhetoric of adoration has merely euphemized contempt. French citizens from other cultures can achieve acceptance, but to be fully part of the nation they must renounce alternative models of identity. Writing by French women from the immigrant communities is fuelled by the need to challenge and extend a national culture which, in the twentieth century, has been richly creative, yet limited by its androcentricity and by its identification of a specific cultural inheritance with universal values.

Literature by women of the 'Beur' community is one area of renewal in a France in which, as a recent article phrased it, 'the frontier between masculine and feminine is shifting',[13] but in which that frontier is still a reality. All the writers referred to in the discussion of *écriture féminine* continue to publish, Duras and Rochefort are in their seventies but still writing, Chawaf, Ernaux, Redonnet may well have long careers ahead of them – and the contemporary French publishing scene includes innumerable women writers for whom there was no space here: Marie Cardinal, Assia Djébar, Claire Etcherelli, Sylvie Germain, Jeanne Hyvrard, Annie Saumont, Monique Wittig, to name but a few. In a society still structured by the power systems and the cultural forms of patriarchy, women's stories, both in the biographical and the literary sense, continue to differ from men's. Women's writing continues in its creative quest to rethink sexuality, language and identity in terms that are neither androcentric, nor simply a reversal of patriarchy's binary logic, but make a virtue of the heterogeneous, unfixed meanings of the word 'feminine'. The tapestry of women's writing is neither predictable in its future patterns nor, by any means, complete.

# Notes

*Introduction*
1 Maïté Albistur and Daniel Armogathe: *Histoire du féminisme français*, vol. 2, p. 450.
2 Richard J. Evans: *The Feminists*, p. 46.
3 Raymond Williams: *The Long Revolution*, p. 55.
4 Stuart Hall in Bennett *et al.* (eds): *Culture, Ideology and Social Process*, p. 29.
5 Colin Radford *et al.* (eds): *Signposts in French Literature* (1988).
6 Virginia Woolf: *A Room of One's Own* (1929). See also *Women and Writing*, ed. Michèle Barrett.
7 See Bibliography.
8 Albistur and Armogathe: *Histoire du féminisme français*, p. 447.
9 Hélène Cixous: 'The Laugh of the Medusa', in Robyn R. Warhol and Diane Price Herndl (eds): *Feminisms: An Anthology of Literary Theory and Criticism*, p. 342.
10 Williams: *The Long Revolution*, p. 64.
11 Resa Dudovitz: *The Myth of Superwoman: Women's Bestsellers in France and the United States*, p. 77.
12 Elizabeth Fallaize quotes a survey carried out by *Le Monde* (23 September 1988) which reached this conclusion – and pointed out that women make up 57 per cent of the working population in France, and read more than men do. *French Women's Writing*, p. 20.
13 See, for example, James F. McMillan: *Housewife or Harlot: The Place of Women in French Society 1870–1940*, Part II.


PART I 1848–1914

*CHAPTER 1 Women in French Society 1848–1914*
1 The phrase is Zola's own, appearing in his preliminary notes for the novel. He also describes his novel as 'the poem of the cunt'. *Nana*, transl. George Holden, Penguin, Harmondsworth 1972. Introduction, pp. 11 and 13. All subsequent references are to this edition.
2 Roszika Parker and Griselda Pollock: *Old Mistresses: Women, Art and Ideology*, p. 14.

3   Olympe de Gouges: Introduction to the *Déclaration des Droits de la Femme*. Quoted in Michèle Sarde: *Regard sur les Françaises*, p. 524.

4   Auguste Comte: *Cours de philosophie positive* (2ᵉ leçon) 1830–42, quoted in Jean Thoraval: *Les Grandes étapes de la civilisation française*. Bordas, Paris 1967, p. 303.

5   Raymond Williams: *Culture and Society 1780–1950* (1958). Penguin, Harmondsworth 1961, p. 322.

6   Chris Weedon: *Feminist Practice and Poststructuralist Theory*, p. 2.

7   Maïté Albistur and Daniel Armogathe: *Histoire du féminisme français*, vol. 2, p. 469.

8   Steven Hause: 'More Minerva than Mars: The French Women's Rights Campaign and the First World War' in Margaret Randolph Higonnet *et al.*: *Behind the Lines: Gender and the Two World Wars*, p. 106.

9   Feminist historians have argued that the possibility of equal partnership between men and women decreased as industrialization progressed. See, for example, Louise A. Tilly and Joan W. Scott: *Women, Work and Family*; and Bonnie G. Smith: *Ladies of the Leisure Class: the Bourgeoises of France in the 19th Century*.

10  Albistur and Armogathe: *Histoire du féminisme français*, p. 472.

11  Ibid., p. 482.

12  Roger Magraw: *France 1815–1914: The Bourgeois Century*, p. 288.

13  In *La Femme* (1858), quoted in Benoîte Groult: *Le Féminisme au masculin*, p.74.

14  Theodore Zeldin: *France 1848–1945. Vol.I: Ambition, Love and Politics*, p. 306.

15  Virginia Woolf uses this title of a popular Victorian poem to designate that selfless, pure feminine ideal which the woman writer had to kill in herself in order to be able to write. See Virginia Woolf: *Women and Writing*, p. 59.

16  For an analysis of the role of the maid within bourgeois sexual mythology, see Anne Martin-Fuguier: 'La Bonne' in Jean-Paul Aron: *Misérable et glorieuse: la femme du XIXᵉ siècle*, p. 33.

17  Smith: *Ladies of the Leisure Class*, p. 107.

18  Quoted in James McMillan: 'Clericals, anticlericals and the women's movement in France under the Third Republic', p. 363.

19  Quoted in Françoise Mayeur: *L'Education des filles en France au XIXᵉ siècle*, p. 186.

20  Smith: *Ladies of the Leisure Class*, p. 177.

21  J. Simon:·*La Femme au vingtième siècle* (1892), quoted in McMillan: 'Clericals, Anticlericals and the Women's Movement in France under the Third Republic', p. 363.

22  Sarde: *Regard sur les Françaises*, p. 86.
23  See Dominique Maingueneau: *Les Livres d'école de la République 1870–1914 (discours et idéologie)*.
24  Jean Alesson: *Le Monde est aux femmes* (1889), quoted in Groult, *Le Féminisme au Masculin*, pp. 76–7.
25  Quoted by Jean Rabaut: *Féministes à la Belle Epoque*, p. 33.
26  Quoted by Groult: *Le Féminisme au Masculin*, p. 85.
27  Quoted by Sarde: *Regard sur les Françaises*, p. 584.
28  'La Tactique féministe', in *La Revue socialiste*, 1 April 1908, quoted in ibid., p. 586.
29  For example, Louis Napoleon made both Mérimée and Sainte-Beuve senators, and Lecomte de Lisle was rewarded for his republicanism by being made librarian at the Senate in 1872.
30  Introductions to the work of Marceline Desbordes-Valmore and Delphine Gay de Girardin can be found in an extremely useful recent book, Sartori and Zimmerman (eds): *French Women Writers: A Bio-Bibliographical Source Book*. The same is true for Marie d'Agoult, Anna de Noailles and Lucie Delarue-Mardrus (see below), as well as for many writers who appear in subsequent chapters.
31  Quoted by Tarna Lea Engelking in her chapter on Anna de Noailles in Sartori and Zimmerman (eds), *French Women Writers*, p. 333.
32  Review by Jacques Fontade in *Le Figaro*, 1901. Dossier Anna de Noailles, Bibliothèque Marguerite Durand, Paris (date and page reference unavailable).
33  Resa L. Dudowitz: *The Myth of Superwoman: Women's Bestsellers in France and the United States*, p. 81.
34  Alexandre Dumas *fils* in *Lettres sur les choses de ce jour*. Quoted in Albistur and Armogathe, *Histoire du féminisme français*, p. 498.
35  Michèle Sarde: *Regard sur les Françaises*, p. 86.
36  These estimates are given in Steven C. Hause and Anne R. Kenney: *Women's Suffrage and Social Politics in the French Third Republic*, p. 42.
37  See Albistur and Armogathe, *Histoire du féminisme français*, pp.523–30.
38  Daniel Armogathe and Maïte Albistur (eds): *Nelly Roussel. l'éternelle sacrifiée*, p. 13.
39  Ibid., p. 59.
40  Evelyne le Garrec (ed.): *Séverine. Choix de papiers*, p. 198.
41  Albistur and Armogathe: *Histoire du féminisme français*, p. 570.
42  Elizabeth Anne Weston: 'Prostitution in Paris in the later 19th century: A Study of Political and Social Ideology', p. 170.
43  Charles Sowerwine: *Sisters or Citizens? Women and Socialism in France since 1876*, p. 8.

44   Ibid., p. 2.


*CHAPTER 2 George Sand and the Problem of Authority*
 1   *Histoire de ma vie* (1854). Calmann-Lévy, Paris 1879, vol. 2, Part
     IV, p. 77.
 2   Ibid., p. 81.
 3   The concept of amassing symbolic cultural capital in order to achieve
     a position of legitimacy within a specific social context is developed
     by the French sociologist Pierre Bourdieu, initially in the 1966 article
     'Champ intellectuel et projet créateur'.
 4   See Toril Moi: 'Appropriating Bourdieu: Feminist Theory and
     Pierre Bourdieu's Theory of Culture', pp. 1037–8, for a clear
     exposition of the concept of the 'miraculé(e)'.
 5   The majority of the critical sources cited in the Bibliography deal
     more with the novels of the 1830s than with the later work.
     These earlier works are certainly the most immediately accessible
     to a feminist reading.
 6   Quoted in Siân Miles: *Introduction to George Sand's Marianne (1876)*.
     Methuen, London 1987, p. x.
 7   Patricia Thomson: *George Sand and the Victorians*, p. 28.
 8   Ibid., p. 61.
 9   Ibid., p. 154.
10   Christopher Robinson: French Literature in the Nineteenth Cen-
     tury, David & Charles, London 1978, p. 105.
11   Episode recounted in *Histoire de ma vie*, vol. 2, Part IV, pp. 121–2.
12   Quoted in Isabelle de Courtivron: 'Weak Men and Fatal Women:
     The Sand Image', in Elaine Marks and George Stamboulian (eds):
     *Homosexualities and French Literature*, p. 211.
13   The 'anxiety of authorship' is a key term used in Sandra M.
     Gilbert and Susan Gubar's study of nineteenth-century English and
     American women writers, *The Madwoman in the Attic*.
14   Miles: *Introduction to Marianne*, p. 53.
15   Ibid., p. 54.
16   Ibid., p. 57.
17   Ibid., p. 52.
18   A translation of *La Petite Fadette* (1849), *Country Waif* does exist (see
     Bibliography), but references here are to the edition published by
     Garnier, Paris 1958, and translations are my own.
19   *Les Maîtres Sonneurs* (1853), transl. as *The Bagpipers*, Cassandra,
     Chicago 1977. References are to the translated edition.
20   *Histoire de ma vie*, vol. 1, Part II, p. 286.
21   It is Naomi Schor who draws attention to the psychoanalytic nature

of Fadette's cure for Sylvain, describing this as a 'talking cure, as she instructs her patient to respect the cardinal rules of what was to become psychoanalysis, the uncensored articulation of all thoughts.' 'Reading Double: Sand's Difference', p. 265. Schor also likens Sylvain's transferral of love from his brother to Fadette herself to Freudian 'transference'.

22  See Note 21.
23  For a more developed and rather different argument on the significance of the Fadette–Sylvain relationship, see Gretchen van Slyke: 'History in Her Story: Historical Referents in Sand's *La Petite Fadette*'.
24  The argument here is limited largely to the novels, since these constitute the bulk of Sand's work, and since discussion of the plays raises questions about performance and production, rather than simply text, which would require more space than I have here. A comprehensive account of Sand's work in theatre can be found in Gay Manifold: *George Sand's Theatre Career*.
25  Pierre Bourdieu: *Distinction: A Social Critique of the Judgement of Taste*, p.252.
26  Toril Moi, 'Appropriating Bourdieu', p. 1022.
27  *Elle et lui* (1859). Calmann-Lévy, Paris 1896, p. 99.
28  *Adriani* (1854). Calmann-Lévy, Paris 1896, p. 142.
29  Ibid., p. 75.
30  *Mademoiselle la Quintinie* (1864). Ressources, Paris & Geneva 1879, p. 31.
31  Ibid., p. 29.
32  Naomi Schor: 'Idealism in the Novel: Recanonizing Sand', p. 65.
33  Ibid., p. 73.

*CHAPTER 3 Feminism, Romance and the Popular Novel: Colette Yver, Gabrielle Reval and Marcelle Tinayre*
1  Jean Larnac: *Histoire de la littérature féminine en France*, p. 223.
2  Resa Dudovitz: *The Myth of Superwoman: Women's Bestsellers in France and the United States*, p. 77. Dudovitz argues that Larnac's figures are conservative estimates, and that of the 25000 professional writers in France in 1909, 5,000 may well have been women.
3  Obituary for Gabrielle Reval in *Nouvelles littéraires*, 22 October 1938.
4  All references are to *The Doctor Wife*. Hutchinson, London 1909.
5  There were 18 female students for 3,479 male students in Parisian faculties of medicine in 1889/90. By 1918/19 there were still only

454 female medical students. Maïté Albistur and Daniel Armogathe: *Histoire du féminisme français.* vol. 2, p. 581.

6 There are close parallels here between the situation of the woman as doctor and as artist. The idea of women painting the nude body provoked anxiety comparable to that induced by the female doctor: in both cases a woman was abandoning a 'feminine' position as object of the (creative/scientific) male gaze, and taking the active role in a process identified with masculine knowledge and creativity. See, for example, Rosemary Betterton: 'How do women look? The female nude in the work of Suzanne Valadon' in Betterton's book *Looking On.* Valadon (1865–1938) belonged to the same generation as the writers discussed here.

7 All references are to *Les Sévriennes.* Albin Michel, Paris 1900.

8 *Avant l'amour* (1897). Calmann-Lévy, Paris 1908.

9 In a lecture at the Université des Annales, 8 March 1924. Dossier Marcelle Tinayre, Bibliothèque Marguerite Durand, Paris.

10 The major exception to this is the more complex *La Maison du péché* (The House of Sin, 1902), in which the conflict between the hero's Jansenist puritanism and the heroine's affirmation of temporal values ends in separation and death.

11 *Hellé.* Calmann-Lévy, Paris 1898.

12 *La Maison du péché.* Calmann-Levy, Paris 1902.

13 *La Rebelle.* Calmann-Lévy, Paris 1905.


*CHAPTER 4 Rachilde: Decadence, Misogyny and the Woman Writer*

1 *Pourquoi je ne suis pas féministe.* Aux Editions de France, Paris 1928.

2 Sandra M.Gilbert and Susan Gubar: *The Madwoman in the Attic,* p. 3.

3 J.K. Huysmans: *A Rebours* (1884). Fasquelle, Paris 1963.

4 Catulle Mendès: *La Première Maîtresse.* Charpentier, Paris 1887.

5 In Barbey d'Aurevilly: *Les Diaboliques* (1874). Garnier, Paris 1963.

6 Villiers de l'Isle-Adam: *L'Eve future.* Brunhoff, Paris 1886.

7 Jean Pierrot, in *The Decadent Imagination 1880–90,* p. 126, uses the expression 'the ball and chain' to designate this figure in Decadent fiction.

8 Luce Irigaray: 'Volume Without Contours', in Margaret Whitford (ed.): *The Irigaray Reader,* pp. 53–68.

9 All stories in Barbey D'Aurevilly: *Les Diaboliques.*

10 Jennifer Birkett: *The Sins of the Fathers: Decadence in France 1870–1914,* p. 161.

11 *Quand j'étais jeune.* Mercure de France, Paris 1947.

12 *Monsieur Vénus* (1884). Flammarion, Paris 1977.

13  *Le Meneur de Louves*. Mercure de France, Paris 1905.
14  All the stories and plays referred to can be found in *Contes et nouvelles, suivis du théâtre*. Mercure de France, Paris 1900.
15  The physical description of Mary is clearly intended to connote a capacity for evil. She is 'pretty, but slightly strange', with eyes set so close to each other that 'the eyebrows formed a single straight line'. Her thumbs are exceptionally long. *La Marquise de Sade* (1887). Mercure de France, Paris 1981, p.16.
16  *La Jongleuse* (1900). Des femmes, Paris 1982.
17  For a more developed analysis of this scene and its significance for Rachilde's representation of female sexuality see Diana Holmes: 'Monstrous Women: Rachilde's Erotic Fiction', in Kate Ince and Alex Hughes (eds): *Desiring Writing: Twentieth Century Erotic Writing by Women*.
18  Nancy Chodorow: *The Reproduction of Mothering* (1978).
19  *La Tour d'amour* (1899). Le Tout sur le Tout, Paris 1988.

CHAPTER 5 *From the Pillory to Sappho's Island: The Poetry of Renée Vivien*
1  Lilian Faderman: *Surpassing the Love of Men: Romantic Friendship and Love between Women from the Renaissance to the Present*.
2  Charles Baudelaire: *Les Fleurs du mal*. Oxford, Blackwell 1959, p. 117.
3  Ibid., p. 148.
4  Ibid., p. 142.
5  Shari Benstock: *Women of the Left Bank*, p. 289.
6  Ibid., p. 271.
7  All page references are to Renée Vivien: *Poésies complètes*, ed. Jean-Paul Goujon 1986.
8  Quotations from the poetry are given in the French, because to render rhythm and sound in translation is virtually impossible. The translations are my own, and seek to provide a close equivalent of the meaning of the original.
9  Isabelle de Courtivron:'Weak Men and Fatal Women: The Sand Image' in Elaine Marks and George Stamboulian (eds): *Homosexualities in French Literature*, p. 210.
10  Alfred de Vigny: *La Colère de Samson* (written 1839, published 1864).
11  Paul Lorenz: *Sappho 1900 Renée Vivien*.
12  Renée Vivien: *La Dame à la louve*, Paris, Régine Deforges 1977, p. 7. All subsequent page references are to this edition.

13  Elyse Blankley: 'Return to Mytilène: Renée Vivien and the City of Women', in Susan Squier (ed.): *Women Writers and the City: Essays in Feminist Literary Criticism*, p. 52.

14  Blankley helpfully points out that Vivien's preference, outside the Mytilène poems, for night, moon and shadow over day, sun and light corresponds to her refusal of the violating phallus, both in its physical and its symbolic senses, for her poems frequently juxtapose 'the basic symbolic bifurcation undergirding western civilisation: the dark lunar female impulse contrasts with the Apollonian sun that stands for male reason' ('Return to Mytilène', p. 53).

15  Hélène Cixous (with Catherine Clément): *La Jeune née* (The Newly Born Woman), p. 162.

16  Margaret Whitford (ed.): *The Irigaray Reader*, p. 55.

17  Marcelle Tinayre: 'Trois visages de Renée Vivien', Schérazade, no. 3, 1910.

## PART 2.

### CHAPTER 6 *Women in French society 1914–58*

1  Marcelle Tinayre: *La Veillée d'armes: le départ*. Calmann-Lévy, Paris 1915.

2  Georges Dupeux: *La Société française 1789–1970*, p. 199.

3  For fully developed arguments on the negative outcomes of World War I for French women, see James McMillan: *Housewife or Harlot: The Place of Women in French Society 1870–1940*; and Steven C. Hause: 'More Minerva than Mars: The French Women's Rights Campaign and the First World War', in Higonnet et al.: *Behind the Lines: Gender and Two World Wars*.

4  Marguerite Durand, quoted in Steven C. Hause and Anne R. Kenney: *Women's Suffrage and Social Politics in the French Third Republic*, p. 192.

5  Steven Hause points out that although the French women's suffrage movement is generally described as a minority phenomenon, in 1914 it had 100,000 adherents, considerably more than the trade-union movement (89,000), which is usually taken more seriously by historians. See Hause and Kenney: *Women's Suffrage*, p. 269.

6  Ibid., p. 238.

7  Hause: 'More Minerva than Mars', p. 104.

8  Ibid., p. 106

9  J.-L. Thaon: 'La Démobilisation féminine', *Demain*, 22 February 1919.

10 Marguerite Thibert, "Crise économique et travail féminin", *Revue internationale du travail*, XXVII, 4 & 5, April and May 1933.

11 Hause: 'More Minerva than Mars', p. 105.

12 Victor Margueritte: *La Garçonne*. Flammarion, Paris 1922. See also Anne Mauron: 'Le Scandale de *La Garçonne*', in Gilbert Guilleminault: *Le Roman vrai de la III<sup>ème</sup> et de la IV<sup>ème</sup> République, 2<sup>ème</sup> partie 1919-1958*, pp. 90–103.

13 *Les Allongés* was reprinted by Gallimard in 1977. Both texts deserve further critical attention.

14 This vision of the war is alluded to, but radically undermined, by Colette in *The Last of Cheri* (1926). See Chapter 7 below.

15 See in particular Henri de Montherlant: *Le Songe* (Gallimard, Paris 1922) and subsequent novels published in the 1920s and 1930s; Pierre Drieu la Rochelle: *L'Homme couvert de femmes* (Gallimard, Paris 1926), several more novels published over the two decades, and finally *Gilles* (Gallimard, Paris 1939). Simone de Beauvoir does a nicely caustic analysis of Montherlant's sexual politics in *The Second Sex*, Book One, Part III, Chapter 2, pp. 230–44. A feminist analysis of the work of both authors can be found in Diana Holmes, 'The Image of Woman in Selected Inter-War French Fiction', (unpublished thesis, Sussex 1977), Chapter 3, pp. 178–255.

16 Evelyne Sullerot: 'Condition de la femme', in Alfred Sauvy: *Histoire économique de la France entre les deux guerres*, p. 424.

17 Theodore Zeldin: *France 1845–1945: Ambition, Love and Politics* p. 359.

18 Maîté Albistur and Daniel Armogathe, *Histoire du féminisme français*, vol. 2, pp. 580–81.

19 James McMillan: *Dreyfus to De Gaulle: Politics and Society in France 1898–1969*, p. 100.

20 See, for example, *Le Droit des femmes*, December 1934. 'Women beware. Your right to work is at risk' was the headline to a report of a speech by the Minister for Employment, in which he had expressed the desirability of giving work to French men instead of '814,000 foreign workers, 774,000 old people, 805,000 women'.

21 Sullerot in Sauvy: *Histoire économique*, p. 428.

22 Sarah Fishman: 'Waiting for the Captive Sons of War: Prisoner of War Wives, 1940–45', in Higonnet *et al.*: *Behind the Lines*, p. 182.

23 Ibid., p. 189.

24 Paula Schwartz: 'Redefining Resistance: Women's Activism in Wartime France', in Higonnet *et al.*: *Between the Lines*, p. 147. Schwartz argues for an expanded definition of 'Resistance' to include those activities undertaken largely by women, and provides

a much fuller account of women's participation than there is space
for here. There are also several books on women and the French
Resistance, among them Union des femmes françaises: *Les Femmes
dans la Résistance*. Editions du Rocher, Paris 1977; and Ania Francos:
*Il était des femmes dans la Résistance*. Stock, Paris 1978.

25  Jane Jenson: 'The Liberation and New Rights for French Women',
in Higonnet *et al.*: *Between the Lines*, p. 275.

26  Claire Laubier: *The Condition of Women in France: 1945 to the
Present*, p. 2.

27  McMillan: *Politics and Society in France 1898–1969*, p. 164.

28  Laubier: *The Condition of Women in France*, p. 13.

29  Jean Vilar, quoted in David Bradby: *Modern French Drama 1940–1980*,
p. 92.

30  'For the young girl, erotic transcendence consists in becoming prey
in order to gain her ends. She becomes an object, and she sees herself
as an object; she discovers this new aspect of her being with surprise;
it seems to her that she has been doubled, instead of coinciding
exactly with herself, she now begins to exist *outside*.' Simone de
Beauvoir: *The Second Sex* (1949), p. 361.

31  Laubier: *The Condition of Women in France*, p. 35.

32  See also Diana Holmes: 'Angry Young Women: Sex and Conflict
in Bestselling First Novels of the 1950s', in Renate Günther
and Jan Windebank (eds): *Violence and Conflict in French Culture*,
pp. 199–214.


*CHAPTER 7 Everyday Adventures, or What Makes Colette a Feminine
Writer*

1  Jean Thoraval: *Les Grandes étapes de la civilisation française*. Bordas,
Paris 1967. *Du Surréalisme à l'empire de la critique*, ed. Germaine Brée
and Edouard Morot-Sir in the *Collection littérature française poche*.
Arthaud, Paris 1990.

2  Jean Larnac: *Histoire de la littérature féminine en France*, p. 223.

3  *Looking Backwards* (*Journal à rebours*, 1941; *De ma fenêtre*, 1942), transl.
David le Vay. The Women's Press, London 1987, p. 17.

4  In an interview with Madeleine Chapsal in Serge Julienne-Caffie:
*Simone de Beauvoir*, p. 212.

5  *The Evening Star* (*L'Etoile Vesper*, 1946), transl. David le Vay. The
Women's Press, London 1987, p. 140.

6  In an article on Colette Yver in the Swiss paper La Femme
d'aujourd'hui in 1930, Yver is said to be a friend of Colette,
'with whom hasty or ill-read people often confuse her – a mistake

which is, after all, entirely understandable'. One wonders whether the journalist had read the work of either Colette.

7 Hélène Cixous: 'The Laugh of the Medusa' (1975), in Robyn R.Warhol and Diane Price Herndl: *Feminisms*, p. 349. The other is Marguerite Duras.

8 For development of this point, see my chapter on 'The Body in the Text', in *Colette* (1991); also Yannick Resch, *Corps féminin, corps textuel* (1973).

9 Cixous, in Warhol and Herndl: *Feminisms*, p. 339.

10 Many of these articles can be found in *L'Envers du music-hall* (*Music-hall Sidelights*) (1913).

11 *References to Les Heures longues and to other work by Colette not easily available in translation, including Aventures quotidiennes, are to Œuvres* (Collected works), vols I–III. Bibliothèque de la Pléaide, Gallimard, Paris 1984–91. Translations in these cases are my own.

12 André Billy in an article published in *L'Œuvre*, 27 January 1918, II, 1429.

13 'They imagine that I could not forbear to burst forth on the world with an opinion on votes for women . . .', writes Colette in *The Evening Star* (1946). 'They think that I have some general ideas. It is not for me to inform them that I exist on those funds of frivolity that come to the aid of the long-lived' (p. 94). Although 'frivolity' is a misnomer for Colette's oblique, rather than discursive, manner of articulating a philosophy, it captures her consistent refusal of solemnity.

14 *Paris-Soir*, 2 April 1939, p. 3. Thanks to David Walker for drawing my attention to this (subsequently unpublished) article.

15 Ibid.

16 Margaret Callander: *Le Blé en herbe and La Chatte* (1992), p. 12.

17 Published in 1942 and 1944. In English in *Looking Backwards* (1987).

18 Although the circumstances precluded any mention of it, Colette herself lived most of the Occupation in a state of anxiety for her Jewish third husband, Maurice Goudeket, who was briefly interned and spent the rest of the war in hiding.

19 *Cheri and The Last of Cheri* (*Chéri*, 1920 and *La Fin de Chéri*, 1926), transl. Roger Senhouse. Penguin, Harmondsworth 1985. References are to 'LC' plus the page number.

20 *The Rainy Moon* appears in *The Collected Stories of Colette*, ed. Robert Phelps. Penguin, Harmondsworth 1985. References are to 'CSC' plus the page number.

21 The passage just quoted continues: 'Marcel Proust, gasping with asthma amid the bluish haze of fumigations and the shower of

pages dropping from him one by one, pursued a bygone and completed time.'

22 Jerry Aline Flieger, *Colette and the Fantom Subject of Autobiography*, p. 185.
23 Julia Kristeva: 'Woman's Time' (1981), in Warhol and Price Herndl: *Feminisms*, p. 445.
24 Ibid., p. 447.
25 See Chapter 8 below.
26 *Break of Day* (*La Naissance du jour*, 1928), transl. Enid McLeod. The Women's Press, London 1979.
27 Kristeva: 'Woman's Time', p. 445.

CHAPTER 8 *Simone de Beauvoir and The Second Sex*

1 Volume I of Beauvoir's autobiography, *Memoirs of a Dutiful Daughter* (*Mémoires d'une jeune fille rangée* [1958], transl. James Kirkup, Penguin, Harmondsworth 1987) gives a full account of this period, and Toril Moi analyses Beauvoir's curious status as one both marginalized by gender and legitimized by intellectual prowess in *Simone de Beauvoir: The Making of an Intellectual Woman* (1994)
2 Penny Forster and Imogen Sutton (eds): *Daughters of de Beauvoir* (1989).
3 *The Second Sex* (*Le Deuxième sexe*, 1949), transl. H.M. Parshley (1953). Penguin, Harmondsworth 1984.
4 On the 1990 BBC programme 'Daughters of de Beauvoir'.
5 Angie Pegg, on the same programme.
6 Marge Piercy, again on the same programme.
7 *Pour une morale de l'ambiguité* (1947). *The Ethics of Ambiguity*, transl. Bernard Frechtman. Citadel Press, New York 1976.
8 *Force of Circumstance* (*La Force des choses*, 1963), transl. Richard Howarth, Penguin, Harmondsworth 1987, p. 136.
9 Woolf visits the British Museum to investigate what books can tell her about the reasons for the inequalities between men and women. Her conclusions in some respects presage those of Beauvoir, particularly the concept of women as men's 'Other'. In ruling and managing the world, Woolf argues, men are enormously helped by the confidence gained from the belief that 'great numbers of people, half the human race indeed, are by nature inferior to [them]sel[ves]' (p. 45).
10 Toril Moi: *Simone de Beauvoir*, p. 180.
11 Ibid., p. 190.
12 Adrienne Rich (1983): 'Compulsory Heterosexuality and Lesbian Existence', in E. Abel and E.K. Abel (eds): *The Signs Reader: Women,*

*Gender and Scholarship*, University of Chicago Press, Chicago 1989.

13  For a detailed study of narrative voice in Beauvoir's fiction, see Elizabeth Fallaize: *The Novels of Simone de Beauvoir* (1988).

14  *The Blood of Others* (*Le Sang des autres*, 1945), transl. Yvonne Moyse and Roger Senhouse. Penguin, Harmondsworth, 1986.

15  *The Mandarins* (*Les Mandarins*, 1954), transl. Leonard M. Friedman. Fontana, London 1986.

16  Toril Moi addresses the question of Beauvoir's own Oedipal drama of separation from/identification with the mother, as evidenced in the texts, in the chapter '*L'Invitée*: an Existentialist Melodrama' in *Simone de Beauvoir*.

17  In 'This Sex which is not one' (1977). This extract in Robyn R. Warhol and Diane Price Herndl: *Feminisms*, pp. 351–2. See also below, Part III, Chapter 11.

18  Carol Ascher: *Simone de Beauvoir: A Life of Freedom*, p. 174.

19  See above, Chapter 7, pp. 143–6.

20  Laura Mulvey: 'Visual Pleasure and Narrative Cinema'. *Screen*, 16 March 1975.

21  Jean Leighton: *Simone de Beauvoir on Woman*, p. 39.

22  Mary Evans: *Simone de Beauvoir: A Feminist Mandarin*, p. xi.

23  Moi: *Simone de Beauvoir*, p. 153.

24  Ibid., p. 152.

25  Ibid., p. 98.

CHAPTER 9 *Elsa Triolet: Stories of Exile and Resistance*

1  Louis Aragon: *Les Yeux d'Elsa*. Seghers, Paris 1942, p. 34.

2  André Breton: 'L'Union libre', in *Clair de terre*. Gallimard, Paris 1926, pp. 93–5.

3  Dominque Desanti: *Les Clés d'Elsa*. Editions Ramsay, Paris 1983, p. 136.

4  Triolet and Aragon have been much criticized in France for their failure to condemn Stalinism or leave the Party at this period. See, for example, Dominique Desanti's treatment of this period in *Les Clés d'Elsa*.

5  References are to *Bonsoir, Thérèse*. Gallimard, Paris 1978. Hereafter BT.

6  Michel Vigault in *Le Cheval blanc* (*The White Horse*, 1943). Gallimard (Folio), Paris 1972, p. 143.

7  Paul Nizan: 'Bonsoir, Thérèse' (15 December 1938 in *Ce Soir*). Reprinted in *Pour une nouvelle culture*. Grasset, Paris 1971, p. 292.

8  Jacques Madaule: *Ce que dit Elsa*. Denoël, Paris 1961, p. 9.

9 *Le Figaro* exemplified the tone of much press commentary at the time of Nozières's trial: 'Violette Nozières is a monster, but it is her life as a "modern girl" that led her into evil ways.' Florence Montreynaud: *Le XXᵉ siècle des femmes*, p. 241.

10 References are to *Mille regrets*. Denoël, Paris 1942.

11 'The Private Life of Alexis Slavsky, Painter' (La Vie privée *ou* Alexis Slavsky, peintre), in *A Fine of Two Hundred Francs* (*Le Premier accroc coûte deux cents francs*, 1944), transl. Helena Lewis. Virago, London 1986.

12 'Cahiers enterrés sous un pêcher', in *A Fine of Two Hundred Francs*.

13 *Personne ne m'aime* (*No one Loves Me*). La Bibliothèque française, Paris 1946.

14 In *A Fine of Two Hundred Francs*.

15 *Les Fantômes armés* (The Armed Ghosts, sequel to *Personne ne m'aime*). La Bibliothèque française, Paris 1947.

16 *Le Rendez-vous des étrangers* (Rendezvous of Strangers – though étrangers also has the equally relevant meaning 'foreigners'). Gallimard, Paris 1956.

17 *Roses à crédit* (Roses on Hire-Purchase, Gallimard, Paris 1959) is the first novel in Triolet's trilogy *L'Age de nylon*. The other two volumes are *Luna Park* (1959) and *L'Ame* (1963).

PART II 1958–94

CHAPTER 10 *Women in French Society 1958–94*

1 Interview with Elisabeth Schemla in the *Nouvel Observateur*, no.1541, 19–25 May 1994, p. 40.

2 Christiane Rochefort: *Les Stances à Sophie*, p. 21.

3 Ibid., p. 19.

4 In a speech announcing the modification of the Constitution on 20 September 1962. Sylvie Guillaume, *La France contemporaine 1946–1990 Vol.2. La Vᵉ République*, p. 70.

5 James McMillan: *Dreyfus to De Gaulle*, p. 164.

6 Ibid., p. 166.

7 Claire Laubier: *The Condition of Women in France*, p. 48.

8 Moulinex marketed their domestic appliances with the slogan 'Moulinex liberates woman', and another brand, Vedette (meaning '(film)star'), used the visual image of a smartly dressed, smiling young woman, basket over her arm, casually pushing the button to start the automatic washing machine as she set off for a day's shopping.

9 Laubier: *The Condition of Women in France*, p. 10.

10 Maîté Albistur and Daniel Armogathe: *Histoire du féminisme français*, *vol. 2, pp. 645–6.*

11 *See Claire Duchen: Women's Rights and Women's Lives in France 1944–1968*, especially Chapter 6.

12 See bibliography, in particular Claire Duchen: *Femininism in France: From May '68 to Mitterrand*, Chapter 1; Françoise Picq: *Libération des femmes: les années-mouvement*; Keith Reader with Khursheed Wadia: *The May 1968 Events in France, Reproductions and Interpretations*.

13 Patrick Searle and Maureen McConville: *French Revolution 1968*, p. 113.

14 Ibid., p. 131.

15 Ibid., p. 105.

16 Duchen: *Women's Rights and Women's Lives*, pp. 199–200.

17 Françoise Thébaud (ed.): *Histoire des femmes en Occident Vol. 5. Le XX$^e$ siècle*, p. 230.

18 La Gaffiche: *Les Femmes s'affichent*, p. 15.

19 Duchen: *Women's Rights and Women's Lives*, p. 208.

20 24 June 1971, in La Gaffiche: *Les Femmes s'affichent*, p. 20.

21 Ibid., p. 60.

22 Duchen: *Feminism in France*, p. 106.

23 For the specific events referred to here and a broader discussion of the relations between MLF feminists and French parties of the Left, see Duchen: *Feminism in France*, pp. 107–19; and *French Connections*, pp. 111–34.

24 Duchen: *Feminism in France*, p. 118.

25 In 1981, in firms with ten or more employees, 25.1 per cent of female manual workers were on the minimum wage as opposed to 7.2 per cent of the men. For office workers, the equivalent figures were 6.4 per cent (women) and 1.8 per cent (men). Laubier: *The Condition of Women in France*, p.125.

26 Yvette Roudy: *A Cause d'elles*, p. 135.

27 Ibid., p. 138.

28 Ibid., p. 163.

29 Katharine Pancol: 'Let us settle our own scores with men', *Paris-Match*, 25 June 1983. Women journalists were given unaccustomed prominence during this debate, as opposition to the Bill clearly looked more convincing, and weakened the feminists' case more effectively, if it came from other women.

30 See Siân Reynolds: 'Rights of Man, Rights of Women, Rites of Identity', in J. Bridgford (ed.): *France, Image and Identity*, p. 212.

31 *Les Femmes s'entêtent*, p. 395.

32 Quoted in Michèle Sarde: *Regard sur les Françaises*, p. 642.

33 Letter to the feminist movement from Lesbian radical feminists from the Questions Féministes collective (1 March 1981) in Duchen: *French Connections*, p. 89.

34 Françoise Picq, in *Les Femmes an 2000* (1988), p. 46.

35 Diane Griffin Crowder: 'Monique Wittig', in Eva Martin Sartori and Dorothy Wynne Zimmerman: *French Women Writers*, p. 526.

36 David Bradby: *Modern French Drama 1940–1980*. Cambridge University Press, Cambridge 1984, p. 196.

37 Morag Schiach: *Hélène Cixous: A Politics of Writing*, p. 131. Sciach's chapter on 'Staging History' provides a succinct and illuminating introduction to Cixous's theatre.

38 Hélène Cixous in *Aller à la mer*, writing of her character Dora in the 1976 play *Portrait de Dora*. Quoted by Celita Lamar in *Our Voices Our Selves*, p. 148.

39 Elisabeth Badinter in the interview cited in Note 1, p. 46.

40 The facts and statistics above are taken from 'Menace sur les femmes', an article by Sylvie Véran in the *Nouvel Observateur*, 15–21 April 1993.

41 'La Pensée en 1993', *Nouvel Observateur*, 30 September–6 October 1993.

42 'L'apprentissage d'Edith Cresson', *L'Express*, 8 August 1991, p. 12.

43 Interview with Edith Cresson, *Nouvel Observateur*, 6–12 January 1994, p. 10.

CHAPTER 11 *Ecriture féminine: The Theory of a Feminine Writing*

1 For a much fuller and admirably clear discussion of the intellectual context within which theories of écriture féminine were formed, see Susan Sellers: *Language and Sexual Difference*, particularly the Introduction and Chapter 1.

2 See Barthes: *The Pleasure of the Text* (1973), transl. Richard Miller, Hill & Wang, New York 1975.

3 Marie Cardinal (with Annie Leclerc): *Autrement dit*. Grasset, Paris 1977, p. 146.

4 The adjective is coined on the model of 'idolatrous', thus 'woman-adoring'.

5 Michèle Sarde: *Regard sur les Françaises*, p. 136.

6 Beauvoir: *The Second Sex*, pp. 740–41.

7 In 'Sorties', which forms one part of *The Newly Born Woman* (1975). This extract can be found in *The Hélène Cixous Reader*, ed. Susan Sellers. Routledge, London and New York 1994, p. 37. Hereafter referred to in text and Notes as HCR.

8   'The Laugh of the Medusa', in Robyn R. Warhol and Diana Price
    Herndl: *Feminisms*, pp. 334–49, 343. Hereafter LM.
9   In 'Speculum of the Other Woman' (1974). This extract appears in
    Warhol and Herndl: *Feminisms*, p. 408.
10  In *Je, tu, nous: Towards a Culture of Difference* (1990), transl. Alison
    Martin, Routledge, London 1993, p. 12.
11  Annie Leclerc: *Parole de femme* (Woman's Word). Grasset, Paris 1974,
    p. 5. Hereafter PF. This extract can be found in Claire Duchen's
    translation of passages from the text in *French Connections*, p. 58.
12  In England, Virginia Woolf had already suggested in 1929 that in
    order to write 'as a woman', a writer would need to rethink even
    the syntactical structure of language, since 'the very form of the
    sentence does not fit her. It is a sentence made by men . . . too
    loose, too heavy and too pompous for a woman's use.' *Women and
    Writing*, p. 48.
13  Irigaray: 'This Sex which is not one' (1977), in Warhol and Herndl:
    *Feminisms*, p. 353.
14  In *Revolution in Poetic Language* (1974). The relevant section on the
    'semiotic' can be found in Toril Moi (ed.): *The Kristeva Reader*.
    Blackwell, Oxford 1986.
15  Irigaray: *Je, tu, nous*, p. 41.
16  Irigaray: 'This Sex which is not one', p. 353.
17  Julia Kristeva: 'Woman's Time' (1981), in Warhol and Herndl:
    *Feminisms*, p. 445.
18  Irigaray: *Je, tu, nous*, p. 113.
19  Ibid., p. 115.
20  Annie Leclerc does not employ the term *écriture féminine*, but her
    contention that a '*parole de femme*', or 'woman's word', must differ
    not only thematically but also formally from 'masculine' language
    takes her on to much the same territory as Cixous.
21  Irigaray: *Je, tu, nous*, p. 36.
22  Irigaray: 'This Sex which is not one', p. 350.
23  Irigaray: *Je, tu, nous*, p. 47.
24  Colette Guillaumin: 'The Question of Difference', *Questions
    féministes*, no. 6. 1979, in Claire Duchen: *French Connections*, p. 65.
25  Ibid., p. 68.
26  Ibid., p. 70.
27  Ann Rosalind Jones: 'Writing the Body: Toward an Under-
    standing of *l'écriture féminine*' (1981), in Warhol and Herndl:
    *Feminisms*, p. 362.
28  Ibid., p. 363.
29  Trista Selous, discussing attempts to claim Marguerite Duras for the

cause of *écriture féminine*, captures the problem well: 'Perhaps feminist attitudes to masculinity need rethinking: is it just something nasty that men have, or is it in us too, and can we put it to good use?' 'Marguerite and the Mountain', in Margaret Atack and Phil Powrie: *Contemporary French Fiction by Women*, p. 93.

30  Margaret Whitford: *Luce Irigaray: Philosophy in the Feminine*, p. 12.

*CHAPTER 12 Defining a Feminine Writing: Chantal Chawaf and Marguerite Duras*

 1  Chantal Chawaf: 'Aujourd'hui', *Roman*, no. 5 (1983), p. 139. Quoted in Elizabeth Fallaize: *French Women's Writing: Recent Fiction*, p. 51.

 2  Chantal Chawaf: 'L'Ecriture', in *Chair chaude* (1976), pp. 80–81. Quoted in Phil Powrie, 'Myth versus Allegory: The Problematisation of Narrative in Chantal Chawaf's *Le soleil et la terre*', in Helen Wilcox et al.: *The Body and the Text* (1990), pp. 80–81.

 3  Chawaf's texts have not been translated into English, but Elizabeth Fallaize's *French Women's Writing: Recent Fiction* contains both a concise and illuminating introduction to Chawaf's work, and a translation of passages from *Blé de semences* [hereafter BS in the text] (Mercure de France, Paris 1976) and from the 1986 *Elwina, le roman-fée* (Elwina, the Fairy-Tale Novel) (Flammarion, Paris 1986).

 4  Fallaize, *French Women's Writing*, p. 55.

 5  Valerie Hannagan: 'Reading as a Daughter: Chantal Chawaf Revisited', in Atack and Powrie: *Contemporary French Fiction by Women*, p. 185.

 6  Phil Powrie: 'Myth versus Allegory', p. 81.

 7  Adèle King: *French Women Novelists: Defining a Female Style*, p. 134.

 8  A text in the form of a dialogue between two female voices, in which neither claims complete authorial control, could itself be seen as an example of *écriture féminine*. The same form was adopted in 1977 by Marie Cardinal and Annie Leclerc with *Autrement dit*. Grasset, Paris 1977. See also Marcelle Marini: *Territoires du féminin, avec Marguerite Duras*. Editions de Minuit, Paris 1977.

 9  Marguerite Duras and Xavière Gauthier: *Les Parleuses*. Minuit, Paris 1974, p. 40.

10  'An Interview with Marguerite Duras', *Signs: Journal of Women in Culture and Society*, I, 2, Winter 1975, pp. 423–34 (p. 423). Quoted in Leslie Hill: *Marguerite Duras: Apocalyptic Desires*, p. 29.

11  Marguerite Duras: *L'Amant* (1984), transl. Barbara Bray as *The Lover* (1986).

12 According to an interview with Duras in the *Nouvel Observateur*, 14–20 November 1986, pp.114–17.

13 Margaret Sankey: 'Time and Autobiography in *L'Amant* by Marguerite Duras', *Australian Journal of French Studies*, vol.XXV, no.1, 1988, p. 61.

14 King: *French Women Novelists*, p. 159.

15 Sarah Capitanio: 'Perspectives sur l'écriture durassienne: *L'Amant*', *Synposium*, vol. XLI, no. 1, 1987, p. 25.

16 Susan Sellers: *Language and Sexual Difference*, p. 160.

*CHAPTER 13 Feminism and Realism: Christiane Rochefort and Annie Ernaux*

1 I am making certain assumptions here, since precise knowledge of who reads a text is notoriously hard to come by. But both the Rochefort and the Ernaux novels discussed here were high in the French bestseller lists in the year of their publication, and have remained available in paperback editions for many years – in Rochefort's case, more than thirty years. This is surely evidence of a 'general' rather than a specialized readership.

2 Christiane Rochefort: Interview with Monique Crochet. The *French Review*, vol. LIV, no. 3, February 1981 (pp. 428–35), pp. 428, 431.

3 Talk given at Birmingham University, March 1994.

4 Talk given at Winchester College, 10 March 1988. Quoted in Siobhàn McIlvanney: 'Ernaux and Realism', p. 55.

5 *Les Petits enfants du siècle*, ed. P.M.W. Thody, Harrap, London 1982. Hereafter PES.

6 *Les Stances à Sophie*. Grasset, Paris 1963. Hereafter SàS.

7 *La Femme gelée*, Gallimard, Paris 1981. Hereafter FG.

8 Between 1953 and 1959 the number of HLM, or social housing units, in France rose from 100,000 to 300,000.

9 Siobhàn McIlvanney: 'Ernaux and Realism', pp. 51–2.

10 To cite just three examples: George Sand's *Indiana* (1828), Rachilde's *La Jongleuse* (1900), Colette's *La Vagabonde* (1911).

11 The development of a consumer society and its definition of personal happiness in terms of the acquisition of goods figures in many French texts of the period, for example Nathalie Sarraute: *Le Planétarium* (1959); Georges Perec: *Les Choses* (1965); Simone de Beauvoir: *Les Belles Images* (1967).

12 Rochefort: *C'est bizarre l'écriture* (Strange Thing, Writing). Grasset, Paris 1970, p. 134.

13 Rochefort in Anne Ophir: *Regards féminins*, p. 90.

14 References are to the French text, but where the quotation is part of the extract translated in Elizabeth Fallaize: *French Women's Writing*, I have used this translation, indicated by the second page reference.

15 The Latin phrase, 'he has two', refers to the practice of verifying the new Pope's masculinity before officially proclaiming his accession to office – a further sign of the Church's respect for the phallus.

16 *Archaos ou le jardin étincelant* (Archaos or the Sparkling Garden). Grasset, Paris 1972.

*CHAPTER 14 An Open Conclusion: Women's Writing Now*

1 Chris Weedon: *Feminist Practice and Poststructuralist Theory*, p. 2.

2 Susan Sellers (ed.): *The Hélène Cixous Reader*, p. 37.

3 Annie Ernaux's talk at Birmingham University, for example, in March 1994, was followed by a lively discussion in which a number of English feminists made the case for the significance of gender in both the theme and the form of Ernaux's writing, but were met with the author's strong reluctance to acknowledge this. Ernaux insisted that 'the "I" has no sex'.

4 Hélène Cixous: 'The Laugh of the Medusa', in Robyn R. Warhol and Diana Price Herndl: *Feminisms*, p.339.

5 See above, Part I, Chapter 1.

6 Sylvie Germain: *Le Livre des nuits* (Gallimard, Paris 1985).

7 Pierrette Fleutiaux: *Métamorphoses de la reine* (Gallimard, Paris 1984).

8 Marie Redonnet: *Rose Mélie Rose* (Minuit, Paris 1987).

9 Elizabeth Fallaize: *French Women's Writing: Recent Fiction*, p. 164. This book contains both a critical introduction to Redonnet's work, and translated extracts from *Rose Mélie Rose*.

10 Farida Belghoul: *Georgette!* (Bernard Barrault, Paris 1986).

11 Soraya Nini: *Ils disent que je suis une beurette* (Fixot, Paris 1993).

12 Alec Hargreaves drew attention to this 'framing' of Nini's novel for a French readership during a talk given at the Birmingham University Day Conference on North African Women Writers, 14 March 1994.

13 Claude Fischler : 'Une féminisation des mœurs?'. *Esprit*, no.196, November 1993, p. 10

# Bibliography

## 1. GENERAL

### WOMEN'S WRITING AND CULTURAL THEORY
Bennett, Tony, Graham Martin, Colin Mercer and Janet Woollacott: *Culture, Ideology and Social Process*. The Open University, London 1981.

Betterton, Rosemary: *Looking On: Images of Femininity in the Visual Arts and Media*. Pandora, London and New York 1987.

Bourdieu, Pierre: *Distinction: A Social Critique of the Judgement of Taste*, transl. R. Nice. Routledge & Kegan Paul, London and New York 1979.

Cameron, Deborah: *The Feminist Critique of Language*. Routledge, London and New York 1990.

Chodorow, Nancy: *The Reproduction of Mothering*. University of California Press, Berkeley 1978.

Duplessis, Rachel Blau: *Writing Beyond the Ending: Narrative Strategies of Twentieth Century Women Writers*. Indiana University Press, Bloomington, 1985.

Gilbert, Sandra M. and Susan Gubar: *The Madwoman in the Attic: The Woman Writer and the Nineteenth-Century Literary Imagination*. Yale University Press, New Haven, CT and London 1984.

Miller, Nancy K.: *Subject to Change: Reading Feminist Writing*. Columbia University Press, New York 1988.

————: *Getting Personal: Feminist Occasions and Other Autobiographical Acts*. Routledge, New York and London 1991.

Mills, Sara, Lynne Pearce, Sue Spaull and Elaine Millard (eds): *Feminist Readings/Feminists Reading*. Harvester Wheatsheaf, Hemel Hempstead 1989.

Moi, Toril: *Sexual/Textual Politics*. Methuen, London 1985.

————: 'Appropriating Bourdieu: Feminist Theory and Pierre Bourdieu's Sociology of Culture'. *New Literary History* 22, 1991, 22 (pp. 1017–49).

Mulvey, Laura: 'Visual Pleasure and Narrative Cinema'. *Screen*, 16 March 1975.

Parker, Roszika and Griselda Pollock: *Old Mistresses: Women, Art and Ideology*, Pandora, London 1987 (first published 1981).

Ward Jouve, Nicole: *White Woman Speaks with Forked Tongue: Criticism as Autobiography*. Routledge, London and New York 1991.

Warhol, Robyn R. and Diana Price Herndl: *Feminisms: An Anthology of Literary Theory and Criticism*. Rutgers University Press, New Brunswick 1991.

Waugh, Patricia: *Feminine Fictions: Revisiting the Postmodern*. Routledge, London and New York 1989.

Weedon, Chris: *Feminist Practice and Poststructuralist Theory*. Blackwell, Oxford 1987.

Williams, Raymond: *The Long Revolution*. Penguin, Harmondsworth 1961.

Woolf, Virginia: *Women and Writing*, ed. Michèle Barrett. The Women's Press, London 1979.

————: *A Room of One's Own* (1929). Oxford University Press, Oxford and New York 1992.

## 2. FRANCE

### (a) FRENCH HISTORY, POLITICS AND CULTURE 1848–1994

Agulhon, Maurice: *Nouvelle Histoire de la France contemporaine. Vol. 8: 1848 ou l'apprentissage de la République*. Editions du Seuil, Paris 1973.

Ardagh, John: *France in the 80s*. Penguin, Harmondsworth 1982.

Bradby, David: *Modern French Drama 1940–1980*. Cambridge University Press, Cambridge 1984.

Copley, Antony: *Sexual Moralities in France: 1780–1980*. Routledge, London 1989.

Dupeux, Georges: *La Société française 1789–1970*. Armand Colin, Paris 1972.

Guillaume, Sylvie: *La France contemporaine: chronologie commentée. 2. La Ve République*. Perrin, Paris 1991.

Guilleminault, Gilbert: *Le Roman vrai de la IIIème et de la IVème République* (2ème partie, 1919–1958). Robert Laffont, Paris 1991.

Günther, Renate and Windebank, Jan (eds): *Violence and Conflict in French Culture*. Sheffield Academic Press, Sheffield 1994.

Hobson, Harold: *French Theatre since 1830*. John Calder and Riverrun Press, London and Dallas, TX 1978.

McMillan, James F.: *Dreyfus to De Gaulle: Politics and Society in France 1898–1969*. Edward Arnold, London 1985.

Magraw, Roger: *France 1815–1914: The Bourgeois Century*. Fontana, London 1983.

Maingueneau, Dominique: *Les Livres d'école de la République 1870–1914 (discours et idéologie).* Le Sycomore, Paris 1979.

Price, Roger (ed.): *1848 in France.* Thames & Hudson, London 1975.

Radford, Colin *et al.* (eds): *Signposts in French Literature.* Hutchinson, London 1988.

Reader, Keith with Khursheed Wadia: *The May 1968 Events in France. Reproductions and Interpretations.* Macmillan, Basingstoke 1993.

Sauvy, Alfred: *Histoire économique de la France entre les deux guerres.* Fayard, Paris 1965.

Searle, Patrick and Maureen McConville: *French Revolution 1968.* Heinemann and Penguin, London 1968.

Sorlin, Pierre: *La Société francaise Vol. I, 1840–1914.* Arthaud, Paris 1969.

Zeldin, Theodore: *France 1848–1945. Vol I: Ambition, Love and Politics.* (1973) *Vol.2. Intellect, Taste and Anxiety.* Oxford University Press, Oxford 1977.

Zeldin, Theodore (ed.): *Conflicts in French society.* Allen & Unwin, London 1977.


## (b) HISTORY OF FRENCH WOMEN AND FEMINISM

Albistur, Maïté and Daniel Armogathe: *Histoire du féminisme francais, vol. 2.* des femmes, Paris 1977.

———: *Nelly Roussel, l'éternelle sacrifiée.* Editions Syros, Paris 1979.

Allwood, Gill: 'Popular Interpretations of Masculinity in Contemporary France'. In Dave Berry and Alec G. Hargreaves: *Women in 20th Century French History and Culture: Papers in Memory of Andrea Cady.* European Research Centre, Loughborough 1993 (pp. 17–29).

Aron, Jean-Paul: *Misérable et glorieuse : la femme du XIXe siecle.* Fayard, Paris 1980.

Beauvoir, Simone de (preface): *Les Femmes s'entêtent.* Collection idées, Gallimard, Paris 1975.

——— (preface): *Le Sexisme ordinaire.* Editions du Seuil, Paris 1979.

Bellet, R.(ed.): *La Femme au XIXe siècle: Littérature et idéologie.* Presses Universitaires de Lyon, Lyon 1978.

Benstock, Shari: *Women of the Left Bank: Paris 1900–1940.* Virago, London 1987.

Bouchardeau, Huguette: *Pas d'histoire, les femmes.* Editions Syros, Paris 1977.

Duchen, Claire: *Feminism in France: From May '68 to Mitterrand.* Routledge & Kegan Paul, London, Boston and Henley 1986.

——— (ed.): *French Connections: Voices from the Women's Movement in France.* Hutchinson, London 1987.

————: *Women's Rights and Women's Lives in France 1944–1968*. Routledge, London and New York 1994.

Evans, Richard J.: *The Feminists*. Croom Helm, London 1977.

Francos, Ania, *Il était des femmes dans la Résistance*. Stock, Paris 1978.

Gisserot, Hélène (ed.): *Les Femmes an 2000* (proceedings of a national conference on this theme January 27 1988). La Documentation française, Paris 1988.

Groult, Benoîte: *Le Féminisme au masculin*. Denoël, Paris 1978.

Hause, Steven with Anne R. Kenny: *Women's Suffrage and Social Politics in the French Third Republic*. Princeton University Press, Princeton, NJ 1984.

Higonnet, Margaret R., Jane Jenson, Sonya Michel and Margaret C. Weitz: (eds): *Behind the Lines: Gender and the Two World Wars*. Yale University Press, New Haven, CT and London, 1987.

Holmes, Diana: 'The Image of Woman in Selected French Fiction of the Inter-War Period' (Unpublished thesis). University of Sussex, 1977.

La Gaffiche: *Les Femmes s'affichent*. La Gaffiche–Syros, Paris 1984.

Laubier, Claire: *The Condition of Women in France: 1945 to the Present*. Routledge, London and New York 1990.

McMillan, James F.: *Housewife or Harlot: The Place of Women in French Society 1870–1940*. Harvester, Brighton 1981.

————: 'Clericals, Anticlericals and the Women's Movement in France under the Third Republic'. *Historical Journal* vol. 24, Part 2, 1981.

Mayeur, Françoise: *L'Education des filles en France au XIXᵉ siècle*. Hachette, Paris 1979.

Montreynaud, Florence: *Le XXᵉ siècle des femmes*. Nathan, Paris 1989.

Picq, Françoise: *Libération des femmes: les années-mouvement*. Le Seuil, Paris 1993.

Rabaut, Jean: *Féministes à la Belle Epoque*. Editions France-Empire, Paris 1985.

Rafferty, F.: 'Madame Séverine: Crusading Journalist of the Third Republic'. *Contemporary French Civilisation* vol. 1, 1977 (pp. 185–202).

Reynolds, Siân (ed.): *Women, State & Revolution: Essays on Power & Gender in Europe since 1789*. Wheatsheaf, London 1986.

————: 'Rights of Man, Rights of Women, Rites of Identity'. In Jeff Bridgford (ed.): *France, Image and Identity*. Newcastle Polytechnic Publications, Newcastle 1987 (pp. 200–19).

Riemer, Eleanor S. and Jon C. Font: *European Women: A Documentary History 1789–1945*. Harvester, Brighton 1983.

Roudy, Yvette: *A Cause d'elles*. Albin Michel, Paris 1985.

Sarde, Michèle: *Regard sur les Françaises*. Stock, Paris 1983.

Sévérine: *Choix de Papiers*, annotated by Evelyne le Garrec. Editions Tierce, Paris 1982.

Smith, Bonnie G.: *Ladies of the Leisure Class: The Bourgeoises of France in the 19th century*. Princeton University Press, Princeton, NJ 1981.

Sowerwine, Charles: *Sisters or Citizens? Women and Socialism in France since 1876*. Cambridge University Press, Cambridge 1982.

Thébaud, Françoise: *Histoire des femmes en Occident Vol. 5.: Le XXᵉ siècle*. Plon, Paris 1992.

Tilly, Louise A. and Joan W. Scott: *Women, Work and Family*. Routledge, London and New York 1989.

Union des femmes françaises: *Les Femmes dans la Résistance*. Editions du Rocher, Paris 1977.

Waelti-Walters, Jennifer and Steven C. Hause (eds): *Feminisms of the Belle Epoque: A Historical and Literary Anthology*. University of Nebraska Press, Lincoln and London 1994.

Weston, Elizabeth Anne: 'Prostitution in Paris in the Later 19th Century: A Study of Political and Social Ideology'. Unpublished thesis. State University of Buffalo, Buffalo 1979.

*Articles and features in the French press*
Dossier: 'Menace sur les femmes'. *Nouvel Observateur* no.1484, 15–21 April 1993.

Dossier: 'Masculin/Féminin'. *Esprit* no. 196, November 1993.

Dossier: 'Les femmes veulent-elles le pouvoir?'. *Nouvel Observateur* no. 1522, 6–12 January 1994.

Badinter, Elisabeth: 'Ici, en droit, nous avons tout obtenu'. *Nouvel Observateur* no. 1541, 19–25 May 1994.


(c) WOMEN WRITERS IN FRANCE
Atack, Margaret and Phil Powrie: *Contemporary French Fiction by Women: Feminist Perspectives*. Manchester University Press, Manchester and New York 1990.

Béalu, Marcel: *Anthologie de la poésie féminine de 1900 à nos jours*. Stock, Paris 1955.

Brécourt-Villars, Claudine: *Ecrire d'amour: Anthologie de textes érotiques féminins (1799–1984)*. Ramsay, Paris 1985.

Brée, Germaine: *Women Writers in France*. Rutgers University Press, New Brunswick 1973.

Crosland, Margaret: *Women of Iron & Velvet : French Women Writers after George Sand*. Taplinger, New York 1976.

Dejean, Joan and Nancy K. Miller (eds): *The Politics of Tradition: Placing*

*Women in French Literature. Yale French Studies* no. 75, 1988.

Didier, Béatrice: *L'Ecriture-femme*. Presses Universitaires de France, Paris 1981.

Dudovitz, Resa L.: *The Myth of Superwoman: Women's Bestsellers in France and the United States*. Routledge, London 1990.

Evans, Martha Noel: *Masks of Tradition: Women and the Politics of Writing in Twentieth Century France*. Cornell University Press, Ithaca, NY and London, 1987.

Fallaize, Elizabeth: *French Women's Writing: Recent Fiction*. Macmillan, Basingstoke 1993.

Holmes, Diana: 'Angry Young Women: Sex and Conflict in Bestselling First Novels of the 1950s'. In Günther and Windebank (eds) (pp. 199–214).

Ince, Kate and Alex Hughes: *Desiring Writing: Twentieth Century French Erotic Fiction by Women*. Berg, London (1996).

King, Adèle: *French Women Novelists: Defining a Female Style*. Macmillan, Basingstoke 1989.

Lamar, Celita: *Our Voices, Our Selves. Women Writing for the French Theatre*. Peter Lang, New York 1991.

Larnac, Jean: *Histoire de la littérature féminine en France* Editions Krâ, Paris 1929.

Marks, Elaine and George Stamboulian: *Homosexualities and French Literature: Cultural Contexts/Critical Texts*. Cornell University Press, Ithaca, NY and London 1979.

Ophir, Anne: *Regards féminins: Condition féminine et création littéraire*. Denoël/Gonthier, Paris 1976.

Sartori, Eva Martin and Dorothy Wynne Zimmerman (eds): *French Women Writers: A Bio-Bibliographical Source Book*. Greenwood Press, New York/Westwood, London 1991.

Sellers, Susan: *Language and Sexual Difference: Feminist Writing in France*. St Martin's Press, New York 1991.

Waelti-Walters, Jennifer: *Feminist Novelists of the Belle Epoque: Love as a Lifestyle*. Indiana University Press, Bloomington and Indianapolis 1990.

Wilcox, Helen, Keith McWatters, Ann Thompson and Linda R. Williams (eds): *The Body and the Text: Hélène Cixous, Reading and Teaching*. Harvester Wheatsheaf, Hemel Hempstead 1990.

(d) STUDIES OF INDIVIDUAL AUTHORS
NB Editions of primary texts are specified in the Notes to each chapter.

*George Sand*

Bouchardeau, Huguette: *George Sand: la lune et les sabots*. Robert Laffont, Paris 1990.

Cohen, Margaret: 'A Woman's Place: *La Petite Fadette* v. *La Voix des Femmes*. *L'Esprit Créateur* vol. XXIX, no. 2. Summer 1989 (pp. 26–38).

Courtivron, Isabelle de: 'Weak Men and Fatal Women: The Sand Image'. In Elaine Marks and George Stamboulian (eds): *Homosexualities and French Literature*.

Dickenson, Donna: *George Sand. A Brave Man – the Most Womanly Woman*. Berg, Oxford, New York and Hamburg 1988.

Frappier-Mazur, Lucienne: 'Nostalgie, dédoublement et écriture dans *Histoire de ma vie*'. *Nineteenth Century French Studies*, vol. 17, no. 3–4, 1989 (pp. 265–75).

Glasgow, Janis: *George Sand: Collected Essays*. Whitston, New York 1985.

Grant, Richard B: 'George Sand's *La Mare au Diable*: A Study in Male Passivity'. *Nineteenth Century French Studies* vol. 13, no. 4, 1985 (pp. 211–23).

Jurgrau, Thelma: 'Autobiography in General and George Sand's in Particular'. *Nineteenth Century French Studies* vol. 17, no. 1–2, 1988–89 (pp. 196–207).

Manifold, Gay: *George Sand's Theatre Career*. UMI Research Press, Ann Arbor, MI 1985.

Rossum-Guyon, F. van: *Une œuvre multiforme*. Cahiers de Recherche des Instituts Néerlendais, Rodopi, Amsterdam 1991.

Salomon, Pierre: *George Sand*. Connaissance des lettres, Hatier 1953.

Schor, Naomi: 'Female Fetishism: The Case of George Sand'. *Poetics Today* vol. 6, no. 1–2, 1985 (pp. 301–10).

———: 'Reading Double: Sand's Difference'. In Nancy Miller: *The Poetics of Gender*. Columbia University Press, New York 1986 (pp. 248–69).

———: 'Idealism in the Novel: Recanonizing Sand'. Yale French Studies no. 75, 1988 *The Politics of Tradition* (pp. 56–73).

———: *George Sand and Idealism*. Columbia University Press, New York 1993.

Thomson, Patricia: *George Sand and the Victorians*. Macmillan, London and Basingstoke 1977.

Van Slyke, Gretchen: 'History in Her Story: Historical Referents in Sand's *La Petite Fadette*'. *Romanic Review* vol. 82, no. 1, 1991 (pp. 49–69).

*Gabrielle Réval*
Dossier *Gabrielle Réval*, Bibliothèque Marguerite Durand, Paris.


*Marcelle Tinayre*
Dossier *Marcelle Tinayre*, Bibliothèque Marguerite Durand, Paris.


*Colette Yver*
Dossier *Colette Yver*, Bibliothèque Marguerite Durand, Paris.


*Rachilde and Decadence*
Dauphiné, Claude: *Rachilde*. Mercure de France, Paris 1991.
Holmes, Diana: 'Monstrous Women: Rachilde's Erotic Fiction'. In Kate Ince and Alex Hughes (eds): *Desiring Writing: Twentieth Century French Erotic Fiction by Women*. Berg, London (1996).
Kelly, Dorothy: '*Monsieur Vénus* and Decadent Reversals'. In *Fictional Genders: Role and Representation in Nineteenth-Century French Narrative*. University of Nebraska Press, Nebraska 1989.

Dossier *Rachilde*, Bibliothèque Marguerite Durand, Paris.


*Decadence*
Birkett, Jennifer: *The Sins of the Fathers: Decadence in France 1870–1914*. Quartet, London 1986.
Brandreth, H.R.T.: *Huysmans* (Studies in Modern European Thought and Literature). Bowes & Bowes, London 1963.
Pierrot, Jean : *The Decadent Imagination, 1880–1900*. University of Chicago Press, Chicago 1981.
Thornton, R.K.R.: *The Decadent Dilemma*. Edward Arnold, London 1983.


*Renée Vivien*
Blankley, Elyse: 'Return to Mytilène: Renée Vivien and the City of Women'. In Susan Squier (ed.): *Women Writers and the City: Essays*

*in Feminist Literary Criticism*. University of Tennessee Press, Knoxville 1984 (pp. 45–67).

Faderman, Lilian: *Surpassing the Love of Men : Romantic Friendship and Love between Women from the Renaissance to the Present*. The Women's Press, London 1985.

Germain, André: *Renée Vivien*. Georges Crès et Cie., Paris 1917.

Lorenz, Paul: *Sappho 1900 Renée Vivien*. Julliard, Paris 1977.

Marks, Elaine: 'Lesbian Intertextuality'. In Elaine Marks and George Stamboulian: *Homosexualities in French Literature* (pp.353–77).

———: '"Sapho 1900": Imaginary Renée Viviens and the Rear of the Belle Epoque'. *Yale French Studies* no. 75, *The Politics of Tradition* (pp. 175–89).

Maurras, Charles: *L'Avenir de l'intelligence*. Nouvelle Librairie Nationale, Paris 1909.

Showalter, Elaine: *Sexual Anarchy – Gender and Culture at the fin-de-siècle*. Virago, London 1992.

Dossier *Renée Vivien,* Bibliothèque Marguerite Durand, Paris.


*Colette*

Callender, Margaret: *Le Blé en herbe and La Chatte*. In *Critical Guides to French Texts*, Grant & Cutler, London 1992.

Flieger, Jerry Aline: *Colette and the Fantom Subject of Autobiography*. Cornell Press, Ithaca, NY and London 1992.

Holmes, Diana: *Colette*. In *Women Writers*, Macmillan, London and Basingstoke 1991.

Resch, Yannick: *Corps féminin, corps textuel*. Klincksieck, Paris 1973.


*Simone de Beauvoir*

Ascher, Carol: *Simone de Beauvoir: A Life of Freedom*. Harvester, Brighton 1981.

Evans, Mary: *Simone de Beauvoir: A Feminist Mandarin*. Tavistock, London 1985.

Fallaize, Elizabeth: *The Novels of Simone de Beauvoir*. Routledge, London 1988.

Forster, Penny and Imogen Sutton (eds): *Daughters of de Beauvoir*. The Women's Press, London 1989.

Julienne-Caffié, Serge: *Simone de Beauvoir*. Gallimard, Paris 1966.

Leighton, Jean: *Simone de Beauvoir on Woman*. Fairleigh Dickinson, Rutherford 1975.

Moi, Toril: *Simone de Beauvoir: The Making of an Intellectual Woman.* Blackwell, Oxford and Cambridge, MA 1994.

### Elsa Triolet

Aragon, Louis: *Les Yeux d'Elsa.* Seghers, Paris 1942.

Desanti, Dominique: *Les Clés d'Elsa.* Ramsay, Paris 1983.

Mackinnon, Lachlan: *The Lives of Elsa Triolet.* Chatto & Windus, London 1992.

Madaule, Jacques: *Ce que dit Elsa.* Denoël, Paris 1961.

Nizan, Paul: 'Bonsoir Thérèse'. In *Pour une nouvelle culture.* Grasset, Paris 1971.

Dossier *Elsa Triolet.* Bibliothèque Marguerite Durand, Paris.

### Ecriture féminine (see also Women Writers in France above)

Jones, Ann Rosalind: 'Writing the Body: Toward an Understanding of *l'écriture féminine*'. In Warhol and Herndl, *Feminisms* (pp. 357–70).

Shiach, Morag: *Hélène Cixous: A Politics of Writing.* Routledge, London and New York 1991.

Whitford, Margaret: *Luce Irigaray: Philosophy in the Feminine.* Routledge, London and New York 1991.

### Chantal Chawaf

Fallaize, Elizabeth: *French Women's Writing: Recent Fiction* (pp. 51–6).

Hannagan, Valerie: 'Reading as a Daughter: Chantal Chawaf Revisited'. In Atack and Powrie: *Contemporary French Fiction by Women* (pp. 177–91).

Powrie, Phil: 'Myth versus Allegory: The Problematisation of Narrative in Chantal Chawaf's *Le Soleil et la Terre*'. In Wilcox *et al.*: *The Body and the Text* (pp. 78–86).

### Marguerite Duras

Capitanio, Sarah: 'Perspectives sur l'écriture durassienne: *L'Amant*'. *Symposium*, vol. XLI, no. 1, Spring 1987 (pp. 15–27).

Hill, Leslie: *Marguerite Duras: Apocalyptic Desires.* Routledge, London and New York 1993.

King, Adèle: *French Women Novelists : Defining a Female Style*. Macmillan, Basingstoke 1989 (pp. 134–63).

Marini, Marcelle: *Territoires du féminin, avec Marguerite Duras*. Editions de Minuit, Paris 1984.

Sankey, Margaret: 'Time and Autobiography in *L'Amant* by Marguerite Duras'. *Australian Journal of French Studies*, vol. XXV, no. 1, 1988 (pp. 58–70).

Selous, Trista: 'Marguerite and the Mountain'. In Atack and Powrie: *Contemporary French Fiction by Women* (pp. 84–95).


*Christiane Rochefort*
Crochet, Monique: Interview with Christiane Rochefort. *French Review*, vol. LIV, No. 3, February 1981 (pp. 428–35).

Holmes, Diana: 'Eroticism and Femininity in the Novels of Christiane Rochefort'. In Jeff Bridgford (ed.): *France, Image and Identity*. Newcastle Polytechnic, Newcastle 1987.

———: 'Realism, Fantasy and Feminist Meaning: the Fiction of Christiane Rochefort'. In Atack and Powrie: *Contemporary French Fiction by Women* (pp. 26–40).


*Annie Ernaux*
Day, Loraine: 'Class, Sexuality and Subjectivity in Annie Ernaux's *Les Armoires vides*'. In Atack and Powrie: *Contemporary French Fiction by Women* (pp. 41–55).

Fallaize, Elizabeth: *French Women's Writing: Recent Fiction* (pp. 67–87).

McIlvanney, Siobhàn : 'Ernaux and Realism: Redressing the Balance'. In Maggie Allison (ed.): *Women Teaching French Papers No. 2. Women's Space and Identity*. University of Bradford, Bradford 1993.

Sanders, Carol: 'Stylistic Aspects of Women's Writing: The Case of Annie Ernaux.' *French Cultural Studies*, vol 4, Part 1, no 10, February 1993 (pp. 15–30).


*Marie Redonnet*
Fallaize, Elizabeth: 'Filling in the Blank Canvas: Memory, Identity and Inheritance in the Work of Marie Redonnet'. *Forum for Modern Language Studies*, vol. 28, October 1992 (pp. 320–34).

Fallaize, Elizabeth: *French Women's Writing: Recent Fiction* (pp. 160–75).

'*Beur*' *writers*

Hargreaves, Alec G.: *Voices from the North African Immigrant Community in France. Immigration and Identity in Beur Fiction*. Berg, London 1991.


3. SELECT BIBLIOGRAPHY OF ENGLISH TRANSLATIONS OF WOMEN'S WRITING

*George Sand*

*The Haunted Pool* (*La Mare au diable*, 1846), transl. Frank H. Potter. Shameless Hussy, Berkeley, CA 1976.

*The Country Waif* (*La Petite Fadette*, 1849), transl. Eirene Collis, intro. Dorothy Zimmerman. Nebraska University Press, Lincoln 1977.

*The Bagpipers* (*Les Maîtres Sonneurs*, 1853), transl. K.P. Wormely. Cassandra, Chicago 1977.

*The Story of My Life* (*Histoire de ma vie*, 1854), multiple transl., ed. Thelma Jurgrau. SUNY, Albany, NY 1990.

*She and He* (*Elle et lui*, 1859), transl. George Burnham Ives. Academy, Chicago 1978.

*Marianne* (*Marianne*, 1876), transl. and ed. Siân Miles. Methuen, London 1987.


*Colette Yver*

*The Doctor Wife* (*Princesses de science*, 1907), transl. Anna, Comtesse de Bremont. Hutchinson, London 1909.


*Renée Vivien*

*A Woman Appeared to Me* (*Une Dame m'apparut*, 1904), transl. Jeannette M. Foster. Naiad Press, Tallahassee, FL 1982.

*At the Sweet Hour of Hand in Hand* (*A l'heure des mains jointes*, 1906), transl. Sandia Belgrade. Naiad Press, Weatherby Lake, MO 1979.


*Colette*

*The Collected Stories of Colette*, ed. Robert Phelps. Penguin, Harmondsworth 1985.

*Cheri/The Last of Cheri.*(*Chéri*, 1920 and *La Fin de Chéri*, 1926), transl. Roger Senhouse. Penguin, Harmondsworth 1954.

*Break of Day* (*La Naissance du jour*, 1928), transl. Enid McLeod. The Women's Press, London 1979.
*Looking Backwards* (*Journal à rebours*, 1941 and *De ma fenêtre*, 1942), transl. David le Vay. The Women's Press, London 1987.
*The Evening Star* (*L'Etoile Vesper*, 1946), transl. David le Vay. The Women's Press, London 1987.


*Simone de Beauvoir*
*The Blood of Others* (*Le Sang des autres*, 1945), transl. Yvonne Moyse and Roger Senhouse. Penguin, Harmondsworth 1986.
*The Ethics of Ambiguity* (*Pour une morale de l'ambiguité*, 1947), transl. Bernard Frechtman. Citadel Press, New York 1976.
*The Mandarins* (*Les Mandarins*, 1954), transl. Leonard M. Friedman. Fontana, London 1986.
*The Second Sex* (*Le Deuxième sexe*, 1949), transl. H.M. Parshley. Penguin, Harmondsworth 1984.
*Memoirs of a Dutiful Daughter* (*Mémoires d'une jeune fille rangée*, 1958), transl. James Kirkup. Penguin, Harmondsworth 1987.
*Force of Circumstance* (*La Force des choses*, 1960), transl. Richard Howard. Penguin, Harmondsworth 1987.


*Elsa Triolet*
*A Fine of Two Hundred Francs* (*Le Premier accroc coûte deux cents francs*, 1944), transl. and intro. Helena Lewis. Virago, London 1986.


*Hélène Cixous*
'The Laugh of the Medusa' ('Le Rire de la Méduse', 1975), transl. Keith Cohen and Paula Cohen. In Warhol and Price Herndl: *Feminisms* (pp. 334–49).
*The Newly Born Woman* (*La Jeune née*, with Catherine Clément, 1975), transl. Betsy Wing. Minnesota University Press, Minneapolis 1986.
*The Hélène Cixous Reader*, transl. and ed. Susan Sellers. Routledge, London and New York 1994.


*Luce Irigaray*
'This Sex which is not one' ('Ce sexe qui n'en est pas un', 1977), transl. Claudia Reeder. In Warhol and Herndl: *Feminisms* (pp. 350–6).

*Speculum of the Other Woman* (*Speculum de l'autre femme*,1977), transl.
 Gillian C. Gill. Cornell University Press, Ithaca, NY 1985.
*The Irigaray Reader*, ed. Margaret Whitford. Blackwell, Oxford 1991.
*Je, tu, nous: Towards a Culture of Difference* (1990), transl. Alison Martin.
 Routledge, London 1993.


*Julia Kristeva*
*The Kristeva Reader*, ed. Toril Moi. Blackwell, Oxford 1986.


*Annie Leclerc*
Translated extracts from *Parole de femme* (Woman's Word,1974) can be
 found in Claire Duchen: *French Connections* and Elizabeth Fallaize:
 *French Women's Writing: Recent Fiction.*


*Marguerite Duras*
*The Ravishing of Lol Stein* (*le Ravissement de Lol V. Stein*, 1964), transl.
 Richard Seaver. Grove Press, New York 1966.
*Destroy, she said* (*Détruire, dit-elle*, 1969), transl. Barbara Bray. Grove Press,
 New York 1970.
*Woman to Woman* (*Les Parleuses*, with Xavière Gauthier, 1974), transl.
 Katharine A. Jensen. University of Nebraska Press, Lincoln 1987.
*The Lover* (*L'Amant*, 1984), transl. Barbara Bray. Collins, Flamingo
 Paperback, London 1985.


*Annie Ernaux*
*Cleaned Out* (*Les Armoires vides*, 1974), transl. Carol Sanders. Dalkey, New
 York 1991.
*Positions* (*La Place*, 1983), transl. Tanya Leslie. Quartet, London 1991.

# Index

LLOYD H. AHLEM

# DO I HAVE TO BE ME?

## THE PSYCHOLOGY OF HUMAN NEED

G/L
REGAL
BOOKS
TM

A Division of G/L Publications
Glendale, California, U.S.A.

© Copyright 1973 by G/L Publications
All rights reserved

Published by
Regal Books Division, G/L Publications
Glendale, California 91209
Printed in U.S.A.

Library of Congress Catalog Card No. 73-79843
Hardcover edition: ISBN 0-8307-0248-2
Softcover edition: ISBN 0-8307-0252-0

# Contents

# 1 Love: a Driving Force

"Would you guys kiss me good night?" It was the last request after a long night's ordeal. A drug episode had gone bad.

The plump, but attractive and lovable, young lady arrived at our home about 11 P.M. Obviously her world had come unglued. Her words could only suggest the grotesque emotions she felt. Wracked with unexplained fear, only half knowing where she was, she had convinced a friend to drive her to our home where, hopefully, some peace might be found.

Slowly her senses returned to normal. But intermittent shrieks signaled a series of delusions, induced by hallucinogens, that erupted in her mind. Gradually we were able to "talk her down." She was "crashing" from a marijuana escapade, but the marijuana had been laced with a hard drug. The resultant trip was longer and more terrifying than she had thought possible.

Five hours passed before her mind cleared enough for her to relate accurately what was happening. We listened intently, not precisely sure how to respond, but we did know that this was a time for tender loving care. We

1

continued giving assurance, being careful not to stimulate guilt in an already troubled mind.

About 5 A.M. she was ready for sleep. We tucked her in bed in our spare room and let her sleep around the clock.

That simple gesture of affection, the kiss good night, was the assurance that someone cared. In life's toughest spots, there is absolutely no substitute for love.

"Love makes the world go 'round,'" so proclaims the ballad most of us have heard. Love is idolized, joked about, even hated. Love is the dominant theme of plays, books, and poetry. Love is fought for, suppressed, stimulated, even prostituted. Probably more human energy is expended in the various expressions and frustrations of love than in any other human experience.

Why? For some reason we were made with the need to give and to receive love. The Bible's creation story describes God's need for an affiliation—some loving relationship. So He made man. He made him in His own image with a need to love and be loved. Other world religions, as well, portray man in some kind of affiliation to his maker. Sometimes they present the relationship as positive, sometimes as negative. Christian faith, however, is always positive. It describes God as loving man so much that He gave Himself to man in order to love him supremely.

Not only do normal human experience and the religions

2

of mankind affirm the need for love, but also current psychological research recognizes empirically this human need. A disease called *marasmus* afflicts severely love-deprived children. The disease manifests itself in a number of physical and psychological symptoms. Physically, the affected children appear to be starving: their abdomens protrude, and their limbs are shriveled. Their complexion is devoid of vitality, and their flesh is like putty to the touch. Psychologically, they avoid all relationships with people, even the establishment of eye contact with others, and instead they occupy their attention with inanimate objects in a decreased range of interests.

Typically, marasmic children have been emotionally abandoned. Their mothers may have parked them in the unwilling care of others or left them in the hospitals where they were born. For the most part, substitute mothers tend only to minimize the child's physical discomforts. They may change his pants and offer him a bottle, but they spare him little affection. Consequently, the child senses early that he has been rejected.

According to some studies, the personalities of marasmic children who experienced prolonged emotional deprivation were damaged for life. Some were so damaged that they died from starvation while still very young. Seemingly unable to consume and utilize the food offered them, they perished. Those who survived to adolescence became withdrawn, weepy types, with little enthusiasm for normal human experience. Others developed schizophrenic personalities as adults, retreating from life, shutting out most interpersonal experience.

When a person's very survival depends on love, the need for love appears clearly established. Because love is essential to life, doctors routinely instruct nurses to fondle and caress babies and young children who may be hospitalized during the psychologically vulnerable days that come early in life. The standard prescription they inscribe on the patients' charts is "TLC"—tender loving care. Such warm attention may spare children great misery later in life.

Through meaningful love experiences, children develop emotional security and confidence in themselves. Having seen love expressed and having felt its assurance, they are able to enter fully into healthy relationships and experiences of their own. The confidence love has given them minimizes their fears of failure.

But what do we mean by the term *love?* In the English language, *love* has many different meanings. When we define love as a basic need, we had better consider which definition we are using. Some experiences that bear the label *love* are not love. Some "loving" relationships, in fact, may be very harmful. Who would prescribe a pseudo love that wounds where healing is needed? Certainly, no one has a basic need for false love. But what kind of love do we really need?

Strolling across our college campus one day, I caught just one phrase of a couple's intense conversation. "Baby," the fellow said to his girl, "I sure would love to love your skin!" Observing this half-nelson demonstration of affection, I doubted that the love he offered was a lofty altruism given for its own sake. His use of the word expressed rather his need for some reduction of a biological drive. To describe the exuberance and desire of adolescence as *love* does not make it the same as loving one's neighbor as oneself. Perhaps the term *lust* better fits the definition of love in this instance. One might seriously question whether emotional development is dependent on this type of love experience.

Just as love and lust are confused in our language, and often in our motives, so love and hostility become confused in the behavior of certain people. In a large metropolitan high school, the teachers and counselors were asked to list the names of students who had reputations for being the lovers in the student body. "Lovers" referred to youngsters

known for necking in public, for brashness in sexual adventure, and for general preoccupation with the opposite sex. When the composite list was completed, personality tests that had been administered to the entire student body were drawn from the files for the student lovers. One dominant trait they exhibited was hostility! The group had a greater than average history of fights on campus and conflicts with teachers; they shared a record of general irritability at school.

Our social conditioning has taught us to reject hostility in most instances. But hostile behavior, contained in the words and gestures of love, may be expressed more easily. These students had found a way effectively to disguise, yet express, their feelings. Hostility disguised as love hardly contributes to the emotional development of its recipient.

Still another definition of love that operates widely in American culture is romantic love. There can be little doubt that many people seek this type of love to bring fulfillment to their lives. Some sociologists who write about marriage have attempted to describe the nature of romantic love.

Let's look at a composite of their efforts to define the term.

1. A strong emotional attachment to a member of the opposite sex. An exclusive affectional relationship with a love partner.

2. An emotional interdependence with the person chosen as the object of one's love and affection.

3. Physical attraction and sexual desire for the loved one. A sense of stimulation in the presence of the chosen partner.

4. Strong emotional reassurance resulting from the love relationship. A sense of bolstering one's own feelings of self-worth.

5. An idealization of one's partner that actually distorts the image of the loved one. The romantic lover deliberately engages in fantasy while contemplating his relationship with his partner.

This definition of love is important for several reasons. First, many normal people hold this conception of love fulfillment. They sincerely believe in the promises of romantic love and seek to be enhanced by it. If theirs has been a healthy emotional development in the early years, they can expect that love and marriage will provide a fulfilling experience. They have observed others for whom this has been true.

Second, a reasonably large number of people enter into romantic love to compensate for some deficit in their lives. They may have been unhappy in the past, or they may have considered themselves inadequate. The prospect of a romantic experience that may answer their needs is appealing indeed. But they want this love for its therapeutic value rather than as a growth experience.

Third, in extolling romantic love, the American culture has constructed an ideal with built-in fallacies. As a result, individuals often find themselves thrown emotionally off balance. In the average marriage, the idealization process goes into reverse as married lovers discover the truth about each other. A starry-eyed husband wakes to find his wife is a witch until she has had her second cup of coffee in the morning. An adoring bride observes that her husband cares more for his own comfort than for hers. Then their strongly emotional interdependence rocks as the partners discover that they fail to meet each other's needs and expectations.

Just as man has no need for love disguised as hostility or lust, so he has no need for the kind of love implicit in the American definition of romantic love. Must a person experience this distortion of love in an attempt to meet his emotional needs? Do the benefits of romantic love so outweigh its harmfulness that we need not be greatly concerned? Or is there a better way?

Let us look now at another definition of love that we may know. This love is more positive in nature and perhaps comes closer to meeting our basic needs.

Brotherly love receives a great deal of current emphasis. For today's turmoil, perceived by almost everyone, it is the easily prescribed antidote.

In the ancient Greek language, several kinds of love were defined and distinguished from one another. The Greek concept of brotherly love involves concern for one another's welfare. It includes the idea of mutuality because this kind of love experience is discontinued, or at least jeopardized, without some agreement that the object of love will return love in kind. Both parties profit from the relationship. Because of the relationship, both are better off than each one is individually.

I recall a missionary's story of two lepers in the Orient. One had no arms; the other had no legs. Both were starving since neither could work effectively alone. The solution to their problem came when the leper who could walk carried the leper who had arms. Together they worked as one and fulfilled each other's survival needs. A warm feeling of kinship arose between them. Brotherly love existed with a kind of wholesome profit in mind. Two could do more than one if they worked together. Further, the profits extended to other areas of life. Since their relationship had solved one problem, other problems suggested themselves for solution through the same cooperation. Brotherly love can grow in depth and significance.

The price of reciprocal love, brotherly love, is the surrender of a certain portion of one's personal sovereignty. Decisions about oneself must be shared, or the relationship collapses. It is at this point that many people balk. The one who seems to need help most may be unable to accept it. The risk of surrendering a little of one's sovereignty seems too great even to accomplish simple things. As a result, the helpless one decides to go it alone, failing increasingly to meet the demands society makes on him. At best, he experiences only minimal satisfactions in life. At worst, he turns completely within himself and, psychologically, perishes.

Brotherly love seems to be so logical an answer to society's ills, yet it is so rarely applied. Is it because people believe that personal sovereignty is more important than the solution of their problems? Is the need to be sovereign in one's experience more potent than the need for love, or does withdrawal obscure needs one had best forget?

# 2 Love: a Developmental Sequence

We have considered briefly the need for love fulfillment. The physical survival of some youngsters depends on it. The healthy psychological functioning of all of us is impaired without it. Our discussion has indicated, however, that not all the experiences commonly called love are exactly that. We do not need love disguised as lust or hostility, we need a purer love, a refined and mature love.

The expression of mature love follows a developmental sequence. It grows from the infant's experience to adult fulfillment. While the whole person is growing, the ability to experience love is growing. Love doesn't begin in the middle of its sequence or start at both ends. It has a fairly normal progression that is identifiable. If an individual fails to attain a developmental stage properly or completely, his ability to love and to be loved is impaired. He must grow into mature love in orderly fashion.

The first step in the developmental sequence is to experience healthy, sensual love in infancy. The more I work with children the more I see the importance of healthy emotional experience early in life.

9

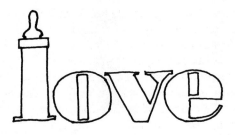

Some years ago I met a boy whose behavior was so extremely offensive that he had to be dismissed from school. He was constantly in trouble for taking off his clothes in school rest rooms or for exposing himself sexually on the playground. No amount of admonition had any effect in correcting him.

The lad was born while his father was away at war. His mother found work to support the family, which included a senile grandmother with an abrasive personality. Born in a military hospital, the boy was rushed home shortly after birth so his mother could return to work. While mother was employed nights as a cocktail waitress, grandmother supposedly kept house. Mother's job, grandmother's confusion, baby's needs, and father's absence combined to create chaos. For months the child's emotional needs were neglected. He often cried himself to sleep and was seldom cuddled and enjoyed by his mother or grandmother. He was like an abandoned child in his own home.

Father's return from the service promised some improvements. Grandmother's death simplified life at home. Father got an adequate job, though he traveled a lot, and mother came home to care for her son. One might have expected that these changes would help, but too much time had passed, and the early experiences of this child had been critical.

Realizing that her son had missed much love as an infant, mother decided to catch up somehow. She fed him, slept with him, cuddled him, smothered him. This abnormal relationship continued until he was in the fourth grade. Now we had a boy who was anxious, obnoxious, and thoroughly confused. He grew hostile—cruel to animals and highly destructive of property. One day his mother phoned. "What shall I do? He's tearing up the bathroom tile with a hammer!" The boy had sensed that he had been used to alleviate mother's guilt and was enraged by it. Finally, lengthy depth therapy and firmly controlled behavior at school alleviated the problem considerably.

What went wrong, specifically? This boy had missed the earliest stage of development of love. Babies and young children have a great need for wholesome, sensual pleasure. They require stroking, fondling, cuddling—lots of physical contact, enjoyed by both parent and child. Healthy experiences like this build self-assurance into children that protects them from hurt for years to come. But this child had been ignored. Now it was too late.

Children are highly sensitive to the attention given them though they lack words to express these feelings until years later. A placid infant placed in the arms of an emotionally disturbed adult will very often become upset and cry. Yet no words have been exchanged, and the adult believes that the child is feeling only pleasure. Warm physical handling and the accepting attitudes of happy parents seem to penetrate to the deepest recesses of children's minds, bringing emotional health and well-being. But these attentions must come early and with wholesome motives. One really cannot catch up later. Timing is all-important.

Because of early deprivation, this boy lacked the roots of emotional growth and became unsure and unstable. Then his mother compensated in a neurotic way, resolving her own guilt rather than fostering his development. He became a problem at school because he was retaliating for mother's early neglect and later neurotic compensations. Aggressive behavior became his symbolic way of resisting

11

her smothering: perhaps misbehaving would make her stop loving in this solicitous way. The absence of the father in the service and on his job left the boy without a clear example to follow. He had never seen a model of mature male behavior at close range. Thus he had no concept of what normal behavior is like. Lacking the foundation of wholesome early experiences, this boy will continue to suffer in attempting to grow to mature love and emotional experience.

Research findings also point up the need for early, wholesome attention. From studies of children reared in institutions where early, sensual love is lacking, we know that such children exhibit at least three general kinds of problems.

First, they show delayed speech development together with a resulting lack of social graciousness. Speech development is a key indicator of early social growth. Infantile speech in older children is a symbolic plea for emotional assurance. When normally developed children hear such speech, they reject the speaking child as "babyish." Thus the deprived child is caught between his need for assurance and his need for social approval.

Second, these children display signs of general emotional impoverishment. They lack emotional spontaneity and seem cold. They tend to hide their emotions and withdraw from uncomfortable situations. In their efforts to avoid being hurt, they lose the benefits of normal social life.

Finally, they show a diminished general intelligence. The social and emotional withdrawal limits attempts at learning. Limited learning, in turn, appears as dullness on mental ability tests. We sometimes call this group of symptoms "institutionalism" or "hospitalism." Where love is diminished, so also is personal and emotional growth.

At least two factors in our history have hindered our understanding of the need for early love. First, the belief that sensual experience was basically evil was a clear setback. The impetus of Puritanism encouraged this attitude. As a result, our culture developed excessive taboos on sex and related sensual experience. But it is important to note that the taboos were possibly a response to unhealthy love fulfillments as much as to sex itself.

Some people try to *fulfill* their love needs sensually and grow no further. When adults preoccupy themselves with physical love, they can fall into the worst type of lust. They exploit the partner physically and emotionally, while focusing their fantasy life continually on sex at an animal level. But sensual love was not designed for fulfillment; it is rather a step toward greater, more mature love, and is fulfilled only in the presence of mature love.

Segments of our society have attempted to legitimatize unhealthy attempts at fulfillment. The current hedonistic Playboy philosophy is a clear attempt in this effort. Suggesting that sensual pleasure is the fulfillment rather than the beginning of healthy love experience, the Playboy is preoccupied with sex, particularly sex of the nonreproductive variety. This is becoming a classical symptom of love development terminated at a most immature level.

The second factor that hindered general understanding of the need for love resulted from the behavioristic psychology of the 1920's. In 1928, J. B. Watson dedicated a book sardonically, "To the first mother who brings up a happy child." Watson was convinced that most of the ills of man could be traced to too much friendliness and warmth from mothers. He believed that if you wanted mature adult behavior, you treated children like pocket editions of adulthood. He failed to recognize that the needs of children are qualitatively different from the needs of adults.

This attitude prevailed so strongly that government publications of the time advised against caring warmly for little children. A significant portion of the population accepted Watson's counsel. It is possible that a measure of today's adult stress results from being raised in an era of bad advice.

When the very young child has been fulfilled through simple, demonstrated love and has felt accepted, he is ready to grow in his experience. He can move on to know mutual love. The Greeks had a word for it—*phileo*. This love was described in the preceding chapter when we considered various definitions of love that exist in our culture. This is the love that the lepers knew when they helped each other overcome their respective handicaps. This is the kind of relationship that makes corporate human activity possible. People acting together in trust solve many problems and achieve many social goals. All of our credit economy is based on mutual trust and help. We can't live without mutually supporting relationships, for when they break down, society collapses.

Little children cannot tell you in words whether they have been loved or not. They lack the ability, for defining one's emotional experience is a highly abstract problem, involving a mature use of intelligence and language. This ability does not begin to function until junior-high-school years. So often the inadequately loved baby looks and acts much like the well-cared-for child. This has led some to believe that early care, therefore, is not important. But by the time that behavioral symptoms of love deprivation appear, the optimum time for that developmental stage has passed. Much work is required to repair the damage, and it is seldom done well.

Reciprocal relationships include risk. The risk comes

14

when we trust others to control us in part or provide for our security. We agree to do as they wish in exchange for their doing as we wish. While doing the will of another, we yield sovereignty over a portion of our lives.

It is striking to observe how difficult it is for insecure people to trust themselves to the will of another. My experience in counseling married couples has confirmed this fact many times.

Recently, a worried young wife approached me concerning the affairs she thought her husband was having with other women. When I asked her what the evidence was, she proceeded to reel off details of scattered experiences that amounted to little. For example, she was sure he took a job as a tree trimmer so he could climb up ladders and view other women in their homes. Also, she checked the odometer on his truck daily to see how far he had traveled. One day he drove six miles to trim a tree. Since it was exactly six miles to the home of a woman friend, it was obvious to her that an affair was in progress. She was sure he had violated the reciprocal agreement of marriage.

The young wife displayed obvious signs of a disturbed personality. During extended counseling, she told of her early life at home. Her mother and father were constantly in conflict, and their troubles had left her insecure and lacking in confidence. Her mother was an unresponsive woman, unable to give warmth and assurance. Her coldness produced an anxiety in the child that dominated her entire life. She feared losing her husband, so she watched his every move. In fact, he lost one good job because she phoned his employer several times a day to find out where he was and what he was doing.

Wearied by this constant overseeing, the husband slowly withdrew from his wife. He didn't realize that he was withdrawing at first, but the daily grilling about his contacts with people brought his reaction sharply to his attention. When he began to spend more time with his wife, she responded by showering him with affection and sexual advances. He thoroughly enjoyed this, of course, but was aware that her motivation was suspect. She was buying him with the gestures of love. She needed to regulate him closely so that she could trust her security to his control.

People who lacked early healthy emotional development find their mutual relationships impaired. Because of lack of self-assurance, they must protect themselves by seeking to control the behavior of those who could hurt them. Since marriage is a trusting relationship, this is the place where the problems erupt most readily.

In this case, the husband was a solid citizen with a very loving concern for his wife. Through counseling he was able to live within her ability to trust, and to respond to her need for assurance. Their problems lessened as a result. The wife, seeing the renewed interest and understanding of her husband, was able to trust him a little more and relax in the greater safety she enjoyed.

This case teaches us two definite things. First, early love experiences affect mutual human relationships by producing assurance and trust. Second, as people understand their limits and live within them, they can grow. When the limits are either constantly exceeded or never tested, growth does not take place. When this husband respected his wife's emotional limits and accepted them, he was able to create a safe environment in which she could extend her trust and safely test her limits.

Attempts to control others are a frequent compensation for lack of trust resulting from lack of love. Teachers of disturbed children know this fact all too well.

One chunky little fellow was an enlightening illustration of this truth. His home had the usual history in cases of disturbed children—cold parents, a frequently absent father, severe and erratic discipline. Unsure of himself, the boy made repeated attempts to capture the attention of his teacher. Not only did he require her attention, but he

16

insisted that she exclude all others from her care as well. He so clung to her that she felt as though she were moving in a prisoner's leg irons.

One day she finally got him occupied with art work and proceeded to help other members of the class. But in a few moments, he was interrupting her every conversation with other students. Finally she "blew her stack." She reprimanded him and hauled him off to the principal's office. Since principals often become father figures to youngsters, you can guess how this boy reacted. He was paralyzed with fear, because his father had been scaring him out of his wits at least twice a week. The principal scolded him severely and sent him back to class.

Now this chunky rascal turned into a hellion. Realizing his physical strength, he threatened everyone who crossed his path. He challenged the teacher's instructions. He threw erasers. He threw a fit. In a few short minutes, he discovered he was in control, not the teacher. Other students responded more dramatically to him than to her. No learning could take place until he permitted it. Truly, he was boss. Only firm physical control and suspension from school restored order.

How many people in the world compensate for lack of mutual love by attempts at control? How many laws are on the books because of distrust and lack of love? How many people seek political power in a quest for love fulfillment? How many troubled souls turn inward in their attentions, imposing self-controls that strangle their emotional growth? I strongly suspect that the extremely legalistic politics and belief systems of many people result from very great emotional needs.

The love experiences of mature, fulfilled people are in striking contrast to the experiences of the troubled persons just discussed. Fortunately, some quality psychological research concerns itself with fulfillment as well as deprivation.

17

In his book *Motivation and Personality,* * Abraham Maslow provides us with a profile of the traits of what he calls self-actualized people. I strongly recommend his book for inspirational as well as scholarly purposes. It gives us a look at the fortunate side of life.

Self-actualized people are those who have achieved a very full development. They are not hung up in any significant way. They have fully explored their talents and applied their energies enthusiastically and efficiently to creative endeavors.

Maslow's research shows that the universal trait among self-actualizers is the ability to be accepting. For these mature individuals no scoundrel is so low that he is not a source of some benefit. The integrity of every human being is treasured. The common humanness of us all is held in deep respect.

In the love relationships of self-actualizers, there is a great desire for psychological as well as physical intimacy. Secret languages and gestures develop between couples that only they understand. Responses toward each other tend to be spontaneous, free from defenses, the tyranny of roles and inhibitions. It is unnecessary to maintain images or appearances. One can be himself completely. No energy is wasted worrying about one's self-presentation or in suppressing anxiety. So accepting of each other are these partners that they become a single personality, yet each is a fully developed individual. Each allows his partner an irreducible, autonomous integrity. Yet each feels the needs of the other as his own. Each fully enjoys the achievements of the other as his own. Attempts to control, to humiliate, or to belittle the loved one are totally unknown.

When students in my classes in mental hygiene and human development finish reading Maslow's work they come away with mixed emotions. They feel that they have

*A. H. Maslow, *Motivation and Personality* (New York: Harper and Row, Inc., 1954), pp. 203-228.

# AGAPE LOVE

glimpsed a goal in life well worth pursuing, but they also wonder if such a rewarding, fulfilling experience is possible for them. Sometimes examples of lofty experience bring a sense of frustration and discouragement. My reply is: a love experience exists that fulfills man, and it is available to everyone. It is expressed in the Greek word, *agape.*

A number of years ago my father was seriously injured in a farm machinery accident. He lost the use of one arm, and his entire nervous system lost some of its resilience from the blows received. In a few short minutes, he changed from being a vigorous, healthy farmer to a retired, physically handicapped bystander.

But this event set into motion acts of love that our family will never forget. These acts began immediately after the mishap. A neighbor found him in the field and took him to the hospital. Other friends immediately took care of the dairy. Still another finished the field work he had left incomplete. They did this not for just a day or two, but for months. Until he could supervise the work of hired men, nearly everyone who knew him seemed to be a volunteer.

The important aspect of this love is that it was given without thought of return. No one asked for pay, no one suggested they were owed a favor. We all felt ourselves recipients of an unmerited love found in few places in the world today.

19

But it didn't end there either. My father became critically ill a few years later, and again the responses were immediate. Nurses volunteered for night duty during this, his last, illness. Friends changed vacation plans so they could provide transportation to special hospitals in neighboring cities. Prepared meals for the family constantly appeared on the doorstep or in the kitchen. Anything that relieved stress and eased the work load was volunteered so freely we could hardly believe it. We were witnesses to agape love translated into human behavior.

For several generations my family has lived in a community that believes profoundly in the experience of agape love. This deep concern for the needs of others has been the mode of life for many of the people. For them, agape love relationships are the usual, normal experiences!

So far, we have defined agape love by showing it in action. Let us now discuss the nature of this love more fully. Agape love is the unmerited favor of God toward all men. It characterizes the personality of God: He has given Himself unreservedly for mankind; He wills to act in man's highest interests. We understand this directly from the New Testament, for no other religion or philosophy has generated such an altruistic concept. In this, the Christian faith stands apart.

Man did not concoct the notion of agape love; he received it by acts of God toward man. Nor did God send man some abstract definition of Himself through ascetic prophets, nor permit philosophers to envision Him in dreams. Instead, He Himself became man. He felt what we feel: loved as no one ever loved before. As the apostle Paul put it, "God was in Christ reconciling the world to himself" (2 Cor. 5:19).

Man's experience of agape love is to receive and repeat the loving acts of God. Those acts are performed in the highest interests of man, without thought of reciprocation.

Thus agape love means unreserved giving of oneself for the benefit of others, even if it costs one's life.

I recently encountered a real estate broker from a Southern state. He had just come to know that he was truly the object of the love of God. The realization had so gripped his imagination that he was doing everything possible to tell others about it. The more he talked, however, the more he understood that he had better translate the love he had experienced into his everyday life. His chief thrust was to try in every possible way to provide the best housing available to people living in oppressive conditions. After several years of work in which he sustained heavy financial loss, the leaders of a dominant community action organization successfully dubbed him a racist. He was driven from his business and left the state, bankrupt.

"How does it feel to get clobbered by those you help?" queried a friend.

"It hurts," my friend replied, "but if Christ endured a cross and was unceasing in His love, I can do no less. I'm no loser in my experience!"

But agape love is more than altruistic social action, wonderful and needed as it is. It is a belief in one's personal worth because God has declared His complete interest in man.

I have been counseling recently with a young woman who is buried in depression and despair. Her marriage has gone sour, she suffers from psychosomatic illnesses, and she is dominated by a hostility that surges uncontrollably. Like so many other troubled people, she felt little love and care as a child. She was shy and afraid to trust others in mutual relationships. Loneliness set in. She sought marriage as an escape, but found it became a trap instead. Acting out her hostility toward her husband and children, she behaved in ways that would make the most callous person feel guilty. Overwhelmed by guilt, she lapsed into depression.

21

What has agape love to do with the needs of a troubled soul such as this? Much in every way. Agape love holds men guiltless. It does not count up their misdeeds and extract judgment or retribution. Agape love, therefore, is the direct antidote to the guilt-ridden personality. It lets ʾ ɔu begin again without handicap.

Bit by bit agape love is soaking into this woman's personality. The other day she offered the thought, "Every once in awhile I find out it is OK to be what I am—without compensations. Sure I'm mean and troubled, but God knows the problems I struggle with. Then I feel a little more free and can trust myself to a little more relationship with my family. It comes out all right when I do. I know I need my family to forgive me, but it's easier to ask when I know all is clear between me and God."

Unlike reciprocal or mutual love, agape love is a "no risk" relationship. You never get to the place where the love has been discontinued because of some fault of yours. You are never reduced in the eyes of God because of some failing. You can't lose this love. God always continues His love toward you in spite of any trait or deed. There is never a time or place where you cannot begin again. As a result you can grow in this love without the fear and inhibition of failure.

In mutual or reciprocal love, failure markedly reduces the motivation to begin again. A few bad experiences, and one party or the other withdraws from the relationship. A couple of instances of unfaithfulness by a husband or wife may endanger a marriage. Only if agape love is brought to bear can the wounds be healed.

In fact, most of us have become so accustomed to conditional ways of relating that we impose on God the same rules we have for our relationships with each other. But when we do, we only deceive ourselves. God's remarkable love for us continues unceasingly. The apostle Paul expresses this contagious truth vividly in his letter to the

Roman Christians: "Who shall separate us from the love of Christ? shall tribulation, or distress, or persecution, or famine, or nakedness, or peril, or sword?" (Rom. 8:35).

Recently a young college girl, whose life was a bundle of moral mistakes and emotional hang-ups, discovered that God loved her anyway. Accepting His love and forgiveness, she shed a heavy load of guilt that had threatened to distort seriously her whole personality. The subsequent changes in her style of living were dramatic. Grades improved. Hostility subsided. Instead of belting her parents with angry accusations for past mistakes, she saw them as people in need of the same great love. They observed the change in their daughter and scarcely believed what had happened. Soon they, too, sought to know this love that remakes man.

What kind of love does man really need? In summary, he needs three kinds. He needs careful, loving, sensual fulfillment as an infant. Out of the assurance derived from being loved, he develops the ability to enter into mutual relationships. With satisfactory relationships, he works effectively, marries well, and participates constructively in society. But what man needs most is to know the redeeming experiences of agape love. We are all subject to the human failures that damage every one of us. No one is free from some hang-up. But no experience of failure removes us from the possibility of knowing the highest love of all. This love is free, unceasing, creative within us, therapeutic. To know it, we simply accept it as a gift from God, allow it to dominate our experience, and live it out in relationship to mankind, knowing that we have in Christ the perfect example to follow.

# 3 Agape Love as Therapy

Several years ago I met a man who returned to his home community because of the strange power of agape love. He had not been there in years—in fact he avoided the place because of the memories it stimulated.

As a youngster he had acquired a reputation for being the most obstreperous, difficult kid in town. Although bright and inquisitive, he was a rebel from his earliest days. Teachers shuddered when they recalled his presence in school. The minister of his parish also was frustrated by his antics in church activities, and finally thrust a significant experience on the boy. In the mind of the lad, it was a totally uninvited experience.

One Saturday morning, the confirmation class of junior high schoolers had gathered at the church for their weekly lesson. Forced to attend, our budding Dillinger made the situation as difficult as possible. He challenged every rule, interrupted every student's recitation, and created chaos until class was dismissed. But on this particular day, out of sheer exasperation, the pastor declared: "Son, I am at my wits' end with you. I can bear you no longer. You cannot come back to this class. But remember, I am going to pray for you *every day* that you are alive!"

Delighted at his release, the boy skipped away and was never seen at church again. Apparently the boy's goal had been to force the minister to reject him. Since he wasn't worried about prayers following him, he considered his relationship to the world of religion effectively terminated.

Life proceeded normally for our rascal. It was a race to see whether he could get through school before the school got through with him. Completing school and seeking adventure, he entered military service shortly before World War II. Adventure he found, experiencing more military combat than most men. But the dangers of war did not seem to nudge him even a little in the direction of the church, or anything or anyone religious.

Following the war, life returned to normal. Our friend had calmed a good deal now; in fact, he had become somewhat reflective. Although he had not thought about the pastor's promise in many years, it had lain dormant deep within his mind. One quiet evening, with no uncommon stimulation present, he began to weep.

"Why am I bawling?" he muttered to himself. "I have nothing to be sad about!" It angered him that his emotions should have slipped out and caught him unaware. "Could it be really true that damned preacher is still praying? How stupid can you get?"

As he fought to control his feelings, the rudiments of his much-resisted religious education returned to his memory. "Unceasing love is ours, never stopping because of any hindrance from us," he dimly recalled the words of the monotone cleric. The words were not very persuasive when he first heard them. Why should they bug him now? But they stuck in his mind, the center of his attention.

"God, if that is so, You're on!" he shouted out loud. "If all these years have not turned You away from me, You deserve the courtesy of a real test."

Simple, unrestrained joy filled the heart of Mr. Rebel. Just for curiosity, he decided to call the old preacher, if he hadn't been planted under the daisies yet. Sure enough, he found him by tracking him through relatives he could locate.

"Are you still praying, preach?" he shouted into the phone without identifying himself.

"If you are who I think you are," returned the old minister, "I haven't missed a day since that last confirmation class."

"Well, I just wanted to let you know you've won," said our friend. Together they wept for joy and shared the greatness of agape love.

The minister was unceasing in his prayers, expecting no reciprocation and no satisfaction when he declared his intention to pray that frustrating day years ago. He would pray no matter what. And that's the way it is when God announces He will love you—no matter what.

There was a joyful reunion in the old home town a few weeks later. The young man's experience led to a renewed fellowship between the pastor and the family, and a re-created relationship among members of the family. Love and forgiveness broke past tensions and led to the exhilaration of new, genuine care.

Let's review the nature of agape love. First, you can't shut it off. It is unceasing, unbroken, unconditional. It continues even if you shut down your perceivers and fail to recognize it. It is a no-contingency relationship. It cannot be bartered, nor purchased, nor earned. It is given freely for our acceptance.

Second, agape love is inconsistent with impurity, hurt, reprisal, or destructiveness. It is uncontaminated by false motive or any other human frailty. As such, it is completely consistent with integrity, growth, openness, awareness, acceptance, and fulfillment.

Most of all, it is personal. It is God becoming man,

identifying completely with him, and regarding him as an heir to all His creation, a joint-heir with His Son. Instead of trying to keep all the adjectives I've mentioned in your head, just think of four words: unceasing, unearned, integrating, personal. If you can manage these, you will have a handy stimulus to refresh your memory.

Human pride may tempt you to forego this simple but marvelous gift. You may have developed well enough through your human successes to think you can make it on your own. If this is the case, here are some thoughts to ponder.

To make a point, let me suggest some ways to keep this love from taking you over. These methods are not uncommon; they hold the attention of a majority of the world's population. Some of the methods are downright attractive. They fatten the ego, puff up the vanity, and let you live in self-conceit. Can you think of anything more delicious?

One of the most acceptable ways of resisting love is to become excessively moral. You can become so upright, clean and dignified that you will earn barrels of social approval. You may be so trusted that you will be elected to public office to end political corruption. Or you may become the dispenser of social and moral judgment in the community. Think of the thrill of censoring movies, hunting down graft in the sanitation department, or being chairman of the citizens' committee to aid the local school in its program to teach moral and spiritual values!

Your image will be impeccable. Successfully comparing your virtues to the qualities of others, you will convince yourself that God will have to accept you. Certainly all this goodness will establish a relationship with Him. His love will be unnecessary in bringing you together; you can buy your relationship with good behavior. His concern for you and His care will then be useless, and part of His nature will be meaningless. And to declare the nature of God to be meaningless is the height of rebellion and heresy.

Morality may get you to think you are about as good as they come. Further, morality can become your effective self-defense and source of pride. It can smother your need for personal knowledge of God and His love. You will set yourself up as an idol to be emulated—a little god. But if being moral is an essentially defensive activity, and not a symptom of healthy growth, it will build a barrier between you and the needs of others. For any large measure of defensiveness in our personalities shuts us off from human need. We grow unaware because we are preoccupied with ourselves, our situation and our images. As a result we are no longer open to people. We no longer sense their needs.

Morality is another crutch we rely on to prove our worth. It becomes a substitute for the highest value that can be placed on man—his value as the personally loved creature of God.

Of course, morality is rejected by some. In rejecting it, people state that they are unwilling to be satisfied with a substitute for true worth and adequacy. But turning to immorality, they find no better answer. They only bring on themselves the scorn of the majority, and perhaps destroy themselves with guilt.

Morality ought to be motivated by the adequacy that springs up in the heart of one who fully senses he is God's own. It should be a by-product of fulfilled experience, not the means to love or adequacy. Out of the enriched sense of worth that agape gives, the motive to disciplined living can operate without raising one's defenses, and without closing one's personality to human need or restricting the sense of fulfillment.

Another, and even more acceptable, way of refusing love is to become very religious. We live in a land where church membership is popular and being religious gets your some-where. It lines you up with the majority. Whatever else people may say about you, they can point to your religious-ness if they are seeking a positive attribute to mention in your eulogy. Further, you may think that you can prove your worth to God by your religiousness and buy His love.

Several years ago, I counseled with a girl who seemed to pursue both ways of attempting to forego agape love. She was *both* moral and religious. This also made her impossible! Acting out her fancied holiness, she became highly unpopular at school, though she was an attractive looking girl. No matter what topic she discussed with her schoolmates, she could not resist making moral judgments and religious pronouncements. No issue nor person was exempt from her judgments. Since her behavior led others to believe that she saw herself as superior, everyone with-drew when she appeared.

The effect of her efforts resulted in serious loneliness. In a short time she was isolated from nearly all her peers. The only people who seemed to approve of her were her sanctimonious elders.

About the time the problem became critical, a new boy moved to town and began to attend the same church. Happily she discovered that he, too, was both moral and religious. What happy communion resulted! These two unwitting youngsters shared the same personality distor-tions, and loneliness had driven them together. Sharing their heavenly neurosis, they fell quickly and deeply in love.

About six months later, reality came crashing through. The girl was pregnant, and her boyfriend denied any re-sponsibility for her condition. He changed churches, never admitting guilt. Their relationship was immediately sev-ered, as were many other friendships. People took sides concerning the young man's character. Obviously the girl was guilty, but people were strongly divided in their opinions of the boy. After all, how could such a religious and moral young man get involved in this way?

Through floods of tears and a broken heart, the girl's experience turned out to be redemptive. She recognized that she was depending upon her image of morality and religiousness for her sense of worth. Having lost her mask of respectability, she was forced to rely totally on the love of God—the God who did not falter in His concern when she got into difficulty. God accepted her because He loved her, not because she was moral and religious. Though she still bears the scars of a bitter lesson, today she is more free of defensiveness than ever before. She is open to the needs of people and has begun to relate in accepting ways and in genuine concern for her friends.

The young man, on the other hand, able to escape the immediate consequences of the problem, further reinforced himself in acceptability. He entered the ministry, and if you ever want to hear a thundering sermon on morality, I can recommend a church for you to attend. Though no one knows for sure, this young man may have found it necessary to distort the whole world to protect his own image—an image he manufactures in an attempt to convince God that he is acceptable.

Still another way to shut down your love receivers is to become very intellectual—not necessarily intelligent, just intellectual. If you are accustomed to critical thinking as we try to teach it in college, this approach should be natural for you. Just start by assuming that all information that exists is within the limits of human understanding. Believe that the human brain is all we need to understand God, ourselves, our reasons for existing. Next, assume that knowledge is expanding so fast that all information worth understanding is known now or lies just beyond the next issue of your favorite scientific journal. Then it is only a matter of time until all these puzzling questions about the meaning of life, about God, or about religious experience are exposed to the light of science, when they will convert to simple psychological, sociological, or scientific principles. Don't be caught admitting that there may be truth existing and available through something as unhuman as divine revelation.

You may have to get a little stubborn about it, occasionally. You are sure to meet someone who insists otherwise. Further, he will declare that he has found a great sense of certainty and personal peace in his faith. He actually seems to enjoy God! What's more, he made his discovery without being very bright. But if you insist on limiting your understanding to things experimentally perceived, you can dispose of him in a few uncomfortable minutes. After all, what you can't see can't possibly be real. Problems that don't fit your notions of experimental verification can't possibly exist. By fiat rule them out! Or at least rule them out of your mental order.

I should warn you about one psychological phenomenon, however. It is called perseveration. When you are sitting by your fireplace following a day of occupational fulfillment at the local loan office, thoughts may erupt without apparent stimulation. This is perseveration. While staring into the flames from the old Yule log, questions about the meaning of life, God and supreme love may sneak up on you. You may wonder, "How do I know that I am *not* the object of great love? What tests could I make to prove this negative hypothesis? Suppose it *is* true that God regards me as worth His supreme efforts to reach me. What then?"

If you are a good intellectual in the defensive, personal sense of the word, you will crush such thinking and relegate it to the mental trash heap. There's no sense facing up to what might be reality when you can protect yourself. Return the old noodle to the sand of uncertainty. Science encompasses all.

One final method of fending off agape love is worth considering. It is a method employed by multitudes today. It is "in." To some degree, it is replacing the intellectual style that is going out of vogue.

This method bears several different names. Turning on, blowing your mind, grooving are some of the young people's terms for it. Getting loaded, stoned, gassed, or lubricated were the words used when I was in college and engulfed in lower-middle-class status. Now that I'm educated in upper-middle-class status it is called transcending, existentially experiencing, or momentarily savoring. No matter, it is all an exploration of the emotions to see how much and how varied human mental experience can be. It is similar to turning up the juice in any complex jungle of electronic circuitry to see all the funny sparks.

Man seems determined to avoid the boring, the mundane. Even if it damages his biological or psychological makeup, he seeks for the experience that stretches human sensation. He feels that if he has explored human capacity for experience to the fullest, then life may be worth something.

To make effective use of this method of substitution for supreme love, you must start with the same assumptions as does the intellectual. You must be your own validating source and limit human experience to your own terms of understanding. You must exclude the possibility of experience that has a divine origin. Try to do that which freaks you out at the moment. Once more hide the noggin in the basket and breathe deeply. What you can't see isn't there. It is only what you feel that counts. And surely you can generate an emotional, perceptual freak-out that compares well with agape love. Certainly there must be some humanly contrived sensation that approaches what God can do in you!

You will have to avoid studiously the testimony of the

apostle Paul when he declares, "What no man ever saw or heard, what no man ever thought could happen, is the very thing God prepared for those who love him" (1 Cor. 2:9). This is the ultimate challenge. It flatly declares there is no equal to agape love. You will have to find this assertion to be either true or false. There is no middle ground.

The possible thought that there *is* an integrating experience available as a gift that maximizes human existence and provides infinite knowledge and guidance for life may throw you off course considerably. You might not enjoy your next experience of turning on, or getting high, knowing that a better alternative is possible, one without the tragic consequences to body and mind.

My point is this. Agape love originates *outside* of human experience, so it is not restricted by human limits of perception or understanding. To fully experience it, we must be open to the simple fact that it is given away freely and requires no striving. God gave it in the form of a person, Jesus, who can live within us. As we open ourselves to Him, we must set aside our favorite alternatives and our most limiting, though delicious, sins.

The best news any of us can receive is that agape love affirms man and declares him worthy. You don't need defenses, polish, morality, intelligence, religiousness. You need a person. When you have Him who is love, He may lead you to these virtues. But they are no substitute for Him.

When you choose to see yourself as God sees you, and let these perceptions dominate your mental experience, a sense of worth and adequacy will begin its stalwart growth in your being. Man is affirmed, not denied by love. "God so loved the world . . ." (John 3:16).

Can you consciously make the choice to receive this love and forgiveness, to supplant whatever substitute you have stuck in its place? When you do, you will begin the greatest adventure in life. You will begin to experience unbartered relationships and enjoy the openness that comes when defensiveness ceases.

People who have little need to protect themselves psychologically lead the most enjoyable lives. They are free to experience relationships fully and free to be empathetic to need. They spend little energy maintaining arsenals of automatic responses to perceived threats.

In one office where I worked, a number of secretaries shared a large working space. Since I passed them each morning as I came to work, I would say hello and josh a bit before getting down to business. One morning, though, I made a serious mistake. I gaily greeted each of them as I passed, except for one who was hidden behind the Multilith, cleaning ink off the floor. About thirty minutes later a sobbing lady, with insult stabbing her psyche, came blubbering into my office. "Why didn't you speak to me?" she muttered. "Am I so small in your eyes that you won't even say good morning?"

"Did I miss greeting you, Harriet? What a shame to start a day without savoring your smiling face!" I thought I was being humorous, but the sarcasm missed nobody. "I'm sorry," I continued. "It will never happen again."

As I considered what I knew about Harriet, I realized that she had a reputation for extreme selfishness. She carefully guarded her interests. She was offended when the telephone was placed an inch or two farther away from her than from the secretary who shared it. She took a day of sick leave when the title of her job was mistakenly entered in an official document as "clerk" rather than "secretary."

It is no accident that protective, defensive people are seen as snobbish, or selfish, or both. They become so preoccupied with the need to prevent hurt that they spend all their energies building defense mechanisms and repertoires of retorts to fend off hurt. Selfishness and protectiveness become the same process. Self-centered people see themselves as protective, but others see them as selfish. And the result is a life almost completely shut off from others.

Although she was physically attractive and a capable employee, Harriet had a continuing problem keeping a job. I also learned that a few years previous to my acquaintance with her, she had been divorced by her husband on the grounds of mental cruelty. Then slowly a change began to take place.

A pastor who saw her as a hurting individual, rather than a selfish snob, began to show her a new set of perceptions that she could choose. Day by day she grew in the understanding that much of her armor was needless because she could experience agape love—love that was free and without threat. He directed her to people who had also experienced this love, and from them she learned what this love means in human experience.

Several years later she was able to chuckle about that weepy day when I had failed to say good morning and she hurt so miserably. She proved that when love comes in, defenses drop. Freedom begins, fatigue moves out. A refreshed energy is available that once was dissipated in self-protection, for protection further removes us from people and heightens our need to defend ourselves. Our efforts can become a vicious circle until our energies are sapped and we have to be tucked away for awhile with a nervous breakdown. Harriet had broken the cycle. She had found resources outside herself and in other people. Healing had begun.

If people have not developed the basic types of love, their defenses are often so elaborate and raised so high that it is difficult to communicate agape love to them by either word or deed. Approaches must be carefully made, or they will be scared away from examining agape love. In any new experience their first order of business is self-defense. With some, you feel as though you have to survey carefully their personal Maginot Line of emotional fortifications and find a way to sneak around it just to get acquainted.

Or you may sense that they have their antennae protruding in all directions, fearfully awaiting the slightest static. With emotional amplifiers turned up high, they perceive every garbled message and react with danger signals. They seem to anticipate getting hurt at any moment. It is a horrible way to live, and it is unnecessary.

Once in awhile, however, the frightened mind is willing to take the risk of experiencing agape love. Instead of settling into discouragement, the person dares at last to trust again. Out of desperation, he finds peace. But ideally, I think that a child should be able to grow in such a way that, as a natural step in his developmental sequence, he enters into God's great love for him.

Agape love affirms man. An affirmed person can afford to be less defensive. With defenses down, he reaches out to others, fully sharing life. This is why I feel that any therapeutic experience we can offer people will help open the way for agape. Any reduction of tension we might bring about, any soothing of troubled minds, is a most valuable experience.

Pure love secures the person as you have discovered if you have accepted God's love for you. Because you know that you are of infinite worth and the object of unceasing love, you move with a new sense of confidence and peace. Your most stubborn feelings of inferiority crumble away. Now that your guard is down, it is possible for you to savor a wider range of your inner experiences. Since you are no longer rejecting your feelings and fighting for the control of your emotions, your subconscious mind frees itself. Mental garbage stored for years beneath your level of awareness may come to light.

A handsome young man began asking me about some strange feelings he was having. He was an intelligent, successful, high-school teacher whose interests in mental health had quickened because of students' problems as well as his own reactions.

He described symptoms of shortness of breath and of an accelerated heartbeat when the situation did not require it. They usually occurred while he was sitting quietly at home or in an audience surrounded by many people. The symptoms frightened him at first, but they subsided shortly after they appeared.

I asked him to tell me some things he believed were significant experiences in his life. He told me that his mother had died in childbirth and that he never knew her personally. When he was still very young, his father had married his mother's sister. She was truly mother to him, and he sensed no loss because of the death of his real mother.

His dad, however, proved to be a stern and bitter man. The boy never knew why, but he was raised with the strictest and most unfeeling discipline possible. Any wish he expressed or privilege he requested was denied. It soon became safer not to ask. If anything went wrong at home, he was made to feel at least partly responsible. As a result, fear of reprisal and guilt stalked him at every turn. He learned to feel guilty even in situations where he was completely innocent.

His stepmother seemed to have a good sense of balance, and while not irritating the old curmudgeon, she gave her stepson much of the assurance he needed. The lad's response was to become an exceedingly good boy. With it he bought the mother's kindness and some freedom from his father's unreasonable demands.

Through the help of a minister, the young man early learned to know the love of God. With this resource, he could resist his father's efforts to induce guilt in a good boy simply to control him.

Arriving at maturity with a sense of personal adequacy and a balanced perspective on his. father, his symptoms began to appear. The question that puzzled him was: "Why these troublesome feelings when I'm at the peak of my life and doing better than ever before? Am I becoming sick?"

My suggestion was that he ought to regard his feelings as symptoms of healing, rather than of illness. He was now a mature person, open and honest with people and enjoying it. Probably the subconscious mind was just now getting around to unloading some of its stress. Our minds occasionally seem to employ time delay as a means of protection. They wait until some time when we can handle the matter, to let us know what they are doing. In a few months, the symptoms this man experienced disappeared entirely and have not returned.

I have heard other people tell of similar experiences. One young woman confessed: "When I dared to open myself to real love and the assurance it brings, I perceived more fear than ever before. But I soon discovered it was fear leaving, not entering, so I quit fighting it and gave it a grand send-off!"

We learned to know another old gentleman who had a reputation for eating nails to feed his personality, but who began to let love capture him when nearly eighty years old. The change was so dramatic that most people who heard about it didn't believe it. While speaking to a Sunday School class one day, he publicly confessed: "More things hurt me now than ever before. I have just awakened to what hurt is all about. For this I am eternally grateful."

When we are no longer perpetually on guard, the subconscious mind begins to speak. "Perfect love casts out fear" (1 John 4:18). When we sense that we are growing in love, experiencing certainty of self, and becoming more open to people, we can be reasonably assured that these symptoms are indicative of healing processes. Love is the great healer, the balm that refreshes the troubled soul. Love releases us to an authentic experience of ourselves and of the needs of others.

# 4 *Seeing Oneself as an Adequate Person*

Insights into human personality often come when one least expects them. Such was the case one smoggy, cold morning in Los Angeles when I boarded an airplane to attend a meeting in Chicago. With awarenesses clouded by a half-comatose condition, I was grousing through my breakfast, which for some reason had been served before we took off. Finishing my cereal, I tried to negotiate a particularly slippery orange slice when a jolt of the aircraft startled me. The orange became the property of the ash tray instead of being impaled on my fork. My awarenesses quickened as I wondered what was shaking this behemoth of the airways.

Apparently, other passengers were equally curious. Subliminal calculations began to click in our brains. What kind of force is necessary to jolt a Boeing 707, especially when the weight is applied so near the center of the cabin? Looking up, we saw a one-in-a-million specimen of humanity clogging the doorway.

At a height of about five feet, sixteen inches, she must have been able to crush elephant scales. Further, she loaded her avoirdupois into tiny shoes with pinpoint heels that were popular a few years ago. More subliminal calculations took place. How many pounds per square inch were crunching the frame of our aluminum bird with each step? Probably only a few tons, but now even the airplane was griping, and for good reason. An aeronautical engineer once told me that normally proportioned women in high heels do more damage to airplanes than all the storms over the Rockies. I was sure we would all disappear into the baggage compartment below.

As the stewardess improvised dance steps to manipulate herself down the aisle, we observed more details: a beehive hairdo with a tiny hat on top; a dark green knit suit that bulged unstylishly. Her face told us which was front and which was rear. She looked like something constructed by a wrangling committee with a big budget.

The man seated in front of me turned and muttered, "Get a load of that!"

"No thank you," I replied. "I think she has decided to sit on someone else."

I was no longer sleepy. I began to think in psychological terms—a habit that keeps me from embarrassing myself when human tragedy stimulates laughter. Now sobered, I pondered this woman's personal grief. How many barbs had she experienced? How many hours of unhappiness had she suffered? Then, how did she see herself? or explain her appearance to herself?

Phenomenological psychology tells us that we tend to behave consistently with the way we see ourselves. If you want to predict what a person will do, find out what picture or image he has of himself. If we view ourselves as adequate people, we have an attitude of self-confidence. We feel good about ourselves. On the other hand, people with a sense of inferiority look and behave the part.

If our self-view is terribly uncomfortable, we distort our images of ourselves and act "out of character," as this woman had done. Most distortions are improvements of

44

the true image. We fancy ourselves better than we are. Or we deny that our less acceptable characteristics exist by not reacting honestly to them. After all, it is common knowledge that large, bulky people should not wear knit suits, high heels, or hats atop beehive hairdos. Yet we have seen people whose dress emphasized every fault of figure and feature. Perhaps this woman thought: If I wear a knit suit, people will know that I don't think of myself as fat, so they won't think that way of me either. Therefore it is all right to wear a knit suit, high heels, beehives, or whatever. So she distorted the self-perceived image into acceptability.

Human thinking tends to follow a number of specific rules, which have been detailed by students of cognitive behavior. In their book *Individual Behavior,* Professors Arthur Combs and Donald Snygg discuss the principles of self-perception and their relationship to self-image. Following is a discussion of some of the principles.*

*Man sees himself in essentially positive, self-enhancing ways.* Unless people think well of themselves, they become discouraged. To see oneself as continually failing or as continually unworthy leads to great unhappiness. Morale

*Arthur Combs and Donald Snygg, *Individual Behavior,* rev. ed. (New York: Harper and Row, Inc., 1959), p. 240.

is maintained by positive self-images. The worthwhileness of life depends on good self-perceptions. As a result, we will automatically attempt to maintain a good image even if we must distort reality to do so.

A few years ago, a certain young man became nationally known for his boxing exploits. His picture was prominently displayed in numerous papers and magazines. He had appeared in international amateur events and achieved an outstanding record. Observers predicted great success for him in professional boxing. As predicted, the young man evolved into a first-class professional fighter. Developed carefully by a skillful manager, he won matches repeatedly. In a few short years, he emerged as the world champion of his weight division.

But now, problems began to appear. Because he had lived so long with the self-picture of a champion, he began to dread defeat. He had held his title several years when these fears came to dominate him. He knew age was slowing him somewhat and that he could never fully regain the abilities of more youthful days. Gradually his personality turned inward. He avoided his friends, the press and even most friendly conversational contacts. Hating to face the world, he employed disguise artists so that he could move freely in the streets without being noticed. He had no more worlds to conquer, and the empire he owned was threatened frequently by young aspirants. Finally he became sullen and sour, and his wife divorced him.

After refusing a number of challenges to his title, he realized that he must face the possibility of defeat or be dethroned by default. One day, an improbably young upstart challenged his title. Accepting this challenge seemed to the champion to be an easy way to maintain prestige, so the fight was on. He prepared badly, and the fight showed it. He fought as though he were already defeated. His moves were halting and badly timed. In the second round, a crushing uppercut caught his chin, and he was counted out. The championship was gone, and a shaky self-image was finally completely shattered.

Very likely, the fear of loss defeated him long before his final match. From that time on, he turned in his loneliness and self-disrespect to dissipation and died a pauper. Even the way of death was a confirmation of his self-perception. Seeing himself as worthless, he acted accordingly and hastened his demise.

The boxer's story shows how desperately people struggle to fend off loss of image. The need for the image to be protected constitutes a fundamental mental health problem. Many business and professional organizations no longer fire the tired and spent executive. They appoint him a vice-president on a consulting basis. We say that he is kicked upstairs. This has become the humane way of dealing with loss of ability or prowess. It preserves the man's self-esteem and still allows his useful talents to be applied.

Children, too, know the need for a good self-picture. The child who continually fails in school does not accept his failure with smiles. Instead he becomes a behavior problem. If teachers reinforce poor images, even the smallest children often respond with rebellion. Obstreperous resistance is actually a sign of vigor and insistence on personal worth. It is the emotionally sick kids who smile and retreat when repeatedly dubbed incompetents in school. A crisis arises, however, when a child becomes a threat to an instructor's need for a good self-image as a disciplinarian. School teachers usually win most of these image battles. The child's psyche generally gets axed first!

So we struggle to see ourselves in essentially positive ways. If distortion of self-image is necessary, we resort to it. We prize our self-perceptions and psychological integrity more than our sanity. When the human mind perceives too much threat, it will resort to psychotic symptoms if necessary. Mental illness is best thought of as the most efficient available means of preserving integrity.

But we see the protective processes in milder form, too. We all have ways of distorting ourselves into more comfortable images. The older a man gets, the faster he could run as a boy, or, with each passing year, the farther he used to walk to school, through deeper snow, to be taught by sterner teachers. Likewise, as I advance in years, the more significant I judge my contributions to the world to be. The meaner I become, the more I blame my family for their lack of consideration. We automatically tend toward self-aggrandizement to fulfill our need for an adequate self-concept.

Note that again we are discussing reciprocal relationships or mutual love. We discover that in our contacts with people this great need for esteem is negotiable. We trade opportunities for enhancement of our self-images. We rely on others to help us not hurt us. If you keep your agreement with me, you will enhance me and not hurt me. If I do not keep my agreement with you and hurt you, you will withdraw your favors and compliments from me. I will allow you to maintain a good image of yourself as long as you allow me to feel good about myself. This leads us to the second rule in self-perception.

*The self-image I perceive is a reflected image.* It is constructed from the reflections of myself that I obtain from others. As I behave in the presence of others, they respond to me with pleasantness or discomfort, or some mixture of the two. As I accumulate years of these reactions I form a picture of myself. The responses of others provide clues to what I am. I know whether I am acceptable or not by the composite picture I devise in my mind.

Here is a little experiment for you to try. Shut your eyes tightly and say the name of a well-known friend. What do you see? A clear image or a foggy one? Because our minds instantly recall pictures or images of familiar persons, no doubt the image was clear. We easily identify these people by some of their prominent features. Try it again, naming a popular public personality. What do you see?

I have frequently asked my classes to try this experiment when we discuss self-image and its problems. Class members close their eyes and I say the letters "JFK." Before his assassination students described a young, vibrant politician with a shock of hair flying in the breeze. Then came the tragedy of President Kennedy's death. The experiment was never quite the same after that. Images were more sedate. Mixed emotions accompanied the figure perceived. The somber days of the funeral often come to mind. Our perceptions were significantly modified by that unfortunate death.

Now let's go back so you can try the experiment again. Close your eyes and say your own name slowly to yourself. What do you see? Is the image as clear as the image of your friend or of the well-known public figure? Probably not. Strangely, we see ourselves indirectly through reflected images, but we see others directly. Therefore our self-images are often unclear. Also, if we need protection from the truth about ourselves, the picture will be more out of focus.

We have two great social institutions that give us more reflected images than any other. These are our families and our schools. When a child is accepted and loved at home, the family reflects these feelings on the child. Consequently, the child early sees himself as wanted and valued and likes himself. If the family sees him as ugly or a nuisance, this too will be reflected and he will see himself as unworthy or undesirable. Then he will act out his self-perceptions with rebellion or withdrawal.

When a child enters school, he must deal with an entirely new set of reflections. He is unknown in school and must establish an image of himself in this new situation. At first he automatically expects school to reflect the same picture his family has furnished him. This expectancy sometimes stimulates remarkable revelations.

Billy was the grandson of one of the elementary school principals in a district near our home. Billy was also the apple of his family's eye. He was the only grandson, and due to unfortunate circumstances there would never be another one. Billy first visited school when he was about three. Healthy, handsome, and full of spirit, he was paraded before the faculty. Every evidence of brilliance was especially noted and vignetted for the boy and any observers who could be corralled.

Then came the day when Billy enrolled in grandmother's school. He was placed with a fine teacher, and academic history was supposed to begin. But Billy would have none of it. Reading readiness became an intellectual hurdle the size of quantum physics. Simple arithmetic had to be delayed until Billy's computer developed some more. In his frustration, he took to sliding all over the floor or daydreaming when confined to his desk. How was the teacher to inform dear Grandmother principal? After all, the teacher's image and reputation were at stake, too!

After many uncomfortable discussions about Billy's quality of performance, the principal called in a psychometrist. He would give a test of intellectual competence and settle the matter—that Billy was just as bright as Grandmother believed and not as incompetent as the stubborn first-grade teacher thought him to be! But the test refused to cooperate. It declared Billy to be about as bright as most kids who have little zest for learning—somewhat below average.

When the testing was over and the results made known, the poor examiner had to endure the projected rage of an insulted grandmother and mother, too. The psychometrist had destroyed an image. He had changed the life picture of an innocent little fellow. How could he be so cruel?

As time went by, continual evidence showed Billy to be a simple, slightly dull little boy who would have to survive schooling as most of us do. But the problem was not over. Billy had to get his self-picture straightened out, too. No more reports of academic eminence would be projected for him. Gone were the promises of a free ride through law school financed by Grandmother's estate. No more lavish feedback about being brainy. Billy would have to get his self-picture to match the real-world picture. Though this was bound to produce stress, the sooner it happened the better, which leads us to the third rule about self-perceptions.

*The individual seeks congruence between the way he sees himself and the way the world sees him.* One of the problems of the seriously disturbed personality lies in his inability to see himself accurately. One Sunday afternoon I attended a worship service in a Midwestern mental institution. The patients attended voluntarily, and it appeared that those more religiously inclined dominated the meeting. Midway through the proceedings, a gentleman rose and announced that he was a prophet of God. He boldly proclaimed, "Hear me, or dire consequences will occur if you refuse my message."

His discourse was rambling and nonsensical, but we all pretended to take it in. Obviously our view of this patient differed from his view of himself. If this man were to recover a normal mental experience, his self-image would have to undergo major modifications.

Another example of the congruence problem came to my attention when a very lovely young woman sought my counsel. She was receiving so much attention from attractive men that she was in a state of anxiety about how to respond. That's a problem, I hear you say? Yes, it was, even though lots of girls would love this kind of attention. But as she revealed her history, her anxiety was easily understood.

This woman had been born with an ugly birthmark that covered most of one side of her face. As a growing young-ster, others constantly called attention to this unsightly disfigurement. She was required endlessly to explain her appearance. Gradually her life become dominated by this unfortunate blemish. Self-rejection tempted at every mo-ment. To compensate for intense feelings of inferiority, she used her brain, which proved to be a most efficient lever to balance the pressures on her life. Intelligent and hard working, she achieved honor student status in nearly every school she attended. But the stares and questions never ceased. Eventually her feelings got the best of her. She longed to hide and avoid people. Anything to avoid the painful, never-ending inquiries!

After high school she was employed as a secretary by a large corporation. Hoping to hide herself in work, she again compensated by using her brain. Because she worked diligently, out of sheer habit, she soon became the most successful person in her unit. She was promptly rewarded with a promotion and more responsibility. But now her inferiorities began to smother her again. Her larger number of personal contacts and duties stimulated such great fear that it threatened to drive her out of the office. She felt unable to handle her feelings about her appearance among so many people. Yielding finally to the painful emotions, she quit work and went to college, hoping to hide among the masses of students.

She reasoned that her brain had worked for her before, and that it would probably work for her again. It did. She obtained recognition for most outstanding scholarship. Invited to join honor societies, she was again thrust into the public eye and into many social contacts. The fears rose once more. She quit school and returned to work. You can guess the next sequence of events. Once again hard work and success thrust her into prominence in her business. Once again, success, the social contacts, and the fear they stimulated drove her out of the office and back to school.

Determined not to get caught in her series of compensations again, she decided to become a teacher of little children. Certainly a group of second-graders couldn't threaten anyone! But once more she had to survive academic success. She graduated magna cum laude, but the prospect of hiding in elementary school with safe little tots made the experience bearable.

Being an able student and worker helped her become an able teacher. After two years of outstanding work, she was notified that her classroom would become a demonstration class. She panicked! Hordes of teachers would be coming to observe! Supervisors, principals, consultants, and state officials would descend upon her classroom! She was back in the public eye! The old emotions of threat and fear arose once more. The school year could not end soon enough. Once more she quit!

By this time she had saved enough money to afford the surgery that would allow her to enjoy a normal appearance. At the time of our counseling session, I noticed only the slightest scar on her cheek. She was actually beautiful.

Believing that her changed face would change her self-image, she thrilled at the prospect of a normal life. But a new problem emerged, the problem that prompted her to seek professional counsel. Never before had she been asked for a date. Never had she found it necessary to fend off the advances of solicitous males. What should she do now?

Much of my advice was merely practical advice about how to play the romantic game. Our culture has devised intricate little rules for this phenomenon, all of them unwritten. But the key to the real problem was to recognize that long established self-perceptions require time and opportunity for new experiences to effect change. Congruence between self-image and the outside world's view of us takes time to develop. No instant results could be available here.

*Established self-perceptions are habits of thought.* The lovely young lady had developed the emotional habit of seeing herself as ugly. She had believed something that became untrue. But beliefs don't shake easily. She had thought of herself in unattractive ways for so many years that it was hard to stop. To react to herself as a beautiful person was to feel like a liar. She knew that delight should be the new and proper response to herself, but habit dictated that she respond with self-depreciation. The conflict of competing emotions occasionally made her think that it was easier just to be unattractive. Her mind was so programmed to see herself as unacceptable that every automatic mental response was geared accordingly. But slowly she began to believe the new truth and to enjoy its blessings. Several years later she surprised me at a conference I was addressing. Still single, but very attractive, she now feared people no longer. Her abilities had brought her much success and joy.

In the previous chapter we defined agape love as the unmerited favor of God, given to all men. This love is unceasing, unchanging, unearned. It never stops even though man does not respond in kind. The example of the young woman trying to accept herself with a new and wonderful appearance is like our experience when we confront the work of God for us. In order to accept it and experience agape love, we must shed habits of long standing. The deeply ingrained tendency to see ourselves as acceptable only if we perform well by human standards must alter.

Only if we were reasonably attractive to God would we be accepted, we think, but the truth of the matter is that God loves us and calls us just, righteous, whole people whether or not we have attained that status with our fellow man. The question is: What perceptions shall I allow to

dominate my mental experience? Shall I accept myself as the forgiven object of unmerited love? Or shall I perceive myself in the tired old way, as working constantly to make myself acceptable in some human system of approval?

God's approval is a free gift. Your challenge is to believe it and let it soak in until all vestiges of guilt, inferiority, and unhappiness have disappeared. Adjust to the real truth about yourself, and let human assessments become clearly secondary. You have a personal, vital choice to make in the matter!

# 5 *Validating Oneself as an Adequate Person*

The adult seeks much of his adequacy through occupational achievements. I once knew a chiropractor who was so concerned about his image as an adequate person that he insisted his children address him as "Doctor."

Successful employment brings an adult prestige, status and income. These results entitle him to purchase certain symbols of success: the classic car, the ultra-modern home and the diet guaranteed to produce an acid stomach.

The usual route to these goals is to establish oneself in a line of work and climb step by step to higher levels of attainment. This is expressly true if formal training leading to a professional career is involved. With continued progress, the achiever receives the prized titles, salaries and plush, thick office carpets that label him a superior person.

In my field of college teaching, specific designations mark our progress. If we perform adequately, or at least get old

57

enough, we reap the rewards of more distinguished ranks and titles. Others accord us a little more deference when we are labeled "Professor" rather than "Assistant Professor." Our vanity inflates, and we can safely assume airs of adequacy.

About May of each year, faculty tension mounts as each person awaits word from the president concerning possible advancement. Sometimes tears are shed when the proclamation arrives declaring success or failure to obtain new status. The threat of failure to obtain the higher ranks devastates some who have chosen rank designation as the criterion of adequacy. Bitterness hounds the footsteps of the critically disappointed. But for the more fortunate, the self-perceived image is enhanced, and life looks rosier. Fed enough of these psychological vitamins, we think we are truly Dr. Somebody.

A graduate professor asked a class I attended a provocative question that reveals the significance of achievement as a symbol and measure of adequacy. "If you could interview someone, but could ask only one question and by its answer determine the maximum amount of information about the individual, what would you ask?" We pondered his query for a time, and then because of the nature of the subject under study, we found the obvious reply. It was, "What do you do for a living?"

The response to this question reveals nearly all the important personal characteristics that relate to achievement. It indicates or suggests the amount and kind of education the person has received. In turn, the level of schooling reveals a clue to the individual's general knowledge and intelligence.

Further, we find that people move toward occupations that fit their self-images as closely as possible. Thus by learning what they do for a living, we obtain an insight into how they see themselves. Jobs become personal theaters where we play our roles before the public. If we are dominant and aggressive, we seek jobs in which we can enact these characteristics. If we are retiring or shy, we choose work that shields us from extensive public view. If we are unable to find reasonable harmony between our self-images and our jobs, one or the other will change. Usually it is the job, for a great change in one's perceived self in a short period of time is unlikely. Employment that is not self-assuring and enhancing is soon abandoned.

The job we hold also places us in a certain level of socioeconomic status. We therefore move in a social class that gives us further designation. Roles are implicit in the various classes and levels of social status, and members tend to act accordingly. Thus a man's job tells us something about the typical mode of public behavior of the individual. A doctor cannot conduct himself publicly in the same way as a labor organizer, nor a public official in the same way as a bartender. So, by his employment a person receives the rewards of society, finding both a role and an identification for himself.

The need for achievement is not confined merely to adult experience, but is shared by the very young as well. Even the tiny tot shows evidence of the need to achieve, to master his world. "Look at me, look at me!" shouts the four-year-old as he ties his shoes for the first time. Having mastered a task earlier than most children, he wants to be recognized as an adequate person as a result.

Tiny infants enjoy manipulating some element of their crib-encaged worlds. Research indicates that we have probably underestimated the learning potential that exists in the very young. Professor Jerome Kagan, of Harvard University, has said, "Babies are novelty-digesting machines that devour change." His studies of the intellectual development of the very young indicate a mastery of more advanced and complex information than we had thought possible. Given the opportunity to manipulate objects and

59

toys in a stimulating environment, they pursue mental experience vigorously and seek the satisfaction it brings.

The school pupil finds his adequacy interpreted very directly to him by his achievements. Symbolized by grades from teachers, school records have blessed or plagued millions of people. Those who succeed are honored, see their names published in the paper, and enjoy the plaudits of school officials as well as of the community. In contrast, those who are labeled failures can find academic life a harsh, bitter experience. A significant number of pupils dubbed inadequate fail because of the imposition of impossible standards. Slow and unable to learn quickly, they receive the disapproval of a massive and socially powerful organization. It may be no fault of their own, but the resulting poor self-image can be a handicap for life. Forced to accept failure, they may turn to other means of determining adequacy. Physical prowess, antisocial behavior, or violence may be their method of retaliation. Much deviant behavior derives from a forced reduction in personal adequacy.

The need to achieve adequacy continues into old age. Observe the professor, who at the end of his career, turns to writing a significant text or takes up an entirely new avocation. Recently, at the time of his retirement, a professor of elementary education launched himself into the field of botany. A beginner with a very late start, he published two stimulating books for gardeners who wanted to understand the scientific aspects of their hobby. As a result, he received more acclaim for his botanical gardening than for his success as a university teacher.

Another professor, whose works I have sampled, was reported to have been working on nine texts at the time of his death. The motive to achieve continues with us until we die.

So we are propelled to achieve. But a most important question arises. What is the true measure of adequacy?

Is it really achievement? or learning? or status? Or are these standard contrivances of fumbling humans? Maybe there is something more valid by which we ought to measure man. I marvel that people struggle all their lives to produce some sense of self-worth and never ask whether the standards by which they judge their worth are valid. My thinking was focused sharply on this matter on one particularly poignant occasion.

I had been privileged to join a group of learned men in a research organization that studied the concerns of public education. These men brought to bear the finest critical minds and the most recent research techniques. It did not take long for me to discover that I was least among the members of this astute body. I learned far more than I contributed. Frequently, I doubted the worth of my contributions to sessions where my talents were lost in the plethora of sharpened skills of my colleagues.

As time went by, a pecking order developed in this little society. This was not an unusual happening; it occurs wherever people join together for any productive task. The people of demonstrable aptitude almost always emerge as the leaders. It is natural for society to rank persons in the order of their worth to the group. So it was with us. The usual sociological phenomenon was evident.

The chairman of our group turned out to be a man of outstanding qualities. He was the president of a corporation engaged in psychological research. As a sideline, he operated an unusually successful school for emotionally disturbed children. He had frequently been a leader in national research organizations. I liked him for his ability to get the best from each of us. It gave us a sense of usefulness and renewed our zest for the work. And I needed that! His philosophical approach to our task was refreshing to us as we dealt with tedious technical problems. He continually observed the possible consequences of our work and kept us sensitive to its meaningfulness.

61

One Thursday morning as we waited for the chairman's arrival, I began to analyze why I thought so highly of him. Clearly he exceeded others in talent and capacity. Perhaps this man was a model one might well emulate. Suddenly my thinking was interrupted. The vice-chairman bluntly opened the session. "The chairman will not be present today," he said. "Last night Charlie put a .38 revolver to his head and blew his brains out."

We sat stunned for a long moment, not daring to venture a word for fear all of us would lose our equilibrium.

As nearly as we could ascertain, Charlie made a conscious decision to end his existence without the precipitating causes that sometimes bring men to this terrible act. He had simply decided that the struggle to live, to be adequate, to amount to something was not worth it. But by most human standards, he "had it made."

Stunned as we were, a second shock wave proved to be even more unnerving. All of us suddenly realized that the goals we sought, our reasons for living, were very much the same as his. If Charlie's reasoning was correct, what was to prevent others of us from reaching the same conclusion about life?

Charlie had apparently decided that achievement as a standard for adequacy was an empty promise. He was educated, wealthy, successful, fulfilled, loved—by human terms of measurement, that is. But the results were not good enough! Dissatisfaction and meaninglessness in life still gnawed deeply at his soul. He had asked supreme questions: What is my reason for existence? How shall I truly determine my worth? Is achievement the key to adequacy? But he had found no satisfactory answers.

At the end of my undergraduate studies, a philosophy professor offered our class this parting thought: "Beware of what you want the most; you may get it." He was simply telling us, "By the time you have spent your life pursuing an objective, it may have lost its savor. Your goals may not have been valuable enough for you to invest in them a lifetime of work and hope. The standard that measures your adequacy and your reason for existence may have gone out of style, or crumbled beneath a weight of research, or tumbled before some social movement. Or like Charlie, you may find life empty even when you possess all the symbols of fulfillment. So how will you determine your adequacy? How will you validate your efforts? What criterion will you choose to measure the outcomes of life?"

It is a key thesis of this book that any *human* standard of adequacy is faulty and questionable. It is inevitably subject to human error. It is always limited to the maximum power of human perception. Instead, a definition of adequacy must be found that exceeds these limits; one that avoids the flaws of man's derived values and limited perceptions. The determination of how man attains true adequacy and of what constitutes a valid reason for existence must rest on eternal verities. Man needs a *revelation* of adequacy, for thus far, human history is poor testimony to mankind's ability either to be adequate or to set standards for adequacy. Time is running out.

One reason for doubting purely human standards of adequacy, particularly the criterion of achievement, is that the competition is unfair. Having spent many hours struggling with the problems of handicapped children, I appreciate the reality of this inequality. Is it fair that some people should be tragically handicapped in the struggle to attain fulfillment through achievement? A number of individuals have problems so great that they become a burden rather than a blessing to society. Their deficiencies preclude any recognized opportunity to achieve. The result is discouragement and a sense of uselessness.

Perhaps the problem of mental deficiency is the one that hurts the most. I vividly recall my experience explaining to two status-conscious parents that their newborn baby

63

was hopelessly retarded. Both parents were highly educated. Both were teachers in well-known colleges. The mother had obtained the finest prenatal care. The baby was born in one of the most up-to-date children's hospital in the world—it served as a training school in pediatrics for a large university medical school. What better place to get started in life?

When the baby was born, it was immediately apparent that he suffered from Down's syndrome—mongolism. The etiology is partly known; apparently a genetic malfunction causes the child to inherit an extra chromosome. The pediatrician who made the diagnosis was one of the world's leading researchers in the field of mental retardation. He was also a skilled person in handling the emotions of people, a fact that helped only a little as we explained the facts to the parents of the child.

At first the mother and father acted as if they were completely in control of the experience. The husband calmly made arrangements to have the child placed in an institution. Rejecting our advice, they would not take him home with them. But the cool control slowly turned to deep bitterness and hate. Each day they became more enraged at the hospital, at the doctor, at me, at life, at God! What sense did it make to allow a retarded child to be born to them—intelligent, educated people whose reputations could only suffer by having a stupid kid around?

The parents placed their child in the institution, and for a time it appeared that they had gained some relief. But it was not so. In sixty days, the couple instituted court proceedings to recover custody of the child, now living in a public institution as a ward of the state. The guilt of the mother in rejecting the child precipitated the action. She had rejected her own offspring and could not bear the hurt.

The parents had two serious problems. Seeking adequacy

through status and academic achievement, they felt unable to tolerate the questions that would be raised by the presence of a retarded child. Surely a retarded youngster would cast aspersions on their intellectual superiority! They were painfully torn between the need to maintain status and the need to reduce guilt. But overwhelmed by the guilt of rejecting the child in an institution, they had him returned to their home.

Their mode of child rearing was pitiful. Afraid to show him to the world, they hid him at home during his early years. Few people knew that they had had a retarded child, whom they were now denying any chance for personal or social development. Bitterness and hostility dominated the parents' lives. Repeatedly they asked, "Why is life so unfair to us and to this child?"

It is clear that if adequacy comes chiefly through achievement, then the present standard is unfair. Since so many can't measure up, this criterion becomes an oppressive goad. Whole segments of our society have experienced the injustice of some handicap. Large portions of the elementary school population in most cities are labeled "disadvantaged," or "unfairly handicapped," in their efforts to find adequacy through achievement.

Whatever standard is in vogue seems to dictate who is to be adequate or perhaps elite. A notable shift in the definition of adequacy took hold of our public schools a few years ago. With the great achievement of the Soviet Union in launching the first space satellite, American schools received a bruising from every possible critic. "Our schools are not turning out adequate students!" was the cry. "We must have tougher requirements!"

Prior to this time, in the view of the students, the adequate youngster was not necessarily an academic. Instead, he was a combination of several elements. He was required to be an early maturing male or an average-to-early matur-

ing female. Physical attractiveness was an important factor in acceptance. Brilliance was revered, but studiousness was not. Grades that were too high could make one suspect. The key to acceptance was athletic prowess. Decorated with letters, sweaters, pins and patches, the athlete was king! Students with this combination of characteristics were most often chosen by their peers to positions of leadership. They obtained the most significant status symbols. In short, they received the label "adequate." They suffered less social stress, and generally enjoyed themselves.

But times changed. Public emphasis shifted to rewarding academic ability. The National Defense Act became law. Scholarships grew in number and were awarded most often to students specializing in science and mathematics. Some schools began to award letters and sweaters to students for academic achievement as well as athletic competence. So now who is adequate? Who now has the advantage of achieving easily a self-image of importance? Suddenly, the egghead found himself in public favor and could hardly believe it.

Because of rising standards for academic competence, some schools experienced an increased drop-out rate. Students found it easier to leave than to face higher probabilities of failure. Other schools found the public less willing to finance the usual sports programs together with other activities.

In short, while we are searching for adequacy, the standards may alter. In times of rapid social change, these standards shift much more quickly. The advantages may go to some other class of persons, so why hunt for an elusive criterion? Further, the achievement criterion always dictates inadequacy for some!

High-school and college-age young people go through periods of intense self-assessment. Questions about the validity of human experience rise forcefully in their minds. These young people begin to look at the standards held for validating themselves and ask a lot of troublesome questions. Perhaps the fatiguing nature of introspection turns them from self-assessment to judgments of the standards they are expected to uphold.

The typical youngster is taking a long look at what the world holds as standards of adequacy. He wonders if there is an alternative to the standard of educational or occupational achievement which gives advantages to some and dictates failure to others, especially when a great increase in general technical knowledge is required of everyone. With every new development, the minimum standard rises a little.

The young person views many different adult models of achievement. He sees individuals of the Charlie-type we mentioned earlier—capable, effective, achieving, but feeling worthless enough to end it all. Then he stumbles on a simple, forthright, sensitive human being who has mastered little of the economic world but who retains a glow for life that defies explanation. In college he encounters the studious philosopher who has no better answer to life's problems than some pushy gadget salesman. Supposedly, the scholar of the metaphysical world would come up with better answers than the peddler, but he does not. Sometimes his answers seem worse. I recall, somewhat dimly now, a poll of professors of philosophy. The results indicated that only a small percentage had committed themselves to a particular philosophy of life. That is scarcely a remarkable symptom of certainty, is it?

Those who obtain the common goals of status, wealth, or educational achievement fare no better than the philosophers. They come to the end of their experiences offering no better judgments than anyone else. The dominant remembrances of the successful are as often those of frustration, threat of loss, and fears accumulated from high risks taken, as those of the joys of self-fulfillment. The successful people of our time are not the glowing examples of life lived for its intrinsic value or meaningfulness.

Why can't human beings create a definition of adequacy, and having achieved it, be assured that life will be meaningful and valid? This question especially spoofs the youngster who decides to become a fully educated humanitarian. He often turns from the usual definition of achievement to a stereotyped life of nonachieving humanitarianism. He may choose to live simply, dress shabbily, accumulate little of life's junk, and do his own thing. In time he accomplishes important tasks. He relieves suffering, improves the educational level of the poor, opens men's eyes to the beauties of nature and themselves. He reflects that he has not contributed to war, violence, or hunger. "What nobler goal could I pursue?" he questions in rationalized thought. "Surely becoming a humanitarian develops intrinsic qualities of adequacy within me."

No one seriously doubts the need for humanitarian efforts. We cannot live long without them. But the fact remains that people who choose humanitarian pursuits do not experience a great deal more fulfillment or sense of adequacy than do others. I have observed many colleagues who chose higher education as a profession in some faint hope that the humanitarian aspects of the occupation would make them become adequate people. This did not happen. Perhaps I could make the same judgment about those who enter the clergy.

Both those who choose achievement as a means to adequacy and those who regard traditional achievement as an obstacle to adequacy conclude their experiences with doubts about their own value. Once a physics professor remarked to me, "What good is it? All I can say is that maybe I didn't hurt anyone as much as if I had done something else!"

My personal conclusion is that the nature of the occupation one chooses is a secondary factor, rather than a primary factor, in our perceptions of our adequacy. While I find it necessary to rule out such occupations as working for breweries, gambling syndicates, or pornography publishers, I cannot look to my occupational choice as a primary determinant of adequacy. The fact that most people *do* estimate their adequacy in terms of their occupations and their achievements does not alter this conclusion.

Occupational choice and satisfaction grow out of a sense of adequacy, not the other way around. An adequate person chooses a job or profession that allows him to enact the sense of adequacy and fulfillment that he already has. While his work may reinforce his sense of adequacy, it is not the primary factor in determining it. This is why two people can enter the same occupational field and have entirely different experiences. One enters the job looking for something he does not have. He has fond hopes that he can live in the sparkle of his title and see himself as Mr. Important. The other man starts with an assumption of adequacy and proceeds to live out an adequate self-life in his world of work. Sometimes the work is reinforcing, sometimes he keeps at it in spite of the feedback he gets. But his self-perception is based primarily on factors other than his achievements. His achievements are by-products of a fulfilled life.

Adequacy, therefore, is *cause* rather than *effect*. Adequacy leads to fulfilled humanitarian experience. It stimulates noble achievement. While achievement may in time reinforce one's sense of adequacy, it is not the chief stimulus. Something more than need for mastery or achievement, something other than success, calls us to fulfilled lives.

Surely the time comes when every farmer must lay down his hoe and call it a day. Achievement ends for us all. Most of us see it terminate before life is over. If our sense of adequacy has depended upon achievements, any curtailment of opportunity can be sheer misery. Many retirements have been cut short by the deaths of persons who lost hold of the means to bolster self-perceptions. But if adequacy was the cause rather than the effect of achievement, how different those days are! The loss of achievement may be painful, but adequacy remains.

If adequacy is cause rather than effect, it suggests a hypothesis about motivation. Adequacy is a stronger motivation to achievement than achievement is to adequacy. The analogy of motivation in guilt reduction supports this idea for it may be argued that guilt and a lack of adequacy are almost synonymous. Guilt motivates a man to seek relief long enough to reduce his stress. When he obtains relief, he stops. Adequacy, on the other hand, is an unceasing stimulus to achievement. Motivation continues because there are always endless worlds yet to conquer. When achievement reinforces an already present sense of adequacy, motivation increases, and it is not terminated by temporary guilt reduction. If you want to be an achiever, seek a basis other than achievement for your fulfillment.

With reasoning such as this I often ask students, "Are you an adequate student because you seek to avoid failure, or because you act out of a sense of achievement and fulfillment?" "Are your A's symptoms of your struggle with guilt, or are they the by-product of an adequate self?"

In lectures before numerous groups of people, I have challenged them to investigate the New Testament thoroughly and determine exactly what God thinks of them.

MAN AGAPE LOVE

I ask, "Does He regard you as adequate or not? What is God's view of you?" (See Romans 8:1, 16, 17.)

The writers of the Scriptures are careful to point out that when God looks at you in Jesus Christ, He sees you as a brother to His own Son. Because of the work of Christ, all the ugliness of humanity is set aside. God has absolutely no attitude of condemnation toward man. You are worth all of God's attention. If you were the only person in the whole world, it would be worth God's effort to make Himself known to you and to love you. He gives you freely the status and adequacy of an heir to the universe.

This is agape love, the unmerited, unconditional favor of God for man. We achieve our adequacy through this unceasing love. We do not *become* sufficient, approved, or adequate; rather we are *declared to be* such! When we believe this, we become achievers and humanitarians as an effect, a by-product of our new-found selves.

How can true adequacy be placed on us simply by pronouncement? Most of us find this difficult to accept. Certainly it would not accrue to us through purely human efforts. People might label us with many titles, but that would not in any way guarantee that we have changed. We are not now dealing with man, however; we are dealing with God. All the conditions of relationship are different so that the usual rules for relationship do not apply. This relationship of love continues unceasingly. You can't lose it by goofing things up somewhere.

Most of us have spent our lives dealing in bartered relationships. We have exchanged good behavior for parental love. Or we have repaid hurt with hurt. We have earned the symbols of adequacy from this world through our achievements. All of these relationships have been mutually dependent. They have existed as long as both parties kept their agreements. We have become so accustomed to behaving in these terms that when conditions change, we hardly know how to act. We perpetually seek to pay for gifts thrust on us, or we give an eye for an eye and a tooth for a tooth.

Have you ever tried to give someone something freely, only to find yourself repaid in spite of all your efforts to the contrary? Some folks cannot get out of the rut of bartering every facet of relationship! One day I found myself in this predicament on a golf course. I had played badly through the early part of the match and lost all the balls I brought along. Seeing my plight, my opponent reached into his bag with two massive hands and came out with over a dozen high-quality balls. He dumped them on the ground by my clubs and simply said, "Take these."

"But I can't take all that!" I countered. "That's too much! Those pellets cost money!"

"Aren't you big enough to take something from a friend?" His voice was strident as he spoke. "Better pick them up or somebody else will get them." With mixed feelings of joy over my treasure of golf balls and humiliation because of my initial refusal, I quickly stuck the balls into my golf bag.

What really happened was this: I was attempting to barter a relationship that he intended me to enjoy on a totally free basis. I had resisted his love. But what hurt me most was the fact that this man had sought me out to get help with a definite problem he faced in his life. And he turned out to be the better man! By his gift, I was sure, he was not buying my help; he clearly wanted that free relationship that exists when both parties give themselves in agape love. He also wanted the gift of help from me as a free expression of love.

So frequently we deal with God on the same basis. We insist on bartering when He would give us His gifts freely. He offers us forgiveness, status, adequacy, direction in life. Instead of responding with thanks and love, we insist on earning the gift or trading something for it. We become so religious nobody can stand us. Or we refuse His gift and say that we do not deserve it. Or we become so aseptically moral that no needy human can touch us. We forget so quickly that Jesus was the one who took care of any shortage of payment we owe, or any bartering that had to be done. He gave Himself so that we could freely receive. You can be adequate. You can be guilt-free! Accept His love. Your doubts about the truth of the matter will vanish when you do. He will put His spirit within you, and honest joy will surprise you.

When a person has accepted adequacy as a gift, he immediately perceives a new standard for achievement. No longer does the criterion of human performance apply, but rather the measure of faithfulness judges us. This is the fair standard, the one that stimulates everyone, frustrates no one, and is administered by the providential will of God.

What is required of a man is that he be found faithful, to paraphrase 1 Corinthians 4:2. He should perform to the limits of his ability in the tasks God gives him to do. He should be free from social pressures to conform to the world's standards of achievement—free to do the things he is truly able and motivated to do.

73

Adopting faithfulness as a criterion has a multiple impact on a person's life. If he has had an uphill struggle trying to amount to something, he experiences relief. By now, his tolerance for failure has probably been well tested, and his motivation may have seriously diminished. For him an impossible standard of human performance, which has dictated inadequacy for so many, has lost its punch. The sock of failure is gone. But now, with a new sense of interest and certainty, he can proceed again, knowing that God is his judge, not a human taskmaster. Doing appropriate tasks judged by more reasonable standards, he finds acceptance from the One who really matters.

For awhile, however, he is probably going to struggle with ambivalence—those bothersome, mixed emotions that slowly resolve themselves. Occasionally he may return to human standards that bring again a sense of failure, because everyone insists on their validity. But surely he can, in time, adjust his sights to measure himself by the sure criterion of faithfulness.

The ambivalence comes from the fact that he must reject long accepted values. And rejection isn't automatic or easy. These values hold on when he would be free of them. It's like trying to kick a stubborn habit. Now he reevaluates people who once stimulated his drive to produce beyond his means. As he sees the way in which they have unwittingly victimized him, he experiences occasional hostility toward those he once revered. He may be tempted from time to time to act out his feelings, but hurting his unthinking friends has no value either. Instead, the relaxation that comes from shedding impossible goals will refresh his mind and relieve his anxiety about his work.

To the person graced with many human capacities, the standard of faithfulness is not easy. He must reckon with new realities and face tough demands. Those performances he accomplished with little effort, but which the community rewarded handsomely, lose much of their luster. The ego fattened by continuous, easily obtained rewards gets an unexpected jolt. The false self-image constructed over the years experiences a humbling discovery. The person gains a new perspective. He sees that more is required than ever before.

Ambivalence again becomes a bit of a problem. The temptation to relax and settle for human judgments that inflate the psyche is hard to resist. But there is something so therapeutic about reality that in time the increased requirement of faithfulness for the well endowed is a refreshing, redemptive experience. One becomes a lover of the truth, even the truth about oneself.

Faithfulness taps the limits of us all. Rather than facing the human standard, which is easy for some and difficult for others, we all are measured by the degree to which we use our God-given capacities. Another impact of the faithfulness criterion is that, freed from human standards, we can pursue endeavors that are also free from human systems of value and reward. We can pursue some improbable missions, attempting creative enterprises because failure no longer looms so deadly as before. We are ready to enjoy pursuits that others would undertake with anxiety, fearing failure.

For example, one may find himself able to leave a promising career in the middle of his best years and do something very unlikely but infinitely useful. I know a number of doctors, teachers, architects, agricultural specialists who left the usual human track of progress and gave themselves away in service to God and man. Traveling to some faraway chunk of foreign soil, they found themselves enriched by faithful living. No longer enslaved by their own success, they became free, faithful men.

The greatest human experience occurs when one can assess oneself both as the object of supreme love and as one who has been faithful in expending all his talents in faithful, agape service to God and man.

While doing psychological work in a large high school, I became acquainted with a nineteen-year-old junior—rather ancient for the third year of high school. The problem was that he had failed U.S. History three times, as well as several other subjects, and just couldn't get out of the place. History was always taught by the same teacher, a hard-nosed fellow who believed in being academically tough. Thanks to this generous supplier of F grades, my friend was at an impasse.

The young man suffered from handicaps that reduced his verbal intelligence significantly, though his other abilities seemed intact. His birth had been most difficult, and he had suffered serious brain damage and facial disfigurement. The usual pattern in such cases is for the handicapped person to reject those who administer failure while venting hostility fully. He often develops an angry, brooding tendency that begins to dominate most of his human relationships. Life becomes a series of unfortunate encounters and further failures.

But this boy had a special kind of motivation. Knowing his limits, he maintained his motivation by recognizing that he need not dread failure so long as he performed to the limits of his ability. He judged himself by the standard of faithfulness in using the talents he had, not by the teacher's inclination to impose an impossible standard.

As we talked, he showed an assurance about his self-esteem that was spiritually based. He was convinced that he had been the recipient of God's grace and that all other assessment factors were secondary. Having known this kind of fulfillment, he insisted on finishing high school so that he could be of maximum use to God and man. His diploma would be a means to help him give himself away.

We were able to make appropriate adjustments in the boy's high-school program and finally got him through history with a passable grade. In due time he graduated and has since done construction work for missionaries in another country. If he had judged himself by the usual standards, I have no doubt that the outcome would have been very different.

# 6 The Need for Authentic Living

Eric Berne's book, *Games People Play,** has captured the attention of thousands of people. Presumably it bears this title because it describes how people relate to each other in non-authentic ways. I recommend it because of the many useful insights it brings. Describing many elaborately contrived modes of behavior, it tells how we learn to transact our business with each other while concealing feelings.

In non-authentic living, there is a behavioral recipe to follow in nearly every social situation. If we know the place where we are going to be and the kind of people who will be there, our behavior can be predicted fairly well. We will unconsciously follow the behavioral recipe that fits the situation.

The roles we play may serve useful functions. Our assumption of roles solves certain problems. It gives others a feeling of certainty about us. When we abide by the social rules, we become predictable people. We are less likely to pull any dramatic surprises. As a result others

*Eric Berne. *Games People Play: The Psychology of Human Relationships* (New York: Grove Press, 1964).

are more comfortable in our presence and we feel more secure. Our minds are relatively free to deal with whatever subject or problem comes up. We are not preoccupied with curiosity or uncomfortableness about one another's actions. So we can temper our actions with love. Therefore, complete honesty or authenticity is not always the best course to follow.

For my own fun one day I taught a college class dressed in a bright orange shirt, yellow alpaca sweater, olive green slacks, red socks, and black-and-white golf shoes. I lectured on the theory of correlation statistics to a graduate seminar, but needless to say, nobody heard a word I said or comprehended any theory. Abstract information on a boring subject produced little interest when the person divulging it looked as though he had fallen into a paint mixer. The glaring colors were completely distracting, for they were inconsistent with the role of the typical professor. So everyone was thrown a little off balance.

My purpose for this stunt was twofold; first, I had a college golf match to supervise after class and, then, I just felt like stepping out of role for a brief time. I had been professorial long enough. Professors get a bit stuffy and become so predictable that too much of the time they interest nobody.

I am reminded of a colleague who dressed almost the same way every day for years. He always wore a blue tweed suit with vest and with his watch chain draped across his paunch. And he never knew what time it was. Nobody ever saw him dressed any other way or ever caught him looking at his watch. I suspect that if I stopped at his home and found him mowing the lawn or carrying out the garbage, he would be wearing a blue tweed suit with watch in place, wondering what time it was.

This man had completely absorbed the professorial role. He was a professor everywhere. When he went to buy garden fertilizer, you could be sure he was a professor, not a gardener. His dress, his manner, his attitude always tipped you off to the fact that he could see himself in no other way. He had been trapped inflexibly in a role and image.

Youngsters learn to play roles early. Boys are taught to play the rough role. Strong boys don't cry, only the sissy ones do. Masculine little men achieve their place in the sun by physical superiority over others. It's all part of the game. Then when they become adults they can't understand why their wives cry over so many things. The wife in turn thinks her husband is a cold, hard, unsympathetic stoic who fails to appreciate her problems.

One professor I knew had been a dean in a large college. When a new president was appointed to the school, he promptly demoted my acquaintance. But the role of dean was so ingrained that he couldn't stop deaning! In department meetings he would "take over" as the dominant personality. He expected his ideas to be received uncritically by his peers. Constantly referring to himself as the senior member of the group, he expected to enjoy status and privilege he was no longer entitled to. As a result, he was an obstacle to solving problems in the department. Furthermore, his feelings were always getting hurt, and he couldn't figure out why.

While playing predictable roles gives us certainty about each other, it can stereotype the uniqueness right out of us. Our freedom to act spontaneously and honestly gets lost. Further, we force ourselves into molds that often fit us uncomfortably in an attempt to absolve conflict between the mold and our true selves. More and more of our behavior becomes patterned uncomfortably after some expected role. To reduce conscious stress, we subdue our sensitivities and our true feelings.

If we are insecure ourselves, or those around us are especially timid, we feel a great deal of pressure to play roles. Any variance in the behavior of others creates questions about how we should behave. We in turn become less predictable and therefore more threatening. Violating expected roles can be very upsetting to shaky people, so we apply pressure to keep us safe either from ourselves or from others.

After playing games for long periods of time, we lose our uniqueness, our authenticity. We become insensitive to our own feelings. When others deal with us, they deal with a person playing a role, not the real person. The difference between our role and who we really are can sometimes become so wide that an observer might think we had a split personality.

Several years ago I counseled with a minister who had denied his feelings through role playing. He was a man with a long history of personal problems and had sought the ministerial role to cover his faults and hurts. As long as he could manifest the appearance of sanctimony, he seemed to get by, for it drove his conflicts underground. In time, however, he developed an illicit attachment for a woman in another city. He was shocked by his own feelings and behavior, but could not discontinue the relationship.

The whole sordid mess eventually came into the open and the congregation he served responded valiantly. Instead of pronouncing judgment and acting punitively, they chose a better way. He had expected that they would treat him as an outcast and strip him of his job. Instead, they dealt with him as a man in great need, and gave assurance and support to his wife who had been sent reeling by the experience. For the first time he began dealing with his own life in authentic terms and getting honest help.

The concealing of his true self in acceptable roles ended. The tension broke. Had he been allowed to deal with his hurts in earlier years, he might never have received this crisis, but as a youngster he had been taught to play always the role of a good boy. Just play the role of a model child.

Never admit that anything bothers you and it won't. Put the lid on troubled feelings. Deny any difficult emotional experience. Always protect your image.

After working in other employment for several years while undergoing counseling and therapy, he returned to the ministry, a healed man with many talents to use productively. With a new sense of freedom, he is ministering more capably than ever before.

The pressure to assume roles can sometimes mount past our ability to endure. The pressure comes frequently from the threat of having to pay a high price for breaking out of a confining role.

A young woman I knew belonged to a certain religious sect that was identified by unusual clothes. Appearing old-fashioned, she suffered under the taunts of her classmates in school. Courses in sewing and home economics were nearly unbearable. She could not work on anything her peers regarded as attractive, and she was forbidden by her parents to use the sewing machines provided at school.

Other problems attended her, too. Physically, her mother was marked by scars caused by a serious accident. She rejected her own appearance and reinforced negative attitudes toward physical appearance in her daughter. Unwittingly she instructed her daughter in the roles of self-rejection and self-deprecation.

Searching for a way to change her low self-estimates, she provoked long theological arguments with her parents. These attacks were unconsciously designed to test the most sensitive and protected areas of the parents' life—a common tactic of troubled youngsters.

Mother made it abundantly clear that rejecting her theology was unforgivable. Furthermore, any challenge to the dress codes of her group was theological rejection. If the daughter insisted on stepping out of the religious role and out from under her mother's projected unhappiness, she was rejecting God. The role of conformity was being reinforced by ultimate weapons: God, family and mother's neurosis.

The result was sad. The girl buckled, absorbing intense guilt and dropped out of school. She was labeled unworthy, and her needs were ignored. Her feelings were completely sacrificed at the altar of mother's need for self-protection. Deeply depressed, she never married or assumed any self-support. She remains totally dependent on her parents even now in their old age.

Suppose that the authentic problem had been faced. If the mother had been given support in facing her own problem of appearance, might the daughter's happiness have been salvaged? If the taunts of classmates had been recognized and faced as a threat, would the youngster have been unconsciously prompted to attack the theological premises of the family and church? Would she have used the theological question to screen her real needs? If the girl could have realistically looked at the mother's projected self-deprecation, would she have absorbed so much guilt? Would she then have had to choose the role of dependency for life to resolve her guilt?

Situations like this, that need honest review and authentic self-presentation, come up in every home at some time or other, although often on a smaller scale. Every home impresses on its children some semblance of required role. The external symptoms may not include rigidly defined dress standards, but nevertheless the role characteristics are there. I can see some of this in my own family as well.

My children's parents are educated well beyond the usual limits. Mother and father have five college degrees between them. The four grandparents have seven degrees. What are the chances that my kids can play any role other than that of children of an overeducated family?

Fortunately, they are doing well in school, and this may

relieve the pressure somewhat. The role may in fact become completely normal and comfortable. But if it does not, I hope that we will have insight and grace enough to recognize the fact and deal authentically with it.

Our culture has developed many professionally described roles. Perhaps the best example of this is conveyed by the medical profession. Careful training in what is known as bedside manner and rigid professional ethics establish the norm for a doctor's behavior.

Suppose your doctor dealt with you authentically on all occasions. When you call him at 2 A.M. to tell him your left big toe hurts, how would he respond? Surely it would be unauthentic of you to make such a call at this hour, but let's be hypothetical. Your friendly purveyor of the healing arts, if acting authentically, would probably order you off the phone so he could get some sleep. But he doesn't respond this way. Instead, he is polite so that when a real crisis arises you won't hesitate to call.

The doctor's assumed role protects him in a number of ways. Since he constantly deals with stress and pain, his own tension could mount to unbelievable heights if he were unable to mask his true feelings. His unauthentic manner protects both you and him. Some shielding is necessary.

But the problem arises when we deal with others *all the time* from behind masks. Then people never know how we really feel. Nor can they tell us how they really feel. We mutually prod each other to play a role or to wear a mask, but we never tell it like it is. In time we are dulled into insensitivity and into predetermined, uncomfortable behavior. Our relationships deteriorate, and we fail to reach each other when we need genuine help.

The temptation to be less than authentic exists in the field of professional counseling as well. Like any other professional, we are tempted to mask many feelings because we know our attitudes are not always helpful. One particular morning stimulated me to hide securely behind a professional mask. I had scheduled a series of appointments to discuss problems of mental handicap with several parents of retarded children. Facing the realities of this difficult problem with parents occasionally is hard enough for a counselor, but struggling through six such cases in one morning was a serious tactical error.

The first parent arrived—dirty, unkempt, foulmouthed and ignorant. My best professional efforts to explain the problem produced only more stress. The parent rejected the problem completely and leveled a barrage of blame at the school system. I suppressed the urge to return in kind and waited for the next appointment.

The second mother arrived—dirty, unkempt, foulmouthed, ignorant and bad smelling. I was licked before I started. Retreating behind my wall of professional tactics, I took a very cool approach. I reflected the mother's feelings mechanically without stimulating any emotion in myself. I also held my breath to avoid the aroma drifting across the desk. My questions were suave. My conclusions were guarded with educational tentativeness. My recommendations were garnished with indefinite psychological gobbledygook. But I didn't get upset. Surely I could get along until a more acceptable client arrived for the next interview. Then I could resume being comfortable. But such was not the case.

Mother number three arrived. She was dirty, unkempt, foulmouthed, ignorant, bad smelling and extremely obese. I prayed for an emergency to call me out of the office. Maybe a teacher somewhere could choose this moment to crack up, and I could be called from my office to a distant school to render advice. No luck; no phone calls.

We were a few sentences into our conversation when this mother sensed I needed some help, too. She diverted from the subject and told me how much I had helped the lady who had just left. I was shocked. How could it be? I was sure I had garbled the whole previous interview and betrayed my frustration. But no, I had been lucky! She must have needed my cool approach.

The woman now sitting across the desk from me was perceptive. She sensed that I was masking something, and it was not helping her need, either. She was right, and I confessed my efforts to deny my own emotions. I admitted that I resisted dealing with people I did not like. The remainder of our conference looked past appearances and hindering feelings, and we were able to develop some solid understandings of the problems she faced.

Looking past appearances is the key to authenticity. It is the only way to stay helpfully vulnerable to people. Man looks at appearances, but God looks at the heart. A paraphrase of 1 Samuel 16:7 was turning over in my mind.

As mothers number four, five and six came through my office that morning, all mathematical probabilities failed. The parents were all the kind of people I was least prepared to deal with that day. But a simple statement by one of them had exposed my reluctant attitudes for what they were. As a result, I was prompted to return to more basic honesty. It was one of the toughest mornings I have ever had. It would have been easier for me to have kept on the mask and played the role of cool professional. But I had been stripped of my facade and I became a little more useful and a lot more tired as a result.

Love and authenticity are inseparable partners in our emotional lives. The security engendered by love allows us to take off our masks and lower the defenses that shut us off from the needs of others and from sensitivity to ourselves. Love allows us to look past the appearances that once protected us because they acted as barriers to reaching others. So love abolishes the mask that distorts perceptions.

The need for authentic living is a challenge to receive agape love and to become honest, sensitive people. And the result is a life rich in experience and full of meaning.

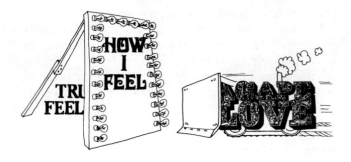

Living past appearances, under the dominating influence of God's love, allows us to enjoy our successes as well. No need to hide them as do some people who are more embarrassed by their achievements than their failures. To admit that one is successful is to risk denying experience again. It has become so popular to be self-effacing and falsely humble that some people can hardly perceive success. But if one has truly achieved, it is just as deceptive to deny success as it is to deny unacceptable feelings or actions.

I recall from my high school days a lad who had artistic ability in sculpting. His works were unusual and creative. But he was different. He matured late and suffered from a lack of physical abilities. Berated by his peers, he settled into social silence. He protected himself by playing the role of a nobody.

But the trouble was that he hid his genuine talents. In a fit of anger over the treatment by his peers, he smashed every object he had made. He rejected even the minimum symptoms of success.

In his senior year, a sensitive teacher encouraged him to return to his hobby. She guarded his feelings carefully, not letting anyone know he was back at work again. With her encouragement he produced a small statue that was displayed at the state fair. It won him immediate acclaim. His name was in the paper, and photos of his work were displayed. But it was more than he or his classmates could bear, for it shattered his facade of being a nobody.

When the news broke, several bullies hoisted him to their shoulders and paraded him around the campus. Shouting derogatory names and taunting him, they finished by dropping him in the fishpond in front of the main building. So great was the pressure to deny legitimate successful experience, that the boy refused to be successful any more. It was safer being nothing than being an achiever.

But love produces certainty of self, because we are the objects of the greatest of all love. With certainty, we sense less need to deny our experiences. This is true whether the experience is success or failure. When the need to deny our identity is reduced, we are free to launch out upon the joys and difficulties of authentic living, the kind of living that puts us in touch with people in redemptive, wholesome ways.

Authenticity, or honesty in living, has certain characteristics that are sometimes helpful to know. Knowing them can stimulate us to growth. Here are the signs of the authentic personality.

1. Adequacy and identity result from his relationships with man and God. The agape love experience is the mode

of his personal conduct. Agape love has affirmed the person, and he has responded in belief and in emotion to this love. He has absorbed this love so that he is now secure, appearing emotionally self-supporting and autonomous.

2. He finds his own personal experience increasingly satisfying and trustworthy. He revels in the joy of his own mental awarenesses. He can trust his feelings and has an accurate sense of judgment concerning the meaning of his experiences.

3. He has a nondefensive attitude toward people. He spends little effort protecting his image, reputation and feelings. He is free of anxiety in dealing with others.

4. He consciously avoids the use of defense mechanisms in painful situations because defensiveness tends to bring distortion of self and others.

5. His security and identity, resulting from agape love, make him open toward people. He sees people as like himself, seeking to make the most sense and meaning of life. As such he shares a common humanity with them.

6. He willingly shares his feelings and attitudes with others. He is not threatened by any subject of discussion. He is not surprised by unusual personal experiences.

7. His understanding of people goes beyond appearances, symbols, images and stereotypes. He regards all behavior as problem solving. He seeks to understand the unique perceptions and dynamics of each person.

8. He avoids categorical judgments of people. Instead, he is mindful of the uniqueness of each person. He regards all people as candidates for genuine growth and the opportunity to receive supreme love.

9. He regards differences of opinion among people as the result of their different backgrounds, experiences and perceptions. Only exceptionally are differences the result of deliberate dishonesty.

10. He crosses the lines of group identity readily: he

is a truly cross-cultural person. Since he understands and appreciates uniqueness, his relationships transcend group stereotypes and definitions.

11. He refrains from imposing his own categories, doctrinal designations, stereotypes, or judgments upon others. Instead he seeks to apply agape love to the unique problems of each person.

12. He tries to remain vulnerable to the widest range of human problems. He sees the need to be open and tentative in his estimation of unusual problems and the people who bear them.

In contrast, let us make a list of the behavioral symptoms of the nonauthentic person.

1. He gains his identity from the image he can construct with his personal occupational achievements.

2. He has a restricted range of contacts with people. He relates most easily to those of similar class designation, stereotype, or group status.

3. Observing rather strict loyalties to his own group, he has a fairly high rejection rate of other people. He deals with those who bear different names, classes, or designations only on remote terms. He sees them as needing to change in order to be included in his fellowship.

4. His conversations deal only with "safe" subjects. He is conscious of the need to make a number of behaviors and topics taboo. He believes that the answers to most human problems are known and, therefore, that further debate is unnecessary.

5. He does not permit himself to experience a wide range of emotions. He regards vulnerability to feeling as a sign of weakness.

6. Since he has predetermined answers to all problems—answers that conform to the mores and taboos of his own group, his emotional growth is steadily toward becoming an authoritarian personality.

7. He perceives those who disagree with him as either

dishonest or unenlightened. They are not to be trusted fully until they deal within the categories he prescribes and come to the predetermined conclusions he dictates.

8. He utilizes defense mechanisms frequently. Defense is the first priority in time of difficulty, for it precludes examination of his attitudes and feelings.

9. He compensates for his imperviousness to people by identifying with a "star" who epitomizes his favorite stereotype. Instead of thinking through a problem, he follows his leader and adopts his approaches and solutions.

10. He lives "in front of himself." One must deal with his image or self-presentation, not the real man. He relates to another person only if his protection is guaranteed.

# 1 The Need to Be Expended

Dr. Paul Carlson, the martyred medical servant of the people of Congo, was a college classmate and friend of mine. We had studied together, traveled together and in general kept in contact with each other for some time before he went to Africa.

Answering the call of the United Nations to furnish desperately needed medical help at the time of Congo's independence and revolution, Paul dedicated himself to do the obviously loving thing. He went to Africa because he was prepared to alleviate the existing need. A godly compulsion to give all of himself characterized his life.

After a couple of years, Paul's work, and that of a medical student assistant, caught the attention of a leading magazine, and a major news feature and picture story was prepared for publication. But as he was assisting the suffering, the great uprising occurred. He was captured by Congolese rebels, the Simbas, who claimed he was a foreign agent. While he was held prisoner in Stanleyville, thousands of us prayed impatiently for his release. After all, the rebels were not known for humanitarian behavior. When he and other prisoners were not released, rescue operations began. Planes were sent in an attempt to return as many captives as possible to safety. When the planes landed, the prisoners broke for freedom. But Paul's life ended in a hail of machine-gun bullets.

Immediately the story and pictures of his work, and the message of the supreme love of God for man that motivated him, was flashed throughout the world. Of his life one television commentator said, "Paul asked only for the opportunity to give, and it cost him his life."

The motivation and inspiration of his work were not lost, however. Today a medical foundation in the Congo continues Paul's selfless giving. His brother assumed his place as a medical servant to needy people. A beautiful science and learning center was built on the campus of our alma mater in his memory. The story of his life, by his widow, has had wide circulation. Paul became an example to the world of fulfillment through loving expendability.

When a person has been assured of his adequacy and worthiness by the loving acts of God, as Paul Carlson was, this assurance begins to permeate his most basic emotional responses. Almost automatically, a desire to expend himself rises sharply and becomes a dominant theme in his life. He yearns to plunge into something totally consuming. He seeks a hill big enough to die on. His life goes on the block: he lets God direct and use it in the most strategic way possible. No longer preoccupied with himself, he is free to surrender himself for others. The need to give himself in agape love moves him as thirst moves a man toward water.

No man who values his ultimate worth and welcomes a release from common anxieties is content with selfish accomplishments. Achievement, as commonly defined, is not engrossing enough. To be known as the richest man in the cemetery would be an unacceptable and repugnant fate. He recognizes as worthless activity the acquisition of life's trinkets or the mere accumulation of academic degrees or other symbols of status.

We need only turn to Solomon to prove his thesis. Flushed with wisdom and laden with gold, he "had it made," yet he was sufficiently discouraged to lament, "Vanity, vanity, all is vanity." Because his motives were selfish, he had spent his life without fulfillment. Until he was restored in relationship to God, misery dogged his life. But even then, his life had been mostly wasted. For he discovered, much too late, that achievement without valid purpose is little more than trash. He ended his life unfulfilled.

Truly unhappy is the person who comes to the end of life with resources unspent. He has missed the opportunity to develop the capacities that were given to him.

Unlike Solomon, the adequate man knows that he must give himself unreservedly to people in agape love. He must achieve that love which is eternally valuable to others and which requires the expenditure of himself. For giving is learned by giving. And usefulness is established by being used. Strong skills and learning factors are involved in selfless giving. Considerable practice is needed to make this mode of life automatic and spontaneous, but with practice the habit of selflessness grows, negating all temptation to return to self-gratification.

Such achievement is spurred by a supreme love of God. It requires the full mobilization of human capacity and creativity, with no resources reserved. This involves loving service, with no thought of reward or reciprocation dominating one's mind. In fact, rewards have a way of detracting from the fulfillment of self-expenditure. Selfless giving can be nullified because others may think that the service was given for reward and not freely.

Instead of visualizing himself as a perpetual giver, the unhappy man perceives himself as a receiver of the symbols of achievement. By constructing a labyrinth of reciprocal agreements, he becomes repository for the Brownie buttons of social recognition: money, status, prestige, achievement. He barters every relationship to produce ego support. In every personal exchange he attempts to secure personal emotional profit. Life is lived as though success consists of a large, identifiable list of credits and assets that the public eye can easily perceive. As a result he has missed the fulfilling joy of total service. Unlike Paul Carlson, his life and his ego are nuclear, not orbital.

What a startlingly different picture we have of Christ. He *emptied* Himself. He allowed Himself to be totally expended in our behalf. It cost Him His life so that we could be the recipients of His supreme love.

In contrast, we spend most of our time trying to *fill* ourselves. Our insatiable appetites seem irreducible. Our consumption of material and psychological goodies appears limitless. We want every emotional kick intensified, and demand endless novelty to keep us satisfied. Soon the supply of life's ticklers is gone, and then we are left with empty cynicism. But what if this insatiable consuming were converted to altruistic, agape-style giving? What would happen?

Obviously our thinking would have to change since the idea of giving ourselves away or of fully expending ourselves is foreign to us. But there is little social pressure on us to be selfless. No current theory of personality or mental health fully accounts for the principle of orbital rather than nuclear personality organization. No body of psychological research has been generated to enlighten us in this area. Hints appear from time to time in humanistic psychology and philosophy, but nowhere is the idea fully developed. Even our humanitarianism, which has obvious appeal because of the great necessity for it, does not satisfy the soul when it is motivated by selfish interests and purely human values. We learn selflessness only through revelation, and it is best explained by the life of Jesus. In selfless giving, He has no peer.

Most textbooks on mental hygiene or human need regard achievement and mastery as ends in themselves. Through achievement man is enhanced and thus satisfied, they conclude. They point to man's continued efforts to produce something or to improve himself as evidence of the need and its validity. But they make no distinction between achievement that is selfish and that which is selfless, a symptom of the life expended in love.

Our thinking, however, must take a different turn. Achievement of ultimate worth is loving self-expenditure, not selfish accumulation. The former is healthy, the latter neurotic. Achievement of living self-expenditure is integrating, wholesome, and redemptive. Achievement for its own sake is selfish, unsatisfying, and ego-inflating. Therefore, two men engaged in exactly the same enterprise, producing the same products or results, can emerge as entirely different psychological and spiritual beings. It all depends on how each man meets his need to be expended.

It is my belief that much of the physical and emotional dissipation we witness derives from a poor and desperate attempt at self-expenditure. It is a neurotic effort, to be sure, but driving needs must be satisfied. We will all be spent, one way or another. Most of us know the problems of someone who has gone down for the final count through alcoholism, mental illness, or even something as socially acceptable as overeating. Failing to expend himself usefully, the person has chosen to dissipate personal resources. The choice is bad, of course, but he had found no other way to be expended.

Some people are so inextricably bound up in themselves that they are unable to consume themselves *except* in dissipation. They have discovered no cause to espouse, no good reason for living. No humanitarian philosophy has satisfied their soul. Hope of fulfillment through agape love and resultant self-expenditure is hidden by ignorance. Nevertheless, their drive to be expended goes unabated. Desperately desiring to be consumed, they make choices that lead to a final resolution.

I believe that this key factor is often overlooked in understanding and treating the alcoholic or addict. While it is well known that the victim may have serious emotional and physiological problems, current theory about healing has not explored the need to be expended. Too many people without serious handicaps, emotional or physical, fall into dissipation. Emotional and physical stress theory is not sufficiently encompassing to explain many of these cases.

In fact, solving some of his emotional problems and achieving physiological stability may deprive such a person of his dissipate methods of expending himself. And this loss hurts terribly. If he has learned to depend on dissipation, he is uncomfortable without it. He is like the neurotic deprived of his irrational behavior. And like the neurotic, he must do *something* to fend off stress. His emotional and physical healing may only sharpen his awareness that life is empty. He is left to face the fact that he knows no reason for his existence. So he returns to dissipation with new vigor, reinforced by a neurotic drive.

In contrast, the New Testament presents a man, the apostle Paul, who is a striking example of one who lived in agape love and productive self-expenditure. He didn't start out that way, however; he changed in adulthood. And this is a most significant psychological fact, for few people reverse the influence of their early lives. Paul's early history must not have been exactly conducive to healthy emotional living. People who turn out as he did have usually been raised by punitive, emotionally cold parents, who also provide a belief system to rationalize their poor child-rearing behavior.

Educated more than most men, Paul was the most feared zealot of his faith. His testimony tells us that he excelled all others in achievement status, religiousness, learning, and pure hostility. The early Christians shuddered at the mention of his name, for he made it his business to jail anyone who opposed him. He consented to the persecution and death of his enemies.

But one day the love of God penetrated his self-righteousness and religious acceptability and turned him around completely. His hostility melted in a new motivation for service. He was so totally permeated with the love of God that he lost no opportunity for self-expenditure. The structure and content of his personality was thoroughly rebuilt. Instead of permitting his life to revolve about his selfish needs and interests, he put his life into orbit around God and loving Him and man.

The degree to which he had been changed is reflected in 2 Corinthians, the fifth chapter. First, Paul carefully explains that who he is and what he is is determined by the love of God and not by human achievements. Then he goes on to tell us what makes him tick. In the thirteenth verse he says, "For if we are beside ourselves (mad as some say), it is for God and concerns Him; if we are in our right mind, it is for your benefit."

Here the apostle Paul implies that he would not struggle or be concerned even to preserve his sanity. His mental equilibrium was God's business, and he was not about to worry himself with the matter. If he was granted the privilege of remaining sound of mind, then it would be totally for the benefit of others. So whether ill or sane, he would give himself away so completely that he would

99

own himself no longer. He reacted as though he had been removed from ownership of self; therefore, he was unconcerned about his personal welfare. He was so completely conscious of his being the object of supreme love, and so totally expended, that he had been released from even the most basic mental concern, the preservation of his mind's equilibrium. His personality had become fully orbital rather than fully nuclear.

Now let's look at another area of expendability.

It is a fact that we become emotionally involved in the things that we own. We attach our feelings of well-being to our possessions. Last winter a mountain cabin we own was threatened by heavy winter snow and rain. We worried about it, wondering if we would lose our investment. Fortunately, no damage was done, and we felt relieved. We had attached feeling to our possession and felt secure when we knew it was safe. But if it hadn't been ours, we wouldn't have worried, for we worry about what we own.

A solution to the worry problem, therefore, is to not be an owner. It is easier not to worry about things we don't own. We can also expend them with much less concern. The same principle applies to our lives. When we are not our own, we need not get excited about our own protection; we can dismiss self-defense. So it was with the apostle Paul. Because he belonged to Christ, he found safety in Him. He also found freedom from self-concern. It became natural for him to give himself away in total expenditure.

If we interpret Paul correctly, we can state a very bold hypothesis. Emotional equilibrium, or peace of mind, or mental health is not an end in itself. Instead it is a by-product of being owned by God and of the loving self-expenditure that so naturally follows. We become so completely free that our very sanity is of little concern. And you won't find a statement like that in any text on personal adjustment!

As a result of our relationship with God, we see our personal stability as a resource to be used in totally consuming altruism. We are blessed with greatly increased ability to give and receive on the basis of agape love. We can take our attention off ourselves and see more of others. Instead of acquiring a tunnel vision, focused constantly on our inner mental gymnastics, we enlarge our horizons to recognize the needs of the world. We see others in need of the same love and freedom from self that we have found. We move toward them, sharing our fulfillment with them, rather than trying to control and rule them and improve their behavior.

You may ask, "What about the person who is on the verge of losing his sanity? Will he not lose it if he surrenders ownership? If he ceases to be concerned for his own stability, will he not slip into psychosis?"

Those of us who have worked with the disturbed and the mentally ill have witnessed their tremendous struggle to keep equilibrium. The sleepless nights, the days filled with tension and fear dominate the mental processes. Raging anger projected on family and friends has strained every relationship. This causes loss of love for the one who needs it most. Few of us are able to supply emotional support for one who is attacking or withdrawing in total fear. Frequently, guilt in the ill person is so great that he indulges in bizarre behavior to alleviate his troubled feelings. How can such a one surrender ownership of self and try to be expendable?

True, there is little available evidence of the therapeutic effects of surrender and expendability in the face of oncoming serious illness. Challenging one to give up sovereignty of self in the face of emotional crisis is not an established therapeutic technique. To make such a challenge requires implicit trust in the direct ability of God to work in a person's life. Further, the method has no evidence in the clinical literature to support it. Instead, the usual approach is to give all possible support to the person in his present understanding. Get him past the crisis and hope that insight can be developed when the situation has calmed.

But I want to share one case with you that suggests the unusual possibilities of expendability as therapy. I was called late one night by a successful executive who wanted help immediately. His wife had been depressed for several weeks and now was in her third day of continuous weeping. Because she hadn't slept nights, every minor incident upset her completely. She couldn't dress the children for school or make out a grocery list. She panicked at the thought of any public appearance, which included stepping outside the house for a minute or two.

This couple experienced added stress because of inability to maintain public appearances. They had stayed away from church for weeks. The husband feared that he might lose his job if the people at work discovered he had an insane wife. And complicating the problem was a compulsion to keep up a good Christian image. After all, when you are a Christian, things like this just don't happen. Isn't it a mockery of your belief and trust? God's strength is supposed to spare or to get one past such troubles.

The husband decided to call me when his wife suggested that either suicide or self-committal to the state hospital was the only answer. Besides, she told him, she was not an adequate wife, and he should have someone as a mate who would be more fulfilling.

When I met with them, we spent several sessions reviewing the personal histories of both the husband and wife, as well as their life as they lived it now. The woman grew up in a large family with a domineering, but withdrawing father. The youngest of eight children, she was lost in the shuffle and suffered a distinct lack of emotional attention. Her mother was the quiet type, always placating the father and keeping the lid on emotional stress in the family.

During college days, the wife had to leave school twice for reasons of fatigue. After a semester of work in business during each period of withdrawal from school, she was able to return and eventually graduated from junior college. In short, her history was indicative of long stress gathered over the years, coupled with low physical stamina. Her tolerance for the current problem was considerably reduced by the same lack of physical stamina.

The difficult birth of their third child precipitated the unceasing tears and sleeplessness. Born prematurely, the child showed no reflex activity that characterizes normal brain function. For three days after the birth she was not shown her baby, nor did she have any word from her doctor. Then suddenly, in a state of high anxiety, he appeared and announced that the child was cerebral palsied. At this point, she nearly lost all self-control.

I spent several interviews with this couple just letting them unburden their accumulated hostility and anxiety. I learned that these people had a genuine knowledge of God and a desire to live for Him. The question became one of how to apply the conceptual knowledge so that it might become a health-giving experience. If this knowledge had not been present, I doubt that we could have taken the adventure that followed.

After some ten hours together, we faced the question of ownership. To whom do we belong? If we are owned by God, then does He not also own our depressed state of mind? Is this not His responsibility? And if He owns us, should we not be willing to accept whatever outcome He has in mind? After considering these questions for some time, I framed the crucial question directly: "Would you be willing to stay in this condition if God, in His sovereignty, so intends? Can ownership of self be so complete that, like the apostle Paul, you will let Him keep you in your right mind if He desires, and if not, let it be His business?"

The crucial question is consistent with the hypothesis we stated earlier: that mental health or peace of mind is a by-product of being owned and expended in agape love. For these folks, this hypothesis had to be acknowledged as critically true or false. If true, they would cease to struggle and take whatever came their way. If false, they would frantically do everything to keep their perceptions intact, making all of life revolve around their critical needs.

Our interviews ceased for about three weeks following the presentation of this important question. Then a call came. "We have decided to try living as Paul suggests," the husband told me. "We believe that God has a direct and personal interest in our welfare."

When this decision was made to put ego into orbit around the will of God, rather than let it occupy a nuclear position, a great sense of peace came. The tears continued to flow for some time, but the fight to resist them was over. The family returned to church even though they could not sit through a service. When they were asked why they always got up and left before any meeting was over, they explained their situation and subsequent decision. Instead of hiding behind masks of tranquility, they began to reveal their true, but difficult lives to friends. The result was an open sharing of problems that brought people together as never before. The fellowship they engendered helped others, who had just as serious problems but who had never had the courage to reveal them.

During the ensuing days, a complete physical checkup was obtained. The family's schedule was modified so that living could be as comfortable as possible. A sister came to live with them and she eased the wife's load considerably. In about three months, recovery was nearly complete.

The decision to expend themselves, both in respect to ownership of self and to service to others, did not magically brush away all the difficulties. Instead it opened a way for healing to occur. It allowed them to reveal themselves and to share both their illness and healing with others. In the years that have followed, this couple has been uniquely equipped to give aid to a number of people who have nearly given up in despair. They now regard those dark days as the greatest blessing God has given to them.

# 8 *Mechanisms and Methods of Adjustment*

The human system of obtaining approval involves our use of a number of mental mechanisms. These are spontaneous, often unconscious habits of thought. We are indebted to the discipline of analytic psychology for our understanding of these mechanisms. Knowing that we normally think in ways that incorporate these habits of thought will help us evaluate our own thinking more clearly. Let us list some of them and discuss them one by one.

1. Rationalization: This is the way we make acceptable some deed or event for which we feel guilty or inadequate. I recall vividly the explanations of graduate students who failed to qualify for admission to doctoral studies in the university I attended. We each had to pass a comprehensive examination in the chief areas of our field. It lasted about sixteen hours over a two-day period, and drained our brains of all we knew. It was frightening just to look at the examination room full of people. Every known student with a master's degree and an A-average was there. When the ordeal was over, half of us would be invited to continue. The rest of us would have to rationalize.

107

"I was just trying out the exams to see how they would go!" offered one unsuccessful venturer. "I plan to give them the full treatment next time they are offered. Now I know what they want from you."

"The University of Colorado seems to have a more realistic approach to these things," suggests another. "I'm already as good as accepted in their program, so this exam doesn't really matter."

"I'm just interested in obtaining the experience," offers another. This last one must have been a masochist. Nobody would endure such agony just for fun.

Rationalization is supplying a seemingly plausible reason for unacceptable behavior. In the face of repeated disappointments, it can become an ingrained process of thought. The habit develops until the person loses his ability to know when he is rationalizing. I have known a few people who rationalize so frequently that their entire mental processes have become distorted. They can seldom think through a problem clearly. Inevitably they choose solutions that seem plausible but that have only a slight chance of being satisfactory. Continually blundering through life, they never understand the reason for their misfortunes.

I once counseled with a police officer who was constantly at odds with his wife. Unable to effect changes in her thinking or behavior, he began to use physical punishment to correct her. He rationalized that her actions were immature. After all, they did not correspond to his authoritative perceptions of the way she should act. Since she was immature, he thought, she should be treated as a child. Therefore, he applied spanking or other punitive measures with increased frequency. Occasionally, she would appear publicly with bruises from her beatings. Needless to say, this marriage ended in a divorce court. Yet the husband could not see any fault of his own. He was merely a concerned mate doing what was obviously best for his wife!

It is obvious to us that serious errors existed in the man's thinking. But he himself didn't see them. His thought system was intact. He had protected his own image as a concerned, caring, thoughtful husband. His rationalization had worked for him. Now he could say that his wife was truly immature and unstable because she was divorcing him. Surely her divorce was a symptom of immaturity!

2. Projection. Blaming others is a simple form of self-defense with which we are all familiar. One summer I coached a Little League baseball team, a venture every father ought to undertake once in his life to learn the full meaning of psychological manipulations of both adults and children. For when we play, we reveal ourselves as we seldom do otherwise.

Our team was blessed with a talented little fellow who in turn was blessed with an overly ambitious mother. She attended every practice, every game, every League meeting, *and* every argument at home plate. In our first critical encounter with cross-town opponents, our budding major leaguer speared a line drive to third base and made an easy double play. All was joy in Mudville for a half-inning! When our turn to bat came, Mr. Athlete, Jr. struck out miserably. He swung at everything including a pitch that landed in the announcer's booth high atop the bleachers. We lost this titanic clash, and mother was livid with rage! Why hadn't proper equipment been provided? Where were the umpires trained? Why were ineligible pitchers allowed to throw to her son? That's right. She was projecting— blaming everyone and everything except the responsible party.

Like rationalization, projecting can become so much a part of thought processes that it is not recognized as such. But a serious secondary aspect of this process should be pointed out. When you project, someone else gets the guff. Someone else's need for protection is needlessly stimulated. No one wants to be crowded into a position of self-defense. Whoever feels the unwarranted blame will return the projections in kind. Have you ever seen much understanding develop in a situation like this? Most fights begin when two people both see themselves as acting in self-defense.

Projection has the distinct disadvantage of creating social stresses needlessly. One may rationalize a good deal as long as no other specific individual is involved. But when we project, others see us as hostile and withdraw from us or retaliate. Our method of protection only complicates the situation. We may save our self-image for the moment, but make enemies doing it.

3. Compensation. The art of building upon our strengths to avoid attention to our weaknesses is called compensation. This can be a useful and helpful way of preserving self-esteem. It can be healthy because growth is frequently involved, and produces legitimate changes in the self-image. We are often better people when we compensate for some flaw. The pages of history frequently describe a great person whose achievements originally began purely as compensation for weakness.

A gentleman I once met was known for his astuteness as a golf coach. His keen eye could detect the subtlest flaw in the swing of one of his students. Professional golfers frequently sought his advice when their games went sour. One day a reporter asked the coach how he had developed such keen abilities. In his reply he related a history of frustration trying to learn the game himself. He simply did not have the physical abilities to execute the complex moves required of a truly great golfer. Instead he compensated. He studied the moves and techniques of all the stars. He trained his eye and his camera to observe the most insignificant detail. The result? Though his own golf game remained good but never excellent, he became a superb teacher.

Compensations, while often useful, can get us into trouble, however. If they contribute to our inability to recognize and correct our weaknesses, we may be better off not compensating. As long as we are reasonably aware of what we cannot do, our compensations will be potentially useful. But when our self-view is badly distorted as the result of compensation, we may have built a trap for ourselves. Our thinking will become habitually unclear, and we may fall victim to the weakness we are trying to overcome.

4. Identification. Recently I read a psychological study about the difference between truly great business executives and those who are mediocre performers or underlings. The study showed that the subordinates and average-quality executives frequently sought satisfaction by identification with more capable men. Rather than achieving purely on their own, they were content to bask in the reflected glory of their superiors and associates. Contrariwise, the outstanding business leaders chose to make their own mark of achievement. While maintaining good relationships with most people, they declined to achieve fame by association.

For example, they avoided certain types of positions. The title "Assistant to the President" carries connotations of reflected glory while the title "Executive Vice-President" carries its own prestige. So the leaders avoided positions with indistinct character and sought out jobs that involved the possibility of unique contribution. Of course, their risk of failure is higher, but their success is not the reflected success of someone else. Success is clearly identified with the person carrying the responsibilities.

As our illustrations indicate, identification is a process of achieving satisfaction through close association with a successful person or organization. While the enjoyment of fulfillment through projection is less than in one's own achievement, the risk of failure is also considerably less. Thus identification meets the needs for protection of the self-image.

When we are identified with a prestigious organization or some famous person, our image improves in our eyes and in the eyes of those who see us. Examples of such identification are everywhere. Students seek an education at Harvard rather than East Overshoe State Technical Institute. Engineers would much rather work for the National Aeronautics and Space Administration than for Ace Doorbell Company. John Q. Adams, IV, will probably attract a different set of girl friends than Joe Schlobowitz. Even the sound of a name attracts or repels people. Most people would rather work for the Peerless Sanitation Engineers than for Bill's Garbage Haulers.

So, our identifications can help us, if they do not block our vision of either our strengths or weaknesses. The reflected glory achieved through stimulating identification spurs us on to meaningful personal achievements. But when our identifications become the chief source of our status and satisfaction, we are in trouble. For then we have traded reality for fantasy and are headed for disaster.

However we may use the mental mechanisms discussed above, or any of the other mechanisms the analytic psychologists suggest, our use of them will probably fall into one of three approaches when we face trouble.

5. Modification. If stress threatens to overwhelm us, we may modify either our perception of the trouble or our perception of ourselves. An example out of today's economic life serves to illustrate.

Newlyweds Cathy and Carl had promised each other the moon. Since both had good jobs, money was no problem, at first. But, as usually happens, Cathy became pregnant, and one income terminated. The fact they had been living on both salaries to make payments on the various parts of the promised moon became chafing sand in their marital bliss. They began sniping at each other and blaming one another for the financial grief. Their strife was at a peak when they glumly sat down before the television set to forget their troubles.

In beautiful living color, a sexy debt merchant showed them how to consolidate all their financial worries in one simple monthly payment and include a new car as a reward for being so intelligent. This seemed to be the answer. Here was a way to modify impending financial doom and postpone the ultimate reality of honeymoon economics. They flew out the door into the clutches of a "financial expert" at the local auto dispensary. The money wizard made good on the TV promise; he sent them home in a new Snortfire Eight with power ash trays and all the other optional equipment. Along with it was a contract for payments somewhat less than they were now expending, *but* with interest, penalties, and a final balloon payoff that would choke a vault at Fort Knox. Cathy and Carl had traded a difficult, immediate problem for an impossible, postponed problem. They had allowed their troubles to modify their perceptions of their difficulties. By modification they temporarily reduced threat and felt more adequate in the present moment. But the ultimate reality was crushing.

Most of us have tried this approach in one way or another. With simple problems it is sometimes useful. We postpone some problems until new, more certain resources are available. But when some major aspect of our lives is at stake, it can be a tragic error. Facing up to tough realities is better than postponing or modifying them into real impossibilities.

6. Denial of self and experience. Once a mother and her eighth-grade daughter sought my counsel concerning a school achievement problem. Apparently the girl had gotten through eight years of elementary education without ever learning to read. Since the initial problem presented to a psychologist is often not the real source of concern, I allowed the conversation to drift into other areas. How was the girl getting along with the other students? What were her ambitions in life?

We had talked rather circuitously for about twenty minutes, when I abruptly asked, "And what does father think about all this?" I should have known better, for any men-

tion of the father in our discussion was conspicuous by its absence. Immediately mother and daughter burst into tears as if I were the little Dutch boy who had pulled his finger out of the dike.

As the discussion continued, I learned that father knew the true nature of the situation, that the child was mentally retarded, but was totally undiplomatic in sharing his knowledge. Instead of being friendly and helpful, he badgered and belittled the child. Though he accepted her retardation, he did so grudgingly.

Mother, suspecting the worst, could not bear the thought that her daughter would never succeed in normal learning requirements. Instead she directed her child to think of becoming a nun where the "only happy life was to be had." A convent would also be a safe place to effect removal of the girl from family embarrassment as well. The approach to the problem was simply to deny that the retardation existed—and to deny father's knowledge of the problem.

Lives that are continually unhappy and disturbed are lives built around a denial of experience. When problems are disclaimed, feelings are swept away and never admitted to conscious experience.

The need to repress many unpleasant emotions leads to insensitivity. Even pleasant feelings can be stifled. People who become insensitive to hurt soon find themselves invulnerable to pleasure as well. The truly free individual hurts a lot because he is willing to admit a full range of feelings to his consciousness. The unruffled stoic often spends great energy denying emotion in order to keep his problems under oppressive control. But while he is doing it, he is temporarily maintaining his image of adequacy and self-control.

A colleague of mine had been a highly successful business executive before entering college teaching. Employed at a high rank and salary, he thought teaching would be a breeze. But his students were bored and bothered with busy work assignments, and nearly revolted one term. The professor, however, refused to recognize the problem. He denied any incompetence on his part and dismissed the students' reactions as frivolous contempt for academic work.

7. Reorganization of perceptions to include the problem. Several years ago we traveled with friends in the mountains, visiting one of our beautiful national parks. Returning from a jaunt to one of the spectacular views at dusk, we marveled at the beauties of the sky. Suddenly a car appeared from the opposite direction, winding crazily up the road. We slowed, pulled to one side, as the auto went by. But then we heard a grinding, scraping sound and the ripping tumult of tires blowing out. The approaching car had struck the vehicle just behind us. Fortunately no injuries occurred, but the collision accomplished some inartistic engraving on both autos.

Both drivers emerged, the man from the offending car indisputably under the influence of liquor. They exchanged information about drivers' licenses and insurance policies. Others helped make arrangements to remove the damaged vehicles and transport the passengers to their destinations.

The event had fairly well spoiled our recollections of a beautiful day as we sat around camp that evening expressing thankfulness that no one had been hurt. We assumed the event was a matter of the past and decided to forget it.

Not so. Two weeks after we had returned home, our doorbell rang, and there stood a constable. He handed me papers that said I was being sued by someone for "permanent bodily damage and grievous physical pain and suffering" to the tune of $15,000. Suing me! I wasn't in any accident! Why me?

My first impulse was to ignore the whole silly business. Obviously it was a mistake and would take care of itself. Furthermore, it was the drunk who was doing the suing, and obviously he couldn't collect! In short, my impulse was either to modify my perceptions into some safe kind of experience or to deny the existence of a problem alto-

116

gether. I was not going to give this trauma the courtesy of being thought of as some honest reality.

I mentioned the matter to my golf partner a day or so later and, to my surprise, he said, "You had better see a good lawyer, buddy." Me, see a lawyer? I didn't believe in paying people to defend me against nothing! My golf partner was adamant. Since I had to do something, I decided to turn the matter over to my insurance carrier, even though the whole business was completely unfair.

When I called my agent that evening, he assured me I had done the right thing and that suits of this kind came up rather frequently. I still struggled to believe it. But it is a good thing I did, for the insurance company spent a substantial number of hours straightening out the whole mess. It seems that the drunken driver who was trying to sue me had mistakenly mixed up the license numbers of the cars. The car he had struck was the same make as mine. Since he also had my name as a witness it was easy for him to get thoroughly confused and direct the litigation at the wrong man.

But suppose I had persisted in my plans just to ignore the whole mess? I might have been involved in endless details and nuisances. It took some stimulating, but I had to accept the fact that I was the subject of litigation and needed to respond appropriately. I had to reorganize my thinking to include the very real fact that a problem was immediately before me and had to be faced. My denial of responsibility did not change the fact I was being sued.

Many people's perceptions are so rigid that they automatically refuse to recognize serious problems. In fact, some persons no longer understand that they are unaware. They have experienced so much stress in the past that their minds block out the truth, making no attempts at reorganization.

The psychologically able individual usually reorganizes his thinking to account fully for the problems thrust upon him. He deals with them rationally, sensing all the related emotions. Then he resumes his normal experience. He is not so insulated from the stress he feels that he spontaneously ignores reality, or modified through safe but unrealistic perceptions.

Another problem occurs in all our lives when we have to choose between perceived alternatives. As we develop from small children into adulthood, we become strongly involved in the lives of our family members. These strong ties frequently involve a considerable mixture of emotions. We are dependent on them and loving toward them, yet often at odds with them and seeking independence from them. In short, the elements of love and hate, hurt and joy, exist side by side in these intense relationships. These competing emotions are probably strongest during adolescence, when emotional divorce from parents and family is a natural and desirable occurrence.

When a loved one dies, however, we struggle with a certainty that challenges us in our perceptual capacities. Only the most confused person can fully deny such reality in his experience. Yet, accepting the full reality is also a difficult step to take. In some way or other, most of us deal with the problem by modifying it into a more acceptable experience. If the loved one has been ill, we may pretend to be glad that he is gone, telling ourselves that he is better off where he is now. Or, as some stoics say, "Everyone's number comes up sometime." In any event, most people modify perceptions first, then ease themselves into the full reality of the experience. I think that this is why some people experience considerable grief long after the event has taken place. They have modified their perceptions by postponing their reactions. Or they have continued certain rituals of their lives, retaining some part of previous experience that involved the one deceased.

Eventually, the full reorganization must come, or life proceeds with distortion and discomfort. Most of us know of someone who, having lost a loved one, closeted himself in his home within his feelings and failed to respond to much of anything forever after.

The denial or modification of our perceptions of experience hampers us in the fortunate experiences of life as well. Earlier, we pointed out that the truly free person hurts a lot because his openness makes him aware of a wide range of human experience. People who have been continually threatened emotionally become so protective that they lose their capacities to revel in joy as well as suffer pain. For them, happiness involves the risk of relationship, and this may be too distressing. Too many unfortunate contacts with people in the past have built emotional callouses to feelings of all kinds.

The mental gymnastics we go through in seeking adequacy become, in themselves, evidence of the extreme nature of our need for adequacy. Ernest Hemingway is reported to have said, in effect, that destruction is more acceptable than defeat. From our observations of the seriously troubled, we conclude that they often choose insanity instead of reality, if reality reveals them to be inadequate. Self is so clearly at the center of existence that the world must be blocked out before it can admit inadequacy. Or self must be distorted into acceptability so the world cannot touch it no matter what its character may be.

# 9 The Nature of the Redemptive Relationship

Listening is the key to the redemptive relationship. Listening is the means by which we gain entry to each other's lives. But what we do on admittance is also critically important. It is possible to play the role of listener and then become destructive when the one to whom we are listening becomes vulnerable to us. Listening must be accompanied by other behaviors to insure that the relationship remains helpful.

A young college girl returned home for Christmas after one quarter in a Midwestern university. It had been a difficult term for her; she had experienced both academic and social difficulties. Her grades were below par, and she had been placed on academic probation. Coming from a protective environment, totally surrounded by church people, she had little knowledge of the worldly sophistication of urbane, mod groups that populate our cities. Lonely and uninitiated, she had fallen for a number of temptations that went against her moral convictions. She had tried to relate to others, but her new friends had only exploited her naiveté.

# LISTENING

She made an appointment with her minister one morning shortly after returning home. She struggled with herself wondering how to get out the words of confession and how to plead for help. When she arrived at the church office at the appointed hour, the pastor invited her in. "How's our pride and joy?" he inquired warmly. "It will be good to hear how you've gotten along."

"I'm a mess," she blurted. "Between liquor and sex, I can hardly stand myself!"

"What? You, the most stable and mature Christian girl in our church! You should be ashamed of yourself," he retorted. She leaped from her chair and ran out the door, tears streaming from her eyes.

The minister lost his opportunity to be redemptive the moment he became judgmental. His spontaneous outburst of rejection of the girl gave himself away. He was a moralist and a legalist who accepted only those people who conformed to his codes. Pharisaical in attitude, he thought he was doing God a favor with his pronouncements.

It is questionable whether he or those in his church had ever been redemptive in the life of the girl. This congregation respected people only if they turned out "right" according to predetermined stereotypes. All others were spiritual inferiors whose faith was suspect.

The girl left the church entirely and turned to a group of self-styled intellectuals for her answers. In their presence, her sin was acceptable and her problems were dealt with in cool philosophical fashion. Ignoring the need for real resolution of guilt, she became a suave sophisticate who was above such silly things as archaic moralisms.

The redemptive relationship is a nonmoralizing relationship. People who seek help from others are often driven by guilt. In remorse they yearn for help. When the first reaction is judgment of guilt or moral disapproval, they feel rejected. Their grief is intensified so greatly that their only recourse is withdrawal. Opportunity for redemption is lost.

In chapter 3, we discussed how you can avoid love by becoming moral. Being moral will make you moralistic if love and guilt resolution are not part of the morality. In your self-styled purity you will either require the same attitude from others or you will reject them. Those who disagree with you will become reminders of your own sin. It is a psychological fact that judgmental, moralistic people are often those with the most unresolved guilt to hide. And people who hide can scarcely be redemptive.

A judgmental attitude toward others puts them on the defensive. They feel insulted or hurt. In this emotional posture, they cannot be open to emotional healing. They are too busy protecting themselves, too occupied with maintaining self-esteem. Defensiveness of personality, therefore, is the antithesis of growth, for growth only occurs when defenses are lowered.

The redemptive relationship is not a coercive relationship. One does not feel overwhelming pressure to be what he cannot be. Instead he has the sensation of being gently led. He is drawn by another who has ventured into growth and who knows the way. He is drawn to move as quickly as he can feel comfortable and as quickly as he can comprehend his own emotions about growing.

In contrast, the coercive person insists that all problems must be solved immediately and on his terms. No latitude for error is allowed. No freedom to approach and withdraw from potential solutions. Just follow the right formula and get on with it. Further, progress must proceed along lines he has already defined with his own jargon. A limited set of terms and concepts must be used. If others are attempted, the coercive person regards it as a form of heresy. Whether any set of terms really defines growth or not is debatable. Sometimes people assume that they have grown simply because they can use the new colloquialisms in their vocabulary.

We run across examples of this problem in counseling psychology. Occasionally I will see a person who uses the jargon of psychology so well that I am tempted to believe they have insight into their problems. They speak in detail of their Oedipus complex, overlays of reaction formation behavior, and resultant neurotic stress. But when it comes to doing something about their condition, they blame their parents and environment, and then seek someone else with whom to have a catharsis. Maybe someone else will equate their use of psychological jargon with growth.

In the New Testament we see Jesus bumping into a similar problem. He had most of his problems with the religious conservatives of his day who knew all the words, but whose lives were a bit of death warmed over. The same is true today. I suspect those who parade religious and theological jargon, but who seldom make any emotional progress in their lives—the hateful heresy-hunters and doctrine-dictators who get along with no one.

Pressure to manifest quickly stereotyped symptoms of progress, along with the use of some particular jargon, usually comes from someone who is more coercive than redemptive. This need to be coercive is itself a symptom of insecurity, an insecurity that the person compensates for by attempting to be dominant or sovereign in the emotional experiences of others.

The redemptive relationship is an equalitarian relationship. While no two people in the world have the same fingerprints, aptitudes, physical characteristics, or social opportunities, a more important quality than any of these is the privilege of all of us. We are equally the objects of the love of God. We are equally entitled to grow in our knowledge of Him and in our personal lives. We are equally entitled to see ourselves as the objects of His grace, and not as advantaged or disadvantaged by some human standard.

When the relationships among a group of people or with another individual become dominated by this sense of equality, a redemptive spirit results that affirms the person. Whatever our backgrounds, we are entitled to affirmation by God and man. To be redemptive is to respond primarily to the equalities of people and their common need for love. While much work is needed in the area of human rights and social justice, it is possible to become so preoccupied with the inequalities of man that we miss the basis for our most redemptive activity, the true equality that exists among men.

Recently we acquired a very standard model of gray kitten in our home. He was only a few weeks old when he arrived, but he quickly caught the attention and affection of our children. They noticed that he had a particular way of becoming acquainted with strangers and with the new items in his environment. He would quietly sneak up on one of them, and then quickly withdraw when a response was made. As he grew in courage, he would come closer and remain longer. Eventually, he became so sure of himself that only a serious jolt could get him off one's lap or away from something breakable.

People behave in much the same way. They approach and withdraw from the objects and persons they are attempting to get to know. In overcoming fears of specific things or experiences, the freedom to approach and withdraw is most helpful. Thus, it is also a characteristic of the redemptive relationship. If we would truly be helpful, we must grant people the opportunity to approach and withdraw from both the problem and the solution required.

Most people have mixed feelings about solving a problem. When problems are solved, relationships change. And this change upsets our stability of perception. An old saying has it that we fear less the devils we know than the angels we don't know. To solve a problem is to risk new terms of relationships. It also usually means deeper and more meaningful relationships with more possibility to both help and hurt. This can create a definite feeling of anxiety. As a result, some people actually resist solving problems while apparently trying to solve them. It's the old story of mixed emotions—as when your wealthy mother-in-law names you as heir and then comes to live with you.

When people do not respect the needs others have to approach and withdraw from a problem, it usually means that the supposed helper or helping group is becoming coercive. They would rather see someone progress and be able to call themselves successful than to allow the troubled individual to work through his situation at his own pace.

But when we become redemptive, we allow others to have as much "wiggle room" as they need. We do not insist on symptoms of progress to prove our own worth as helpers. In fact we must be willing to let the person fail, if he insists. If we do not, we are usurping the rights of sovereignty over the person's life. And only God is entitled to that. Further, only the person himself can give back to God his personal sovereignty.

A redemptive relationship is a series of shared experiences. As such, it is not always smooth and velvety. Sharing some things precludes easygoing occasionally. When life is fully shared, things get abrasive from time to time. If they don't, there is some evidence of withholding oneself in the relationship. And this leads us to a problem.

I was speaking on the subject of marriage and home matters in a church one Sunday evening. Prior to my address, the group had gathered for coffee and cake. We chatted awhile, getting acquainted with the people and enjoying good fellowship. During the conversation, one particularly affluent gentleman announced that his only problems were financial, and that most of those could be laid at the feet of organized labor. He was happy that I was there to speak about marriage, but he assured me that most of what I said probably wouldn't apply to him.

Announcements like this always make me wonder a bit, perhaps even stimulate me to do a better-than-average job with the subject. At any rate, we did have a very good session. I felt happy about my presentation, and the audience entered into a question-and-answer period with considerable enthusiasm. Especially involved was the man who had announced that his only problems were financial. From time to time he would make a statement or ask a question that revealed a bit of his hidden self. Then after the meeting he cornered me and we began an hour's discussion.

"My wife is very nervous," he indicated. "She always seems upset, especially at bill paying time and tax time. I tell her not to worry, everything will go all right, and we'll have plenty to live on. We always do, too, you know."

"You share your financial worries with her, then?" I questioned.

"Yes, but I don't really bother her with them. I just let her in on enough to keep her interested in my work."

"What else do you share with her in your life?" I continued. Counselors find that the problem presented to them is often a test case to see if the real problem will be carefully handled. Perhaps financial problems were only an opening scene to the real drama in this life.

The gentleman was visibly shaken by my question, though it seemed innocent enough to me. Instead of pursuing an answer, he talked disinterestedly again about money matters. Then he thanked me for my presentation and dismissed himself.

I learned later that his wife had sought the counsel of

her minister because of feelings of great loneliness. She was completely left out of her husband's life. When he mentioned financial problems to her, it made her anxious, not because money worried her, but because it was the only part of his life she really knew about. When the subject came up, she was hopeful that it might be a beginning of extended discussion in other personal areas. In her hopefulness she was showing her anxiety. The response of her husband to the anxiety was not to open up more, but to limit even the discussions of money. As a result they shut each other out of their inner lives, and the wife found herself a lonely woman with no one to share life with her.

I learned later, too, that the husband had had a serious problem getting along with his employees. He either ingratiated himself with them or provoked them sorely. Then I began to wonder how his life and his marriage might have been different if this abrasive problem had been shared with his wife rather than hidden. It might have been tough to discuss a personal weakness and arguments might have ensued. But had the effort been made, the wife would have not experienced loneliness and her husband might have found real help in their relationships. The opportunity for redemptive relationship in marriage had been missed because only the pleasantries had been exchanged and none of the abrasiveness was allowed admittance.

When we act redemptively toward others, in marriage, in personal encounter, or in fellowship and sharing groups, we come out best by sharing the full spectrum of our lives. This requires a good deal of risk, for in admitting others to areas of our personal vulnerability we can get hurt. But if the final outcome is to be growth, the risk must be taken.

For the sake of easy moments, and perhaps for the appearance of social acceptability, we often become limited-spectrum people. Only those areas of life that are already comfortable to us are open for examination and relationship. The full spectrum of our experiences is kept available. To escape this truncated growth, there are at least two steps we must take.

First, recall that the words of Jesus were, "I am come that you might have life and have it more abundantly." (See John 10:10.) It is a solemn promise of God to give you life if you will have it. But you must make the move to open yourself to Him. And He is no threat. He accepts us for what we are without retribution and makes it safe for us to go into His presence without anxiety. Then as we become sure of ourselves with Him, we can begin to work through our problems on a no-risk basis, knowing that He will act redemptively toward us.

The second step follows the first. When we have been assured by God of our acceptability to Him, it is easier to share our lives with other people, especially with those who have decided to pursue a course similar to the one we have taken. God uses other people to help us. And in sharing redemptively with them, we help them, too.

The redemptive relationship is one in which no one calls the shots. No one prescribes behaviorally defined objectives that all must pursue. The prevailing attitude is that each person is a unique creation, to be perfected in God's own way and manner, and that anything short of this is a truncated growth experience. Each grants the other maximum freedom to be uniquely individual in the hands of the Master Creator.

Too often more limited results occur. It is easy for us to become so preoccupied with the behavioral definitions of our belief systems that we look only for certain behaviors as symptoms of growth. Further, we insist that growth and feeling must be expressed in rigid concepts, using a standardized vocabulary. A kind of personal theology appears more trustworthy than the Person of God. Systems then take priority over people, even in religious and psychological experience. It ought not to be so.

When we impose limited objectives and specifically defined behavioral requirements upon people, we lapse into the tendency to become coercive. We subtly insist that we would like to have a bit of control over others. Somehow we cannot trust ourselves to other people until we have at least a limited sovereignty over their lives. Again, this is the antithesis of growth. Sovereignty of persons belongs to God alone, or to the person himself, if he is so shortsighted as to not give it up to the Creator.

Finally, the redemptive relationship is one that can be terminated without guilt. This condition of relationship is consistent with our understanding of agape love. This love is freely given and freely received. It is reciprocal love that solicits obligation. Reciprocal love is a necessary love in the conduct of human affairs, but for fully redemptive purposes, a higher order of relationship must exist.

Some relationships must be discontinued simply because we move about, change human status, play new roles. Sometimes growth depends on terminating a relationship that has outgrown its redemptive and helpful characteristics. If relationships continue only to fulfill mutual obligation, they quickly lose any capacity for redemptiveness they might have had. Thus they are best terminated.

We have friends who live in Asia that we rarely see. Further, we correspond once every two years, if at all. But when they come home, we immediately seek each other out and have the time of our lives. We can pick up the conversation where we left it five years before when they were last home. We help them some, financially, but otherwise we make little contact while they are away. Their friendship has been one of the greatest sources of help and blessing to our lives. But one important factor is apparent. We are free to take leave of each other and to resume fellowship with each other on the freest of terms.

We begin and end in a redemptive way, and our lives are far richer for the experience.

Perhaps the best description of conditions for redemptive relationships is found in 1 Corinthians 13:1, "If I speak in the tongues of men and of angels. . . ."

# 10 *The Need for Physical Well-Being and Security*

I was beginning my first responsibility as a school psychologist when one of our principals called me for quick assistance. He did not explain his problem fully, so I hurried to his school as rapidly as possible. Arriving just as classes were beginning, I found one teacher and her class locked out of their room. The principal and teacher were struggling with the lock, which some unknown culprit had obviously jammed from the inside. The janitor came by shortly and was able to get us into the classroom. The first of the children filed in, then burst back into the corridor shrieking. Flying music books barely skimmed their heads as they attempted to enter.

Shielding myself, I volunteered to recapture command of the halls of academia. Once inside I found a husky boy, music books in hand, standing on top of the upright piano ready to let fly. When he saw me, he quickly ducked away, hiding behind the piano and window draperies close by. I approached him carefully, seeking an explanation for the small riot he had created. He cowered in the corner, muttering that he knew I was after him and must be intent on punishing him. He was partly correct, but I assured him

133

that I wanted to hear what he had to say before I took any action.

The principal ushered him to the office and we spent several minutes calming him down. Then I questioned the teacher about her experiences with the child previously. "Is this the first such outburst you have experienced?" I asked.

"No, not really, I had him in kindergarten a couple of years ago and he was a terror then," she replied. "His school record is written in teachers' sweat."

The boy, whom we'll call Richard, was the best-known student in this elementary school. Every teacher who had taught him, or had been on yard duty, knew of his antics. He was usually referred to as the worst behavior problem in the school and with a near perfect attendance record! His fame spread to the neighborhood as well. He had the reputation of a sulking bully who believed everyone was picking on him.

A day later, I called at the home to see how the parents had been able to work with him. Mother proved to be a weary and frustrated woman, not knowing where to turn for help. She wasn't sure she wanted to see anyone from school because such visits just meant more trouble. As is customary in case work, I also asked some details about the boy's health history and emotional development. Giving the mother the details about the recent incident at school I asked, "What is Richard's usual reaction to difficult situations?" With this she sensed that I was not there to level judgment, but to learn all I could about her boy.

The story was a long one, but the salient points were very meaningful and formed a diagnostic constellation frequently found in high-strung children like Richard. While living in another state, the boy had been seriously ill with a kidney infection. The resultant high fever and delirious condition warranted immediate hospitalization. The boy lapsed into a coma for several days, and doctors wondered whether he would recover. But the crisis passed and Richard returned home, apparently recovered. Shortly after hospitalization, he experienced several severe convulsive episodes. Later neurological examinations confirmed that some brain damage had probably resulted from his serious illness.

The mother also indicated that Richard's personality underwent considerable change after the hospitalization. He had been a placid child until that time, but now many things upset him. His emotions seemed to be on a Yo-Yo, and his moods were unpredictable. He seemed possessed by a hair-trigger temper that flared at the most inopportune times. In school he had the most difficulty learning to translate his thoughts into writing as they came to him. Writing a simple paragraph, dictated by the teacher, was an impossible assignment. But his mathematical abilities seemed to have remained intact. Summer vacations took an unusual toll in loss of learning. It seemed as though he had to learn to read all over again every fall.

But the most difficult factor to deal with was the explosive personality. Class members could never predict his reactions, and because he was strong and husky, they learned to fear him. As a result, they withdrew, and Richard found himself with very few friends. This fact became important in his outlook on life, for he began to feel inferior and easily hurt. In retaliation for his injured feelings, he would abuse classmates, often hurting them painfully.

Richard and his family were advised to seek the services of a diagnostic center at a large hospital, where both psychological and physical factors could be evaluated. This study would give us full information on how to help Richard make the most of school as well as of his personal life. As we suspected, significant brain damage was noted, along with the usual corresponding symptoms: moodiness, temper, impaired general coordination, flight of attention, to mention a few. With a carefully controlled medication

135

program consisting mainly of anticonvulsants and mild depressants, behavior was brought under control, and the boy's attitude improved markedly. He no longer flared at slight provocations. Children lost much of their fear of him, and his social life returned to near normal. No longer a sulking bully, he felt as though he had achieved a major personal victory in life.

It would have been easy to label Richard an obstreperous boy and prescribe only punishment. I often wonder how many other needy boys have never had the benefit of full understanding and modern facilities, and so have lived out their lives in unhappiness. It became clear that Richard's problem was basically a physical problem, not a psychological one. His behavior was merely a symptom of an underlying physical condition.

As I worked with the family for several years, I was impressed with their stability and genuine concern. The parents were not the kind one would expect to have a boy with difficult behavior. But behavior, all behavior is built upon a physiological basis and this basis must not be overlooked. In Richard's case it provided the key to a most happy solution, not only for Richard, but for the parents who were feeling guilt and failure that was unjustified.

No behavior, including thought and emotion, occurs apart from tissue. Mind and body are one in structure, and highly related in function. When one goes out of kilter, the other is affected. No psychological diagnosis is complete without full recognition of the physiological factors underlying behavior. And no one can be a fully developed person without proper physical well-being. Man clearly needs physical security and stability.

Few machines run in such a delicate balance as does the human body. The smallest change in functioning is often felt immediately. As I sit typing this chapter, I am mindful of the fact that I forgot my thyroid pill this morning. I'm a little slow of mind and keep pressing the wrong keys. Something is out of balance and I'll need to correct matters shortly. But the best example is how we feel when our body temperature varies about two degrees. How do you feel then? If you are normal, a two-degree elevation will put you in bed for at least twenty-four hours.

Yet I see many people who take very poor care of themselves and wonder why they are upset, depressed, or just miserable. This is especially true of college students who delight in burning the candle at both ends. One young psychology major stopped by my office to complain that he was losing interest in school. He liked his major and wasn't thinking of changing, but he just seemed to lack motivation. "Give me an idea of your schedule," I said.

"Oh, I am taking nineteen units this quarter and working part time," he replied.

"How long and when?" I asked.

"I finish classes about four-thirty, and I work at a laundry from six in the evening until one in the morning. I sleep until seven and get to school at eight."

"How much sleep do you actually get?" I questioned further.

"Well, I'm engaged, and have to see my girl some time, so I usually stop by her house after work for about an hour."

"Then you sleep?"

"Yes, about four hours a night, if I'm lucky!"

"And you are wondering why you are not motivated? Can I make a guess?" My question obviously rubbed him the wrong way.

As it turned out, he was unhappy about being engaged, and he was using the work excuse to keep from seeing his girl any more than he had to. He seemed to lack the courage to break off the relationship. He just hoped she would get tired of his visits at one o'clock in the morning and perform the break-off surgery herself. In time, however, they managed to separate, and the boy's motivation increased markedly, as well as his sleeping time. He got another job, happily resumed his studies and obtained outstanding grades.

A psychiatrist friend of mine who works in a large university reports that he frequently sees students who eat poorly, sleep little, indulge in undisciplined fun, and then wonder why they are depressed. "The fact is," he says, "you just can't get kids to realize that feelings are based on physical functioning. If you tax your physical capacities, you are going to feel bad."

One quiet evening the phone rang as we were about to retire. A friend I had known for a long time was calling, and it was obvious that he was in a state of controlled desperation. "Ever have your wife talk of committing herself?" he asked, trying to insert a little humor into his desperation. "I know some guys who would relish the idea, but I don't! What do I do, Doc?"

"Tell me what's going on," I replied.

"Well, she feels so low she won't risk leaving the house. She cries all the time and doesn't want me to go to work. Then she says she can't pray, feels nobody could love her, and wants me to put her away. I've never been through anything like this. It just doesn't seem real. I hear about others having such troubles, but I never thought it would happen to us."

I asked a number of questions to sort out possible emotional factors from physical factors before making a suggestion. Since the surface indications were that no great psychological trauma was present, I urged them to seek out a specialist in internal medicine. Sure enough, he found the answer. The woman was seriously lacking in thyroid production. After several sessions of lab work, the doctor prescribed medication, principally thyroid. In a matter of weeks, the depression had gone, and the family was back on an even keel.

Obviously, not every case responds to treatment so dramatically as this one. But whenever there is some significant shift in emotional well-being, you should have a thorough checkup by a medical doctor. Take a look at the following list of symptoms. These describe a significant number of people who request appointments with me.

—Appointment usually sought by a woman. Men scarcely ever call psychologists. They come after their wives get involved.
—Feelings of depression and worthlessness.
—Seriously overweight or underweight.
—Inability to sleep.
—History of uncertainty as a child resulting from emotionally unresponsive parents.
—Many financial and social obligations that seem never to end.
—Several children born within a short period of years; little time between pregnancies.
—Some major surgery accompanying onset of symptoms. Often a hysterectomy, or other procedure involving glands.
—An unsupportive mate who retreats in time of stress.

Just reading the list makes me tired. No wonder people with such a parade of symptoms hurt emotionally. They are pooped, exhausted, joyless. Even faith seems to have vanished, and they have run out of theological answers to life.

I was discussing this list with physicians at a nearby mental health center as we were reviewing the kind of patient who seeks help. One of the doctors piped up, "Sounds like fifty percent of my practice!"

"Mine, too," said another.

Obviously, you shouldn't do any self diagnosing from this list, but anytime a significant emotional change occurs in just a few weeks, a thorough checkup is highly recommended. I have seen too many people change theology, assume highly modified self-concepts, break up marriages, or fight with their in-laws as a result of a physical disorder. It is amazing to see the reaction when the problem is corrected. I recall one particularly distraught woman, who divorced her husband and abandoned her children only to find that she had been given some very bad advice and that essentially she had a physical problem, not an emotional one. It took months, but eventually the hurts were healed sufficiently for the couple to remarry and resume a normal home life.

Following is another list. These are cases I have known in the past with their chief symptoms and causes. All were more complex than I am indicating, but I am oversimplifying to make a point.

—A kindergarten girl with a subnormal IQ. After three years of specific endocrine treatment, her intelligence returned to normal.

—A leader in a women's organization was known for her extreme Christian enthusiasm and high rate of activity. Nobody could keep up with her. A glandular condition propelled her until she was exhausted and had to be hospitalized.

—A junior-high-school boy developed a serious inferiority complex. He piled on fat about the waist, but not on his extremities. Embarrassed about his appearance, he became painfully shy. Studies revealed a serious hypothalamic condition.

—An elderly woman seriously considered suicide as a result of episodes of depression. Hating all doctors except veterinarians, she refused medical attention. Eventually she lapsed into a coma and was rushed to a hospital where severe diabetes was diagnosed.

—A fourth-grade boy frequently appeared to experience mild seizures. Referred to a diagnostic center, he was found to suffer from extremely serious vitamin deficiencies.

—A third-grade boy couldn't read, and failed every subject. He fell over objects and ran into things. He was referred to the psychologist as possibly retarded. When fitted with a pair of glasses with a built-in hearing aid, his IQ and achievement returned to normal.

When the need for physical stability is not met, a number of psychological factors come into play. These factors are attempts at solving the problem, but will always prove unsatisfactory until the root problem is solved. Occasionally we are able to detect subtle physiological difficulties by closely observing the psychological processes of the mind. Under persistent physical stress, any one or several of the following psychological symptoms may occur.

1. Reduced mobility. We easily identify this symptom in the aged. No one really wonders why an elderly person does not leave the house very much. It exposes him to illness and danger. But when a younger person spends too much time at home, we have cause to wonder. Reduced mobility shuts off the individual from people. Thus he lacks the reassurance of friends. He fails to achieve the proper rewards for his efforts. His personal life becomes impoverished, and he is lonely. In his withdrawal, he becomes unhappy and wonders why the world is such an unfriendly place. In time, his whole personality suffers distortion.

2. Restricted interests. When physical problems plague

a person, too much of his attention must be given to his own body and mind. Busily introspecting about how he feels, he becomes preoccupied with pain and discomfort. Self-concern soon permeates his personality, and he focuses almost entirely on his selfish interests. As a result, he loses touch with current happenings in his social world and is less conversant about happier matters. Others find him uncomfortable to be around and withdraw, leaving him to his loneliness. One oldster in a retirement home complained, "All I hear about around here are problems of the lower intestinal tract and the way the Democrats are ruining the country."

The person who has successfully overcome a physical handicap knows that he must constantly work at not thinking of himself in terms of his handicap. It is quite a different matter to think of oneself as a handicapped person rather than as a person with a handicap. A person with a handicap does not lose his ability to think straight, or his ability to make acquaintances, or his capacity to establish fulfilling activities in his experience.

3. Truncated judgment. This is a subtle process, but it exists nevertheless. By *truncated,* we mean restricted, accounting for less than the whole of the matter. A physically beset individual tends to make decisions about himself in terms of his limits rather than his possibilities. In so doing, he probably restricts his life and limits himself needlessly.

Examples of distorted judgment related to deprivations are documented in psychological research. We know for example that very poor children perceive coins to be larger than they really are. We know that starving people dream of steaks and caviar rather than hamburger and beans. Impoverished people see moderately built homes as fine estates. All of our judgments reflect our problems, and our problems can so preoccupy us that we make bad decisions.

Changes in ability to make judgments occur slowly and

often without the awareness of the person. Efforts are necessary to guard against this possibility. Anyone constantly bothered by a serious problem would do well to seek professional counsel just to check his judgment ability.

4. Resistance to correction. To make a satisfactory correction in thinking requires the admission of possible error in judgment. This can be guilt-provoking and therefore may be resisted, especially if the judgment was particularly bad. For some, the cure is more painful than the kill. Further, to correct an underlying physical problem is to risk finding out how serious things may be. Thus the problem may be doubly resisted.

I recall the case of a woman who was feeling very low and began to blame her husband's employment for her stress. If only he would change work so they could live somewhere else. So they moved, but no relief came. She nagged for a second move, then a third, and still no relief. In time, medication and rest affected a satisfactory solution. Now she was very chagrined because of the insults and nagging she had leveled at her husband for not appreciating how she felt and suggesting that the problem was within

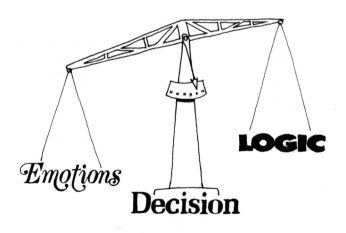

143

her and not him. We both assured her that we were happy she was well and that she should forget her embarrassment. But it wasn't enough. Now we get a box of candy every Christmas to atone for the misbehavior during counseling sessions.

The fact remains that we believe in the way we feel. Our feelings take precedence over logic in personal decision-making. And when we are ill, we make decisions that correspond with that illness and not always with the inherent logic of the matter. It takes considerable self-objectivity to seek correction in thinking and feeling, even when obvious physical ills may explain the condition.

# 11 *Biblical Grounds for Self-Identity*

In chapter 4 we pointed out that all of us need to see ourselves as adequate people. Without perceived self-adequacy, we are largely doomed to failure. The inadequate self-picture becomes the self-fulfilling prophecy of disappointment. On the other hand, a self-image of adequacy gives rise to feelings of success and optimism. Again a self-fulfilling prophecy is at work. One who predicts success for himself tackles tough projects, attempts difficult tasks, and often obtains elusive and valuable goals that most others miss.

A good self-image does not mean lifting oneself by one's bootstraps. A good self-image develops out of valid information about oneself. If a person has a good self-image, he has fully accepted the truth about himself, and that truth is not demeaning. Neither is it a delusion of success where none exists. A good self-image must be based on a genuine and honest self-appraisal. Otherwise the resulting disappointments will be doubly damaging, and ultimate recovery will be most difficult.

Self-appraisal is the way you value yourself. It's the way you see yourself, both implicitly and explicitly. It's the kind of terms you choose to describe yourself. It's the picture of yourself you carry in your mind. But the question is, is it a true picture or a false one? By what standard do you judge yourself—by man-made goals and values, or by enduring, eternal truth? What is the hard ground of reality about you? What is the most believable thing that can be said about you?

My attention was first drawn to this question when I was a freshman in college. It was Christian Emphasis Week on campus, and a guest speaker in chapel had posed the question, "Who do you think you are, anyway?" It is not unusual for a college freshman to tackle this question. In fact, life away from home with new friends and peers and new intellectual expectancies is bound to raise questions about self-identity. The first year of college provides both an unusual opportunity for self-discovery and a risky trial for the more uncertain student.

The basic tenet of Professor Arthur Combs' book, *Individual Behavior,* is that we behave in terms of the way we see ourselves. If we want to predict anyone's behavior, we must know how he sees himself in the situation where the behavior is going to take place. No other single bit of information about a person is so vital and useful for prediction purposes. Knowledge about IQ, grades, socioeconomic status, and the like is helpful, but not nearly so useful as the knowledge of self-image. Our Christian Emphasis speaker put it this way:

The philosopher says, "I am what I become. . . ."
The capitalist says, "I am what I own. . . ."
The scholar says, "I am what I know. . . ."
The existentialist says, "I am what I perceive and feel. . . ."
The moralist says, "I am what I do. . . ."
The radical says, "I am not what I reject!"

But Paul, the apostle says, "I am the least of the apostles, unfit to be called an apostle, because I persecuted the church of God. But by the grace of God I am what I am" (1 Cor. 15:9-10).

The point of the text is that Paul had learned to see himself primarily as an object of God's grace. No longer

# GOD

## RIGHTEOUS GOD

did he view himself as a Jew, a Pharisee, an intellectual, or a persecutor, for now he was an object of the supreme love of God. All other evidence to the contrary, his first business was to assume that he was as like Christ as possible, because that is the way God regarded him.

The fact that Paul could identify himself as the object of the grace of God in no way denies other possible facets of self-image. He was not covering up anything, he was simply acquiring a more important, more dominant factor in his self-description than he had known before. As a result he could spare himself completely from self-condemnation and self-depreciation.

The diversity of Paul's self-image is apparent in his writings. For example, in Romans 7:24 he says, "Wretched man that I am! Who will deliver me from this body of death?" While regarding himself as wretched, he did not measure his true value for himself in these terms. He simply recognized the reality of his human condition. Later on, when his personal situation had probably deteriorated even more, he writes in lofty terms unequaled in the New Testament. Ephesians 1:3 declares, "Blessed be the God and Father of our Lord Jesus Christ, who has blessed us in Christ with every spiritual blessing. . . ."

These words of exultation to the Ephesians were written while Paul was ill and in jail, awaiting execution, and nursing back to health a sick friend who had come to visit him. Obviously he had something to react to other than his own physical circumstances or his status as an educated Jew turned Christian martyr.

Even his successes as a Christian were open to some question. From his jail cell, he wrote to several of his churches admonishing them to refrain from such hideous sins as drunkenness, adultery, incest, pagan worship, and the like. His visible achievements as a church leader would sadden many a bishop's heart. The conclusion has to be that Paul saw himself clearly as an object of the grace of God privileged to do His work. So dominant in his mind was this fact that nothing else really mattered. Not even his sanity was worth protecting in light of who he was as a Christian. (See 2 Cor. 5 and Eph. 1.)

A number of things characterize us who are objects of the love of God. First of all, we are *known people.* Nothing in the mind of any of us is unknown to God. He reads us clearly and completely—better than the most skilled analyst. It is only we who know so little about ourselves. God has far outdistanced us in getting to know us—every well-concealed motive, every latent behavioral tendency, every unresolved conflict, every unsanctified inhibition is clearly understood.

In *The Transparent Self** Professor Sidney Jourard makes the point that it is the unrevealed life that is the troubled

*Sidney M. Jourard, *The Transparent Self: Self-Disclosure and Well-Being* (Princeton, N.J.: D. Van Nostrand Company, Inc., 1964), p. 21.

life. The more secretive we are with ourselves, the more protective we need to be; the more deeply hidden are our most treasured sins, the more likely we are to be candidates for emotional and spiritual trouble. To be open to both God and man is to be on the way to healing. Paul makes the point clearly in 2 Corinthians 5:11: "What we are is known to God, and I hope it is known also to your conscience." He hid nothing of himself, even his personal foibles, to those who needed his spiritual nurture.

I remember reading a study of the school records of high-school dropouts in one large city school system. The most significant finding was that these students were largely unknown people. Teachers had trouble recalling their names; their cumulative records in the office were the thinnest and often lacking important information. In the minds of others, they were nobodies, unrevealed people who hid from the world and from others.

In several instances in the New Testament, Jesus is spoken of as revealing Himself to His disciples. I am not sure of the full implication of these references, but I have wondered how well Jesus' disciples knew Him. If Jesus was truly human as we are, was He not also subject to the same need to share Himself with His closest friends? Did He need the same feedback from friends about how He was getting along in life? I suspect He did, and that does not diminish for one moment His full divinity as the Son of God. It simply illustrates how deeply into our lives His redemptive power can go and how it should permeate our Christian fellowship.

The koinonia movement in the church today offers genuine hope for more fully developed lives and more fully operative redemption experiences for all of us. In its best forms, this movement encourages openness and assures us of progress in our growth. Out of it can come deep relationships and mutual understandings that quickly circumvent suspicion and possible breaches in fellowship. By being known men we, too, can affirm, ". . . by the grace of God, I am what I am."

Second, we are ambivalent men. A bundle of mixed-up emotions seems to characterize most of our waking moments. Seldom do we respond to any situation with a clear, pure motive. Competing feelings are our lot. I, for example, enjoy my job, but hate the schedule. I find the people I work with honorable and devoted people—mostly. Some days they would be easier to handle if they weren't such great Christians, then I could clobber them without much misgiving. My wife is a wonderful and charming person, but she's bugging me at the moment about a plumbing problem. My kids are a pleasure, especially when they're asleep. Otherwise they want the car, stay out too late, and think that Sunday School is less than terrific.

Psychologists discovered long ago that love and hate aren't opposite ends of the same pole. In fact, love and hate exist strongly side by side. We often love and hate the same people. Consider troubled marriages, for instance. Every marriage has some ambivalence in it. It's in the marriages ending in divorce that most ambivalence shows up. So intense are the competing emotions that the couple splits up. That takes care of the hate. Now all they have left is the love. So they date each other after the divorce, sometimes sleep together, sometimes even remarry. That gets the hate back. Now they are more mixed up than ever.

How do you feel about your faith? Do you ever have mixed feelings about that? I've known Christians almost strangled in ambivalence about their faith. They know faith is the means of salvation, but they can't seem to shed the guilt they feel. Somebody is always telling them what they aren't and what they ought to be. So they are miserable. Usually that somebody wants everyone to repeat the atonement all over again just for the theological misery of it. To some it just doesn't seem fair that the gift of eternal

150

life is really a gift. So they make themselves miserable trying both to accept the gift and then to repay God for His grace. Nonsense! The gift is free, and loving service is the appropriate response, but not miserable servitude trying to gain spiritual Brownie points to earn one's salvation.

Paul's life was one of ambivalence, too. In Romans 7:15 he writes, "I do not understand my own actions. For I do not do what I want, but I do the very thing I hate." Then he thanks God that in spite of the way he feels and acts, God gives the victory, and as a result there is no condemnation for those who are Christians!

Even Jesus struggled with ambivalence, too. Though we sometimes deny His humanity, the Bible is pretty clear on this point. In fact, at the time that He faced the cross we have perhaps the strongest of all expressions of ambivalence. In Luke 22:42 we hear Him pray, "Father, if thou art willing, remove this cup from me; nevertheless not my will, but thine, be done."

Our most difficult decisions often provoke the greatest ambivalence in us. If we are growing, productive people, our choices are usually between alternatives that are both good and attractive. Therefore to choose one is to let another worthwhile opportunity pass. So often that has been the case as we have decided to move or to stay in one job or location or another. Only with the passing of time and some firm commitment to God has our loss been sustained, even in good moves we have made.

So the first step in handling ambivalence is to recognize that it exists. Don't deny it. No spiritual progress occurs that way. You'll only drive the ambivalent feelings underground, and they will operate anyway in your subconscious mind. Face the fact of mixed emotions. They were known to Paul, as well as to Jesus, and He will go with you and give you the victory you need.

The person apparently without ambivalence is the one

who is in most trouble. Lack of this human conflict is symptomatic of a lack of awareness of some important aspect of one's own experience. Therefore, when genuine mixed emotion stirs us up, it can be a healthy sign. It may mean that we are becoming more sensitive to the real subtleties of a problem that needs our attention. Respect yourself as an ambivalent soul, and know that God cares how you feel.

Third, we are common men. In spite of the fact that much attention is given nowadays to the fact of our uniqueness, we are still all one kind of person, apart from God and without hope except the hope He gives us. If that sounds dire, wait for the rest of the story. It's probably better news than you had imagined.

One of the most misused Bible verses is found in Romans 3:22,23. Usually these verses are quoted to prove the sinfulness of us all and therefore our need for salvation. While this is true about us, it is the secondary premise of this Scripture. The intent of the verse is to cap a discussion Paul has been having with the Romans. He was about to go to Rome for trial and would meet some fellow Christians for the first time. Since he was a Jew and they were Gentiles, he was anxious to point up some similarities between them. So he discussed the fact that since the coming of Christ there is no more advantage to being a Jew. Now they were all the same, just sinners needing a lot of help. "Since all have sinned and fall short of the glory of God." Or so we often quote it, leaving out the first phrase, "For there is no distinction," meaning no difference between Jews and Gentiles.

The point about being a common man is that there is a lot of experience we all know about. Many of our awarenesses are universal. Therefore, when we share ourselves with others it is not as odd an experience as it may seem. There is scarcely a human spiritual need or frustration we know that most others haven't known. Certainly, the cultural differences among people are often great, but we have made so much of this lately that it seems as if we lived in separate worlds entirely. In the common need for relationship with God and each other, little is uncommon. We ought to feel much less reticence in sharing the good news of Jesus Christ. As someone has put it, we are only beggars who have found bread telling other beggars where to find it.

But being a common man means that God knows a lot about us. He once was one of us, too. He was tempted and tried in every way we know, and didn't slip off His·throne in the process. We sometimes get the false notion that there are human experiences God doesn't recognize and that therefore He cannot help us in them. But it isn't so. The basis for our fellowship with both man and God is broad and common. The only real differences that count are those between the seekers and the finders, and all of us have been seekers at one time or another.

Paul illustrates his commonness when he declares that he wants to be all things to all men in order to aid in their salvation. It is apparent that he had acquired a great deal of adaptability during the course of his spiritual growth. Once a bitter Jew, spewing hate everywhere, he was transformed into a loving, caring child of God. He was able to be a barbarian to the barbarians, yet argue philosophy with the Greeks on Mars Hill. Using their thought systems and categories, he expounded to them the unknown God and declared Him to be the Christ. In the synagogues and temples, he opened narrow-minded eyes to see the Messiah of prophecy given in the Old Testament. As a Roman citizen, he argued his case before several tribunals, always declaring his faith in Christ.

The common man is an adaptable man, in Christ. I doubt that there is any theory of cultural adaptability anywhere in the psychological literature that accounts for the abilities of Paul. His background was anything but conducive to such flexibility. In fact, rigidity, not flexibility, was the goal of his unconverted mind, for he wanted to make everyone a narrow legalist. His conversion and growth are examples of the possibilities that exist for common men, like you and me. Nowhere in Scripture is there any indication of any limit on what we can become under the grace of God.

So, when God looks at you, what do you think He sees? A common man? A common man, yes, but more. In fact, when God looks at you, do you think He can tell any difference between you and His own Son? I'm not concerned about whether you answer the question yes or no. You may even want to get into a theological argument with me at this point. But if you will study your Bible diligently, I doubt that you'll be able to find any evidence that when God looks at man He sees anyone other than the Son He sent, Jesus. So pull yourself up to your full rights and privileges as a joint-heir with Christ.

The final point I want to make about our identity in Christ, and the most important one, is that we are *righteous men.* You *are* a righteous person—in Christ. Apart from Him, you have no hope. But if you have chosen to be His person and assumed His forgiveness and status, you are entitled to call yourself righteous.

Perhaps that sounds a little presumptuous. I know a number of people who become wary when I suggest this idea to them. They seem to feel that they can call themselves Christians, all right, but they also feel they have to do something, or be something other than what they are, to claim an identity of righteousness. They feel they must gain church status, or spend a few pious years of service, or make some sacrifice before they can attain such an attribute. But the fact is, Christ attributes His righteousness to us and it is not mixed with one whit of our human accomplishment. That's what grace is all about!

In John's Gospel we are told that the function of the Holy Spirit is to convict of sin, of righteousness, and of judgment. Universally guilty man doesn't have too much trouble with the conviction of sin and judgment. He is painfully aware of his problems in this regard. He has been working on his guilt-reduction problems as long as he has been alive, always saying "excuse me," always playing the acceptability games that make one tolerable to society. So to simply assume the identity of righteousness because of the historical act of God seems farfetched and very unconventional.

But the Holy Spirit keeps plugging away at us. He keeps reminding us that there is no righteousness in us on the basis of our own efforts or merits. No amount of "please excuse me for living" will get us anywhere. The same old shortcomings keep dominating our lives, and we get little relief. Oh, once in a while some existential philosopher will come along and smooth things over for an hour or two, but when that reprieve wears off we are back to our old natural state again. But through Christ, the Holy Spirit gives us a gift of assurance that Someone has made up all the differences between what we are and what we ought to be. As a result, we can assume ourselves to be righteous people. And when that fact dawns on us in all of its God-prompted force, a lot of things begin to happen.

I was in the college several years before the reality of this truth got through to me. School had been pretty much of a drag. I had found myriads of friends, lots of intellectual stimulation, and the opportunity to work through many problems, but the real glow of confident life just wasn't there. I suppose I was still achieving my own atonement. I was a Christian, at least in my belief system and behavior, mostly, yet I found it difficult to assume any assurance of genuine freedom in life. But God was at work, chipping away at my assumptions both about Himself and about me. And then one day the truth dawned! I could really be free and assume full status as a righteous person.

This experience came as I was transferring from junior

college to a four-year university. A genuine spiritual awakening had come to the campus, but had missed me completely. I was tired of my efforts to keep things going on the Christian front, and I was not sure of what I should do in life—I had run out of gas spiritually and emotionally. The moment of change came, not in church nor in the stimulus of a great spiritual exercise complete with stereophonic intonations, but on a bright, clear day, when I was home on my parents' farm between school terms. I was feeding the cows, mulling through all my assumptions about life in general, and once more feeling the frustration of my experiences. At that instant, I heaved a pitch fork into the haystack and muttered, "OK, God, you're on! You get whatever is in me, both good and bad."

Changes difficult to describe began to take place. I soon discovered it was all right to be happy. Why inhibit simple joy any longer? I began to lose some of my unsanctified inhibitions. My attitude changed from that of a loser to that of a winner in life. No longer was I willing to accept the put-downs I had felt from those who were still struggling for status. I didn't bother to put them down either, because now I understood the mess they were in. Instead I had a way out of the situation. And I found a lot of people quite willing to listen when they discovered I had received a genuine gift.

Some intellectual changes began to take place, too. My faith had rested at least partly on a fairly airtight, logical, scriptural, orthodox theology. Somehow this seemed necessary to keep God from falling off His throne. I really felt that the right system was important, and it is, but not to keep God on His pedestal. I soon discovered that He has a way of staying put no matter what my intellectual questions may be. As a result, I was able to think through other systems without fear of being done in spiritually. When I hear people haggling about this or that doctrinal insignificance, I wonder if they aren't caught in the web

156

of having to protect God from Christians and themselves from full atonement! But for me, the Bible became an open book, and my relationship to God was affirming, building, and joyous, no longer condemning and wearying.

You *can* safely assume the righteousness of Christ, if you are His. I know of no other grounds for reworking so completely one's self-identity. It will positively change life. Eventually, personal feelings of inferiority and worthlessness will vanish. Fear and a sense of inadequacy will disappear, for it is virtually impossible to hang on to them when one lives continually with the God-given assumption of righteousness!

"From now on, therefore, we regard no one from a human point of view; even though we once regarded Christ from a human point of view, we regard him thus no longer. Therefore, if any one is in Christ, he is a new creation; the old has passed away, behold, the new has come" (2 Cor. 5:16,17).

# 12 *Mind Changes in Christian Experience*

At one time I served as a consulting psychologist for a Christian ranch attempting to help teen-age boys who were either predelinquent or on probation from the courts. These youngsters had many things in common. Unloved, some had come from homes where there had been little restraint; others from homes where there had been an excessive amount of restraint, even brutality. Uniformly, the boys' morale was low. Many were bitter. They assumed that they were not heirs to a life that mattered; the usual opportunities available to teen-agers could never be theirs. So, what use was there in planning for the future? The boys lived totally for the present moment, often in fear. To endure that moment was oppressive enough—no need to worry about tomorrow's trouble.

The boys refused, too, to discuss such an immediate problem as the remaining months in high school. They failed to see education as a means to an end. To them school was a drag, a pain to be endured. Frequent failure and disappointment blurred time-perceptions. Time was merely a moment crowded with hurt; time was something to be done with, to ignore. Thinking about time became an uncomfortable mental exercise. The more disturbed the

boy, the more he lacked ability to plan ahead, to make reasonable self-predictions about the future. This abnormal attitude in regard to time became a symptom of emotional disturbance.

I became aware of this symptom again when I was teaching a class in child and adolescent psychology. A large class, it had its share of distractable, uneasy students. In the front row sat five disinterested young women, who insisted on smoking during the lecture. They came and went as they pleased during the class hour. But as we progressed through ideas about how normal youngsters grow, as documented by research, their interest picked up remarkably. To their surprise, they discovered that they lived outside the bounds of usual, normal human experience. The most revealing jolt came when we discussed the normal youngster's perception of time and how it changed with growth.

The very young child is frequently confused about the

future. He learns first to differentiate between time periods of the present and the immediate past. Learning to differentiate between the present and the future takes more time. In fact, it takes some youngsters years before they realize that time, apart from their own life, exists at all.

Many ten-year-olds cannot conceive of time as it existed between World War I and World War II. In the same way ancient history is totally incomprehensible to most teen-agers. And accurate prediction of personal experiences as they relate appropriately to plans for the future comes rather late in the high-school years.

The girls in my class learned that their perceptions of time and their ability to plan appropriately for the future had been significantly distorted. Living in a constant uproar and disturbance had given their minds tunnel vision, which focused only on the present. They constantly made planning errors. They had difficulty choosing a major. A couple of them could not readily tell when they were going to be graduated, or if they were. In fact graduation appeared so far away it could not be related to present experiences. These girls deferred making a vocational choice, too. What choices were made often had little bearing on the subjects they studied. Poor timing in these choices led most of them to graduate late, to drop out of school, or to exhaust financial resources before their education was completed.

Yet, their discovery that they deviated from the normal concepts of time opened avenues for discussion. On several occasions we talked about the Christian's dimension of time and eternity and its implications in planning one's life. One of the girls experienced a great deal of emotional healing, which was evidenced in meaningful management of time and planning for the future.

Note one wise man's observation about the matter of time:

"As a child, I crawled and time crawled.

As a toddler, I walked and time walked along.

161

As a youth, I ran, and time ran, too.
I'm older now, I walk again, but time flies.
Life is done, where has time gone?"

It does seem that the older we grow the more quickly time passes. In fact, now my days fly so fast I frequently question my stewardship of time. How about you? Do you recall elementary school days? Time passed slowly then. You could hardly wait for school to be dismissed. The clock on the wall marked the time—3:35 P.M. You buried your face in your book and read fast and furiously in an effort to hurry the clock. When you thought you could stand it no longer you looked at it again. Do you remember its shout? 3:38!

Now I think that perhaps the ground of experience in perceiving time is shifting. World events occur more quickly. Significant social revolutions come and go several times in a lifetime. Social change that previously occurred slowly now flashes on the screen and off again with such lightning speed that we cannot comprehend it.

I recall the lecture of an anthropologist who had visited an island in the South Seas and observed the customs of its primitive people. Their mode of living and social life style had changed little in hundreds of years. Yet, in the very center of the main village, in an open area created especially for it, sat an American-made freezer in all its glory. The island had no electricity with which to use the appliance, but the invention became a symbol of the dreams of the community. It signaled the fact that as much change could take place in the next forty years as had taken place in the past four hundred.

Our ability to manage our time and our life span indicates the quality of our mental and spiritual lives. The Scriptures admonish: "So teach us to number our days, that we may apply our hearts unto wisdom" (Ps. 90:12). How we manage our time reveals how mature we are.

In my studies I have observed a number of approaches

to the management of time. The first is evidenced in an individual I'll call the *time-grinder*. I once worked with a time-grinder, a man who, knowing he wasn't going to live forever, made every minute count. Sometimes I thought he tried to make some moments count twice. He could be found in his office every morning at seven. He seldom left before seven in the evening. After dinner he either attended school or taught in a local university. By the time he was fifty years old, he had chalked up thirty-two years of experience in public service and had earned two doctoral degrees. He rarely took a vacation. In one seven-year period, he was away from his job only one day. Nothing but exhaustion could deter him.

This may sound like devotion and diligence, and in most people's minds, it was. Yet this man was a highly frustrated person, and those around him who picked up his dissonant vibrations became frustrated, too.

There is also the man who is a *time-killer*. Call him a sluggard if you will. He's like one of my more inept colleagues who always arrived at appointments and meetings fifteen minutes to a half hour early.

"Why?" I asked him one day.

He shrugged. "I just like to kill time, I guess," he said. "Nothing else to do."

This man didn't realize that time is the stuff life is made of. When you kill time, you kill a little of yourself. Life is what's happening while you are making other plans. Time-killing anesthetizes sensitivity to what's happening presently.

It's surprising how many people in the world place no value on the time they have been given. They kill it and go blindly to a disappointing demise.

When I think of the time-killer, I think of a class reunion I emceed several years ago. Twenty-five years had passed since graduation, so we were all eager to see how each person looked and to learn what he had accomplished.

One of our classmates was noticeably absent, however. Because he had been an outstanding student, we were disappointed. Later we learned that fear had kept him from the reunion. He felt that he had done nothing significant with his time and his talents. Guilt-ridden, he dreaded reviewing his life with anyone. Although steadily employed, he had had no real purpose in life and had just gone along killing the clock. Should he ever surmise what he might have been, could he stand the shock?

Now let's consider the *time-preserver.* He's radical in a different sense. He believes that the present moment must be enjoyed, and if possible, retained forever. The past has no value, nor can the future equate with the now.

In his *Study of History\** Arnold Toynbee talks of the savior of the time machine, the preserver of the now. Certain civilizations chose this approach as a means to prevent cultural and political demise. Take China as an example. To preserve the present moment for what was once the world's greatest society, this country built walls to prevent any outside influence from penetrating and changing the status quo. The walls became the time machine. *Now,* these people said, will be *forever.* But history has shown that, for hundreds of years, progress was stymied. Only recently has change occurred, and violently, too.

We see examples of time-preservers all around us. The most common are the people who insist on preserving all our institutions in their present form without modification. This is true particularly of our churches, our schools, and their programs. Selfish sacredness is equated with cultural experience that must not be tampered with.

Inability to accept change in institutional life is a symptom of genuine uneasiness about time. A fixation upon a certain time-and-space experience seems necessary to protect oneself from the passing of life. The struggle to

*Arnold J. Toynbee, *A Study of History* (New York: Oxford University Press. 1945), p. 538.

hold onto the good old days results in an attempt to spiritualize present institutions. Their structure, styles, and functions are theologically rationalized. When this happens, those who seek change are forced to become involved in theological battles. But the theological conflict is a charade. The true issue is not theological, but personal and emotional. Unfortunately, many believe the theological rationalizations, and those who seek change begin to question whether or not they have fallen into unbelief. False guilt, which might have been avoided, engulfs both reformer and defender. As a result, progress is impeded and institutions flounder.

Finally, there is the *time-exploiter.* To many of us he is the most recent phenomenon. The rise of existential philosophy in everyday life and among common people has helped promote this approach to the handling of time. Even television commercials advise us to exploit time. You only go once through life, so make your grab while you can and with as much gusto as possible. This is the boob-tube's beer-can philosophy, which represents the thought pattern of many people. Enjoy the *now.* Buy *now,* pay *later.* Live it up!

In some instances, individuals have used their inability to reconcile themselves to a proper handling of time as an excuse for riot. History's been a bum steer, they shout. Let's tear up our institutions. Down with tradition. Unseat the establishment. Whatever takes place after the revolution is bound to be better than the present. This clamor for change has come from segments of society, past and present. Again the problem involves deviate living in time. Since eternity is unknowable, or nonexistent, why think about it? In a sense the drug addict says this, too. The present is all there is. So, cop out; lay waste institutions, traditions, and cultures. Do something new. Life is transient at best.

Dr. Theodore W. Anderson, the late president of the

Evangelical Covenant Church, refused to accept this philosophy. In one of his sermons, he said, "I would live as though I had but one day; I would plan as if I had a thousand years." In his own way he paraphrased the Scripture quoted previously: "So teach us to number our days, that we may apply our hearts unto wisdom" (Ps. 90:12).

Because the Christian holds an eternal perspective, he understands this kind of counsel. He knows that all things will be reconciled, in Christ, eventually. Therefore he ought to be more comfortable in the presence of time than anyone else. His life is limitless, his destiny eternal. He is not compelled to settle all issues of the world in his threescore and ten years. He enjoys genuine relaxation, and economy of energy and resource, in the eternal perspective. He knows that nervous tensions need not develop over that which is temporal. When we choose to recondition our emotions with an eternal view of time and institutions, and for that matter, all other things, a lot of our psychosomatic illnesses will subside and the peace of God will reign once more.

The key is the *redemption of time.* As Christians we ought not yield to wasteful resignation in our consideration of time. Neither should we give ourselves to frantic rushing through God's kingdom. Were heaven to move at as hectic a pace as most local churches, it would not be a place of rest. We have much to learn about the appropriate, Christian, gut reaction to time.

Another mind change that occurs with growth involves a change in one's priorities. Different things become important. Certain once-critical questions no longer hold crucial significance. Newly discovered needs come into focus making the adrenalin flow in response to new stimulations.

In a study of priorities, I once tried an interesting experiment. For one week I kept a record of the opening lines of people who came into my office. Almost half of the conversations began with the words, "I know you are busy, but. . . ." As if to say, "I know that your highest priorities do not include me at this time, but if you can spare a minute I'll apologize for bothering you with my problem."

After one such obsequious greeting from a good friend and colleague I replied, "Baloney! I'm not busy, and you're not busy. So why hedge? What's more important than my talking to you right now?" My friend was so stunned he forgot his mission. When he remembered what he came for, he couldn't find words to express himself. We both lapsed into silly laughter every time he tried to talk. You see, we realized to what extent priorities had gone awry. We acknowledged that the many mistaken concepts we hold about what is most important make us feel as though we have to apologize when we want to talk to each other.

Recurrently I find this true. Once I worked in an institution where my office was only a few yards from the office of the chief administrator. But it took two weeks to get an appointment with him. He hibernated for months at a time. When he did open his door, he was so preoccupied with the stack of junk on his desk that he scarcely heard the reason for a subordinate's call. Needless to say, he didn't last many years as an administrator. There were too many broken connections that occurred between people because too much time elapsed between contacts. Delay caused ambiguous dialogue about muddled problems. Relationships were strained and stress heightened by silence. The man didn't know his priorities.

On the other hand, when there is grace in our lives, people become more important than functions. A few years ago I was part of a team of school psychologists who visited several California guidance administrators in search of good innovative ideas. One person we met was head counselor of a large junior high school that was suffering from growing pains. Double sessions, scores of new teachers, and lack of room complicated the guidance program immensely. When we queried the counselor about her role, she clutched a box of registration cards and in a shrill harried voice countered, "As long as I keep track of this, I'm OK! When I don't have this, I'm lost!"

We realized immediately that this woman, and two full-time assistants, were so inundated by growth in their work load that registration cards had become more important than people. They had no time to see anyone. Students became intruders in their lives. They upset the counseling office!

The function of a schedule or of any administrative process is to facilitate relationships among people in the presence of time limits. Yet it is easy to become such a slave to functions and schedules that people get lost in the rush to make time units mesh properly. In our hectic lives of complicated time slots, it is often better to junk the appointment list and just listen to the person at hand.

Nationals in some countries understand this time-priority concept. Our Latin-American neighbors say that time is friendship. Missionary friends tell me that if Africans sense distress in an individual's life, they will come and sit with him. They don't plan to say anything, nor to solve anything. By their presence they just want to convey concern. This is a good example of a proper perspective regarding people, presence, and time. When we learn to put people first in our time allotments, we'll be much more redemptive in our influence. Let God be our guide. He puts people ahead of functions, persons above time slots, life above organizational patterns.

Priorities involve attitudes, too. Under grace, the attitude of affirmation takes precedence over the attitude of negation. The reason for this is soundly biblical. The essential message of God to us is one of hope, love, deliverance, redemption—all attributes of affirmation. Our life is no longer shaped by death, failure, and lack of forgiveness. That's negation and a valid reason why our relationships should be characterized by grace, not by impunity. We affirm people; we do not negate them.

Several years ago I conducted a study of the statements made by junior-high-school teachers to their classes. My colleagues and I found a way to classify each subject and predicate uttered by a teacher in a thirty-minute teaching session. The statements were rated on a five-point scale. A *1*-rating meant that a statement was warm, supportive, and encouraging to the student. A *5*-rating meant the statement was hostile, punitive, or discouraging to the student. A *3*-rating classified statements of neutral character, usually made in explanation of a lesson. Ratings of *2* and *4* represented intermediate values on the scale. A *2* indicated a moderately supportive statement; a *4,* a moderately unsupportive statement.

We were pleased to find that most teachers were more often warm than they were hostile. Perhaps this speaks well of the teaching profession. In another test we measured the relative degree of anxiety and tranquility experienced by students. The results confirmed what we had believed to be true. When teachers were hostile and unsupportive, anxiety rose. When they were supportive and friendly, anxiety diminished.

In this same experiment, we also asked principals to rate their teachers according to the quality of teaching they believed prevailed. Again, affirming teachers rated higher than those who were inclined to be negative.

One might ask if it is possible for a person to change attitudes of this kind. Yes, it is. Benjamin Franklin is supposed to have claimed that he changed from a curmudgeon to an affable gentleman by consciously changing the nature of his responses to people. Through this action his acceptance by others improved. So it can be with us. When we choose to affirm people, they respond affirmatively to us. When we are punitive, we drive men away. Recall that Jesus attracted a motley assortment of men around Him.

169

Winebibbers and gluttons ate with Him. The poor received friendship and help. The sick flocked to Him. These people were recipients of the affirmation and redemption that He allowed to flow from Him. Like Christ, let us affirm and love people; let us put impunity aside. Redeemed people lose their need to punish. They are not driven to correct every visible sin. Instead they earn the love of men who, because of affirmation, choose to sin no more.

Another change in priority involves a change in relationship with God. If we choose the best, we enter into a first-name relationship that is more personal, less abstract, less theologically burdened.

I've often noticed how, when some people pray, they seem unable to talk to God without first repeating long theological affirmations that He exists, exists in three persons, lives in heaven, has become incarnate in human flesh, has pretty well established his superiority over angels, earthquakes, demons, and the fate of the human race. I don't know who is supposed to be impressed, but I wonder if God doesn't chuckle when He listens to such discourse from the mouths of His saints. How would you like to have someone establish your ancestry, address, attributes, past history, and role in society before he says, "Hello!"

To be personal does not mean we are disrespectful. On the contrary it means that we show our respect more fully in a personal relationship. To be personal implies a state of openness and a vulnerability to one another. In an open relationship, respect is felt more keenly than an insult would be. So the fact that one uses personal terms in conversation does not, in and of itself, evidence disrespect. Rather it is one's conduct, when it is personal, that matters.

Many people have trouble being personal with God. They have been conditioned to experience Him only in worshipful awe. Or they have known Him only in great theological contexts which, to the human mind, seem incompatible with personal relationships. But one need not

of their sensitivity, bring themselves to accept the recom-
mendation. It hurt them, too. Yet, because they ducked
the immediate pain, they had to face a more serious backlash.

The truth remains, however, that as we grow, we hurt
more, we fear more, we experience more. We become
sensitive, more vulnerable, more acquainted with the sor-
rows and the griefs of other men.

Do you recall that I began this line of thought by saying
that it was a joy to perceive an ever-widening array of
human experience? But how can increased fear be joyous?
Am I inconsistent in my arguments? It seems so, I know.
Yet such perception is joyous—not in some ascetic sense,
either. As we learn to perceive more of life and feel needs
more keenly, we become more realistic, more reality
oriented. It is a fundamental truth that reality, and the
accurate perception of it, is therapeutic even if it does hurt.
This is because as we perceive more fully, we are also
able to experience our joys more fully. And for Christians,
there is much more joy than sorrow. This must be what
Paul meant when he told us to count it joy when we find
ourselves in tribulation. If Paul hadn't proved that he
believed this, he would long ago have been chalked off
as a masochistic nut, or at least as a foolish ascetic who
got big kicks out of pain.

And what about experiences that effect the entire universe? Isn't it surprising that God has entrusted to us the
solutions to these pressing problems—matters like the population explosion, worldwide pollution, transplants of
organs, and altered genetic structures? I find it amazing
that the Bible is more silent than vocal about these matters.
Oh, I know that some individuals insist that the Bible gives
precise direction regarding them, but really, much is left
for us to figure out. Have you ever wrestled with the
theology of organ transplants, for instance? When science
finds a way to preserve your gifted, experienced, well-ad-

justed brain and to place it in the body of a person thirty years younger than you, whose soul becomes whose? Who goes to heaven? You or the recipient of your mind? Work on that for awhile and when you figure it out, write me and tell me what your answer is. If you are driven up a wall because you can't come up with an answer and aren't able to chuckle about it, I'll say your salvation is missing an important ingredient—the ability to experience joy in a dilemma.

Some people can't afford to be joyful. They are so busy guarding themselves against hurt while working out their salvation that they forget that joy is part of the Christian experience. If they felt joy, they would also feel hurt, and then they might lose their cool. How about you? Do you find it better to be miserable than to lose your cool? Think again. Maybe your cool is preventing an experience of grace. You might consider letting God have your cool, too.

I knew a college dean who was known for his unemotional approach to every problem. Nothing bothered or upset him. But nothing made him happy, either. To him hilarity involved nothing more than a slight quiver of the upper lip; extreme sadness, a slight quiver of the lower lip. Poor Dr. Cool! He never knew what a good emotional airing meant, nor did he know the warmth of close personal friendships. He lived and died alone.

I'm glad I've found joy in the long straight flight of a golf ball; in the smile of a daughter who just beat her best backstroke record in the local pool; in a cool evening breeze as I sit on the back steps of my home.

At present I'm trying to find joy in winds whipping off Lake Michigan. Maybe I'll make it. I'm also trying to find joy in running out of gas on the expressway at rush hour in 98 degree temperature and 99 percent humidity in downtown Chicago. Maybe I'll learn that, too. But I'm not sure I want to. It's that old problem of ambivalence again. I only know life is a lot richer when I open my emotions to God who is involved in everything.

Emotional constriction is a symptom of generalized hang-ups in life. When we feel neither joy nor pain, we are in danger. It is the unmoved soul who is headed for trouble, not the one who feels a wide range of experiences. If we work hard to contain a single emotional experience, chances are we will constrict a lot of other feelings, too. But when we fearlessly let God in on all of our feelings, He redeems us and sets us free—free to sense all that, in His omniscience He has provided for us.

# 13 A Case in Point

Not long ago I learned to know a man by reading the record of his life. Though he lived in another time and in another part of the world, his personal story illustrates most of the ideas presented thus far. As I tell you his history, try to put yourself in his shoes. See if you can feel as he must have felt.

I first discovered him as a middle-aged man. It's that time of life when one makes many personal assessments. I'm middle-aged myself so I can identify quite readily with our friend's experience. We tend to aggrandize our experiences as we grow older. We subtly add significance to things we have done. We forget our failures. Our sterling qualities emerge virtually without blemish.

But the friend of whom I speak had occasion to be a realist. In middle age he suffered from reasonably severe physical handicaps. His vision was impaired, possibly because of an epileptic or diabetic condition. We are not at all sure of this, but we recall there were problems of loss of consciousness associated with poor eyesight. Naturally this presented problems. Being alone and having to

177

communicate through writing must have been very difficult. Imagine his frustration trying to find someone who would take a few minutes to read his mail for him! He was in jail at the time. And the outlook was grim. Further, the literacy rate was low where he was confined, and it is doubtful that many of his keepers could or would honor his literary requests.

Our friend was a man of letters. He had studied in the outstanding schools of his day. An excellent student, he had majored in history and theology. His academic reputation was well known. In fact, his perceptive writings were regarded as treasures and passed from group to group so that many could profit from his ideas.

But he was a peculiar man, peculiar in the sense that he acted on his beliefs. In this he was different from us. We aren't quite so involved with what we know. More often we stumble over some truth and get up and go on as though nothing ever happened. Not so our friend. Something propelled him to act upon what he learned. When his ideas changed, his actions changed. And people were startled by his altered behavior. He might well have borne the radical label had he lived in the contemporary scene.

As a result of his profound commitment to ideas, he became a leader among men. At a young age, his church conferred on him leadership roles often reserved for men many years his senior. And while young, he was elected to the highest authoritative body of his religious order. In some ways it seemed that he was an eccentric, single of mind and purpose—a zealot in the true sense of the word.

We know little of his early history and background. We know nothing about his relationships to parents or about early successes and traumas. We can only guess what his childhood was like. It would seem that the personality he developed could have used some help. As a young adult, he acted like a hostile religious intellectual. People held

178

him both in esteem and in fear. We find no sense of loving closeness from descriptions we have of him. When he writes about himself, he avoids all reference to early childhood and youth. I suspect that he was deprived of a great deal of early healthy emotional care. This dearth of information about his childhood may be significant in view of what happened later.

Often the hostile intellectual becomes a leader. It is strange, but sometimes emotional illness entices men more than health does. How many times have you seen a religious leader with a burr in his saddle and a message of stress on his heart win large followings wherever he goes? It happens over and over again, and our friend may have been one who exercised these psychological propellents. In fact, so punitive had his personality become that he often sought legal redress in the courts for those who opposed him. Often they were cast into prison. Even death sentences were meted out to his adversaries in the name of the Kingdom of God. One wonders how long this could go on without conflicts building in his mind and perplexing his soul.

Then at the very height of his punitive religious career, he experienced an about-face. A blinding, mind-blowing, ego-assaulting jolt discomposed him. The latent conflict that had been brewing now burst upon him with tempest fury. And he changed as few men have been known to change. Both his followers and his victims were astounded. No one could comprehend what had happened. Nor did anyone know how to deal with him. Incomprehensible as it was, the public was forced to wrestle with the change. Now the man loved his enemies. They, in turn, felt he should be accepted, though they still feared him. On the other hand his friends ostracized him. He no longer carried out the repugnant orders of his sect. Instead he disappeared from view for several months, no doubt in an effort to collect his own thoughts.

However, regardless of circumstances, no man with leadership aptitude loses his ability to gather a following. In his change, this man had lost none of this latent talent. But now his zeal was redirected. Genuine love had replaced hostility. New relationships began to develop for new reasons. Everywhere he went people listened to his story. Some argued with him. They provoked him in any way they could to test the validity of his experience. But his character was firm. He could not be shaken.

In time, a number of groups formed that were sympathetic to his teachings. These people adopted his new life style as theirs. His new-found zeal became the incentive that caused him to travel to all the great trade centers of the world. Here his ideas were challenged in every marketplace of thought.

Later a time of disappointment set in. Some of his followers fell into moral disrepute. His teachings became an excuse for the grossest immoralities, sexual deviance and lust. Besides, there arose a group who challenged his authority and his logic. Jealous peers tried desperately to discredit him. They wanted to appropriate some of his popularity for themselves. Eventually nearly all of the groups that fanned around him disintegrated, never to be heard from again, except in written epitaphs.

The legal principles in his part of the world were quite different from ours. We say a man is innocent until proved guilty. But where he lived, men were presumed guilty until proven innocent. Such was the case in this man's life. His ideas finally caught the attention of civil authority. So much clamor arose when he taught that public disturbances were common. The authorities finally decided that something had to be done to curb these outbreaks. Consequently he was brought to trial on several occasions. The first trials were generally insignificant. He was regarded as an odd one who really did nothing wrong—it was just the manner in which he went about it. So cool it, admonished the counselors of the law! But cool it, he could not. He just wasn't made that way!

Trial followed trial, usually in a sequence of appeals to higher courts. Finally a conviction from the highest court was obtained. He must die for his crime.

So we find him at middle age—convicted and sentenced to die. With his followers in disrepute for their immorality, his personal career could be regarded by most as shipwrecked. No assets accumulated. No retirement plans made. No family that cared. Little visible impact made on the society in which he lived. What now?

Are you able to identify with our friend? How would you feel if this were your situation? Another thought—how would you explain the tremendous change that had taken place in his life—a change that made a loving shepherd out of a hostile zealot?

These are not farfetched considerations. At middle age you have either obtained an education, or you have not. You have successfully married and raised a family, or you have not. You have achieved some stability of career, or you have not. You have achieved early aspirations, or you have settled for less. The opportunities have diminished with the years, and now there is no turning back.

It isn't surprising that many people become depressed at this stage of life. At least one researcher of my acquaintance claims that beginning middle age—from about forty to fifty—is the age of maximum mental depression. Most of the dreams that might have been probably will never be realized. This is the age of the man we have described. How does he feel? In a very real sense, it is difficult to empathize fully with him. Most of us do not have a death sentence hanging over us, so our condition is not so acute as his. Nevertheless, I challenge you to put yourself emotionally in his place.

We are fortunate in that we do have a record of our friend's feeling at this moment. We can read about it simply by turning to chapter 1 of the book of Ephesians in the New Testament. Listen to these words in verses 3 and 4. "Blessed be the God and Father of our Lord Jesus Christ, who hath blessed us with all spiritual blessings in heavenly places in Christ: According as he hath chosen us in him before the foundation of the world, that we should be holy and without blame before him in love."

Depressing words? Far from it!

I'm sure you recognize that what you have been reading is a nonspiritual interpretation of the life of the apostle Paul, before and after his conversion. The verses quoted represent the loftiest emotional expression of Paul anywhere in the New Testament.

This passage creates a problem for the serious student, however. How can a man react with such elation having come through a turbulent life such as his? Here he was, awaiting his doom, reviewing a life of personal failure, with no family that cared. The Bible does record that one friend visited him in prison. But he got sick. In fact the visitor, Epaphroditus, became so ill that Paul feared he would not live. Fortunately he recovered, but such illness could scarcely have contributed much elation to the moment!

It would be normal procedure for a psychologist to question Paul's reaction to the whole situation. Was he in his right mind? Can a sane man exult under such stress? Normally we expect people's emotional reactions to match their experiences. When they do not match, but seem too much out of character, we presume some serious distortion of thought process has occurred. In Paul's case we must face the fact that either he was seriously misperceiving as a result of his stress or something most unusual had happened to change the emotional dynamics of his life. Can we assume that the earlier dramatic change in his life had something to do with it?

Having considered this question regarding Paul's ability

Depression

to rejoice under stress, a friend of mine, a psychiatrist, simply says that Paul was a schizophrenic whose reactions had so departed from reality that he was experiencing emotional delusions. No sane man would react to such dire circumstances with such elation.

What do you think? Are there other clues to the problem? Was Paul's experience potentially so renewing and transforming that all the psychological rules of human emotional reaction must be reviewed? Is there a personality dynamic in force in the lives of Christians, but not in others? Perhaps Paul gives us a clue in other writings.

In all Paul's writings, one chapter of Scripture gives particular insight into the psychological workings of the conversion experience. The passage is found in 2 Corinthians 5. Beginning with verse 11, note the statements from which we can derive principles about the converted personality.

Paul had no loss of reality about his life situation. He talks of it freely and openly. In chapter 4 he pulls no punches about feeling uncomfortableness in his experience. For example, verses 8 and 9 say: "We are troubled on every side, yet not distressed; we are perplexed, but not in despair; persecuted, but not forsaken; cast down, but not destroyed."

The fact that Paul clearly perceived reality precludes any real notion that he was not in his right mind. This was no schizophrenic experiencing delusions of grandeur or persecution. This was a man with his full wits about him, never denying his suffering, but so taken with God's promises that suffering was of little consequence to him. In fact, a casual reading of the entire book of 2 Corinthians underscores this truth. He had a better grip on reality than most Christians. As a result he could vindicate both his apostleship and his enthusiasm while encouraging the faltering Corinthian Christians.

Back to chapter 5. In verses 11 and 12, Paul deals with the the first of several psychological principles. The first is the principle of identity—finding out who you are, finding out who you are in the full context of the love and judgment of God.

In chapter 4, we talked about the need to see oneself as an adequate person. This is what identity is all about. When we come to see ourselves as the objects of God's unmerited love and pull ourselves up to that full image, we have established the most important basis for seeing ourselves as adequate persons. When we respond in faithful service, without much regard to whether our service is humanly regarded as worthwhile achievement or not, we establish the other most important basis for identity. Accepting the love of God makes us realize that we are worthwhile. No inferiorities are permitted here. If God thinks you are somebody, you are somebody, no matter what society has to say about it. When you respond in faithful service, you meet every expectation of God. He wants you to serve, not to achieve as men commonly understand achievement in an economic, status-conscious world.

Paul then contrasts this identity with the identity obtained by others. In verse 12, he speaks about those who feel that achievement is better than service, or status better than the nature of one's heart. Apparently there were those who still thought they could earn enough Brownie points to make themselves acceptable to God. No way! You must start where you are, be what you are, let God make up all the differences, and then in love serve Him.

Paul says, "By the grace of God, I am what I am" (1 Cor. 15:10). When you are God's nothing else really matters! Your identity is cast in the simple fact that you are the object of boundless love, regardless of any human assessment.

The second principle of the Christian psychological life that Paul deals with is the principle of nonownership of self. This is the principle that is likely to be hotly contested by theorists of personality. Ours is the day when it is a great thing to be one's own person. In various ways you have heard men say, "I want to be my own man!" The courts attempt to balance individual rights with the rights of society, a balance that needs periodic reexamination. Education sets as its goal the development of the individual so that he can obtain a state of psychological autonomy. Political scientists assume that all nations have the right to determine their own destinies.

But Paul is of another mind. He assumes that it is better to be dead to oneself, not to live for oneself. To be dead to oneself is to cease owning oneself. And it is no secret that we become pretty much wrapped up in what we own.

This is true whether we own property, children or position. Conversely, we lose involvement when ownership ceases. I no longer worry about the heater in the house I sold a couple of years ago. I don't get excited if the neighbor's window breaks in a windstorm, though I might help him fix it. I feel far less deeply about the welfare of other people's children than I do about my own. So what might happen if I ceased ownership of myself? Suppose I could give up ownership of my fears, my talents, my concerns about health. Would that help?

Apparently Paul had been able to transfer title of himself to God. In fact, the effect of his words is to say, "So what if I'm crazy? That's God's business. So what if I'm sane? Then I can live for you." (See verse 13. The Amplified New Testament has an especially good treatment of the passage.) Apparently Paul had given up even the ownership of his own sanity. Ah, sanity, that most prized of men's possessions! What struggles a man will endure so as not to lose his mind!

But if a man does not own even his own sanity, doesn't it stand to reason that he'll be a lot less self-involved? Won't he worry a lot less about how he appears to others? Shouldn't he be able to stop about half his struggle with life? Wouldn't a lot of psychotherapy be cut short if the object of that therapy were suddenly unimportant, or at least of secondary value?

Some years ago I counseled with a young man who was just beginning the ministry. Problems of depression beset him to the extent that he could not continue his service to his church. The climax came when in the middle of a sermon he began to weep. Unable to control himself, he closed the service and ran home. He believed his life had ended.

His loss of occupation greatly multiplied his problem. Now he was unable to support his family. As a result he lost much self-esteem. His wife went to work as a secretary

186

and kept the family going for almost a year. Needless to say, the depressive episodes increased, and he considered institutionalizing himself. Before many weeks had passed, he refused even to go outside his home, fearing what friends and neighbors would say.

As we began to converse about the problem, I learned that success and the esteem of parishioners were critically important to this man. He was well educated in the Christian faith and frequently preached on successful Christian living, but now his message was fading rapidly. In his darkest moments he considered suicide as a way out. But this would not do either. What about those victorious messages? What about the family? He was afraid to live and afraid to die.

Depression is often a mask for deep hostility, and as we counseled it became apparent that this man was unconsciously hiding a lot of anger. Apparently one of his motives for going into the ministry was to prove himself worthy to both God and man, particularly to a very spiritual father who had demonstrated little approval of his son. Since neither God nor his dad seemed pleased by the young minister's efforts, the result was murky depression.

After much venting of hostility and verbalizing about his relationship to his father, he felt relieved. Yet he still did not know what to do next. "If I could only feel free to go crazy," he muttered one evening as we talked, "I think half the battle would be over."

"Why don't you see if you can," I suggested.

"That sounds as crazy as I do," he retorted, "but it makes a silly kind of sense!" At this point we entered into some meaningful discussion of what it means to be owned by a God who is utterly in charge of our affairs, a God who cares deeply and one to whom we can fully abandon ourselves. Then we talked about Paul in 2 Corinthians. Was his principle of self-abandonment really a valid one?

In succeeding sessions, this young man began yielding

ownership of himself. Yielding meant also surrendering his problems and emotions. One doesn't give God only the nice-looking things inside the head. He gives all. When my friend did this in sweet release and abandonment, half the battle was won. Since he was now acceptable to God, he no longer needed to please an over-expecting dad.

Bit by bit, health returned. A call to a new charge came, and he was able to respond with genuine enthusiasm. Today he has a freedom and sensitivity to people known by few Christians. He is not his own, he has been taken over by God. Paul writes in 1 Corinthians 6:19,20, "Ye are not your own, for ye are bought with a price: therefore glorify God in your body, and in your spirit, which are God's."

If the two principles we have stated are true, then a whole new theory of personality must emerge. If it is true that identity can be gained simply by replacing the usual efforts at attaining a good self-image with the recognition that God loves us, then hope is available for untold numbers of people. Every major theory of personality in today's textbooks regards identity as some kind of achievement, and almost never as a gift. Secular theorists cannot conceive of the idea that "by the grace of God I am what I am."

Further, if it is true that one can relinquish self-ownership thus reducing markedly self-anxieties, then current psychotherapy must be reevaluated. Most anxiety reduction for therapy clients is obtained by accomplishing something, never by giving something away.

The implication for current personality theory is that the Christian can postulate a theory that does not have human ego at its center. Instead of being in nuclear position, the ego of man is orbital in the organization of himself. So far this idea is unheard of in today's psychology systems. Virtually every sophisticated theory of human personality supposes that man was made with ego as the central fact of the human life. The goal of all development of the person is to see that this ego is protected, fulfilled, enhanced and valued. But Paul says no. Instead the Christian must come to understand that God is nuclear in human personality and ego is orbital. Thus the Christian view contradicts most of what is known in the psychological theories of man.

God is not just an idea. He is not just a concept to be used to cover the unexplainable. Nor is Christian faith an alternative among alternatives. It is not a system alongside other systems—an idea that can readily be accepted or rejected without consequence. Rather, how one deals with the God of the Bible and the Christ who is His Son has vital implication for the very structure of one's personal and emotional life.

In most psychological theory, the goal of existence is to experience an integrated wholeness with ego at the center of life. Therefore mental health and emotional well-being become all-important. But not so with the Christian. For him, his faith is not just a means of achieving a state of mental well-being to be discarded when that function is not fulfilled. Instead, mental health and emotional well-being are by-products of an experience wherein God is nuclear in life, ego is orbital, and the purpose of living is giving honor and praise to God, who alone is capable of receiving such adoration. If in turn, God gives one mental wholeness, well and good; but it is not first in God's spiritual and mental economy.

The pursuit of mental health is a secondary effect of a yielded life. In fact, pursuing it as an end in itself only reinforces the ego centrality of most people's experience. When well-being comes as a by-product, it comes in greater simplicity, in greater quantity, and in total harmony with the ultimate purpose of man.

If we trust God and seek to bring honor to Him, the problem of peace of soul will largely take care of itself. In 1 Corinthians 2:9 Paul says: "What no man ever saw or heard, what no man ever thought could happen, is the very thing God prepared for those who love him." Further, in Philippians 4:6,7 he says (and this is my own paraphrase), "Don't worry about anything, pray about everything, give thanks for anything, and the peace of God, which exceeds all human ability to understand, will take care of both your mind and your emotions through Christ Jesus."

When Jesus was about to leave this earth He gave a similar promise to His disciples. It is found in John 14:27. "Peace I leave with you, my peace I give unto you: not as the world giveth, give I unto you. Let not your heart be troubled, neither let it be afraid."

# 14 The Need for Worship

Most people think of worship as a religious phenomenon without implication for psychological life. It has been viewed by many as one of those things religious people do for no rational reason except that the church seemed to get started on it and couldn't let it go. It is seen as an esoteric and quaint religious exercise with only symbolic meanings. Most people are right. It is an esoteric happening without much sense unless the fact of genuine conversion has taken place. Then the dynamics change altogether. Once God moves in, perspectives on what is real or rich and what is esoteric or meaningless do an about-face.

My attention was firmly fixed upon this matter a number of years ago when A. W. Tozer, writing in a magazine article, pointed up the fact that most people today have lost the concept of the Shekinah glory of God radiating through temple worship. Christians have become introspective to the point that all religious experience is ego involved, internal in the soul, and judged by what I get out of it. Any Christian experience that does not focus upon some personal need has been effectively eliminated but this is not the nature of worship.

About the same time I was pondering the fact that

worship and related religious experience is one of the few universal forms of behavior. The worship of God in some form is present nearly everywhere in the world. Every culture has it, except the highly educated culture. It is in this culture alone that atheism thrives. One of the unfortunate aspects of human educational progress is the cessation of worship by sophisticated people. Actually, cessation is concerned only with the religious elements of worship. The human being secularized by learning still worships; he has only switched objects. Man may think that he has advanced his understanding enough to eliminate the necessity of religious experience but he is only deceived. Worship is still with him even though forms have changed and objects replaced. Man can no more live without worship than he can live without love.

My awareness of the need for worship was further heightened by noting the great prayers of Scripture. There are four prayers commonly regarded as the great petitions of the Bible. The first is David's prayer when he was refused the privilege of building the Temple. Too much blood was shed in his time, and God reserved the right of building the Temple for Solomon, David's successor. David seems disappointed but, nevertheless, accepts the injunction of God. His response is not one of introspective soul searching as much as one of a great worship experience. He honors God for who He is, puts aside his self concerns, and proceeds to collect the materials neceessary for temple construction at a later date.

David was able to set aside pampering his own emotions and utter the phrases that describe the greatness and holiness of God. In a time of stress, David points upward rather than inward. There is no great analysis of his own spiritual condition to explain why God had acted in His sovereign way.

Solomon later was granted the right to build the great edifice that evoked awe in every beholder. The description of the temple in the Old Testament sends the calculators of the mind whirling. The expense was fantastic, the designs magnificent. When dedicated, thousands of voices in united choir appeared twenty-four hours a day as part of the dedication ceremony. In the midst of the celebration, Solomon prays. And his prayer is a model of worshipful experience. All the majesty and grandeur of God is acclaimed. In hearing the prayer, no mind could miss the priorities for spiritual experience that were apparent. No building committees were congratulated, no slaves who cut timbers or mined gold were named, no heartfelt thanks for the pledges of the church membership were mentioned. Instead the Shekinah glory of God was clearly set forth in a way that only the most obtuse observer would miss.

Likewise, in both the great prayers of Jesus the worship elements are present. "Our father who art in heaven, hallowed be thy name. . . ." No immediate mention of human introspective experience is màde. It does come later, but it is not first. First the glory of God. First the recognition of who is sovereign. First the declaration of who God is.

I have come to recognize these prayers as models of Christian mental experience. The Christian mind must be so programmed that the immediate response to all human experience is a response of worship. Whether that experience is one of joy or sorrow, it matters not. Worship is the modus operandi of the mature spiritual mind.

Such a mind existed in Job. You may recall that Job received, with the permission of God, one of the most severe tests of character. He was plagued with the loss of livestock, the loss of sons, and the loss of health. Grief was his lot in overwhelming measure. His personal losses were so great that even his wife could not sustain them. "Curse God and die" was her encouragement. Three friends of Job picked up the chant as well.

What did you do at your most grievous moment? What advice did you get? The inquisition that Job's friends conducted may have been more troublesome than his losses. His losses obviously did not sway him from his worshipful commitment to God. Nor did loss even suggest such a response. His friends did. Obviously Job was guilty of something and they advised a spiritual self-search into every gloomy cavern of his mind. What fun that might have been. But Job was not so disposed. Instead, he stripped himself of all other symbols of status and wealth and entered into worship. In sackcloth and ashes, with heart and mind bare before God, he declares that though God slay him, yet will he trust. Neither would he enter into personal introspection to falsely identify guilt when there was none. Instead, worship was his response!

Since I regard worship as the fundamental frame of mind for the Christian and as the modus operandi of mature spiritual experience, I want to advance five propositional statements concerning the psychological nature of worship.

First, you will worship something. Whether you are Christian, heathen, atheist, or syncretist, or of any other persuasion, you will worship something. At some point in your life you will give yourself to something. It may not be an altogether conscious experience, but you will give yourself to something. And whatever claims you will be your object of worship.

Earlier in the book we talked about the nature of agape love, a love that is given without merit on the part of the receiver. It is unearned. Similarly, you will set up something as a recipient of your attention and devotion. You will make a conscious or an unconscious commitment of your life to something, some cause, some purpose, some person, or some combination of all of these and never mind the validity of the object or its worthiness. Something will occupy the center of your life and claim your devotion even if that claim seems to occur by default.

The apostle Paul points out that people set up agape relationships with all kinds of unworthy objects. Men may

194

decide that they are economic creatures and spend virtually all of their lives in economic pursuits. Many are successful and die known as the richest men in the cemetery. But you don't have to be rich to worship money. Sometimes being poor calls so much attention to money that poor men worship the not-so-almighty buck. An unmerited object is chosen for an unfortunately overrated relationship.

It is easy to demonstrate that money is not worth the worship it gets. Testimonials exist all around us to this effect. People observe the evidence and hope to do better. So the search for objects to worship is incessantly pursued. Several alternatives have been found and today are claiming the devotion of many.

In one of my classes in human growth and development I raised the question about valuable reasons for living. "Why grow up, anyway," I chided. "What's the reason?" A middle-aged gentleman who had returned to college to "find himself" was hooked by the question. It made him restless and uncomfortable because he had no real answer, yet he knew it was the most important issue he faced. He saw his life running out without purpose, and without this he knew he faced a most unpleasant demise. Strange isn't it that the people with the least reason to live have the hardest time dying! Unfortunately, this gentleman decided that the only alternative left to him was the devotion of all his resources to existential experience. He would seek to make meaning out of life by consuming himself in sensory experience and the exhaustion of his resources in a wide range of mind-blowing episodes. So he chose to worship the exploration of his sensual life. He could hardly have taken a wilder ride to hell. He knew full well what was in store, but he was fresh out of alternatives. He felt nothing was worth anything so why worry about the value of anything. And blow his mind he did—all in the search for something to abate his need for an object of worship.

Unfortunately this man represents a trend overtaking thousands of young people. The worship of economic success, the history of warfare in man, the injustices of the world—all have left man without alternatives. The worship of sensory or even illusory experience is a dominant trend, not because it represents so great an alternative, but simply because so many other things have been tried and found wanting.

Yet another object of worship is political system and ideology. The rational and objective merits of these systems certainly don't explain the devotion attached to them. They are as hollow and unfulfilling as any of man's futile experiences. But what most people don't recognize is that the merits of the object of their devotion matters little. A person must be devoted to something. He must worship or he will disintegrate! So the best of a poor lot of alternatives is chosen. An ideology or political system with even the remotest possibility of improving matters is going to be chosen by many.

In a similar way people yearn to devote themselves to anything that promises power over people and events. I am both amused and alarmed by the tremendous impact of behavioral psychology these days. B. F. Skinner's book *Walden Two* set off nationwide, even worldwide discussion of a theory that promised to make events controllable and predictable. Interestingly enough, the principles involved in the psychological system underlying *Walden Two* work rather well in quite a number of situations. I have personally seen undisciplined classes of disturbed children brought under control by the operant conditioning techniques suggested in behavioral psychology. Obstreperous behavior has been abated, teachers' anxiety reduced, and praises to Skinner—hallelujah! Extrapolate the principles and you have a world under control. This is not too different from what the Marxists are telling the world. They say man is a product of his conditioning and by consciously

manipulating him you can make of him what you will—
presumably an equalitarian social animal where only productive motives prevail.

But then Nietzsche had similar ideas and so did Rous-
seau, Hegel, Aristotle and Plato. Plato thought that if all
men would turn seriously to philosophy, human events
would be both controllable and predictable. Thus the philosophers have had incessant following down through the
ages, not so much because their points were either valid
or invalid, but because men needed something to worship—something to command total devotion.

The second premise is that without worship, life disin-
tegrates. Some object of worship must be present to organize the human personality. It is a matter of secondary
importance, psychologically, whether or not the worship
object is valid. There must be a something around which
to bind and build all of life. Something besides self must
be in the middle of things. While men seem to build life
around themselves, what they are unconsciously doing is

seeking a replacement for their ego-centered experiences. The need for worship explains this impulse to replacement.

My interpretation of both Bertrand Russell and Jean Paul Sartre is that both had run so far out of options for objects or worship they turned to despair as the organizing point of human experience. Life had to be built out of the firm ground of despair, since neither had found anything else in life but despair. What a gloomy way to go. Why bother at all, one wonders. But we must recognize that if life had only despair left, then despair must be used to organize the human experience. If our assumption is correct, the alternative to despair for these men was personality disintegration. That was the only identifiable choice.

In any contest between the need to keep one's mind on a logical course and the need to worship, the motive to worship will win. I can find no other way to explain the great devotion to absurd objects, causes and movements. Witness the tremendous growth of astrology as a serious hobby of intelligent people. I believe the interest in astrology is nonsensical, at best. It makes me wonder what has happened to minds that otherwise seem capable of rational inquiry. The only explanation seems to be that man must have some system of ultimates, some object of devotion to give his life meaning and interpretation. He seems willing to worship most anything regardless of its absurdity.

The giving up of an object of worship in the face of rational insight is often most difficult. Sometimes invalid objects of worship are exposed by rational inquiry and a serious stress point in life is identified. Whole civilizations of people have been known to reject education because such a choice had to be made. Millions have lived in intellectual darkness rather than pursue inquiry which might result in the deprivation of one of life's greatest needs.

This leads us to the third premise about worship. The object of worship must be ultimately and finally valid. It must not be untrue or destructible. While even invalid objects of worship will give an organizing base to life, ultimately despair will follow if the object loses its truthfulness. Thus theology, based on sound presuppositions, is still the queen of the sciences and comparative religion is no idle parlor game.

I recently worked my way through Francis Schaeffer's book, *The God Who Is There*. The book responds to the great need to unaerstand suppc  tions, logical processes and biblical evidence to establish with firmness a valid object of devotion and worship. Schaeffer clearly makes the point that when the validity question goes unsolved or unanswered, despair is the inevitable result.

Fortunately the hand of God often participates in establishing validity for Himself in the minds and hearts of people. We witnessed this fact not long ago in a tribe of jungle dwelling Indians in South America. A serious epidemic had taken several lives and left others disabled. This group of people had recently embraced Christ as Saviour but tended to revert to spiritism in the face of this disaster. Two men, at least one of whom was a professing Christian, decided to seek revenge for the illness that had gripped their tribe. To appease the spirits they thought responsible, they stalked two residents of their tribe at night and drove spears through them.

One mature Christian in the tribe apprehended one of the men and warned the assailant that God would deal seriously with him. In less than an hour the culprit was dead, having laughed derisively when warned. A somber audience of tribespeople heard the story and thanked God for protecting their new found faith, even by this drastic means.

One of the reasons for the near demise of some theological seminaries lies in their inability to clearly establish the validity of the God they worship. In one prominent seminary, it is possible to graduate with a divinity degree without ever having taken a course in biblical literature. Instead this school has devoted itself to a study of matters far less than ultimate in character. It competes with other social institutions who better relieve many of the world's social ills. Thus appearing second best as an instrument of social change and presenting an uncertain voice with regard to the validity of God, the school finds it difficult to draw men for study or to promise hope from the despair that encircles humanity. A clear and valid Saviour together with a sense of redemption ultimates in life is required if despair is not to follow.

The fourth premise is that valid worship regenerates both mind and soul. In the course of counseling and psychotherapy, I often give my clients a program of worship experience. This is not necessarily public or formal worship, but rather a personal expression. With some instruction in how to pray and how to read Scripture, I ask them to think about ideas that do not center on their illness with its accompanying drain of emotional resources.

For one seriously depressed woman I selected a series of psalms of praise that made no reference to oneself at all. I suggested that she make no mention of herself in her prayers, simply praise God, enjoy his awe and greatness and give thanks for who He is. She expressed great resistance to the idea. To enter upon such a program meant abandoning the preoccupations with self that had accompanied her spiritual exercises. She wasn't sure whether she was really ready to give up her own concerns and relate to God in this way. But she had to make her choice or realize that her therapy would become meaningless. Reluctantly, at first, but with increasing joy as she went along, she began to find her way out of her private emotional pit. Worship was regenerating her heart and mind.

I have noted that some of the most delightful people

I know are constantly in a worship frame of mind. One day I enjoyed a round of golf with a minister who was gifted in many ways: an athlete, musician and able preacher. On the first hole of our match he hit two crisp shots to the green and sank his first putt to go one under par. If you're a golfer you know what joy there is in making a birdie on the first hole! His response? He stood atop the mound that elevated the green and sang joyfully, "A Mighty Fortress Is Our God"! His immediate response even to a simple joy of life was to worship. Most people would think him silly, but I learned a lesson I never forgot. Worship removes oneself from the center of attention and replaces self with the joyful awe of God. No longer can guilt and selfishness occupy the personal stage front and center. No longer can emotional energies be sapped on miserable introspection. Worship is the mental frame of the mature person.

The fifth premise is that the only valid object of worship is the triune God, revealed in Jesus Christ. It is not my intention to present a systematic theological argument and apologetic for this statement. Rather, I want to declare with Scripture simply that in Christ all things in heaven and all things on earth will ultimately be reconciled in Him. I know of no more encompassing statement or principle that can be made. If Christ is that, then he is the worthy object of your devotion and worship. And since the statement is so final, it leaves you with a choice. The choice is to either accept it as true or as false. There is no partial acceptance or middle ground with such a statement. You must either assume truth or deny validity. It is not my statement, it is the statement of the Scriptures.

The Scriptures don't stop with this, however. They further insist that the person of Christ was *both* fully God and fully man. Who can envision or comprehend an idea like that? The processes of human mental imagery won't let it happen. So it is necessary to take a giant step of faith and start believing that these statements are true. Believing means that God will then personally validate Himself for you as He did for the tribespeople spoken of earlier in this chapter. It means accepting the limits of logical thought and intellectual process. It means a willingness to begin trusting a revelation given in holy writ. When you do you will arrive at the beginning of the greatest adventure you have ever known. Worship will be the most renewing experience of your life and you'll begin a life of adventure that will take you beyond your finest expectations.